Stakeholder Management and Social Responsibility

The main objective of this book is to provide an innovative set of concepts and tools regarding company management, internal and external stakeholders and social responsibilities, reflecting the necessities and opportunities generated by the digital transformation, the transition to a knowledge-based economy, and the COVID-19 crisis. The book, based on a holistic vision and contextual approach of business, contributes to the development of company management and stakeholder and social responsibility theories and practices, being structured in 12 chapters.

The original company management vision, approaches, and tools are based on three pillars: a new "manager–relevant stakeholder" rather than "manager–subordinate" managerial paradigm; a new type of company social responsibility rather than corporate social responsibility; and a new concept of company-relevant stakeholder rather than that of salient stakeholders. The book contains two innovative managerial mechanisms: the managerial synapse and company-relevant stakeholders-based management system able to help companies and stakeholders face successfully the challenges of digital transformation and the COVID-19 crisis and to generate greater organization functionality and performance.

The book will be of interest to company managers and management specialists, management academics, consultants and researchers, and MBA students interested in a style of management with social responsibility at the forefront.

Ovidiu Nicolescu is Professor Emeritus at Bucharest University of Economic Studies and President of the Romanian Academic Management Society, Romania.

Ciprian Nicolescu is Professor of Management at Bucharest University of Economic Studies, Romania.

Routledge Advances in Management and Business Studies

Chinese Business and the Belt and Road Initiative
Institutional Strategies
Jerry J. Zhang

Management Control Systems, Decision-Making, and Innovation Development
The CDI Model
Dawid Szutowski

Competition, Strategy, and Innovation
The Impact of Trends in Business and the Consumer World
Edited by Rafał Śliwiński and Łukasz Puślecki

Critical Perspectives on Innovation Management
The Bright and Dark Sides of Innovative Firms
Edited by Patryk Dziurski

Operations Management in Japan
The Efficiency of Japanese Manufacturing
Hiromichi Shibata

Stakeholder Management and Social Responsibility
Concepts, Approaches and Tools in the Covid Context
Ovidiu Nicolescu and Ciprian Nicolescu

Japanese Business Operations in an Uncertain World
Edited by Anshuman Khare, Nobutaka Odake and Hiroki Ishiruka

Entrepreneurship and Culture
The New Social Paradigm
Alf H. Walle

For more information about this series, please visit: www.routledge.com/Routledge-Advances-in-Management-and-Business-Studies/book-series/SE0305

Stakeholder Management and Social Responsibility

Concepts, Approaches and Tools in the Covid Context

Ovidiu Nicolescu and
Ciprian Nicolescu

Routledge
Taylor & Francis Group
NEW YORK AND LONDON

First published 2022
by Routledge
605 Third Avenue, New York, NY 10158

and by Routledge
2 Park Square, Milton Park, Abingdon, Oxon, OX14 4RN

Routledge is an imprint of the Taylor & Francis Group, an informa business

Library of Congress Cataloguing-in-Publication Data
A catalog record has been requested for this book

ISBN: 978-1-032-10920-6 (hbk)
ISBN: 978-1-032-10923-7 (pbk)
ISBN: 978-1-003-21770-1 (ebk)

DOI: 10.4324/9781003217701

Typeset in Sabon
by MPS Limited, Dehradun

Contents

Figures

Tables

Preface

The main objective of this book is to provide an innovative set of concepts, approaches, and tools regarding company management, internal and external stakeholders, and social responsibilities, reflecting the necessities and opportunities generated by the digital transformation, the transition to a knowledge-based economy, and the COVID-19 crisis.

The authors, based on a comprehensive analysis, have identified **a set of key points regarding company management and stakeholder and social responsibility theory and practice** in the last decade, representing **major challenges** that should be taken into consideration by specialists.

A The digital transformation, industrial revolution 4.0, the transition to the "smart economy", ecologization and other mega shifts in the society, and the economy generate for companies and their stakeholders numerous and unexpected opportunities, threats, and challenges that place the management of organizations in very complex and, very often, stressful situations.

B There are multiple and essential changes in the theoretical and pragmatic approaches to company management and stakeholder and social responsibility as feedback to the contextual opportunities, threats, and challenges that are only partially performant and sustainable.

C There have been very innovative and performant developments in the theoretical and pragmatic elements of certain areas of management, such as strategy, human resources management, management tools, stakeholder relationships (customer relationship management [CRM], supply chain management [SCM], corporate social responsibility [CSR]), and others, which should be developed further and correlated.

D There exist notable limits and weak points in company management, and stakeholder and social responsibility theory and practice, with significant negative impacts on a company's competitiveness and sustainability, and their stakeholders, as recently emphasized by the COVID-19 pandemic.

E In many respects, company management, despite some notable advances, remains too traditional, and not sufficiently able to change deeply or to reshape in order to valorize to a large extent the new contextual opportunities and the high quality of human resources. It is necessary – as many renowned specialists (G. Hamel, R.E. Freeman, D. Kiron, M. Reeves, C.D. Pringle, and others) have asked – to reinvent management.

The new holistic vision and innovative approach to company management and stakeholder and social responsibility developed by the authors in this book involves **nine milestones:**

- Digitalization, industrial revolution 4.0, the transition to a knowledge-based economy, and other contextual mutations have radically changed businesses, companies, management, and people, generating essential changes in all components of the society at macro-, meso-, and microlevels.
- In the context of digitalization and transition to the "smart economy", information and knowledge, which represent the content of intellectual capital, have become the most important resources in company development, influencing decisively individual and organizational performance. Information and knowledge will have (as they already have in many top companies in the United States, western Europe, and Japan) a determining impact on an organization's functionality, competitiveness, and sustainability.
- Internal stakeholders (managers, shareholders, and executants) and external stakeholders (customers, suppliers, consultants, informaticians, finance providers, local communities, etc.) are the main holders of information, knowledge, and tangible resources and have increasing impacts on a company.
- A company's survival, functionality, development, and performance in the medium and long term depend decisively not only on the company shareholders and top managers but also on the main stakeholders within and outside the company.
- All companies have stakeholders who heavily influence their activities and performance (of course, the number and importance of stakeholders increase concomitantly with the size and complexity of the organization). Consequently, the placement of the main stakeholders on the frontline is necessary in every company, not only in corporations and large enterprises.
- A company should be approached as an entity with multiple strategic objectives, determined according to the interests of the relevant stakeholders. The company's multiobjective should be multidimensional – financial, technical, social, ecological, moral, legal, and others. It is recommended that strategic company objectives should be focused on the company's and the relevant stakeholders' long-term sustainability. Such objectives motivate relevant stakeholders to be

involved and productive and, concomitantly, to promote in the company a long-term approach that is beneficial for all. The multiobjective approach and the way to plan it could generate stakeholder and company synergy and competitivity.

- Company management focused on the manager–subordinate relationship, which involves only two main stakeholders, has reached its limits. This type of management is not able to realize to a great extent access to, and use (necessary and possible) of, the information, knowledge, and tangible resources of the other external and internal stakeholders. Company management must be centred on the relationships with all main stakeholders, which determines the "de facto" organization's functionality, performance, and sustainability.
- Corporate social responsibilities should be exercised in all types of companies, not only large companies, because all have obligations, demands, and responsibilities towards society, the local community, their employees, the ecological environment, and others.
- Approaches to company management and stakeholder and social responsibility should be reconceptualized and reshaped according to a new integrative vision. The entire company management should be refocused on the main stakeholders together with social responsibilities, and this requires the design and implementation of new strategies, leadership, managerial mechanisms, organizational culture, performance criteria, and other elements.

Based on these milestones, we have elaborated a new vision and approaches regarding the company management and stakeholder and social responsibility. **The most important innovative contributions** are the following:

- Identification among company stakeholders, based on a set of rigorous criteria, of a special category – the relevant stakeholder – which influences significantly the organization's functionality, development, and performance; the new management approach is centred on the relevant stakeholders.
- Extension of the focus of company management from two stakeholders (shareholders and top managers) to all relevant internal and external stakeholders. This means changing the managerial paradigm from the manager–subordinate relationship to a new managerial paradigm: manager–relevant stakeholder.
- Extension of the stakeholders taken into consideration by management, from large companies to all companies irrespective of size; we propose this because all companies depend on the relevant stakeholders, and their functionality, development, and performance are decisively influenced by them.

- Extension of corporate social responsibility to be taken into consideration, and this approach as a major element in the organization, from corporations and large companies to those of all types. We propose this because all companies have obligations and responsibilities towards the local community, region, and country in which they operate, to the ecological environment and population involved, etc. All companies face the same societal challenges. Instead of corporate social responsibility, we propose a new concept: company social responsibility.
- An increase in the scope of company social responsibilities from the economic, social, legal, and moral aspects to include a fifth element – the ecological aspect – concomitantly with a focus on the relevant stakeholders and reconfiguration of the relationships between the elements of social responsibility. The theoretical background of the change is the replacement of the responsibility pyramid (see Carrol, Baden, and others) with the responsibility pentagon, a new concept elaborated by us.
- Extension of the specific approach based on collaboration, motivation, flexibility, etc. (as used in recent decades, especially in large companies, with two relevant stakeholders – CRM for customers and SCM for suppliers) to the other relevant stakeholders. Starting from these very performant best practices, we have conceived a new concept and mechanism, namely the managerial synapse, which could be used with all relevant stakeholders. Of course, a specific managerial synapse should be designed for each internal and external stakeholder category.
- Designing a new management system focused on stakeholders – a management system based on company-relevant stakeholders – which integrates the new with the previous elements. This system valorizes to a large extent stakeholders' information, knowledge, and other resources both in the company and in the interests of stakeholders; motivates internal and external stakeholders to work together more closely and efficiently based on a win–win relationship; and encourages the intensive fulfilment by the company of its social responsibilities with multiple economic, social, ecological, moral, and legal benefits for all.

These innovative elements regarding company management, relevant stakeholders, and social responsibility are able to generate **huge beneficial effects** in the companies – both in their economic and social context – and to relaunch the economy after the COVID pandemic. Synthetically, they could be grouped into three categories:

- Suplementary resources for the company;
- Much better work processes reshaped in the company and its stakeholders;

- Higher and multidimensional and sustainable performances in the company, community, economy, and society.

Theoretical and pragmatic innovative approaches incorporated in this book represent just the beginning in the development of a new integrative vision on company's management, relevant stakeholder, and social responsibility. There are numerous aspects in our approach that should be further analyzed and developed. The growing societal challenges, digitalization, industrial revolution 4.0, transition to the smart economy, ecologization, and other mutations have continous and deep implications for an organization's management, stakeholder, and social responsibility, which should be taken into consideration.

These elements and many others indicate the need for further research, both theoretical and pragmatic, in order to generate new concepts, approaches, and tools capable of determining much better multidimensional performances in organizations, valorizing to a high level of the potential of the relevant stakeholders, and practising more moral and efficient social responsibilities and human management in all types of organizations, in accordance with the revolutionary changes of our times.

1 Instead of Introduction: Why Is Stakeholder Management Necessary and Possible in the Present Context?

Why Is Stakeholder Management Necessary Now, in the Present Context?

Organizational Arguments

1 **Perception and understanding of organizations, including companies of course – as social constructions.** This means that they are artefacts created by human beings to serve their ends. They are shaped by human purposes, and they do not exist interdependently of human minds and actions. Companies are systems of human action in which means and ends are guided by intentions, strategies, and hoped-for incomes. They are in effect created by meaning with a rich tapestry of cultural rules, roles, and intentions (Coghlan, 2016).

2 Companies should – according to a recent study (Schwartz et al., 2019) – **reframe the future of work**, with the aim of generating more value and meaning for the customer, the workforce and other partners, and greater earnings for the company over time. In order to succeed with this vision, organizations must shift focus from company to customer, workforce, and other important stakeholders.

3 Development of a new type of company focused on knowledge – as resource, product, asset, and competitive advantage – which are quite different compared with the classical capitalist company; it is called a **knowledge-based company**.

4 **Companies' contextualization** by amplification of the external environment influences their objectives, resources, activities, functionality, performance, and sustainability on concomitantly with the multiplication and acceleration of the companies' inputs and outputs.

5 Awareness that financial performance should no longer be the sole pursuit of enterprises. Companies – according to Ignatius (2019) – are being pushed to consider the interests of all their stakeholders, including employees, customers, and the community, not just those of their shareholders.

DOI: 10.4324/9781003217701-1

6. **Intellectual capital plays a decisive role** in the survival, functioning, and development of modern, knowledge-based companies.
7. **The resources of a large proportion of the companies have changed profoundly** in recent decades through:

    - the emergence of two new categories of resources – information and knowledge;
    - the components, the structure, and the functionality of "classical" resources – human, technical-material, and financial – have substantially changed;
    - the human resource, very closely associated with information resource and knowledge resource, has a major role in modern organizations, much more than in classical companies.

8. **Companies' activities have changed** enormously in recent decades through:

    - the formation of consistent activities focused on the creation, purchasing, use, share, valorization, etc. of knowledge; all these operations constitute the content of the new company knowledge-function; this function is a transversal company function, different from vertical company functions (research and development, commercial, production, finance and accounting, and human resources);
    - the content and dynamics of classical activities (supply, production, sales, accounting, finance, etc.) have also changed profoundly;
    - human resources training, because of its size and major impact within an organization, gradually becomes – especially in large- and medium-sized companies – a distinct company's function fulfilled and partially externalized outside the organization.

9. **Modern companies based on knowledge** – this is quadro-dimensional, trying to achieve concomitantly **four types of objectives:**

    - economic;
    - social;
    - ecological;
    - educational.

10. A knowledge-based society is an **ecosystem** presenting the following features:

    - a system made up of interactive parts that act together;
    - a multidimensional community – human, economic, and ecological;
    - networking endogen complex;
    - a system interconnected with other systems and with its environment.

11 The background of the performance and sustainability of a knowledge-based company is represented by the **sustainability diamond based on knowledge** (Figure 1.1).

12 Manifestation of the **new organizational paradox** was discovered by Hamel (2009) – the organization should become more adaptable, innovative, and inspirational, without being less focused and disciplined or less oriented toward performance.

13 The 2020 Future of Leadership Global Executive Study and Research Report finds that **leaders may be holding on to behaviours that might have worked once but now stymie the talent of their employees.** "Organizations must empower leaders to change their ways of making to succeed in a new digital economy" (Ready, Cohen, Kiron, & Pring, 2020).

14 Awareness of the fact that the success of a firm is determined by its ability to establish and maintain **relationships within the entire stakeholder network** (Post, Preston, & Sachs, 2002).

15 In the context of the pandemic, in **the majority of companies, the connection and collaboration with many important external stakeholders, especially the customers, suppliers, bankers, and local communities, have been affected and need to be restored on a new basis** taking into consideration the "new normality".

16 **Deterioration in many companies of work relationships and co-operation between internal stakeholders** – particularly between managers and subordinates – because of the massive increase in work online, social distancing, and other major changes caused by the COVID-19 pandemic. In order to restore good and even more performant work relationships between shareholders, managers, and subordinates, their approach should be reconsidered and rebuilt against a new and more motivational and innovative background.

17 Frequently, **the survival of companies that are mostly affected by the COVID-19 pandemic is not possible without implications for stakeholders.** In many countries, even the state becomes a major stakeholder for companies, developing national strategies and policies, focused on helping them to survive and to continue to work, making products and services, and protecting jobs and maintaining their capacity to generate incomes for the state budgets in the following period. Many states – and EU states are a very good example – have allocated huge amounts of money as grants and subvention credits, by subsidizing the costs for companies and the population.

18 **Companies' reinvention** taking in consideration the multiple changes and challenges occurred at mondo, macro, and micro systems. A recent study suggested that it is no longer about how companies should thrive, but rather how they must reinvent themselves to survive, because that is the key issue today (Weill & Woerner, 2018).

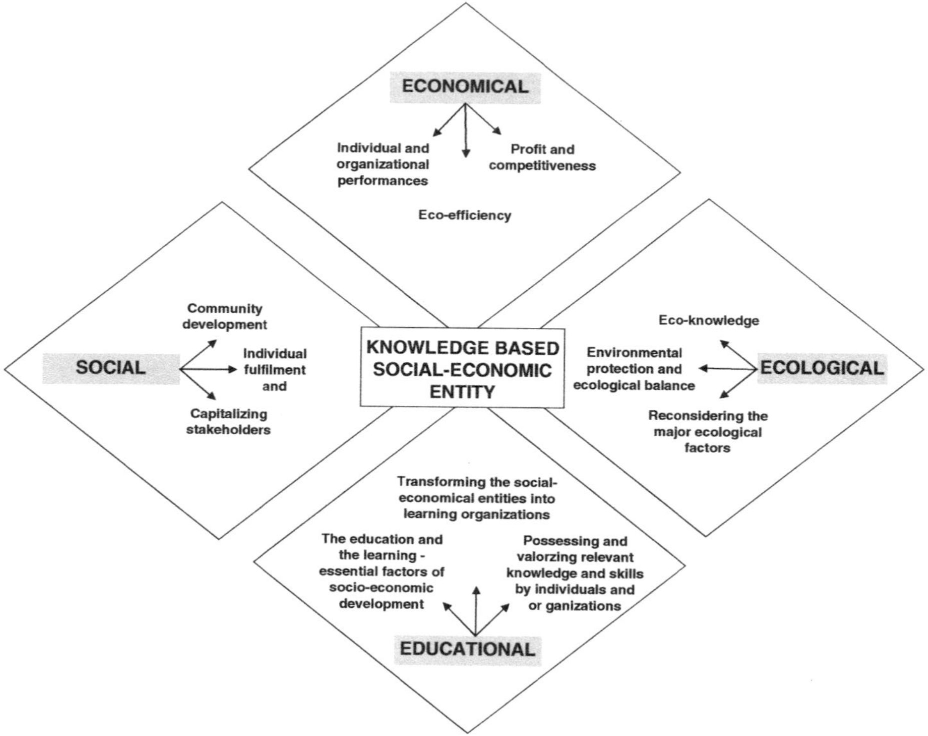

Figure 1.1 Sustainability diamond (knowledge-based entity).

Adapted from New Approach – Quadrangle of Knowledge-Based Sustainability, by O. Nicolescu and C. Nicolescu, 2017, *Proceedings of International Conference "Knowledge-Based Organization,"* *23* (1), 414. Retrieved from https://www.researchgate.net/publication/318732098_New_Approach_-_Quadrangle_of_Knowledge_Based_Sustainability

Managerial Arguments

1 **Awareness of the existence of a comprehensive network of stakeholders** – inside and outside companies – who have a major impact on their functionality, performance, and sustainability.
2 Traditional management, still predominant in the majority of companies, is based on the absolute primacy of the owner or shareholders' interests, with the **needs and expectations of other stakeholders being ignored or only sporadically taken into consideration.** A partial exception to this refers relatively often to companies' top managers.
3 In a recent study, well-known specialists Bailey, Reeves, Whitaker, and Hutchinson (2019) asked for **indirect forms of management instead of command-and-control techniques.**
4 It is – as Schein and Schein (2019) asserted – **time for a new model,** one that is built on close professional relationships, openness, and trust.
5 **The potential of large number of the companies' endogenous stakeholders** – managers and especially executants – is used for sustainable organizational development **only to a small extent.**
6 **The traditional managerial relationship, i.e. manager–subordinate** – involving two of the most numerous and important company stakeholders, which is based on hierarchy and on the "strong" authority of the manager – **is not sufficiently performative** in the majority of organizations. As a consequence, in many companies, new managerial elements have been developed based on participation, flexibility, collaboration, and strategic agility, which may solve this problem only partially and not sufficiently.
7 **The potential of most companies' exogenous stakeholders** – clients, suppliers, investors, bankers, consultants, etc. – is **frequently ignored or used only to a small degree.** Because of this situation, these stakeholders do not contribute enough to generating value added for the company and to obtaining competitive advantage.
8 **The ascertainment by many reputable specialists of the need to elaborate and to practice a new type of management** that is radically different from the management predominant in the present – management focused on stakeholders. This idea is very well formulated by the renowned Freeman (2017, p. 7) in the foreword of a well-known book edited by Andriof, Waddock, Husted, and Rahman (2017): "the need for a new era of management thinking and one based on the idea of stakeholders. We need to rewrite management theory and practice".
9 Reconceptualization, based on the stakeholder theory, of a **firm as a "multi-purpose entity"** (Crane, Palazzo, Spence, & Matten, 2014). This reconceptualization "opens" the door for "de facto"

integration of the stakeholders in the company's strategy, functioning, and performance.

10 **Refocusing of the top managers' cooperation on all stakeholders.** "Statement on the Purpose of Cooperation" (International Council for Small Business, 2019), adopted by 185 leading USA CEOs in 2019, states: "We share a fundamental commitment to all of our stakeholders. We commit to:

- Delivering value to our customers. We will further the tradition of American companies leading the way in meeting or exceeding customer expectations;
- Investing in our employees. This starts with compensating them fairly and providing important benefits. It also includes supporting them through training and education that help develop new skills for a rapidly changing world. We foster diversity and inclusion, dignity and respect;
- Dealing fairly and ethically with our suppliers. We are dedicated to serving as good partners to the other companies, large and small, that help us meet our missions;
- Supporting the communities in which we work. We respect the people in our communities and protect the environment by embracing sustainable practices across our businesses;
- Generating long-term value for shareholders, who provide the capital that allows companies to invest, grow and innovate. We are committed to transparency and effective engagement with shareholders.

Each of our stakeholders is essential. We commit to deliver value to all of them, for the future success of our companies, our communities and our country.

11 **The pandemic has caused many changes in the management of companies.** Among these, we mention the modification to a large extent of the work conditions for managers and subordinates, new business difficulties, challenges, and opportunities with customers, suppliers, partners, bankers, and communities. These elements – and many others – **make necessary new and performant managerial approaches in the relationships with all major endogenous and exogenous company stakeholders.** Already, many specialists (Levenson, 2020; Teece, Raspin, & Cox, 2020) are asking for new business models capable of attracting and using better competences and other resources of companies' stakeholders to the benefit of all parties involved.

12 In the context generated by COVID-19 crisis, certain specialists (Battilana & Casciaro, 2021) argue the need to revamp boards in the companies and to **give more power to employees and stakeholders.**

Societal Arguments

1 Harvard University mathematical biologist Martin Nowak, in 2006, discovered **that natural cooperation is the third fundamental principle of evolution** besides mutation and natural selection (Nowak, 2006).
2 **Human beings are more cooperative and less selfish** than most people believe. Organizations should help us embrace our collaborative sentiments (Benkler, 2011).
3 Societal requirements – formulated by many prestigious specialists based on valuable studies – **propose to reframe capitalism in terms of stakeholder theory** so that we come to see business as creating value for the stakeholder. We should move stakeholder theory to the centre of our thinking about business (Freeman, Harrison, Wicks, Parmar, & De Colle, 2010).
4 More recently Edward Freeman and Heather Elms argued that **the social responsibility of business is to create value for stakeholders,** indicating customers, suppliers, employees, communities, and other shareholders (Freeman & Elms, 2018).
5 **Transition in the national and international economy, from competition between companies to competition between networks of companies' stakeholders.** We have competing networks of stakeholders, where one competing network is in competition with others (Freeman et al., 2010). As a consequence, all relevant companies' stakeholders should be integrated in networks capable of competing successfully in local, regional, national, and international markets and environments.
6 Increase in the societal challenges and requirements versus companies in the context of the COVID-19 pandemic, which is a global societal crisis (Boston Consulting Group, 2020). In many countries, the state has acted in order to help companies to maintain supply chains, jobs, distribution networks, financial capacities, etc. Consequently, **companies need to make many changes in their relationships with stakeholders** involved in these processes – suppliers, subordinates, customers, bankers, financial intermediaries, and others (see, e.g., BCG, 2020; Carlsson-Szlezac, Reeves, & Swartz, 2020; Gjaja, Fæste, Hansell, & Hohner, 2020; King, Wald, & Manly, 2020; Waldron & Wetherbe, 2020). Better and effective work and business relationships with major stakeholders will decrease the negative effects for companies, people, communities, businesses, and for the entire society in the future.
7 Corporate leaders, according to several reputed specialists, are rethinking the role of business in society. **Companies need to add a lens to strategy setting, one that considers what we call total societal impact,** which is the total benefit to society from company's

products, services, operations, core capabilities, and activities (Beal et al., 2017).

8. In the context of the COVID-19 pandemic, the necessity **to rethink the role of business in society** has been emphasized by important organizations and specialists (BCG, 2020; Ghose, 2020; Levenson, 2020; Radjou, 2020).
9. In the context of the COVID-19 pandemic, even **the replacement of capitalism with a new system called a "frugal economy"** has been proposed. **"A frugal economy centred on stakeholders"** strives to create more economic, social, and ecological value while simultaneously wisely optimizing the use of all available resources. A frugal economy aims to do better with less, by making the most of all existing resources to maximize the value for all stakeholders (Radjou, 2020).

Why Is Stakeholder Management Possible Now, in the Current Context?

Organizational Arguments

1. Manifestation in companies of a **very strong tendency of modernization** of resources and activities is becoming and acting as ecosystems capable of, and open to, intensive innovation and change.
2. **Transformation of an increasing proportion of companies into knowledge-based organizations**, which possess the necessary vision and resources, especially the knowledge and information, to remodel them according to the new challenges, necessities, and opportunities.
3. **Transformation of a large percentage of companies into learning organizations**, amplifying substantially companies' and their managers' and executants' capacity to innovate and to remodel themselves.
4. **Rapid digitalization of companies and the business environment, at a faster rate in the pandemic context**, enhances and accelerates the use of knowledge and information, the communication and the consultation with the companies' stakeholders, both internal and external, actually and potentially.
5. **Amplification of the information and knowledge is retained, shared, and used by the companies**, their components, and the other stakeholders.
6. **Proliferation at the level of companies focused on sustainability and corporate social responsibility**, which make them more open and proactive to their stakeholders.
7. In the COVID-19 pandemic context, many companies, in every country, in order to survive and to continue their activities, have successfully made, in just a few months, many major changes, proving their **remarkable organizational transformation capability**.

8 **The pandemic crisis has emphasized companies' openness and willingness to change their receptiveness to new elements** from both inside and outside the organization.
9 **Increasing openness of companies to make organizational changes.** According to a survey published by Harvard Business Review, in 2018, 47% of companies reported that in order to survive they needed to reinvent their business every three years or less, and in 2020, the number jumped to 58% (Zhexembayeva, 2020).

Managerial Arguments

1 **The deep transformation of the management practices** in numerous companies – corporations and large companies being in pole position – by quasi-continuous innovation and change. The transformation of management practice has been amplified and accelerated during the pandemic crisis.
2 **The appearance in quite a large number of companies of new managerial dimensions** – previsional, innovational, flexible, motivational, methodological, informational, formative, participative, systemic, and international – but still not sufficiently used and valorized by companies.
3 Seizing, taking into consideration and valorizing to a large extent by numerous companies' managers of the huge potential of the **new organization resources – information, knowledge, and intellectual capital.**
4 Awareness of a large number of managers of the company's **many categories of stakeholders' existence and the major impact** on it – clients, suppliers, managers, executants, shareholders, investors, bankers, etc.
5 Discovering that **managers can more effectively respond to hardship when they activate a shared emotional connection** – referred to as "shared passion for **place**" – with the internal and external stakeholders. This represents a new path to organizational resilience (Hernandez, 2019).
6 Development in numerous companies of **specific and effective managerial mechanisms for certain important stakeholder categories** is very useful and capable of generating high performance. The most widely used and most performant of such mechanisms are the Customer Relationship Management (CRM) and Supply Chain Management (SCM).
7 Developments under environmental challenges and demands for certain stakeholder categories (e.g. local communities, company employees) are of **specific managerial approaches with human and ecological dimensions** like corporate social responsibility (CSR).

8 The recent formulation of "the thesis that a **combination of the focus on the management process with the stakes of the companies' stakeholders** could represent to the present necessities and realities an alternative solution for obtaining sustainability" (Sadun, Bloom, & Reenen, 2017).
9 **Remodelling of the organization and employee culture,** placing emphasis on the novelty, creativity, change, flexibility, participation, and adaptability amplified by the impact of the COVID-19 pandemic.
10 Manifestation, because of the mutations in the company environment associated with the transition to the knowledge- and digitalized-based economy and society – both in management science and management practice – of **numerous innovative ideas and approaches, which continue to be amplified and diversified,** in order to increase company performance and sustainability.
11 **Identification of the necessity and possibility of radically remodelling an organization's management by the great number of renowned management scientists and top managers** from prestigious companies and the formulation by them of appeals and urges in this respect. Among these, we mention the "Renegade Brigade" (Hamel 2009) and the strategic document adopted at the Davos Forum in 2017 called "The Compact for Responsive and Responsible Leadership – A Roadmap for Sustainable Long-Term Growth and Opportunity" (World Economic Forum, 2017). In the Renegade Brigade Manifesto (Hamel, 2009), 136 leading professors, consultants and managers from the USA, Europe, and Canada concluded that "the modern management" (management 1.0), which dates back to the late nineteenth century, has reached the limits of improvement. They have laid out a roadmap for reinventing management proposing to construct management 2.0, taking into consideration 25 management's grand challenges, which are summarized in Table 1.1.

According to the Renegade Brigade, the management should solve the following paradox: organizations must become more adaptable, innovative, and inspiring, without getting any less focused, disciplined, or performance oriented.

The strategic document "The Compact for Responsive and Responsible Leadership – A Roadmap for Sustainable Long-Term Growth and Opportunity" has been elaborated by 100 leading businesses and was finally adopted by all participants at the Davos Forum 2017 (World Economic Forum, 2017). According to this document, there is a need for a compact that **recalibrates the relationship between public corporations and their major investors** and conceives of **corporate governance as a collaboration among corporations, shareholders, and other stakeholders** working together to achieve long-term value and resist short termism.

Table 1.1 Management's grand challenges

1.	Ensure that the work of management serves a higher purpose
2.	Fully embed the ideas of community and citizenship in management systems
3.	Reconstruct management's philosophical foundations
4.	Eliminate the pathologies of formal hierarchy
5.	Reduce fear and increase trust
6.	Reinvent the means of control
7.	Redefine the work of leadership
8.	Expand and exploit diversity
9.	Reinvent strategy making as an emergent process
10.	De-structure and disaggregate the organization
11.	Dramatically reduce the pull of the past
12.	Share the work of setting direction
13.	Develop holistic performance measures
14.	Stretch executive time frames and perspectives
15.	Create a democracy of information
16.	Empower the renegades and disarm the reactionaries
17.	Expand the scope of employee autonomy
18.	Create internal markets for ideas, talent and resources
19.	Depoliticize decision-making
20.	Better optimize trade-offs
21.	Further unleash human imagination
22.	Enable communities of passion
23.	Retool management for an open world
24.	Humanize the language and practice of business
25.	Retrain managerial minds

Adapted from "Moon Shots for Management" by G. Hamel, 2009, *Harvard Business Review*, *87*(2), 91–98. Retrieved from https://hbr.org/2009/02/moon-shots-for-management

Disagreement among stakeholders is best resolved in a transparent and respectful manner, de-escalating conflictual stances wherever possible. Each manager participant as a responsive and responsible leader has undersigned and committed to acting within the remit of his/her responsibilities, duties, and influence to promote meaningful engagement between the board, investors, and other **stakeholders who builds mutual trust and effective stewardship**, and promotes the highest possible standards of corporate conduct, and to implement policies and practices within the organization that drive transformation towards the adherence to long-term strategies and sustainable growth for the benefit of all stakeholders.

12 **Enhancement of the managers' professionalization trend**: professional manager possesses the high management and business knowledge level and a vision focusing on change, innovation, and participation, being capable to initiate and practice a new management type in the relationship with the companies' stakeholders, and valorizing their large potential in a win-win approach. The companies managed by

high-level professional managers have been able to face much better the COVID-19 pandemic challenges and threats and to “catch” and use better the new opportunities.

13 **Development in the COVID-19 pandemic context of new managerial approaches** regarding the company strategy, leadership, management of human resources, organizational culture, CRM, SCM, and others **allows the company management to cooperate better and in a more performant manner with many major internal and external stakeholders** – managers, subordinates, suppliers, customers, local communities, state authorities, etc. Among these new or substantially remodelled concepts and approaches, we mention the HEART framework (Waldron & Wetherbe, 2020), an agile strategy (Heichler, 2020; Romeo, Moukanas, & Rung, 2020; Teece, Raspin, & Cox, 2020), resilience (Chaturvedi, Dey, & Singh, 2020; Kaplan, 2020; Levenson, 2020), adaptive leadership (Ramalingam, Nabarro, Oqubay, Carnall, & Wild, 2020), contingency planning (Levenson, 2020), transformational response (King et al., 2020), and multi-stakeholder capitalism (Romeo et al., 2020).

Societal Arguments

I This category of arguments is represented firstly by **tendencies in an organizational environment that enable and make possible the implementation of stakeholder-based management.** They are presented largely in Chapter 3 of this book. Here we just enumerate them:

1 Increase of business environment complexity, dynamism, and volatility.
2 Economy and society digitalization.
3 Work intellectualization.
4 Internationalization of all activities.
5 Multiculturalization of the labour force.
6 Nanotechnologization and biotechnologization.
7 Comprehensive networking in the society and economy.
8 Sustainable ecologization.
9 Intensification and diversification of state interventions in the economy.
10 Development of a powerful educational-formative dimension.
11 Multidimensional remodelling/reshaping of the markets.

Some of these trends are very complex, influencing not only the possibility of company management focusing on the stakeholders but also the need to do this in order to survive and be sustainable.

II **From a societal point of view, the COVID-19 pandemic** has increased the awareness of the society regarding the need to make profound changes in all its components, including the business environment and companies. Because of this, the society is more open to profound changes in all fields. Moreover, many specialists (Narayandas, Hebbar, & Li, 2020; Romeo et al., 2020; Tarabishy & Carayannis, 2020) **have stressed that given more attention and consideration to stakeholders represents the main option to remodel society, business, and especially companies.** The Global Risks Report 2020, presented at the World Economic Forum 2020 in Davos, stresses the need for a multi-stakeholder approach to addressing the world's greatest challenges (World Economic Forum, 2020). In fact, at the World Economic Forum's 50th annual meeting in Davos-Klosters, the focus was "Stakeholders for a cohesive and sustainable world".

III More than this, according to Joly (2021) – one of the best American companies CEO – has started **stakeholder era**, in which we need a refoundation of business and capitalism, and business leaders who prioritize common good and recognize the humanity of all stakeholders.

References

Bailey, A., Reeves, M., Whitaker, K., & Hutchinson, R. (2019). *The company of the future – Winning the '20s*. Retrieved from https://www.bcg.com/publications/2019/company-of-the-future.aspx

Battilana, J., & Casciaro, T. (2021). Power sharing can change corporations for the better. *Harvard Business Review*. Retrieved from https://hbr.org/2021/05/power-sharing-can-change-corporations-for-the-better

Beal, D., Eccles, R., Hansell, G., Lesser, R., Unnikrishnan, S., Woods, W., & Young, D. (2017). *Total societal impact: A new lens for strategy*. Retrieved from https://www.bcg.com/publications/2017/total-societal-impact-new-lens-strategy.aspx

Benkler, Y. (2011). The unselfish gene. *Harvard Business Review*, *89*(7–8), 76–85.

Boston Consulting Group. (2020). COVID-19 BCG perspectives series: Facts, scenarios and actions for leaders. Retrieved from https://media-publications.bcg.com/BCG-COVID-19-BCG-Perspectives-Version13.pdf

Carlsson-Szlezac, P., Reeves M., & Swartz, P. (2020). Understanding the economic shock of coronavirus. *Harvard Business Review*. Retrieved from https://hbr.org/2020/03/understanding-the-economic-shock-of-coronavirus

Chaturvedi, H., Dey A. K., & Singh, N. (2020). Coping with COVID-19. *Global Focus the EFMD Business Magazine*. Retrieved from https://www.globalfocusmagazine.com/coping-with-covid-19/

Coghlan, D. (2016). *Inside organizations: Exploring organizational experience*. London, UK: Sage Publications. 10.4135/9781526402424

Crane, A., Palazzo, G., Spence, L. J., & Matten, D. (2014). Contesting the value of "creating shared value." *California Management Review*, *56*(2), 130–153. 10.1525/cmr.2014.56.2.130

Freeman, R. E. (2017). Foreword. In J. Andriof, S. Waddock, B. Husted, & S. S. Rahman (Eds.), *Unfolding stakeholder thinking: Theory, responsibility and engag*ement (Vol. 1, pp. 7–8). New York, NY: Routledge.
Freeman, R. E., & Elms, H. (2018). The social responsibility of business is to create value for stakeholders. *MIT Sloan Management Review*. Retrieved from https://sloanreview.mit.edu/article/the-social-responsibility-of-business-is-to-create-value-for-stakeholders/
Freeman, R. E., Harrison, J. S., Wicks, A. C., Parmar, B. L., & De Colle, S. (2010). *Stakeholder theory: The state of art*. New York, NY: Cambridge University Press.
Ghose, S. (2020). Are you ready for the quantum computing revolution? *Harvard Business Review*. Retrieved from https://hbr.org/2020/09/are-you-ready-for-the-quantum-computing-revolution
Gjaja, M., Fæste, L., Hansell, G., & Hohner, D. (2020, April 16). COVID-19: Win the fight, win the future. Boston Consulting Group. Retrieved from https://www.bcg.com/en-hu/publications/2020/covid-scenario-planning-winning-the-future-series
Hamel, G. (2009).. Moon shots for management. *Harvard Business Review*, *87*(2), 91–98. Retrieved from https://hbr.org/2009/02/moon-shots-for-management
Heichler, E. (2020). Seize the moment. *MIT Sloan Management Review*. Retrieved from https://sloanreview.mit.edu/article/seize-the-moment/?og=Fall+2020+Issue+Horizontal
Hernandez, M. (2019). A shared passion for place can make a business more resilient. *MIT Sloan Management Review*. Retrieved from https://sloanreview.mit.edu/article/a-shared-passion-for-place-can-make-a-business-more-resilient/
Ignatius, A. (2019). Profit and purpose. *Harvard Business Review*, *97*(2), 10.
International Council for Small Business. (2019). ICSB's humane entrepreneurship initiative adopted by CEOs of nearly 200 companies. Statement on the purpose of cooperation. Retrieved from https://icsb.org/200ceos/
Joly, H. (2021). How to lead in the stakeholder era. *Harvard Business Review*. Retrieved from https://hbr.org/2021/05/how-to-lead-in-the-stakeholder-era
Kaplan, S. (2020). Why social responsibility produces more resilient organizations. *MIT Sloan Management Review*. Retrieved from https://sloanreview.mit.edu/article/why-social-responsibility-produces-more-resilient-organizations/
King, K., Wald, D., & Manly, J. (2020, April 21). Advantage beyond the crisis. Boston Consulting Group. Retrieved from https://www.bcg.com/en-hu/publications/2020/building-business-advantage-beyond-covid-19-crisis
Levenson, A. (2020). A long time until the economic new normal. *MIT Sloan Management Review*. Retrieved from https://sloanreview.mit.edu/article/a-long-time-until-the-economic-new-normal
Narayandas, D., Hebbar, V., & Li., L. (2020). Lessons from Chinese companies' response to Covid-19. *Harvard Business Review*. Retrieved from https://hbr.org/2020/06/lessons-from-chinese-companies-response-to-covid-19
Nicolescu, O., & Nicolescu, C. (2017). New approach – Quadrangle of knowledge based sustainability. *Proceedings of International Conference "Knowledge-Based Organization*," *23*(1), 411–417. Retrieved from https://www.researchgate.net/publication/318732098_New_Approach_-_Quadrangle_of_Knowledge_Based_Sustainability. doi:10.1515/kbo-2017-0068

Nowak, M. A. (2006). *Evolutionary dynamics: Exploring the equations of life*. Cambridge, MA: Harvard Business Press.

Post, J. E., Preston, L. E., & Sachs, S. (2002). *Redefining the corporation: Stakeholder management and organizational wealth*. Stanford, CA: Stanford University Press.

Radjou, N. (2020). The rising frugal economy. *MIT Sloan Management Review*. Retrieved from https://sloanreview.mit.edu/article/the-rising-frugal-economy/

Ramalingam, B., Nabarro, D., Oqubay, A., Carnall, D. R., & Wild, L. (2020). 5 principles to guide adaptive leadership. *Harvard Business Review*. Retrieved from https://hbr.org/2020/09/5-principles-to-guide-adaptive-leadership

Ready, D. A., Cohen, C., Kiron, D., & Pring, B. (2020). The new leadership playbook for digital age. *MIT Sloan Management Review*. Retrieved from https://sloanreview.mit.edu/projects/the-new-leadership-playbook-for-the-digital-age/?gclid=CjwKCAjwg6b0BRBMEiwANd1_SE8dUmZetK_peLCkKB-I6abknYo6vYcKUtSDNbE_MYo5CTuqs4SF6yRoCxlwQAvD_BwE

Romeo, J., Moukanas, H., & Rung, G. (2020). The age of accelerating strategy breakthroughs. *MIT Sloan Management Review*. Retrieved from https://sloanreview.mit.edu/article/the-age-of-accelerating-strategy-breakthroughs/

Sadun, R., Bloom, N., & Reenen J. V. (2017). Why do we undervalue competitive management? *Harvard Business Review*, *95*(5), 120–127.

Schein, E. H., & Schein, P. A. (2019). A new era for culture, change, and leadership. *MIT Sloan Management Review*, *60*(4), 52–58.

Schwartz, J., Hagel III, J., Wooll, M., & Monahan, K. (2019). Reframing the future of work. *MIT Sloan Management Review*. Retrieved from https://sloanreview.mit.edu/article/reframing-the-future-of-work/

Tarabishy, A. E., & Carayannis, E. (2020, September 12). Democratization of knowledge. *International Council for Small Business*. Retrieved from https://icsb.org/democratizationofknowledge/

Teece, D. J., Raspin, P. G., & Cox, D. R. (2020). Plotting strategy in a dynamic world. *MIT Sloan Management Review*. Retrieved from Review Special Collection: https://sloanreview.mit.edu/article/plotting-strategy-in-a-dynamic-world/

Waldron, T., & Wetherbe, J. (2020). Ensure that your customer relationships outlast coronavirus. *Harvard Business Review*. Retrieved from https://hbr.org/2020/04/ensure-that-your-customer-relationships-outlast-coronavirus

Weill, P., & Woerner, S. L. (2018). Surviving in an increasingly digital ecosystem. *MIT Sloan Management Review*, *59*(2), 26–28.

World Economic Forum. (2017). World Economic Forum annual meeting. The compact for responsive and responsible leadership – A roadmap for sustainable long-term growth and opportunity. Retrieved from https://www.weforum.org/events/world-economic-forum-annual-meeting-2017

World Economic Forum. (2020). *The global risk report 2020*. Retrieved from http://www3.weforum.org/docs/WEF_Global_Risk_Report_2020.pdf

Zhexembayeva, N. (2020). 3 things you're getting wrong about organizational change. *Harvard Business Review*. Retrieved from https://hbr.org/2020/06/3-things-youre-getting-wrong-about-organizational-change

2 Transition to the Knowledge-Based Economy and the Digital Economy – The Context of the Company Management, Stakeholder, and Social Responsibility Approach

Knowledge Revolution

The formulation "knowledge revolution", although increasingly used in recent decades, is not sufficiently well known and utilized at international level. Certain people could see it as just a replacement for the "information revolution" or a "tautology", while others could replace "knowledge revolution" with "digital revolution". Although there is a close connection between the information revolution and the knowledge revolution, the latter is quite different from several points of view: genesis, scope, foundation, nature and economic, social, scientific, education, and ecologic performances (Burton-Jones, 1999). In the last few years, the "formula industrial revolution 4.0" has frequently been used. In this book, we continue to utilize the term "knowledge revolution", because we believe that it suggestively reveals the new essential element involved in the present revolution – knowledge. The term "industrial revolution 4.0" hides the new content of the knowledge revolution and does not help to seize, understand, and take it into consideration.

Essentially, the **knowledge revolution** refers to a fundamental change from an economy based mainly on physical resources to an economy based predominantly on knowledge (Foray, 2009; Nicolescu & Nicolescu, 2011; Stewart, 1998b). This revolution is based on the determinant roles of knowledge within the modern economy. During the last few decades, we have noticed and taken into consideration the increasing economic impact of technology, information, economic processes, human capital, organizational capabilities, and competences, all very closely connected to knowledge. Each of these factors separately approached reveals the extremely valuable elements with huge pragmatic implications. Their common denominator is represented by knowledge, and these factors are actually being the ways to individualize and operationalize that knowledge.

From ancient times, wealth and power have been associated with the possession of physical resources. Traditional production assets – land, machinery, buildings, etc. – were predominantly of a physical nature.

DOI: 10.4324/9781003217701-2

For this reason, the need to have comprehensive and deep knowledge has been limited. Industrial revolutions in previous centuries were based to a large extent on steam power, the physical strength of human beings, and financial capital.

In recent decades, this situation started to change significantly, and the wealth and power of the twenty-first century – especially in the developed economies – are generated mainly by intangible intellectual resources, by knowledge capital. The knowledge revolution is a comprehensive and profound process generating essential mutations in all components of social activities, similar as intensity with those produced by industrial revolution.

Today, we are in the first stages of a knowledge revolution. The products and services are – from the knowledge point of view – more intensive than in the previous periods. Knowledge tends to become the main characteristic of many activities, more than the products and services produced (Cairncross, 1997). The impact of the knowledge revolution becomes visible through the market's volatility, the uncertainties regarding the direction of economic activities, the change in the knowledge structure of product costs and prices, the modification of jobs and careers, the perceived uncertainties of many people, and so on.

A knowledge-based economy is the result of the knowledge revolution, which is rapidly growing in the developed countries and – gradually – in other countries.

The knowledge revolution fulfils the change from a capitalist economy to a knowledge-based economy,[1] and it is, according to experts from the Denmark Ministry of Economy and Public Finance, a very complex process (Burton-Jones, 1999). In their opinion, informational technology and communication have an essential role in fulfilling the knowledge revolution. The new information and communication technologies determine radical changes in economic and social activities and, concomitantly, in the ways to acquire, create, disseminate, and use the knowledge. The new informatics and communication technologies determine the substantial modifications in organizations and in the methods used by producers of goods and services. The proliferation of these new technologies and the changes in the role and function of knowledge generate profound mutations in the modalities in which people work, learn, entertain, and communicate. In the economy, as a general result of the changes mentioned, knowledge becomes the essential factor in the attainment of high productivity and competitivity by companies, industries, national economies, and the world economy.

According to the renowned specialist Hamel (2002), the economic revolution in the twenty-first century is characterized by complex and non-linear behaviour in technology, competition, and global markets, which are very closely interconnected and demand continued innovation

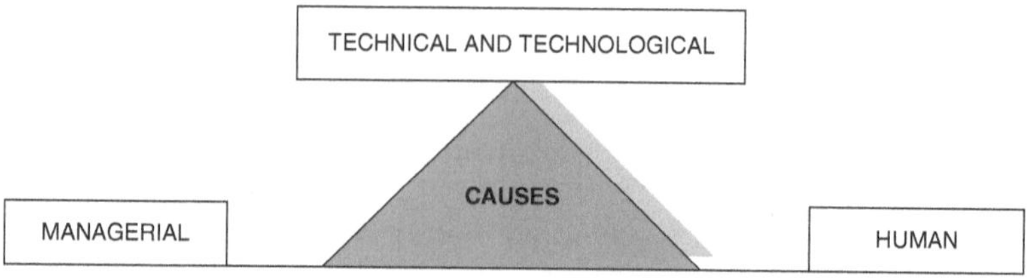

Figure 2.1 The typology of the causes.

Adapted from Organizația și managementul bazate pe cunoștințe (p. 156), by O. Nicolescu and C. Nicolescu, 2011, Prouniversitaria.

in order to create competitive wealth. In his opinion, the transition in the last few decades from an industrial-type economy to the new economy has involved three stages: innovations in products and services, innovation in business processes, and innovation in the entire economic thinking.

In the rich literature dedicated to the knowledge economy and knowledge society, the approach of causes generating a knowledge revolution is – in our opinion – only sporadic and not comprehensive, usually indicating mainly the new information and communication technologies. According to our analysis (Nicolescu & Nicolescu, 2005; Nicolescu & Nicolescu, 2011), the knowledge revolution is generated by **three categories of causes** (see Figure 2.1).

A **Technical and technological causes** refer to the essential changes made in the material factors of production, both in the hard equipment and in the soft technologies. In our opinion, the profound technical and technological changes contributing to the generation of the knowledge revolution deal with:

  a **Mutations in information processes,** based on informatic technologies, are often digital, which generate a huge increase and acceleration of the information and explicit knowledge collection, recording, transportation, dissemination, use, and deposit. In the economy, informatization determines the co-evolution of the demand and offer and radical changes in the business nature and dynamics (Mertens, 2004).

  b **Profound changes in communication processes,** which have as a consequence, greatly increased the capacity to transmit and to receive complex information and knowledge, despite distance, frequently in real time and often in ways similar to direct human communication, among a large number of individuals and organizations. Telecommunication has become more and more important, effective and efficient in the present economy.

c **Atoms process mutations, mainly by using new technologies – nanotechnology** – generating new materials, intelligent raw materials, micro mechanisms, etc., having amazing properties and performances. Nanotechnologies influence the economy and social development in multiple ways.

d **Living cells process mutations, through biotechnologies,** which are able to generate genetic changes in all components of the animal and vegetable kingdom. As a consequence, the yelling of plants and animals is substantially increased, and new superior plant varieties and animal breeds are created. All these biological products, which are very productive, incorporate quantities of big knowledge.

e **Unconventional energy (ubiquitous energy) production and use** – solar, wind, geothermal, and green energy, which are unlimited, cheaper, and cleaner than the classical energy.

Recently, the study "An MIT SMR Executive Guide" by Segars (2018) was disseminated, which deals with the content and impact of new technologies. It announces "**the universal technological revolution,** one that is fundamentally altering four key realms of our world: commerce, health care, learning and environment". In this study, seven classes of technology that are driving by a universal revolution are revealed:

- Pervasive computing: embedded proactive, networked digital processes;
- Wireless mesh networks: high bandwidth, dynamic, wireless, smart connectivity;
- Biotechnology: technologically created and enhanced life forms and system;
- 3D printing: digitally designed, chemically manufactured objects;
- Machine learning: augmented, automated data analysis;
- Nanotechnology: engineered atoms, super-materials;
- Robotics: precise, agile, intelligent mechanical systems.

According to the author, each of these technologies exhibits three distinctive and rapidly evolving capabilities:

> intelligence – the ability to sense or predict an environment or situation and act on that knowledge; natural interface – the ability to align with the actions, traits and intuitive schemes of humans, as well as the physics of nature; ubiquity – the ability to be omnipresent in previously discrete transactions, objects, machines and people. (Segars, 2018)

All presented elements regarding the new technical and technological mutations indicate an increase in their influence on the society and the economy, based on the high incorporation of new productive and sophisticated knowledge.

B **Human nature causes**, which reflect major changes in human resources, in work processes, in the capacity, and modalities to innovate and to generate value added in organizations. We synthesize these mutations in the following manner:

a **Quantitative and qualitative changes in the human resources level of education and knowledge.** From a quantitative point of view, we can see – especially in the developed countries – that the entire population is involved in the education system and in the lifelong learning process. From a qualitative point of view, we can see the radical changes in the teaching and learning processes at every level of the educational system. The theoretical dimension of education is decreasing, concomitantly with the amplification of the methodological pragmatic dimension, with active training methods becoming, gradually, predominant in all educational system components.

b All the aforementioned changes in the educational processes have, as a direct effect, the acquisition by all people – albeit to different degrees – of a **higher capacity to create, assimilate, use, and valorize knowledge.** As a consequence, the productive capacity of human resources is much higher than in the last century, concomitantly with the transformation of knowledge into the main economic "fuel", and it determines decisively the productivity and the performance of individuals and organizations.

c **In this context, the innovation availability and capacity of human resources are increasing.** Innovative people represent one of the three determinant factors that contribute to innovation (Manso, 2017). New types of education, new technologies, and actual market demands generate simultaneously extremely high possibilities and necessities for innovation. In all fields – technical, commercial, production, finance, education, ecologic, legislative, social, etc. – innovation is quasi permanent.

d **Intellectual work becomes, in almost all economic activities, predominant and/or makes a decisive contribution to achieving performance.** As a result, major challenges are taking place regarding jobs, social composition, the structures, and institutional mechanisms in the economy, science, education, administration, politics, etc.

Because of all these causes, the nature of work is radically different to the work done in the previous millennium. To an increasing degree, work means collection, combination, generation, and use of knowledge, while the percentage of physical processes is decreasing. Work tends to be based predominantly, both quantitatively and qualitatively, on knowledge and information becoming intellectualized.

C **Managerial causes** that reflect the major changes produced in the managerial processes and relationships in the ways used in order to combine and to utilize the material production factors and the human resources. The professional management practised in the last few decades contributes to the knowledge revolution and to building a knowledge-based economy and knowledge-based society through its new dimensions and operational modalities (Nicolescu, 2001):

a **Previsional management,** consisting in the anticipation of changes and in the designing of managerial solutions, allowing organizations to deal with these changes and to valorize their potential for enhancing performance.

b **Methodological-applicative management,** practising decisions and actions using to a large extent management systems, methods, techniques, etc. that increase the organization's rigour and efficacity.

c **Innovational management,** which consists in the permanent renewing of the managerial processes and relationship content and the modalities to implement them, having many and substantially direct and indirect positive effects on the functionality and performances of the entities involved (companies, clusters, networks, regions, countries, etc.) (Mitra, 2017). A 2017 PwC poll of 1,379 CEOs in 79 countries indicated that innovation was the aspect of their business that they most wanted to strengthen (PricewaterhouseCoopers, 2017).

d **Flexible management,** acting through quasi continued and intensive modification of the constructive and functional parameters of organizations' management, generating dynamism and efficacity in the organizations.

e **Motivational management,** managers' decisions, actions and behaviours taking into consideration permanently and at a high level, using special concepts, methods, and techniques, the interests of the organization's components and the other stakeholders, with a direct and significant positive impact on the organization's functionality and performance.

f **Informatized and digitalized management,** reflected in the use to a large extent, and intensively, of modern informatics, hard and soft, in designing and operating managerial solutions in organizations, having direct and substantial effects on the speed, rationality, and efficacy of the business and social processes in these organizations.

g **Formative management,** consisting in managers taking into consideration, in practising their managerial processes and relationships, the specific formative requirements, through adoption and implementation of decisions capable of increasing the level of knowledge and the potential of employees, seen as major vectors of the organization's development.

h **Participative management,** through the implication of the organization's employees and other stakeholders, directly and indirectly, using certain managerial bodies, methods and approaches, in the analysis and in the solution of many complex and important problems of the organization, generating more efficiency. Certain specialists already believe that today there is a collaborative revolution (Adler, Heckscher, & Prusak, 2011).

i **Systemic management,** consisting in the approach to, and solution of, problems faced by organizations taking into consideration their interdependences, placing in a central position the organization's strategic objectives, and considering the principal endogenous and exogenous variables involved, generating high multidimensional efficiency.

j **Internationalized management,** by using in the design, adoption and implementation of managerial solutions, knowledge and information regarding managerial, commercial, financial, educational, fiscal, scientific, ecologic, etc. evolutions of the world economy and its important components, and managerial concepts, methods or approaches from other countries.

All these types of causes presented determine the knowledge revolution, which is generating profound and rapid changes in society and the economy.

Knowledge: Main Characteristics and Roles

The knowledge revolution and the new knowledge economy are based on knowledge, information, and data. American specialist Burton-Jones (1999) believes that these three concepts are related as illustrated in Figure 2.2.

Data is defined as a signal that can be sent from a transmitter to a receiver – human beings, computers, etc. **Information** represents intelligent data for a receiver, which brings something new to them. According to Stewart (1998b), **information is different from knowledge** in four respects:

- **Size,** information is usually smaller than knowledge, representing its components;

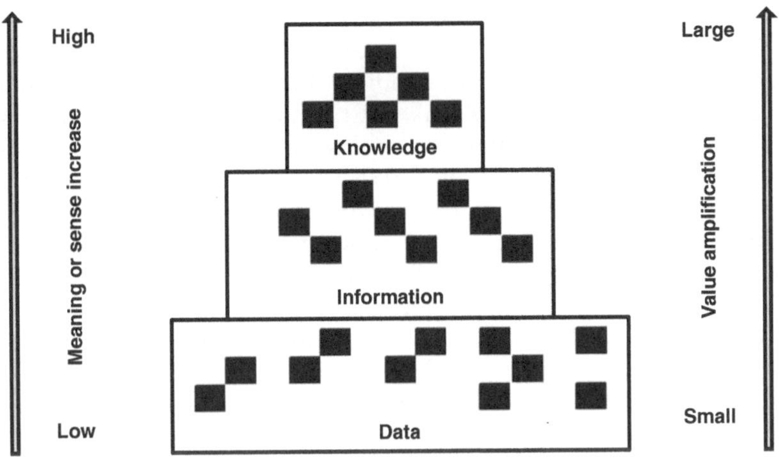

Figure 2.2 Interrelationships among knowledge, information, and data.

Adapted from *Knowledge capitalism: Business, work, and learning in the new economy* (p. 6), by A. Burton-Jones, 1999, Oxford University Press.

- **Nature,** because knowledge always contains "expertise", elements that could be used, generating solutions;
- **Temporal,** since knowledge "expertise" involves time-consuming implementation, giving it a processual character;
- **Intelligence,** because knowledge makes the objects in which it is incorporated smart and quite frequently smaller and slighter. The modern mobile phones are a very good example in this respect.

Despite all these differences, in an organization, separation between information and knowledge is not always easy to fulfil in practice, especially when there are more persons involved who interact. There are situations when what is information for one person represents knowledge for another, as they have higher intellectual capacity and/or operational capabilities.

Taking into account the elements presented above, we can assert that in order to be correct, the **delimitation between information and knowledge should be done contextually,** taking into consideration the framework, the factors involved, and the results generated. In this regard, the specialist Cairncross (1997) demonstrated that distance plays an important role in the generation and use of knowledge and it "did not die", despite the statements made by numerous informaticians.

Burton-Jones (1999) defines knowledge as "cumulative stocks of information and abilities generated by the receiver's use of information". In our opinion, this definition should be completed with two aspects. When the receiver is a human being, knowledge reflects his/her perception and judgment on information received as raw material. Knowledge is also different from information because it depends on the intellectual capacity of the receiver, on his/her competencies regarding the perception, understanding, and use of the information (Bouchez, 2012; Ichijo & Nonaka, 2007). Knowledge incorporates information as its main input. Knowledge and information are substantially complementary (Foray, 2009). The second specification refers to the fact that knowledge is always different from information due to its **capacity to generate value added** (Adler et al., 2011; Bouchez, 2014; El-Korany, 2007; Mertens, 2004; Russ, Fineman, & Jones, 2010; Seeley & Davenport, 2006). It is not easy to identify this capacity, but it is always present in knowledge. Without this capacity, we are dealing with information or data.

Based on the previous elements, we can say that knowledge has **two dimensions – human and economic**. In a company, there is knowledge in human resources (human capital), in clients' preferences and demands (clients' capital), and in its products, processes, organizational capabilities, and system (structural capital). As a result, the value of knowledge assets could significantly surpass the value of company tangible assets (Burton-Jones, 1999; El-Korany, 2007).

A few years ago, a group of researchers from several North American universities (Russ et al., 2010, p. 8) defined knowledge using a mathematical formula:

$$K = P \times (P + S + P \times S)$$

in which:

K = knowledge
P = people
S = systems
P × S = synergy generated by people and systems.

This formula indicates that the processes and systems multiply everyone's capacity to create knowledge.

Analyses carried out by many specialists have revealed that in the present economy, knowledge achieves four essential roles or functions (see Figure 2.3).

Knowledge as **raw material** contributes to a large extent to producing modern products. It is obvious that in manufacturing a computer or TV, besides metal and plastic, a lot of knowledge is involved. Moreover, knowledge represents a major part of the value of these products.

Knowledge also represents an **essential production factor**, because together with classical production factors – labour force and production means – knowledge, often structured as technology, plays a part in all production and commercial phases. Of course, the more modern a company is, the more contributions the knowledge used makes as a production factor.

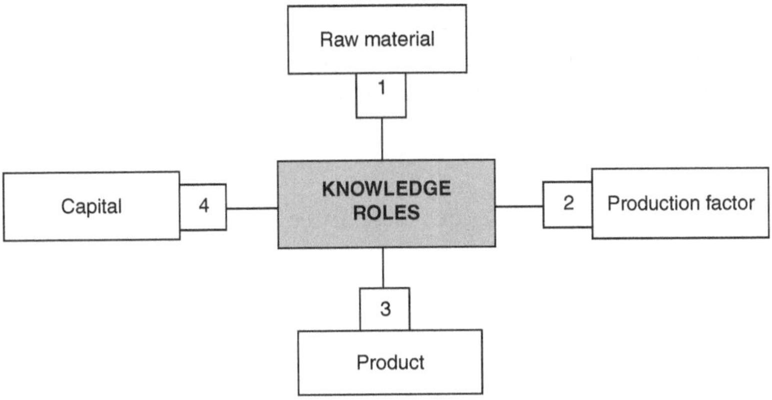

Figure 2.3 Knowledge roles in economy.

Knowledge represents very frequently a **finished product itself**, such as software, a technical project, card, patent, quality standard, marketing analysis, business plan, ecological project, management project, etc. In recent years, we have witnessed in the fast diversification of knowledge products, concomitantly with an increase of their weight in companies' turnover and in countries' GNP.

It is worth mentioning that at the same time, the majority of physical products incorporate much more knowledge. High-tech products – computers, telephones, satellites, TV sets, drones, robots, etc. – are "richer" in knowledge, which determines "de facto" their high performance and value.

In the total value of modern companies, **knowledge capital** tends to represent a high weight. Although intangible, the knowledge of companies, human resources, technologies, commercial management, financial know-how, etc. has high value, which is more frequently evaluated and taken into consideration in the companies' value on the stock exchange.

All the elements presented in this section demonstrate the multiple and essential roles of knowledge in companies, national economies, and the world economy. In practice, without knowledge none of the socio-economic entities – micro, mezzo, macro, international – could survive and work successfully. Knowledge represents in the modern economy the main stock of accumulation and the major source of wealth (Bouchez, 2014). Moreover, "knowledge not only makes for a more productive and resilient economy but it can also lead to the kind of agility and problem-solving ability that is especially needed in the face of sudden unanticipated shocks" (Mokyr, 2020), like the COVID-19 pandemic.

Knowledge-Based Economy Concept

Before defining and characterizing the knowledge-based economy, we consider it useful to present the three elements that in the opinion of Stewart (1998a, pp. 14–18) represents **the pillars of this type of economy:**

a **Knowledge becomes the main content of the purchase, sale and production processes.** In order to demonstrate this, Stewart presents numerous figures regarding the economy of the USA.

b **The knowledge asset – a component of intellectual capital** – becomes more important than financial and techno-material assets. In the past, when we referred to a company we indicated the building, deposits, etc. – mainly physical assets. In the present we usually indicate its brand.

c **In the process of valorizing the knowledge and the intellectual capital,** and obtaining **the intellectual property are needed new terminology, new managerial methods and techniques, new technologies, and – not the last – new strategies.** In other words, the knowledge-based economy is a new type of economy that needs new concepts and approaches in order to be able to describe, explain, understand, and – against this new background – valorize its huge potential.

Of course, we may have some doubts about these three pillars, especially regarding their capacity to synthetize the quintessence of the knowledge-based economy. We consider them very useful, as they are able to bring to the foreground the essential features of the knowledge-based economy, which is very necessary to understand its content.

Specialists' opinions regarding the **definition of the knowledge-based economy or the new economy are rather different.** For example, Soete (2002), in a very well-known book edited by Archibugi and Lundvall, defines the knowledge-based economy as an economy dominated to a large extent by global influence and information and communication speed, often in real time despite the distance. They believe that its main features are globalization and digitalization, which confer intangibility on international transactions, both commercial and direct investment. The knowledge-based economy involves the emergence of new companies and new industries.

Examination of this definition reveals that actually the specialists approach the new economy almost entirely from informatization and internationalization perspectives. They do not realize the essential difference between information and knowledge, and without this landmark, the "new economy" refers less to the economy (except its international dimension) and more to the development of communication within the economy. Although their approach contains valuable elements, it is not satisfactory because it does not grasp and take into consideration the major changes in the business processes. We appreciate that their approach represents a very interesting and useful definition of the "new economy" in the transition phase towards a knowledge-based economy.

Stewart approaches the knowledge-based economy in greater depth, always using this denomination without referring to the "new economy". He specifies that the knowledge-based economy has money in view – because it is an economy – in the context of purchasing, producing, and selling knowledge. The knowledge-based economy has its background intellectual capital (Stewart, 1998a). Knowledge – the foundation of the knowledge-based economy – is important not only for high-tech companies but also for companies with a low technical level, non-profit organizations, governmental agencies, etc. Stewart's definition outlines the fact that in the knowledge-based economy, the elements of an economic nature, reflected in the priority given to business performance, remain essential. This is changed only for obtaining business performance. Stewart's second major contribution is "knowledge debunking", outlining that knowledge is not limited only to high technologies, sophisticated software or hardware etc. Knowledge is an approach with an emphasis on economic finality, on its capacity to generate value added, despite its nature, modernity or incorporated information.

The knowledge-based economy also means the development of a new culture in the society, which determines profound changes in our way of thinking, working, and living (Caspar, 2014). The very well-known international organization the **OECD** has formulated the following definition of a knowledge-based economy: "an economy based directly on the production, distribution and use of knowledge and information". This definition has been adopted in many countries and also by the European Commission. It was included in a study edited by the European Union (European Commission – Directorate-General for Enterprise and Industry, 2004, p. 5). In such an economy, there is a high degree of connectivity among the involved agents, and knowledge is used and exploited in all ways possible in business activities (Atkeson & Kehoe, 2007).

World Bank specialists have elaborated another definition: "[A] knowledge economy is one where organizations and people acquire, create, disseminate and use knowledge more effectively for greater economic and social development" (World Bank, 2017). It calculates the knowledge index, which evaluates countries' ability to generate, adapt, and diffuse knowledge.

We have started from these definitions; we have analyzed other approaches to the knowledge-based economy (Castells, 2010; Dumova &

Fiordo, 2010; Foray, 2009; Jouyet & Lévy, 2007; Mallovan, Liquète, & Verlaet, 2015; Powell & Snellman, 2004); we have taken into consideration certain definitions of previous economic types (capitalism, feudalism, etc.); and, based on these, we have formulated **another definition for the knowledge-based economy.** Essentially a knowledge-based economy is characterized by the transformation of knowledge into essential raw material, capital, product, and production factors of an economy, and by economic processes within the knowledge generation, purchase, sale, learning, use, development, sharing, storage, and the protection become predominantly, and decisively determine the productivity, the profit, and the long-term sustainability.[2]

We believe that this definition of a knowledge-based economy brings **some important supplementary elements compared with the previous variants of definitions:**

a It indicates the role and economic functions of knowledge within economic processes, outlining its multidimensionality and comprehensive character never found so far for other elements involved in economic processes;
b It specifies that knowledge transformation represents the main content of economic processes, the types of knowledge operations, and their major contribution to the generation of value added;
c It asserts the conditioning relationship between the obtaining of economic performance and sustainability on the one hand, and the carrying out of the set of knowledge processes and the using of intellectual capital on the other, integrating, of course, classical resources (technical-material, labour force, financial, etc.).

The highlighting of the superior qualitative nature and the specificity of the knowledge-based economy does not mean a unilateral approach to the economic system. Naturally, a knowledge-based economic system could not be reduced only to knowledge. All inputs necessary for economic activities are maintained. They changed their weights in the economic circuits and partially their nature and manifestation ways because of the major impact of the knowledge.

Without any doubt, although the economic processes will change, they will always need human, technical-material, and financial resources, but in superior configurations and mechanisms, determined by the progress in previous periods by new elements. It is very important that political factors from numerous countries have picked up on the need to construct a knowledge-based economy. At the Lisbon Summit in 2000, EU countries decided through the Lisbon Strategy to build a knowledge-based economy (The Lisbon European Council, 2000). Ten years later, in the EU Strategy 2020 for 2010–2020, it is planned to develop a knowledge-based economy or smart economy

(European Council, 2010). Today's engine of economic growth, represented by the knowledge-based economy, "may lessen the long-term economic impact of the COVID-19 pandemic" (Mokyr, 2020).

Knowledge-Based Economy Features

The identification and presentation of the main characteristics of the knowledge-based economy contribute to the better understanding of its specificity and of the many and major impacts on all economic and social elements in the society. In Figure 2.4, we have indicated what the **most relevant characteristics of the knowledge-based economy** are, according to our research (Nicolescu & Nicolescu, 2019), which are largely different from the characteristics established by other specialists (European Commission – Directorate-General for Enterprise and Industry, 2010; Garmise, 2006; Grant, 2007).

Of course, these features of the knowledge-based economy are not exhaustive and some of them are more difficult to fully understand due to their specific nature. But all together, they provide valuable elements in order to grasp the specificity of the knowledge-based economy and the essential differences compared with the economy that is still predominant at present.

Digital Revolution and Digital Economy

The digital revolution started a few decades ago, and there are many and very diversified approaches. Recently, the specialists Unruh and Kiron (2017) proposed a framework for understanding digitalization and its implications, which in our opinion is very helpful (Figure 2.5).

In fact, in this framework, **the three phases of the digital revolution** are presented:

- The first phase is **digitization, which refers mainly to the products and services changed** from analogue to digital format. Digitization has happened first in sectors where products and services rely just on information (publishing, music, finance), and it has been slower, for more tangible, physical products. **The main result of the first phase of digital revolution has been digitized products and services.**
- The second phase – **digitalization – has focused on organizational level,** involving industries in which have been developed new business models and business processes capable of valorizing the benefits to the newly digitized products. In this phase, new types of companies, like Apple, Amazon, etc., have started and developed rapidly. Digitalization has not been limited only to the business sector but spreading to the public sector too. **The main result of this phase is new organization models and processes.**

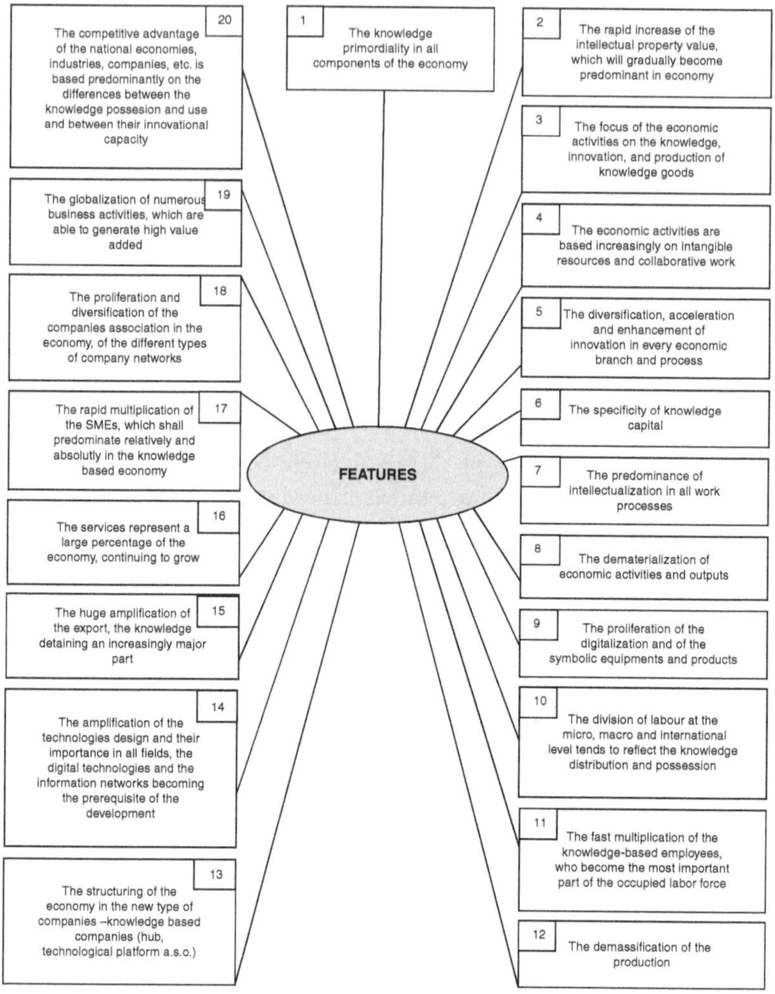

Figure 2.4 Knowledge-based economy features.

Figure 2.5 A framework for understanding digitalization.

Adapted from "Digital transformation on purpose" by G. Unruh and D. Kiron, 2017, *MIT Sloan Management*, p. 3. Retrieved from https://sloanreview.mit.edu/article/digital-transformation-on-purpose/

- **The third phase – digital transformation – has occurred at the level of the entire economy and society**, because of the large-scale diffusion to the new technologies. Digital technologies alter individual and group values, decisions, actions, and behaviours. Digital technologies transform everything (Nicolescu & Nicolescu, 2005) at the individual, organizational, and societal level. They even transform the human genome (Unruh & Kiron, 2017). The main results of this phase – which is continuing rapidly – are the **major changes in the economy and in the society, structures, mechanisms, behaviours, and performances**. These transformations are both positive and negative.

The technologies that make a major contribution to digital transformation, and will have a tendency to increase their impact in the next decade, are the following: the Internet of Things (IOT) and connected devices, artificial intelligence (AI), big data analysis and cloud, custom manufacturing and 3D printing, robots and drones, pervasive computing, biotechnology, machine learning, nanotechnology, social media and platforms and autonomous vehicles (Ben-Ner & Siemsen, 2017; Fisher, 2017; Pigni, Piccoli, & Watson, 2016). According to a recent study (Segars, 2018), combining the capabilities of these technologies will give rise to even more powerful super-technologies that will open a new digital frontier.

The digital revolution has multidimensional effects, not only technological but also economic, ecologic, human, etc. Certain specialists, like Becerra (2017) from the Boston Consulting Group, in his speech at the Davos Forum in 2017, believe that the digital revolution is not about technology, but it is about people.

We present a selection of the **major effects** of the digital revolution based on the works of representative specialists and organizations in the field (Bukht & Heeks, 2017; Dahlman, Mealy, & Wermelinger, 2016; Meyer, 2017; Rifkin, 2016; Schwab, 2016; World Economic Forum & Accenture, 2018):

- change of consumer expectations;
- cheap and better technologies;
- falling cost of advanced technologies;
- product enhancement;
- development of collaborative innovation;
- cheap connection and a more connected world;
- rapid proliferation/extension of networks;
- three big impacts on the labour markets: substitution, augmentation, and creation;
- disruption of existing economic processes, systems, and sectors;

- reshaping of existing consumer behaviour, business interaction, and business models;
- restructuring of the economy and society;
- deepening inequality in society;
- decreased trust in all technology sectors;
- positive contribution to the decoupling of economic growth from an increase in emissions and resources;
- increased productivity in many sectors;
- new opportunities for leisure, artistic expression and a healthier future;
- generation of new risks, challenges, and opportunities for individuals, organizations, economies, and societies.

The generic results of the digital revolution are – according to its three phases – a **digital sector, digital economy, and digitalized economy**, as we can see in Figure 2.6.

The figure reveals explicitly the content of each of them and the relationships among their content. **The digital economy** is defined as "that part of economic output derived solely or primarily from digital technologies, with a business model based on digital goals and services" (Bukht & Heeks, 2017, p. 1). The digital economy "encompasses both the core digital sector and also the broader range of extensive digital activity, without claiming that all digitized activity is part of the digital

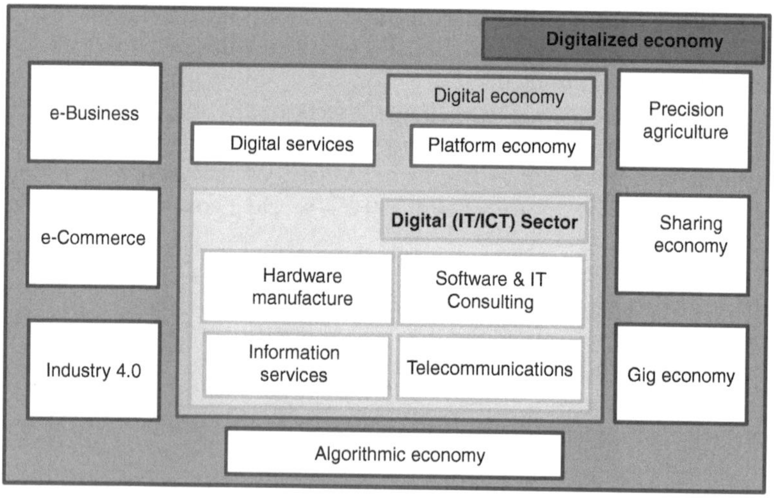

Figure 2.6 Scoping the digital economy.

Adapted from Defining, conceptualising and measuring the digital economy (p. 13), by R. Bukht and R. Heeks, 2017, https://diodeweb.files.wordpress.com/2017/08/diwkppr68-diode.pdf.

economy" (Bukht & Heeks, 2017, p. 13).[3] The dimension of the digital economy is huge: its total value reaches USD 2.9 trillion (Gada, 2016). **The digitalized economy** is the result of the digital transformation, and it is more comprehensive quantitatively and higher from a qualitative point of view than the digital economy.

Digital business is different from traditional business in many respects. According to a recent investigation (Kane, Phillips, Copulsky, & Andrus, 2019), the biggest six differences are the following: pace of business (speed, rate of change), culture and mindset (creativity, learning risk taking), flexible, distributed workplace (collaboration, decision-making transparency), productivity (streamlined processes, continuous improvement), improved access to use of tools (greater data availability, technology performance), and connectivity (remote working, always on). During the recent period, within COVID-19 context, digital business development has accelerated, proving again its unique features and advantages.

Relationships Between Digital/Digitalized Economy and Knowledge-Based Economy

In the previous paragraphs, we presented the main elements that characterize the knowledge-based economy: digital economy, digitalized economy, knowledge revolution, digitization, digitalization, and digital transformation. In order to better understand the complex relationships between them and their influence on management, economic, and societal processes, we analyze comparatively a digital–digitalized economy and a knowledge-based economy. We identified **five main differences** (Nicolescu & Nicolescu, 2019) as indicated in Table 2.1.

Based on these elements, we can state that the **relationships between the knowledge-based economy and digital/digitalized economy are relationships between the whole and the part.** A knowledge-based economy is more comprehensive, complex, and multidimensional than a digital/digitalized economy. The knowledge-based economy incorporates entirely the digital and digitalized economy. At the same time, it is important to emphasize that the digitalized economy is an essential component of the knowledge-based economy, and it plays a major role in its development.

In the near future, the digitalization of the knowledge-based economy will increase, with many positive effects on it, but also with increasing challenges and risks. The present knowledge-based economy, according to reputed professor Jeremy Rifkin, is characterized by

> digital interconnectivity. Social capital is as vital as market capital, access is as important as ownership, sustainability supersedes consumerism, collaboration is as crucial as competition, virtual

Table 2.1 The main differences between a digital and digitalized economy on the one hand and a knowledge-based economy on the other

No.	*Criteria*	*Digital and Digitalized Economy*	*Knowledge-Based Economy*
1.	Genesis	A digital and digitalized economy are the results of the digital revolution having digital technologies as its main content.	A knowledge-based economy is generated by the knowledge revolution,[4] which involves five technical causes, four human causes, and ten managerial causes (see Section 2.1).
2.	Scope	A digital and digitalized economy contain a core digital sector (IT/ICT) and the other components of the economy where digital technologies are used (see Figure 2.6). The potential for development is very large. For example, a study by strategy consultant Roland Berger, cited by Schweer and Sahl (2017), concludes that the digital transformation could add around 1.25 trillion euros to Europe's industrial value creation by 2025. Another evaluation presented at the Davos Forum in 2017 estimated that digitalization could generate a value of around 100 trillion over the next decade globally (World Economic Forum & Accenture, 2017).	A knowledge-based economy unfolds at the level of the entire economy, where the economic processes are focused increasingly on knowledge. It is much larger than a digitalized economy, because of the large amount of knowledge – primarily tacit knowledge – that is not digital and could never be digital.
3.	Foundation	Digital and digitalized economies are focused on the use of digital technologies: Internet	A knowledge-based economy is focused on knowledge (creation, purchase, store,

(*Continued*)

Table 2.1 (Continued)

No.	*Criteria*	*Digital and Digitalized Economy*	*Knowledge-Based Economy*
		of Things (IOT), artificial intelligence (AI), data analytics and cloud, 3D printing, drones, robots, technological platforms, etc., and their impact on the level of product, organization, and – to a less extend – the economy and the society. In these types of economy, it is not done the difference between information and knowledge, and it is not emphasizing the essential capacity of knowledge to create value added.	dissemination, use, share, learning, protecting, valorizing, etc.), taking into consideration both explicit and tacit knowledge, the latter not being organically associated with digital technologies.
4.	Nature of processes involved	A digital and digitalized economy deal mainly with information processes, where digital technologies and to a smaller extent their impact on business processes are largely used.	A knowledge-based economy deals with all economic processes based on knowledge; economic and social processes are approached taking into consideration their multidimensional nature – economic, social, ecologic, etc.
5.	Performance	Digital and digitalized economy performances are evaluated to a large extent by specific indicators, which reflect the particularities of the digital technologies used: for example, digital traction metrics, presented at the Davos Forum in 2017 (see Table 2.2). Of course, they are usually filled with some financial indicators.	Performance of the knowledge-based economy is evaluated multidimensional – economic, social, ecologic, and educational. For example, the Knowledge Economy Index (KEI) is based on the average of four subindexes, which represent the four pillars of the knowledge-based economy: economic, innovative, and institutional regime

(*Continued*)

Table 2.1 (Continued)

No.	*Criteria*	*Digital and Digitalized Economy*	*Knowledge-Based Economy*
			(EIR); innovation and technological adoption; education and training; information and communication technologies (ICT) infrastructure. Each of them is calculated using many and diversified indicators.

Table 2.2 Company digital indicators

Company Digital Indicators			
Size	*Number of Active Users*	*Rate of Users*	*Implication*
Examples	*Examples*	*Examples*	*Examples*
• Total conversions • Overall traffic • Number of users • Chanel specific traffic	• Total site visits • Number of monthly active users • Number of weekly active users	• Ratio of new users to repeat users • Click through rates • Lead to close ratio • Abandon rate	• Return of digital investing • Top technical talent attracted, promoted and retained • Interactions per visit • Client satisfaction index

Adapted from Digital transformation initiative (p. 23), 2018, World Economic Forum. Retrieved from http://reports.weforum.org/digital-transformation/wp-content/blogs.dir/94/mp/files/pages/files/dti-executive-summary-20180510.pdf

> integration of value chains gives way to lateral economies of scale, intellectual property makes room for open sourcing and creative common licensing, GNP becomes less relevant and social indicators become more valuable in measuring the quality of life of society, and an economy based on scarcity and profit vies for a Zero Marginal Society Cost, where an increasing array of goods and services are produced and shared for free in an economy of abundance. (Rifkin, 2016)

In the last few decades, the knowledge-based economy has developed fast, especially in the developed countries. The European Union, in order to accelerate the construction of the knowledge-based economy, has adopted two strategies – the Lisbon Strategy in 2000 and the 2020 EU Strategy in 2010. Unfortunately, these were not very successfully implemented.

For the next period, it is necessary, using systemic and realistic approaches, not reactive but proactive, at the world and organization level, to harness the huge potential of all types of knowledge, of a digital transformation. The Davos Forum 2017 (World Economic Forum & Accenture, 2017) and many specialists (Bukht & Heeks, 2017; Dahlman et al., 2016; Kiron & Unruh, 2018; Meyer, 2017; Mosco, 2017; Schweer & Sahl, 2017; Unruh & Kiron, 2017) have provided many essential elements capable of unlocking knowledge value to society.

Knowledge-Based Company – The Essential Component of the Knowledge-Based Economy

The knowledge-based economy has as its principal component a knowledge-based organization. The majority of knowledge-based organizations are **knowledge-based companies** that could be defined as companies that rely on an equilibrated approach from an economic, ecologic, social, and educational point of view and are able to highly valorize knowledge and other available resources, generating long-term efficiency and multidimensional performances, validated by the market and recognized by the society. The knowledge-based company is a sustainable enterprise, which establishes long-term economic, social, ecologic, and educational objectives and has the capacity to fulfil them through intensive use of knowledge, producing multiple positive effects for an organization, its stakeholders, and environment.

A digital company is a very important type of knowledge-based company that is characterized by the widespread use of digital technologies and by intensive use of digitization, digitalization, and digital transformation. Digital companies are very innovative and flexible, focusing on up-to-date knowledge, closely associated with digital technologies. Usually, a digital company is a networking-driven company. There is a large variety of digital companies, such as hubs, technological platforms, living labs, etc.

Analysis conducted by specialists, as well as the activities and performances of companies, reveals that a **knowledge-based company presents** specific features that are quite different from classical enterprises, which still predominate. In Table 2.3, we display these features, synthesized from the many studies (Burton-Jones, 1999; Cairncross, 2003; Fabbri, Glaser, Gaujard, & Toutain, 2016; Iansiti & Lakhani, 2017; Nicolescu & Nicolescu, 2011; PricewaterhouseCoopers, 2017; Schneider, Wickert, & Marti, 2017; Weill & Woerner, 2017; Weill & Woerner, 2018; Williamson & De Meyer, 2012).

Table 2.3 The features of the knowledge-based company

No.	*Features*
1.	Decrease of physical assets, activities, and employees, concomitantly with the development of the internal knowledge base and the amplification of the relationships with clients, suppliers, and external human resources.
2.	Externalization of activities that are not essentially for the company, concomitantly with internalization of other activities, essential for organization
3.	Change of the relationships with external human resources necessary for the company, by asking them to fulfil less important activities, like office works and maintenance operations.
4.	Amplification and diversification of the knowledge treatment processes – creation, purchase, dissemination, use, share, storing, learning, sale, protection, etc. – that have a decisive impact on the company's competitivity.
5.	Large scale of the innovation processes in the company's activities, being technical, commercial, human resources, managerial, etc.; innovation becomes a precondition of the company's survival and performance.
6.	Strategic development of the company relies on increasing the organization's knowledge (vertically and horizontally), which supposes that the company has the capacity to develop its own knowledge and to seize the opportunities for synergetic cooperation with other enterprises in the knowledge domain.
7.	Intensive preoccupation of the company with implementation of digital technologies and other up-to-date technologies, methods and techniques.
8.	Internal organization model of the knowledge-based company is to a large extent similar to the human cognitive model, involving structural networks, semi-autonomous team, flexibility, organizational and individual abilities for learning, etc.
9.	Proliferation of participative and collaborative approaches, with the company acting to develop collaborative communities.
10.	Reduction of the number and roles of middle and low-level managers and, gradually, externalization of peripheral works, concomitantly with the integration in the company of "knowledge managers", who frequently start their work with the company as change consultants and agents.
11.	Amplification of the learning processes of human resources, with the company becoming a learning organization.
12.	Remodelling of the company's managerial and economic capacities, in order to exploit better the knowledge and digital technologies.
13.	Training investment directed to a certain extent at external labour force used, in order to replace their own company employees, who are not developing skills sufficiently.
14.	Restructuring of the company's motivation system according to the following requirements: • increase of the stimulants given to all employees, according to their proven performance and merits; • increase of the stimulants based on individual performance for peripheral employees;

(*Continued*)

Table 2.3 (Continued)

No.	*Features*
	• enhancement of the concomitant use of organizational, group and individual stimulants for the company's core employees; • widespread use of promotion as a stimulant for internal and external company human resources.
15.	Development of an open culture, with the company communicating and inviting clients, suppliers, and other external stakeholders in the organization in order to follow how it implements the decisions regarding their entities.
16.	Use of transparent and correct approaches in the company relationships with internal and external company stakeholders, paying close attention to building and maintaining "trust capital".
17.	Implementation of multiple collaborative ways with other organizations participating in networks, ensuring company has better resource access, time, and cost conditions.
18.	Diminution of barriers between the different types of company, between human enterprise resources and persons, and between home work and work organization.
19.	Gradual decrease of the boundaries among companies.
20.	Maximization of the company's efficiency and effectiveness is based concomitantly on highly cohesive teams and on the moderate interaction among them.
21.	Company focus on intellectual capital obtaining, use, protection, and valorization.
22.	Organization focus on the achievement of multidimensional performances – business, social, ecologic, and educational – which are conditioning decisively the company's sustainability.

There are **two ways to create a new type of enterprise – a knowledge-based company:**

a **Business transformation of "classical" enterprises,** sometimes by digital transformation, fulfilling, according to specialists, a complex process, structured in six steps:

- knowledge identification and evaluation
- knowledge re-engineering
- knowledge networking
- knowledge-based motivation
- knowledge enhancement
- knowledge-based company maturization

The number of "classical companies" that transform themselves into knowledge-based companies is increasing rapidly, because – as outlined recently by the renowned specialists Weill and Woerner (2017) – today "companies must reinvent to survive".

b **Creation of knowledge-based companies, usually digital companies.** A major characteristic of this type of company is the strong emphasis on internal and external stakeholders, using a wide range of approaches. These start-ups are built from the beginning as ecosystems, taking different forms: hubs, living labs, fab labs, technological platforms, etc. Frequently these are very competitive, with some of them becoming famous – Apple, Microsoft, Uber, etc.

Knowledge-based companies should be sustainable organizations, and their activity and management should **rely on the quadrangle of knowledge sustainability** (see Figure 1.1 in the chapter "Instead of introduction" elaborated by Nicolescu and Nicolescu, 2017). The quadrangle highlights the four dimensions of the efficiency and effectiveness of a knowledge-based company. In our opinion, this quadrangle synthesizes in a systemic way the essential elements regarding economic and social utility and the impact of a knowledge-based organization. The four dimensions on which the model is structured represent axes that must be considered by company managers and other stakeholders, in order to harness the huge knowledge potential and to generate accelerated and sustainable development.

The eight key lessons formulated recently by a group of specialists (Kiron et al., 2017) could be very useful for achieving company sustainability. Also, super-technologies will offer rich opportunities for companies (Segars, 2018).

Business Ecosystems – The New Performant Structures of the Knowledge-Based Economy

A business ecosystem represents a new form of knowledge-based company developed in the last few decades that is radically different from classical companies. **A business ecosystem** is a flexible and adaptable network of organizations – suppliers, producers, distributors, customers, competitors, and other stakeholders – interacting on the delivery of specific products or services, both through cooperation and competition. The ecosystem is generated by transforming companies from being product-driven to networking-driven. The **main characteristics** of the ecosystem (Puranam, Alexy, & Reitzig, 2014; Uden, Wangsa, & Damiani, 2007; Williamson & De Meyer, 2012) are the following:

- ecosystem products and/or services are complex, not standard, involving a large amount of, and specific, tacit and explicit knowledge;
- each organization component affects and is affected by others;
- each organization is proactive in developing mutual relationships with other ecosystem components;

- one organization is the lead company and uses "smart power" to play an active role in directing, stimulating and shaping the business ecosystem around it;
- the ecosystem structure, activities, and interactions are flexible and can be rapidly reconfigured;
- the ecosystem's organizations are embedded in a specific flexible business environment and they need to co-evolve together;
- the business ecosystem is an informal system, flexible, innovative, adaptive, and dynamic, focused on satisfying the changing demands in certain market niches and on engineering effective ways to capture profit for its components.

In the context of digital transformation, special attention has been paid to the **digital ecosystem** (Briscoe & De Wilde, 2006; Dini et al., 2005; Puranam et al., 2014; Uden et al, 2007; Weill & Woerner, 2018; Zhu, 2015), which represents a new type of ecosystem. The **digital ecosystem** is an open socio-technical system, based on the collaborative community model, focused on the production and distribution of knowledge-intensive products and services, using largely digital technologies. The properties of the digital ecosystem are self-organization, scalability, and sustainability. In the last few years, artificial intelligence ecosystems have proliferated quickly (Bughin & Hazan, 2017; Halper & Stodder, 2016;). In the world economy, a large variety of digital ecosystems has developed (Almirall et al., 2016; Coyle, 2017; Dini et al., 2005; Dushnitsky, Guerini, Piva, & Rossi-Lamastra, 2016; Fabbri et al., 2016; Iansiti & Lakhani, 2017; Puranam et al., 2014; Van Alstyne, 2016; Van Alstyne, Parker, & Choudary, 2016; Visnjic, Neely, Cennamo, & Visnjic, 2016; Williamson & De Meyer, 2012):

- hubs
- digital platforms
- industrial mash-ups
- global digital centres
- "smart" cities
- fab labs
- living labs

In digital ecosystems, a digital culture is developed that is characterized by impact, speed, openness, and autonomy (Westerman, Soule, & Eswaran, 2019). The fast extension of the digital ecosystem is caused by the **multiple advantages** generated for its components and for economic development. Williamson and De Meyer (2012) have identified six very consistent key advantages (see Figure 2.7).

Elements presented in this section provide convincing arguments for understanding that the ecosystem represents a new form of knowledge-

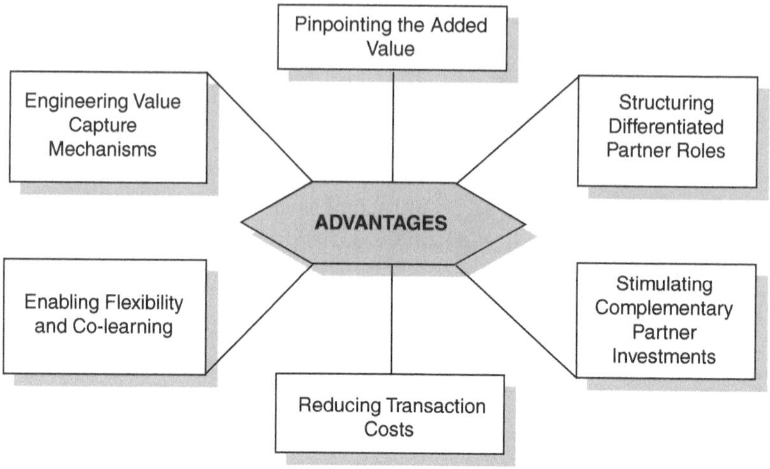

Figure 2.7 Key ecosystem advantages.

Adapted from "Ecosystem advantage: How to successfully harness the power of partners" by P. J. Williamson and A. De Meyer, 2012, *California Management Review*, *55*(1), p. 33. Retrieved from https://ink.library.smu.edu.sg/cgi/viewcontent.cgi?article=4518&context=lkcsb_research

based organization, capable of solving sustainable, very complex challenges in the knowledge-based economy, by developing comprehensive relationships with certain important stakeholders. In the context of the COVID-19 pandemic, many ecosystems have proved superior resilience and performance compared with the "classical companies".

Challenges of COVID-19 Pandemic Context

Under the impact of the COVID-19 pandemic, the world economy faces a deep societal crisis. In almost all countries, a so-called "real economy freezing" has occurred, which is reflected in decreased GNP, increased unemployment, state budget income reduction, increased budget deficit and public debt, etc. Analyses realized by numerous specialists in many countries regarding the crisis generated by COVID-19 have revealed **five essential elements:**

a Medical and business situations are, and shall be, very different from one country to another, because of diversified characteristics and influences of medical, economical, managerial, social, cultural, and ecological determinants, both national and international.

b Every country needs a specific approach, as a function of the particular/national context and of the business and social resilience at the national, sectoral, and territorial levels.

c Countries should collaborate and coordinate certain essential medical and business elements, taking into consideration the fact that the world faces not only a medical pandemic but also an economic crisis, which is very complex and challenging.
d Combating the pandemic and its many negative effects, getting out of the crisis, and relaunching the economy are conditioned by comprehensive and substantial state intervention in the socio-economic activities.
e Getting out of the crisis and relaunching the economy also depend to a large extent on companies, which are the main providers of value added, GNP, jobs, and incomes to the state budgets in every country. In order to be able to do this, many companies should reinvent themselves and remodel their management.

Under the influence of the COVID-19 pandemic, there are many major changes in the economy, which have a powerful impact on companies and represent **challenges for their management**. Among these, we mention the following:

- Notable decrease in direct demand for certain products and services (tourism, transport, entertainment, etc.).
- Reduction and/or delay of the supply with certain raw materials, spare parts, and finished goods.
- Increased risk of being blocked or delayed with public or private economic and social ongoing projects.
- Decrease in the indirect demand (especially industry, service, and trade) for many products and services caused by the previous changes.
- Notable fluctuation in orders and prices for certain important product types, like drugs, medical equipment, oil, some raw materials, etc.
- Decrease or major modification of alternative financing (stock exchange, venture capital, equity funds, business angels, etc.).

Under these conditions at the national and international level **new societal priorities** are emerging:

- Health population protection at a high level.
- Maintaining the functioning of the economy at all its levels – national, regional, sectoral, local, and company – as close is possible to its normal standards and performances, in order to be able to satisfy major individual and organizational needs, both economic and social.
- Normalization of the entire society's functioning.

- Preservation of the national economy sustainability in the long run, in the present and future medical, commercial, financial, social, etc. conditions.
- Rapid recovery of the economic growth in each country.

In order to cope with these challenges and priorities, it **is necessary to project and implement a new type of management** that is able to increase the resilience of all economic and social entities at national, sectorial, regional, local, microeconomic, and international level.

In the crisis and post crisis, management will be effective and efficient if it has at least the following six capabilities:

- The ability to have realistic perceptions of the processes developing in the economy and society and of their consequences on the people, companies, business, etc.
- Capacity to provide rapid, flexible, and effective feedback on new situations (Dykes, Hughes-Morgan, Kolev, & Ferrier, 2020; Romeo, Moukanas, & Rung, 2020).
- Resilience capacity in the face of multiple stresses (medical, social, economic, political, etc.).
- Capacity to be innovatively performant in the short, medium, and long run.
- Capacity to cooperate with other entities, in order to take into consideration the present and future societal priorities, threats, and opportunities.
- Capacity to conceive an innovative strategy that is able to cope with the new contextual threats and to valorize the new opportunities, contributing decisively to the rapid and performant recovery of the company.

A new type of management should be able to valorize the potential of all the organization's main stakeholders – external and internal – as was stressed at Davos by the World Economic Forum (WEF, 2020) and numerous specialists (see, e.g., Chaturvedi, Dey, & Singh, 2020; Chima & Gutman, 2020; Radjou, 2020; Romeo, Moukanas, & Rung, 2020), who believe that this is the key for a performant management in the present and post-COVID context. In their implementation, managers should bear in mind that the return to normality, which will be a "new normality", will be a long process (Levenson, 2020), and the contribution of each important stakeholder is very much needed.

Notes

1 We mention that not all specialists who approach the future changes of the economy and society, agree with de knowledge revolution and the knowledge-

based economy. For example, in a book largely debated at the international level a few years ago – G. Balakrishnan (Ed.). (2003). *Debating empire*. London, UK: Verso – is proposed a transition through revolution to the empire, at the world level, without taking into consideration "de facto", the impact of the last economic, scientific, etc. developments, although they mention some of them.

2 Of course, there are some authors who denied the existence of the knowledge-based economy (Azam, G. 2006. L'utopie de L'économie des Connaissence. *Problèmes Economiques*, *2901*, 33–39; Foray, D. 2004. *The economics of knowledge*. Cambridge, MA: MIT Press).

3 Definition formulated by Bukht, R. and Heeks, R. is not only corelated with the three phases of digital revolution, but also based on the analysis of 21 definitions of digital economy (Bukht, R., & Heeks, R. 2017. *Defining, conceptualising and measuring the digital economy*. Working Paper Series, Paper No. 68. Retrieved from https://diodeweb.files.wordpress.com/2017/08/diwkppr68-diode.pdf).

4 The knowledge-based economy is the result of the knowledge revolution, which is more comprehensive than digital revolution (see comparatively 2.2 and 2.5 content). In our study, we choose to use the term of knowledge revolution and not fourth industrial revolution (see, e.g., Schwab, K. approach) or third revolution (see, e.g., Rifkin, J. approach). We prefer the concept of knowledge revolution, for several reasons: the knowledge represents the essential element of the radical transformation in economy and society; industrial represents just one dimension of the economy and it is not able to express the essence of the last decades deep mutations which include all economy branches and sectors. Industrial is something "déjà vu", which not reflects the novelty of what happens in the last decades, the radical new content of the economic and society processes is represented by the knowledge.

References

Adler, P., Heckscher, C., & Prusak, L. (2011). Building a collaborative enterprise. *Harvard Business Review*, *89*(7/8), 94–101.

Almirall, E., Wareham, J., Ratti, C., Conesa, P., Bria, F., Gaviria, A., et al. (2016). Smart cities at the crossroads: New tensions in city transformation. *California Management Review*, *59*(1), 141–152. doi:10.1177/0008125616683949

Atkeson, A., & Kehoe, P. J. (2007). Modeling the transition to a new Economy: Lessons from two technological revolutions. *The American Economic Review*, *97*(1), 64–88. doi:10.1257/aer.97.1.64

Becerra, J. (2017, March 14). The digital revolution is not about technology: It's about people. *World Economic Forum*. Retrieved from https://www.weforum.org/agenda/2017/03/the-digital-revolution-is-not-about-technology-it-s-about-people

Ben-Ner, A., & Siemsen, E. (2017). Decentralization and localization of production: The organizational and economic consequences of additive manufacturing (3D printing). *California Management Review*, *59*(2), 5–23. doi:10.1177/0008125617695284

Bouchez, J. P. (2012). *L'économie du savoir: construction, engeux et perspectives*. Bruxelles, Belgium: De Boeck Superieur. doi:10.7202/1025094ar

Bouchez, J.-P. (2014). Autour de "l'économie du savoir": ses composantes, ses dynamiques et ses enjeux. *Savoir*, *1*(34), 9–45. doi:10.3917/savo.034.0009

Briscoe, G., & De Wilde, P. (2006). Digital ecosystems: *Evolving service-oriented architectures*. Retrieved from https://arxiv.org/pdf/0712.4102.pdf

Bughin, J., & Hazan, E. (2017). Five management strategies for getting the most from al. *MIT Sloan Management Review*. Retrieved from https://sloanreview.mit.edu/article/five-management-strategies-for-getting-the-most-from-ai/

Bukht, R., & Heeks, R. (2017). *Defining, conceptualising and measuring the digital economy*. Development informatics, Working Paper Series, Paper No. 68. Retrieved from https://diodeweb.files.wordpress.com/2017/08/diwkppr68-diode.pdf

Burton-Jones, A. (1999). *Knowledge capitalism: Business, work, and learning in the new economy*. Oxford, UK: Oxford University Press. doi:10.1093/acprof:oso/9780198296225.001.0001

Cairncross, F. (1997). *The death of distance: How the communications revolution will change our lives*. Boston, MA: Harvard Business School Press.

Cairncross, F. (2003). *The company of the future*. London, UK: Profile Books.

Caspar, P. (2014). Times are changing... *Savoirs*, *1*(34), 7–8. doi:10.3917/savo.034.0007

Castells, M. (2010). *The rise of the network society* (2nd ed.). Malden, MA: Willey-Blackwell.

Chaturvedi, H., Dey A. K., & Singh, N. (2020). Coping with COVID-19. *Global Focus, the EFMD Business Magazine*. Retrieved from https://www.globalfocusmagazine.com/coping-with-covid-19/

Chima, A., & Gutman, R. (2020). What it takes to lead through an era of exponential change. *Harvard Business Review*. Retrieved from https://hbr.org/2020/10/what-it-takes-to-lead-through-an-era-of-exponential-change

Coyle, D. (2017). Precarious and productive work in digital economy. *National Institute Economic Review*, *240*(1), R5–R14. doi:10.1177/002795011724000110

Dahlman, C., Mealy, S., & Wermelinger, M. (2016). *Harnessing the digital economy for developing countries*. OECD Development Centre, Working Paper No. 334. Retrieved from https://read.oecd-ilibrary.org/development/harnessing-the-digital-economy-for-developing-countries_4adffb24-en#page1

Dini, P., Darking, M., Rathbone N., Vidal, M., Hernandez, P., Ferronato, P., et al. 2005). *The digital ecosystems research vision: 2010 and beyond*. European Commisssion, Bruxelles, Position Paper.

Dumova, T., & Fiordo, R. (2010). *Handbook of research on social interaction technologies and collaboration software: Concepts and trends*. Hershey, PA: IGI Global.

Dushnitsky, G., Guerini, M., Piva, E., & Rossi-Lamastra, C. (2016). Crowdfunding in Europe: Determinants of platform creation across countries. *California Management Review*, *58*(2), 44–71. doi:10.1525/cmr.2016.58.2.44

Dykes, B. J., Hughes-Morgan, M., Kolev, K. D., & Ferrier W. J. (2020). Responding to crises with speed and agility. *MIT Sloan Management Review*.

Retrieved from https://sloanreview.mit.edu/article/responding-to-crises-with-speed-and-agility/

El-Korany, A. (2007) A knowledge management application in enterprises. *International Journal of Management and Enterprise Development*, 4(6), 693–702. doi:10.1504/IJMED.2007.014989

European Commission – Directorate-General for Enterprise and Industry. (2004). *Innovation management and the knowledge driven economy.* Bruxelles, Belgium: Publications Office of the European Union.

European Commission – Directorate-General for Enterprise and Industry. (2010). *European competitiveness report 2009.* Luxembourg: : Publications Office of the European Union.

European Council. (2010). *A new European strategy for jobs and growth.* EUCO 13/10, Brussels.

Fabbri, J., Glaser, A., Gaujard, C., & Toutain, O. (2016). Espaces collaboratifs d'innovation: au-delà du phénomène de mode, de quoi parle-t-on? *Entreprendre & Innover*, 4(31), 5–7. doi:10.3917/entin.031.0005

Fisher, B. (2017, August 9). *Realizing the promise of artificial intelligence. Forbes.* Retrieved from https://www.forbes.com/sites/kpmg/2017/08/09/realizing-the-promise-of-artificial-intelligence/#127f7a1e485e

Foray, D. (2009). *L'économie de la connaissance.* Paris, France: La Découverte.

Gada, K. (2016, June 16). The digital economy in 5 minutes. *Forbes.* Retrieved from https://www.forbes.com/sites/koshagada/2016/06/16/what-is-the-digital-economy/#2088cd737628

Garmise, S. (2006). *People and competitive advantage of place: Building a workforce for the 21st century.* Armonk, NY: M.E. Sharpe.

Grant, R. (2007). Knowledge management and the knowledge-based economy. In L. Prusak & E. Matson (Eds.), *Knowledge management and organizational learning* (pp. 15–29). Oxford, UK: Oxford University Press.

Halper, F., & Stodder, D. (2016). *Marketing analytics meets artificial intelligence: Six strategies for success.* Retrieved from https://www.sas.com/content/dam/SAS/en_us/doc/whitepaper2/tdwi-marketing-analytics-meets-artificial-intelligence-108556.pdf

Hamel, G. (2002). *Leading the revolution: How to thrive in turbulent times by making innovation a way of life.* New York, NY, and Boston, MA: Plume & Harvard Business School Press.

Iansiti, M., & Lakhani, K. R. (2017). Managing our hub economy: Strategy, ethics, and network competition in the age of digital superpowers. *Harvard Business Review*, *95*(5), 84–92.

Ichijo, K., & Nonaka, I. (2007). Glossary. In K. Ichijo & I. Nonaka (Eds.), *Knowledge creation and management: New challenges for managers* (pp. 275–299, 286). Oxford, UK: Oxford University Press.

Jouyet, J.-P., & Lévy, M. (2007). *L'économie de l'immatériel: La croissance de demain.* Paris, France: La Documentation Française.

Kane, G. C., Phillips, A. N., Copulsky, J., & Andrus, G. (2019). How digital leadership is (n't) different. *MIT Sloan Management Review*, *60*(3), 34–40.

Kiron, D., & Unruh, G. (2018). The convergence of digitalization and sustainability. *MIT Sloan Management Review.* Retrieved from https://sloanreview.mit.edu/article/the-convergence-of-digitalization-and-sustainability/

Kiron, D., Unruh, G., Kruschwitz, N., Reeves, M., Rubel, H., Meyer, A., et al. (2017). Corporate sustainability at a crossroads. *MIT Sloan Management Review*. Retrieved from https://sloanreview.mit.edu/projects/corporate-sustainability-at-a-crossroads/

Levenson, A. (2020) A long time until the economic new normal. *MIT Sloan Management Review*. Retrieved from https://sloanreview.mit.edu/article/a-long-time-until-the-economic-new-normal

Mallovan, M., Liquète, V., & Verlaet, L. (2015). De la gestion des connaissances à l'économie des connaissances. *Communication & Management*, *1*(12), 5–12. doi:10.3917/comma.121.0005

Manso, G. (2017). Creating incentives for innovation. *California Management Review*, *60*(1), 18–32. doi:10.1177/0008125617725287

Mertens, L. (2004). *Training, productivity and labour competencies in organizations*. ILO, Cintefor, Montevideo. Retrieved from https://www.oitcinterfor.org/sites/default/files/file_publicacion/mertens_trazos_eng.pdf

Meyer, H. (2017, June 12). *Understanding the digital revolution and what it means*. Retrieved from https://www.socialeurope.eu/understanding-digital-revolution-means

Mitra, J. (2017). *The business of innovation*. London, UK: Sage Publications.

Mokyr, J. (2020). Why our knowledge economy can survive the new age of pestilence. *MIT Sloan Management Review*. Retrieved from https://sloanreview.mit.edu/article/why-our-knowledge-economy-can-survive-the-new-age-of-pestilence/

Mosco, V. (2017). *Becoming digital toward a post-internet society*. Bingley, UK: Emerald Publishing Limited.

Nicolescu, O. (2001). *Management comparat* (2nd ed.). Bucureşti, Romania: Editura Economică.

Nicolescu, O., & Nicolescu, C. (2011). *Organizaţia şi managementul bazate pe cunoştinţe*. Bucureşti, Romania: Pro Universitaria.

Nicolescu, O., & Nicolescu, C. (2017). New approach-the quadrangle of knowledge based sustainability. *Proceedings of International Conference – Knowledge-Based Organization*, *23*(1), 411–417. doi:10.1515/kbo-2017-0068

Nicolescu, O., & Nicolescu, C. (2019). Relationships between digital/digitalized economy and knowledge based economy. *Proceedings of the 13th International Conference "Management Strategies for High Performance"*, *13*(1), 457–465.

Nicolescu, O., & Nicolescu, L. (2005). *Economia firma şi managementul bazate pe cunoştinţe*. Bucureşti, Romania: Editura Economică.

Pigni, F., Piccoli, G., & Watson, R. (2016). Digital data streams: Creating value from the real-time flow of big data. *California Management Review*, *58*(3), 5–25. doi:10.1525/cmr.2016.58.3.5

Powell, W. W., & Snellman, K. (2004). The knowledge economy. *Annual Review of Sociology*, *30*, 199–220. doi:10.1146/annurev.soc.29.010202.100037

PricewaterhouseCoopers. (2017). *20 years inside the mind of the CEO... What's next?* 20th CEO Survey. Retrieved from https://www.pwc.com/gx/en/ceo-survey/2017/pwc-ceo-20th-survey-report-2017.pdf

Puranam, P., Alexy, O., & Reitzig, M. (2014). What's "new" about new forms of organizing? *Academy of Management Review*, *39*(2), 162–180. doi:10.5465/amr.2011.0436

Radjou, N. (2020). The rising frugal economy. *MIT Sloan Management Review*. Retrieved from https://sloanreview.mit.edu/article/the-rising-frugal-economy/

Rifkin, J. (2016). *The 2016 world economic forum misfires with its fourth industrial revolution theme*. Retrieved from https://www.huffingtonpost.com/jeremy-rifkin/the-2016-world-economic-f_b_8975326.html

Romeo, J., Moukanas, H., & Rung, G. (2020). The age of accelerating strategy breakthroughs. *MIT Sloan Management Review*. Retrieved from https://sloanreview.mit.edu/article/the-age-of-accelerating-strategy-breakthroughs/

Russ, M., Fineman, R. J., & Jones, J. K. (2010). Conceptual theory: What do you know? In M. Russ (Ed.), *Knowledge management strategies for business development* (pp. 1–22). Hershey, PA: Business Science Reference (IGI Global). doi:10.4018/978-1-60566-348-7

Schneider, A., Wickert, C., & Marti, E. (2017). Reducing complexity by creating complexity: A systems theory perspective on how organizations respond to their environments. *Journal of Management Studies*, *54*(2), 182–208. doi:10.1111/joms.12206

Schwab, K. (2016, January 14). *The fourth industrial revolution: What it means, how to respond*. Retrieved from https://www.weforum.org/agenda/2016/01/the-fourth-industrial-revolution-what-it-means-and-how-to-respond/

Schweer, D., & Sahl, J. C. (2017). The digital transformation of industry – The benefit for Germany. In F. Abolhassan (Eds.), *The drivers of digital transformation. Management for professionals* (pp. 23–31). Cham, DE: Springer.

Seeley, C. P., & Davenport, T. H. (2006). KM meets business intelligence: Merging knowledge and information at Intel. *Knowledge Management Review*, *8*(6), 10–15.

Segars, A. H. (2018). Seven technologies remaking the world. *MIT Sloan Management Review*. An MIT SMR Executive Guide. Retrieved from https://sloanreview.mit.edu/wp-content/uploads/2018/03/00c59a8098.pdf

Soete, L. (2002). The new economy: A European perspective. In D. Archibugi & B.-Å. Lundvall (Eds.), *The globalizing learning economy* (pp. 21–23). Oxford, UK: Oxford University Press. doi:10.1093/0199258171.001.0001

Stewart, T. A. (1998a). *Intellectual capital: The new wealth of organizations* (2nd ed.). London, UK: Nicholas Breadley Publishing.

Stewart, T. A. (1998b, April 13). Leading edge: A new way to think about employees. *Forum Magazine*.

The Lisbon European Council. (2000). *An agenda of economic and social renewal for Europe*. DOC/007, Brussels.

Uden, L., Wangsa, I. T., & Damiani, E. (2007). The future of e-learning: E-learning ecosystem. *Proceedings of 2007 Inaugural IEEE International Conference on Digital Ecosystems and Technologies*, pp. 113–117. Retrieved from https://www.academia.edu/2983170/The_future_of_E-learning_E-learning_ecosystem

Unruh, G., & Kiron, D. (2017). Digital transformation on purpose. *MIT Sloan Management Review*. Retrieved from https://sloanreview.mit.edu/article/digital-transformation-on-purpose/

Van Alstyne, M. W. (2016). How platform business are transforming strategy. *Harvard Business Review*. Retrieved from https://hbr.org/webinar/2016/04/how-platform-businesses-are-transforming-strategy

Van Alstyne, M. W., Parker, G. G., & Choudary, S. P. (2016). 6 reasons platforms fail. *Harvard Business Review*. Retrieved from https://hbr.org/2016/03/6-reasons-platforms-fail

Visnjic, I., Neely, A., Cennamo, C., & Visnjic, N. (2016). Governing the city: Unleashing value from business ecosystem. *California Management Review*, *59*(1), 109–140. doi:10.1177/0008125616683955

Weill, P., & Woerner, S. L. (2017). Is your company ready for a digital future? *MIT Sloan Management Review*. Retrieved from https://sloanreview.mit.edu/article/is-your-company-ready-for-a-digital-future/

Weill, P., & Woerner, S. L. (2018). Surviving in an increasingly digital ecosystem. *MIT Sloan Management Review*, *59*(2), 26–28.

Westerman, G., Soule, D. L., & Eswaran, A. (2019). Building digital-ready culture in traditional organizations. *MIT Sloan Management Review*, *60*(4), 59–68.

Williamson, P. J., & De Meyer, A. (2012). Ecosystem advantage: How to successfully harness the power of partners. *California Management Review*, *55*(1), 24–46. Retrieved from https://ink.library.smu.edu.sg/cgi/viewcontent.cgi?article=4518&context=lkcsb_research 10.1525/cmr.2012.55.1.24

World Bank. (2017). *A framework for knowledge based economy*. Retrieved from http://www.worldbank.org//Wbsite/external/WBI/WBIPrograms/KFDLP/O.contentMDK:20269036_menu.PK461205-pagePK:64156158-PLPK:64152884-theSitePK:46119800.html#knowledge

World Economic Forum. (2018). *Digital transformation initiative*. Retrieved from http://reports.weforum.org/digital-transformation/wp-content/blogs.dir/94/mp/files/pages/files/dti-executive-summary-20180510.pdf

World Economic Forum. (2020). *The global risk report 2020*. Retrieved from http://www3.weforum.org/docs/WEF_Global_Risk_Report_2020.pdf

Zhu, P. (2015). *Digital master: Debunk the myths of enterprise digital maturity*. Morrisville, NC: Lulu Publishing Services.

3 Contextual Main Changes and Influences on the Company and Its Stakeholders

Approach to the Changing Business Environment

A company's foundation, development, performance, and sustainability are influenced decisively by the business environment. For this reason, the environment's evolution is very important for all companies and should be analyzed in depth and its changes are taken into consideration carefully.

The business environment includes an organization's all exogenous elements of a different nature – technical, economic, demographic, cultural, scientific, ecologic, political, medical, legal, etc. – that influence the prevision of the objectives, obtaining the resources, the decision-making, and implementation in order to be performant. The **main categories of factors** that can be separated into business environment or company environment are as follows:

- **Economic factors** (domestic market, international market, banking system, inflation, exchange rate, population incomes, etc.);
- **Technical and technological factors** (digital technologies, available machinery and equipment, number and quality of licences and patents, potential of R&D branch, etc.);
- **Management-administrative factors** (national strategy and policy, quality of the central and local administration, available managerial systems, methods and techniques, quality of management consultancy and training, e.tc.);
- **Demographic factors** (population number and its socio-professional structure, share of occupied population, birth rate, mortality rate, etc.);
- **Sociocultural factors** (social structure of the population, educational system, health system, national culture, etc.);
- **Medical factors** (health system, pandemic disease, drugs, etc.);
- **Ecological factors** (natural resources, climate, water, vegetation, fauna, etc.);
- **Political factors** (national policies [economic, social, educational, science, etc.], international bodies' policies [United Nations,

DOI: 10.4324/9781003217701-3

International Labour Organization, International Monetary Fund, Word Bank, etc.], policies of the most powerful countries [USA, China, Russia, Germany, etc.]);
- **Legal factors** (business laws, governmental decisions, quality of judiciary bodies, etc.).

The intensive internationalization during the last few decades has determined an increase in the impact of environmental factors from outside countries on companies, their activities, and performances. Without any doubt, the last hundred years have been characterized by the numerous and profound changes in all environmental factors. The COVID-19 pandemic – a medical factor – is the last major change that has caused many and important shifts in all components of the business environment. COVID-19 has influenced to a large extent the manifestation of the majority of the other eight categories at least in the short and medium term. Never, in the history of mankind, have changes been so comprehensive, fast, and intensive.

In this chapter, we focus on the global changes in the business environment, generated to a large extent by the **transition to a knowledge-based economy and by digitalization**. Our analysis has revealed that, in the context of the transition to a knowledge-based economy, of the persistence of specific elements of the capitalist economy and society and – in the less developed areas – of the previous socio-economic systems, we can identify certain **essential trends in the organizational environment at the world level**: so-called "**megashifts**".

We will present the main megashifts identified by us starting from the consultation of a large number of studies (Attali, 2007; Brătianu, 2015; Broadman, 2015; Brown, Adams, Larsen, & Roney, 2015; Griffin, 2012; Lichtenthaler, 2016; Markoff, 2016; Naqvi, 2014; Nicolescu, Popa, Nicolescu, & Ştefan, 2019; Nicolescu et al., 2019) and based on our own analysis.

The background of the megashifts is represented by the intensification, diversification, and acceleration of innovation. Numerous papers (Birkinshaw, Hamel, & Mol, 2008; Burkus, 2013; Christensen, Raynor, & McDonald, 2015; Grossman, 2016; Hamel, 2006; Pisano, 2015) have proved that innovation represents the engine of the revolutionary changes taking place in all fields of society. The trends presented in the following sections represent the essential innovations developing in the business environment at the global level that predominantly influence an organization's activities, functionality, and performance (see Figure 3.1).

The environmental tendencies influence **companies in many areas:**

- Company inputs (knowledge, information, raw materials, energy, human resources, product and service demands, machines, equipment, credits, etc.).

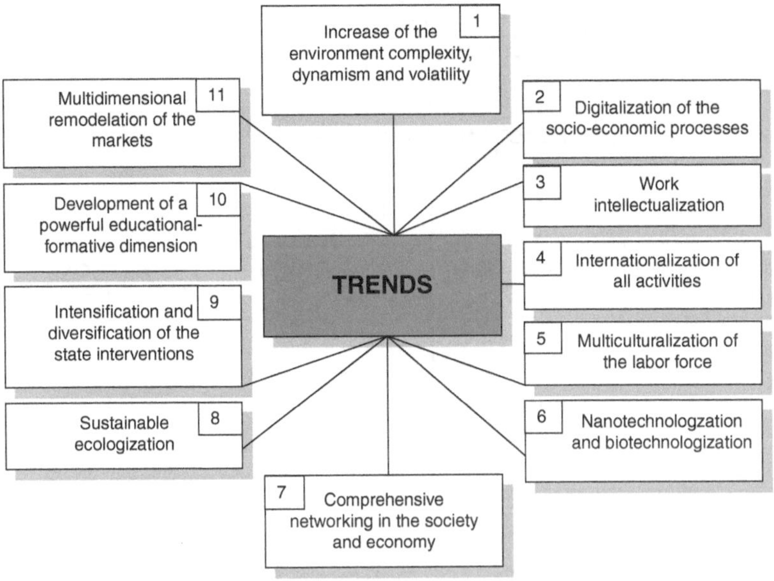

Figure 3.1 The main trends – "megashifts" – in the organization changing business environment.

- Company activities and works (content, structure, duration, quality, cost, etc.)
- Company outputs and performances (products, services, turnover, productivity, market share, profit, dividends, competitive advantage, sustainability, etc.)

Bearing in mind all these influences, we will indicate in the following sections some of the most influential mutations in the global business environment that should be taken into consideration by companies' management in order to achieve competitive advantage and sustainability. We will try to approach each of the tendencies identified and analyzed according to the elements incorporated in Figure 3.2.

The changes in the global business environment heavily influence not only companies but also national economies and the world economy. Their effects and influences are interrelated on multiple levels, increasing the difficulty of their perception and of performant feedback from all types of entities. In order to face these challenges, to stop the negative effects and to valorize the opportunities, global approaches have been developed through international organizations – United Nations Organization (UNO), International Labour Organization (ILO), World Trade Organization (WTO), International Monetary Fund (IMF), World Bank (WB), etc. The above-mentioned organizations and other

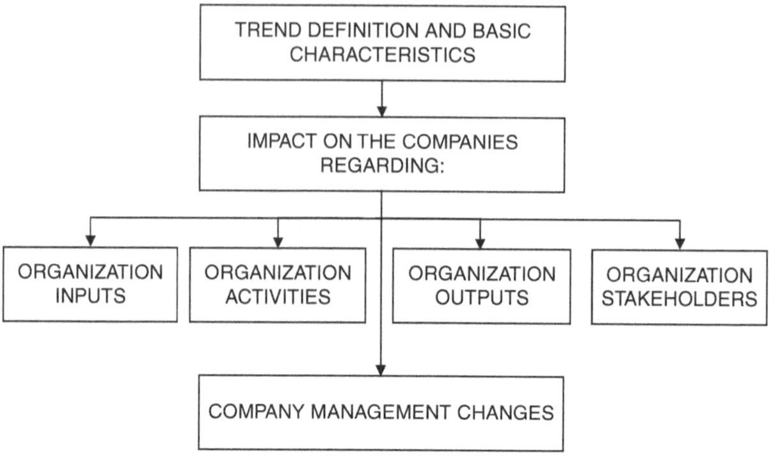

Figure 3.2 Main elements regarding the approach of the business environment trends.

international bodies have developed strategies, agreements, protocols, resolutions, and recommendations regarding future global evolutions or in certain major fields – trade, finance, labour force, banking, ecology, military, and others – trying to contribute to better activities and performances at all levels (international, national economies, and companies).

Without any doubt, the COVID-19 pandemic is the contextual element with the most influential impact on the business environment in this period. It has multiple very intense and often unexpected influences on the society and economy, compared with megashifts that occurred in the last few decades.

We consider it necessary to make **two remarks regarding the approach to the changes generated by the COVID -19 pandemic** in the business environment:

a In the present and next period, the COVID-19 pandemic produces, and will continue to produce, substantial changes that shock us, providing major threats to, and difficulties in, the economy and society, concomitantly with some opportunities. However, the direct impacts of the pandemic will decrease gradually in the next few years, because of the diminution of the pandemic's intensity and because the management of various entities (state, region, company, etc.) will learn how to face the pandemic and its effects.
b Manifestations of all megashifts are influenced by the COVID-19 pandemic, quite often notably so. We consider it useful to make the point that all the megashifts mentioned above will continue to

operate in the future, because their roots are in the objective evolution of the economy and society. In our approach, we shall try, at the level of each megashift, to reveal some of the pandemic's influences that are closely conected with the objectives and problems of our book.

Main Trends in the Changing Business Environment

Increase in the Business Environment Complexity, Dynamism, and Volatility

During the last century, the organization business environment changed very fast and intensely. Recently four major changes in the business environment were proposed in a new concept known as VUCA – volatility, uncertainty, complexity, and ambiguity (Bennett & Lemoine, 2014; Garrow & Varney, 2015). We adopt a partially different approach in considering that the relevant mutations in the business environment are complexity, dynamism, and volatility.

Complexity means that the business environment incorporates numerous elements and their numbers increase rapidly; the size, nature, and dynamics of these elements are diversified, and the interrelations among components are rapidly amplified. There is a vast amount of information and knowledge about the majority of business components, but some of them are difficult to understand and time-consuming for analysis, prediction, and decision-making. The number of variables and the interrelationships among them, which should be analyzed and taken into consideration by management bodies, are huge and rapidly increasing.

Dynamism means that a large proportion of the business environment components are moving very fast. The most rapid are changing the technical elements, especially those connected with digitization, digitalization and digital transformation. This is a major reason why it is very difficult to measure and evaluate precisely the characteristics of the environmental factors and components. Anticipating their evolution is even more difficult, and the probability of getting reliable information and knowledge on these dynamic elements quite frequently is not very high. In this situation, the design of strategies and policies for the environment components becomes more difficult, with negative consequences for their quality and efficacity. Also, the implementation of the entities' strategy and policies faces many challenges and difficulties, involving a lot of rapid changes that are not easy to manage properly.

Volatility is mainly a consequence of the previous two environmental characteristics. In essence, volatility means that the environmental elements are very unstable and their evolution is quite often unexpected. The instability of the environmental factors makes it very difficult to catch them and to evaluate their parameters. Also, the unexpectedness of the environmental factors and their characteristics often surprises managerial bodies, finding them not ready to copy with the situations and to generate efficient solutions. Both instability and unexpectedness are generated by the actions of some variables that are not known, or not sufficiently well known, frequently without a history record. Quite often the variables are strongly related to innovation, especially to disruptive innovation. Information regarding the variables is fragmented and not sufficiently reliable, making it difficult to identify correlations and to achieve rigorous analysis.

For an organization's management the environmental volatility creates risk situations, making the decisional processes and operational activities very tough, and decreasing the company's performance and sustainability.

The others two components of VUCA – ambiguity and uncertainty – we do not consider as being characteristic of the business environment, at least in the manner explained by these authors: "ambiguity characteristics: cause relationships unclear. No precedents exist, you face unknown unknowns" (Bennett & Lemoine, 2014, p. 27). These explanations refer in fact not to characteristics of the environment but to our capacity to identify and analyze causal relationships in a complex, dynamic and volatile environment. It is obvious that causal relationships exist in the environment. Also, we do not believe that uncertainty is a characteristic of the environment. It is exactly the same situation as for ambiguity.

The complexity, dynamism, and volatility in the business environment influence organizations mainly on **three levels:**

- **organization inputs** – much of the information and knowledge, and many clients' demands, etc., are entirely new, sometimes unexpected, and for the other inputs partially changed (inflation rate, exchange rate, raw materials, machines, people, laws, etc.);
- **organization activities and works** – which are impacted by new commercial, financial, human, technical, etc. variables, often not sufficiently well known;
- **organization outputs** – which should be very frequently modified, although it is not always very clear how, in order to respond to the changing conditions of the markets, competitors, bankers, community, investors, etc.

The increase of the environment's complexity, dynamism, and volatility has several impacts directly on the **stakeholders:**

- all stakeholders, both internal and external, need to make more efforts and be more innovative, in order to face the environmental changes;

- the number and importance of the company's external stakeholders will increase, involving more time and resources to cultivate the relationships with them and to valorize the new opportunities associated with them;
- the stakeholders' feedback should be faster than in the previous periods, because of the higher environmental dynamism and volatility.

Great efforts should be made by organizations' managers, shareholders, employees, and other stakeholders in all these processes, involving very diversified and high competences.

The COVID-19 pandemic influences especially the complexity and volatility by increasing their intensity. This makes it more difficult to conduct performant management in an organization and to construct and develop productive and durable relationships with all major stakeholders.

Digitalization of the Socio-Economic Processes

The digital revolution is – without any doubt – one of the most important and influential megashifts of the present times. As we have already indicated in Section 2.8 of the previous chapter, the digital revolution mainly involves three processes: digitization, digitalization, and digital transformation (Unruh & Kiron, 2017). Their effects on the economy and society are multiple and profound. However, there are renowned specialists – like Rifkin (2016) – who believe that the evolution of digitalization has barely begun its course and that its new configuration in the form of the Internet of Things represents the next stage of development. Digitalization is very closely connected with other revolutionary technologies – artificial intelligence, big data analytics, cloud computing, 3D printing, etc.

Digitalization – like informatization previously – presents significant variation in intensity, content, and effects worldwide. Of course, in the most developed countries digitalization is at the forefront, but many other countries are rapidly recovering. Because of digitalization, the quantity of information, the information storage capacity, the degree of information processing, and the circulation speed have made huge progress in a very short time. The identification, codification, circulation, use and valorization of information, and knowledge – two of the most valuable resources in the present times – are increasing very fast. Digitalization and informatization profoundly change the content of all activities and of the socio-economic entities in which they are achieved.

Digitalization frequently renders business models and processes obsolete. Many value chains are being transformed by digital technology, some of them evolutionary, some of them disruptive (Schweer & Sahl, 2017). At the societal level, in order to capitalize more on digitalization it is necessary – as very well argued by Unruh and Kiron (2017) – **to promote digital transformation with the purpose of** "leading the world toward a better digital future". It requires proactive scanning of the emerging landscape for both social and environmental risks, while simultaneously looking for opportunities to use digital technologies to resolve global challenges. In the European Union, the Commission has already prepared a roadmap of the digital transformation that contains five parts: change management, intent and priorities, responsibilities and skills, vision, and – last but not least – the age of the consumers.

For companies, it is recommended to have a proactive approach to facing digitalization, not the reactive approach that is still predominant today. Company management is necessary to take into consideration both positive and negative digitalization effects. Digitalization provides **many advantages** for companies:

- more new product and services,
- high potential digital technologies,
- faster and more efficient information and knowledge flows,
- digital interconnectivity,
- easier access to potential clients and to markets.

Concomitantly, digitalization generates **many challenges and risks** for companies: profound changes in customers' demands, obsolescence of products, services or technologies, major changes in human resources skills and behaviours, need for large investments, etc.

Digitalization greatly **influences companies at three levels:**

- **inputs**, affording a company rapid access to a large amount of knowledge and information, contributing greatly to the modernization of its technologies and equipment, and helping the organization to construct and to be part of networks with external and internal stakeholders;
- **activities**, the speed of all the company's decisional and operational processes is higher, the quantity of knowledge and information available is much larger, the capacity of each organizational field to approach and solve problems is higher;
- **outputs**, generated by the company through participation in digitalization – quality, turnover, productivity, incomes – are higher.

Digitization, digitalization, and digital transformation influence **company stakeholders**, essentially, **in the following ways:**

- appearance of new company stakeholders – informatics companies, digital consultants, digital designers, etc. – which are specialized in providing digital means, approaches, and solutions to organizations;

- stakeholders' capacity to receive, process, and use information increases and speeds up;
- all stakeholders' decisions, actions, and behaviours change to a certain extent, because of the digital techniques and technologies utilized in their work;
- increase in all company stakeholders – internal and external – networking among themselves and in the company involved;
- increase in information and knowledge use by, and impact on, all company stakeholders, due to digitalization and digital transformation.

It is obvious that the digital trend manifests a strong amplification and acceleration in recent years, which, without any doubt, will continue in the next period. Threats and difficulties generated by the COVID-19 pandemic provide new incentives for accelerating the development of digitalization and its use in organizations all over the world. Company managers and other stakeholders should strive – using a proactive approach – to cope as well as possible with the opportunities, challenges, and risks generated by digitalization.

Work Intellectualization

The proliferation of intellectual work processes represents one of the most challenging mutations that have occurred in the last half century in the socio-economic organization environment.

Work intellectualization incorporates mainly information processes and knowledge processing without using – or at least using minimally – human physical effort. The main "tools" used are the human brain, informatics and automatized or robotic equipment.

Work intellectualization is expanding very rapidly in all countries. The USA was the first country in the world, from around 1957, where intellectual work became predominant, overcoming physical work, with the number of white-collar employees surpassing the number of blue-collar workers. Today, the digital revolution and the proliferation of new technologies – robotics, Internet of Things, artificial intelligence, drones, 3D printing, big data metrics, cloud computing, etc. – generate more intellectual work in all organizations. These technologies are based mainly on the use of more and more sophisticated and productive knowledge. The human resource, which is involved in intellectual work processes, is represented by knowledge workers. They possess intellectual capital and they work collaboratively.

Work intellectualization radically changes the coordinates and the parameters to be taken into consideration by every human being and organization, generating multiple shifts in the relations among all systems involved. Work intellectualization focusing on knowledge use, sharing, and valorization generates much higher productivity compared to the previous period. Because of this, intellectualization will determine profound changes in human life and the activity of organizations, facilitating the enhancement of living standards and socio-economic development in every country.

Work intellectualization has **significant impacts on companies** regarding:

- **inputs** – the quality of human resources is much better and more intellectualized, human resources have huge potential to valorize knowledge and information, to be innovative;
- **activities** – the knowledge and information used by intellectualized human resources in the fulfilment of each activity are greater and the quality of analysis and solutions is better, increasing the efficiency of activities;
- **outputs** – products and services generated by work intellectualization are richer in knowledge, their quality is higher, and they are better correlated with the market demand.

Work intellectualization also influences **companies' stakeholders** in several ways:

- significant increase in all stakeholders' knowledge and intellectual capital;
- improvement of all stakeholders' work quality and productivity;
- enhancement of stakeholders' capacity to understand, to analyze, and to design solutions for new individual and organizational challenges, opportunities, and threats;
- development of stakeholders' communication and interaction skills and competences.

At the company level, work intellectualization involves a new type of management. Company strategy and policy should be focused on intellectual capital generation, development, and valorization. Human resources, especially knowledge workers, should be the core of the company management. In the company, specific organizational structures, information systems, decision-making mechanisms, motivational approaches, etc. should be created in order to valorize the multiple qualities of intellectual work. A new type of organizational culture should be practised, in order to obtain maximum benefits from knowledge workers, and from their very productive intellectual capital.

The COVID-19 pandemic has helped people and organizations to understand better the importance and advantages of intellectual work, contributing to its increase in many organizations.

Internationalization of Activities

Without any doubt, comprehensive internationalization is an essential megashift of the present times. This internationalization involves hundreds of states and independent territories, thousands of extremely diverse regions, with many strong particularities, which are not easy to perceive and take into consideration by socio-economic entities. All kinds of flows among states and regions – human, technical, managerial, commercial, financial, scientific, cultural, sporting, ecological, juridical, political, etc. – are permanently multiplying and accelerating. During the last few years, the speed of internationalization has increased – the digital revolution and telecommunications making major contributions – and, concomitantly, it has continued to diversify. Internationalization generates increasing globalization by involving more territories, fields of activities, organizations and individuals and by amplifying impacts of different natures at the level of mankind (Broadman, 2015; Ernst & Young, 2015; Turcan, 2013; Wall, Rees, & Minocha, 2011). Internationalization **increases companies' access to different resources:**

- information and knowledge
- raw materials
- labour forces
- new products and technologies
- machines and equipment
- energy

The opportunity of penetrating markets in other countries, despite their distance, is very important. Based on these elements, internationalization generates new business opportunities, either for existing companies or for new entrepreneurs and investors, in all countries. In the meantime, internationalization produces a lot of challenges and risks for companies, such as new, better and/or cheaper products and services from foreign producers and suppliers in local and national markets, new foreign investment in the company field, migration of the local labour force, proliferation of new competitive management, marketing, financial, etc. approaches, methods and techniques coming from other countries, fluctuation of exchange rates for major currencies, etc. In this context, all company activities change profoundly, starting with raw materials, energy, machine, and technology supply and finishing with the sale of products and services and incomes obtained. Organizational activities are more open to foreign markets, to technical and technological changes from other countries, to international financial and human resources, ecological trends, etc.

Internationalization determines certain **significant shifts** at the company stakeholder level:

- modification of all company stakeholders' thinking, action, and behaviour under the impact of internationalization;
- increase in the level of direct and indirect influence of external company stakeholders from other countries, especially for medium-sized companies;
- enhancement of international interest from a large proportion of external and internal company stakeholders;
- increase of company stakeholders' potential and productivity because of their access to international information, knowledge, and other resources.

Company management should update their approaches, implementing innovations in all fields in order to be performant and to ensure the sustainability of the organization in such an international complex and dynamic environment.

Internationalization, in the context of the pandemic, faces numerous challenges. It has become more obvious that internationalization presents some important limitations, even disadvantages, for numerous countries and companies. In our opinion, internationalization will continue, but it should be remodelled in order to be more beneficial for all parties involved, for all stakeholders.

Multiculturalization of the Labour Force

The intense and heterogeneous multiculturalization represents one of the recent striking mutations that have developed in the society and in the economy. Multiculturalization means the establishment of human and work relations among individuals, groups and communities belonging to different national, regional and local cultures. The cultural differences among people from different areas are frequently large in terms of traditions, habits, rituals, mentalities, social value systems, communication methods, education, religion, social status, etc. All these generate specific and heterogeneous life visions, work approaches, individual and group values, decisional and actional approaches, individual and group behaviours, etc. Multiculturalization, from the organizational environment point of view, **takes two forms:**

- interstate multiculturalization, which deals with relations among people from different states, but who have a permanent residence in their home countries.
- intrastate multiculturalization, which includes people from different countries, but who live in the same state.

Both types of multiculturalization strongly influence – although partially in a different manner – the configuration and especially the functionality of the organizational environment (Broadman, 2015; Ernst & Young, 2015; Turcan, 2013; Wall, Rees, & Minocha, 2011).

Multiculturalization **influences companies** by some inputs: companies have access to a cheaper, more or less skilled labour force, usually with a better salary–quality relationship. Also, employees with different cultures provide supplementary information and knowledge, which could represent new resources for the company. In companies, a multicultural labour force involves specific human resource management, certain modifications in internal and external communication, partial remodelling of the organizational culture and specific types of social responsibility. Quite often, multiculturalization determines certain changes in the approach of the domestic and international markets.

Multiculturalization **influences company stakeholders** in the following ways:

- increase in the number of company stakeholders with cultures other than the culture dominant in the company;
- modification to a certain extent of the company stakeholders' own culture under the impact of the multiculturalization of the organization's human resources and their relationships;
- development of new behaviours and of new decisions, approaches, and actions among company stakeholders because of the multicultural labour force involved;
- increase in the complexity of relationships with internal and external company stakeholders due to the multicultural influences involved.

The trade-off for companies from the multiculturalization of human resources could be large: decreased costs, especially in terms of the labour force; better access to markets, mainly in the areas where these employees come from; increase of the company's capacity to internationalize its activities, etc. The benefits of using multicultural individuals motivate the company's management to cope with the challenges and risks associated with working with human resources with different cultures from other countries or regions.

Nanotechnologization and Biotechnologization

Nanotechnologization and biotechnologization are two of the most spectacular megashifts that substantially modify global economic and social activities. Both regard, directly and indirectly, all fields of human activities (Brousseau & Curien, 2007; Ciocoiu, Borisov, Dobrea, Burcea, & Târţiu, 2012; Day & Schoemaker, 2016; Markoff, 2016). **Nanotechnologization** elaborates and uses technologies at the atom level, creating new intelligent raw materials and small-size equipment and machines, with high yield and productivity, much higher than those achieved previously.

Biotechnologization, through genetic changes at the life cell level, determines the substantial improvement of animal breeds and plant varieties, generating very high production on the surface unit and on the animal capita (Brousseau & Curien, 2007).

In companies – especially in industrial ones – nanotechnologization provides many new inputs: raw materials, new smart technologies, products, knowledge and miniaturized equipment and machines. In agriculture and in food industry companies, biotechnologization offers as inputs new technologies, products, raw materials, animal breeds, plant varieties, equipment, etc. Many of the company activities are changing because of these new inputs. The most frequently found changes are focused on production, R&D, commercial activities, and the training of human resources. Changes in company inputs and activities generate much better outcomes at the organization level: higher quality of products and services, more competitive products, increased company sale prices and income, development of a competitive brand, higher prices of company shares, etc.

Nanotechnologization and biotechnologization determine some **significant shifts at the level of company stakeholders.** Among these, we mention the following:

- major changes in internal stakeholders' work, especially those involved in production, R&D, and human resources, in order to implement nanotechnologies and biotechnologies;
- appearance of new external stakeholders, who provide the nanotechnologies, biotechnologies, and all equipment and services necessary to use them in the company;
- partial modification of the relationships of company managers with the majority of external stakeholders, in order to fully valorize the beneficial effects of the nanotechnologization and biotechnologization.

In order to achieve all these changes generated by nanotechnologization and biotechnologization, companies' management should elaborate and implement specific strategies and policies and update the management of all fields mentioned above – R&D, production, commercial, and human resources. By performing these managerial operations, companies' outputs are better – higher-quality product, increased productivity and yield, lower unit cost – thereby obtaining competitive advantage and sustainability.

We appreciate that both nanotechnologization and biotechnologization are only in the beginning phase of their development. In the next few years, nanotechnologization and biotechnologization will produce many more outstanding innovations, which will have more impact, and in ways difficult to anticipate now, on companies and on numerous other socio-economic entities. Company management should be very anticipative, productive, and innovative in order to face the new challenges and opportunities generated by nanotechnologization and biotechnologization. It will manage based on new business models, involving more and diversified smart stakeholders, with rich top knowledge and using high-quality intellectual capital.

Comprehensive Networking in the Society and the Economy

Society and economy networking has grown fast in the last few decades, reflecting the structuring of an increasing number of business environment components as networks. Social practice reveals that network – structured as clusters, hubs, technopolis, technological platforms, network companies, commercial chains, multinational companies, holdings, federations, professional, scientific, sporting, etc. associations – are more frequent and more important in all domains. Networking has developed as an organizational feedback to the division of labour, deepening in the society and economy, structured in numerous components, many of them small in size, and frequently specialized. As a consequence, efficient and permanent work with other entities becomes more and more difficult. Networking is trying to overcome the limitations and difficulties associated with small-sized and/or specialized entities, concomitantly with better valorization of the new opportunities generated by the knowledge revolution. Informatization, digitalization, internationalization, nanotechnologization, etc. are providing powerful information, knowledge, communication, human, and technical support for performant networking.

The large proliferation of networks and the increase of their importance and impact are reflected in the emergence of a new profession, "**netocrat**", i.e. people who control the networks.

The main inputs generated by these networks **in companies** are: easier and faster access to suppliers, clients, production partners, financial entities, consultants, trainers, investors, etc.; more access to information and knowledge about network components; more interconnectivity with external company stakeholders and easier collaboration with them.

Company activities are changing to a certain extent in order to be able to communicate and work with other network components. Quite often a company develops its supply chain and improves customer relationships. Participation of the company in a network involves significant changes in managerial decisions, actions and behaviours, in order to respond to the specific requirements of the networks in which the company is integrated, and to get "de facto" network benefits. Company management could also develop easier, performant specialized systems for important domains. The most frequently developed are supply chain management (SCM) and client relationship management (CRM). Sometimes it is beneficial to build a matrix structure in the company.

The business model for a company integrated in networks should be remodelled, transforming the enterprise from being product-driven to networking-driven. This helps the company to maximize the advantages of being a network member: higher-rated company brand, better-quality products and services, superior position of the company in the market, and more profitable relationships with external stakeholders (Becerra, 2017; Inkpen & Tsang, 2016; Jarvenpaa & Välikangas, 2014; McIntyre & Srinivasan, 2017; Perry-Smith & Mannucci, 2017).

The present intensification of the comprehensive networking in the economy and the society has some **important influences on company stakeholders:**

- development of the co-working and the relationships of the company stakeholders, especially of the external stakeholders;
- increase of the intellectual capital of the company stakeholders, mainly of the relational capital;
- enhancement of the stakeholders' capacity to integrate the company's activities in the business and social environment, and to be engaged more successfully in the enhancement of performances.

The proliferation of networks – both business and social – fosters and develops new ecosystems in the economy and contributes to the fast development of a collaborative and shared economy (Lichtenthaler, 2016).

In the context of the COVID-19 pandemic, networking reveals **two contradictory faces:**

- the virtual network based on working online has been less affected by the effects of the COVID-19 pandemic and it helps organizations to solve many problems, decreasing the risk of people infection.
- the physical network has been blocked or decreased notably because of restrictions associated with the fight against the pandemic.

Without any doubt, the COVID-19 pandemic has stimulated the development of virtual networking inside and outside organizations, contributing to the increase of the degree of networking in society and the economy.

Sustainable Ecologization

Many analyses reveal that the environmental protection against the negative effects of human activities (primarily of economic activities), the more efficient and equitable use of non-renewable natural resources and the resetting of ecological equilibriums at the world, continental, and regional level represent the main components of ecologization. All these processes mean new inputs, restrictions, and outputs for numerous types of organizations. For the majority of them, ecologization determines significant changes in strategies, policies, systems, mechanisms, activities, and outputs.

Sustainability is a new dimension of ecologization developed in the last few decades. **Sustainable ecologization** means the approach of ecologization in a long-run perspective and providing the necessary resources for its implementation. Sustainable ecologization determines the amplification of the requirements and pressures on all types of organizations. Notwithstanding, sustainability is essential for the survival of mankind and for its continued development, valorizing the huge opportunities generated by the knowledge revolution. On the other hand – as Brown, Adams, Larsen, and Roney (2015) have outlined – there is a big danger of an ecological decline and, as a consequence, of economic and social decline.

In all countries, in order to achieve sustainable ecologization, special laws and other regulations have been adopted regarding environmental protection, health security for human resources and ecostandards, in accordance with the numerous international agreements and protocols in this field.

At **the company level**, there are substantial changes in inputs, concerning: prohibition of certain raw materials and technologies; mandatory characteristics for many raw materials, technologies, machines, equipment, etc.; generation and use of energy; production, use, storing, and reuse of waste; special taxes and penalties for the utilization of pollutant substances; higher limits regarding carbon dioxide, and other noxious emissions.

Many of company activities should be changed in order to respect the legislation and to be able to utilize profitably the new inputs. The most frequent changes affect production, supply, sale, R&D activities, storage, human resources security and transportation. Sometimes, especially in industry, new activities should be organized in companies for waste storage, reuse of waste, waste transportation, environmental and health protection, etc. Previous requirements and changes involve significant shifts in company management strategies, policies, systems, methods, approaches, operations, etc.

In company outputs, we can see two categories of changes. The first refers to the making of ecological products and services, reduction of noxious waste, reuse of waste, and better protection of the company and local environment. The second category, regarding economic aspects, are increased costs of raw materials, technologies, machines, and supplementary investments or decreased profits. This category has been neglected to a certain extent during the COVID-19 pandemic, because of the emergence of new priorities and restrictions.

The ecologization megashift also **influences company stakeholders** in several ways:

- rise of the new category of external stakeholders, like local communities, "ecological" NGOs, protection agencies focused on the ecological field, which promote requirements, rules, standards, etc. in order to preserve and protect the ecological environment;
- development of new approaches at the level of company stakeholders through which sustainable ecologization is promoted;
- building of some special kind of stakeholder networking focused on waste and on the circular economy.

Companies' and stakeholders' compliance with the ecological requirements and standards is necessary for company survival and sustainable development, for population security and health, and for the protection of the local, national, continental, and global environment.

Intensification and Diversification of State Intervention

In recent decades, state interventions in the society and economy have increased dramatically at the national, regional, and world level. The COVID-19 pandemic has increased state intervention at a high level, never previously seen during peacetime. State interventions from the point of view of their **scope can be divided into three categories:**

a **State intervention at the country level**, usually dealing with the preservation and increase of the business environment functionality and predictability, with decent life standards and social peace. These interventions were increased during the 2009–2011 world economic crisis, which continues in many countries, attaining a peak during COVID-19 pandemic.

b **State intervention at continental level**, where there are multi-state systems of international economic integration. The European Union is the best such example. This type of state intervention is directed at the development of the regional environment, enabling economic and social development and valorizing at a higher level the specificity of each country involved and their complementarities.

c **Global intervention**, usually through international organizations, whose members comprise all or a large number of world states.

The UN, ILO, IMF, and WB are the most comprehensive and best-known such types of international bodies. A major role is also played by certain groups from the most powerful and influential states, like the G7, G20, OECD, and NATO. Their interventions at global, continental, regional, or national level usually deal with the prevention and/or elimination of crises and/or major political, economic, military and social dysfunctionalities, or the improvement of the economic and societal environment and/or development at the international level.

The global societal crisis generated by the COVID-19 pandemic necessitates concomitantly these three types of state interventions. Analysis reveals that state interventions **influence companies mainly in two ways:**

- **Modifying the entire business environment.** The business environment, from the point of view of companies' activities and performance, could be enabling, permissive, or unfavourable. In an enabling environment, it is easy to create new companies and, for existing enterprises, there are good conditions in order to be performant and sustainable. Normally, all state interventions should be focused on the development of an enabling business environment. Unfortunately, in real life, sometimes state interventions damage the business environment with very negative effects on the business and society;
- **Changing only some components of the business environment.** This happens when a state intervention is focused on a specific field or domain, like fiscality, labour force, industry, agriculture, etc. In this case, company activities are impacted, positively or negatively, only partially.

It is very important that every state intervention, through strategies, policies, laws, administrative regulations, standards, etc., is preceded by *ex-ante* impact analysis, in order to avoid negative effects on the economy and society and to contribute to developing an enabling environment for all kinds of companies.

Changes in the business environment caused by state interventions have multiple impacts on companies. The **most frequent impacts** of state interventions on companies relate to:

- taxes and fees
- investment conditions
- environmental protection
- work security
- access to certain resources
- exchange rates

- utilities tariffs
- storage and use of waste

All these elements determine changes in company inputs, activities, and outputs.

Company management should carefully analyze and take into consideration such state interventions, should prepare and operate all necessary changes in order to make them profitable for the company, or – at the very least – be tolerable well, without decreasing the organization's competitive capacity and sustainability.

State interventions influence **company stakeholders mainly in the following ways:**

- Modification to a certain extent of the relationships between the company and its stakeholders, because of the changes in taxes, fees, security requirements, investment conditions, etc.
- Facilitation of the appearance and/or development of new company stakeholders, like investors, suppliers, distributors or customers, when state interventions enable investments, increased production and sales, as well as exports and imports, etc.
- Contribution of the elimination or reduction of certain company stakeholders when state taxes, fees, tariffs and requirements regarding environmental protection, investments, etc. demotivate them or make their activities non-profitable.

In our opinion, based on previous tendencies, in the future state interventions will be more intense and more varied in terms of their content and ways to implement them. These state interventions will continue to be predominantly strategic, but the operational dimension will increase too, being essential for social, economic, ecological, military, etc. equilibrium at the regional, national, and international level, for sustainable and peaceful development. State feedbacks in the COVID-19 pandemic context confirms these predictions.

Development of the Powerful Educational-Formative Dimension

The quality of human resources represents the determinant element for the manifestation of all the above-mentioned business environment trends. All types of evolutions – economic, technical, political, scientific, ecological, managerial, etc. – are the result of human thinking, decisions, actions, and behaviours. The last few decades have been characterized by comprehensive and profound progress regarding human resource education and training. Access of the most part of population to the education, and its substantial improvement, becoming more pragmatic, innovative and entrepreneurial, provide higher quality human resources, more dynamic and productive. Education, training, and lifelong learning have become conditional for organizations' survival and performance, for the proper functioning of society and for competitive development. Numerous researches and studies have proved that education and training investments are the most productive ones. For this reason, in the future education and training will intensify in order to provide a labour force capable of assimilating and valorizing knowledge, the most productive resource of the knowledge-based economy and society. This trend has, and will continue to have, major **positive effects** on all types of organizations' activities and performance.

The **influence of human resources on a company is decisive in many respects**. First, the employees represent one of the most important inputs in the enterprise. The skills, knowledge, methods, techniques, creativity, engagement, work capacity, behaviour, etc. of employees determine the effectiveness and efficiency of every resource in the company (raw materials, machines, equipment, buildings, cash, patents, etc.). Second, the company activities' content and results are substantially influenced by the characteristics of the human resources employed. The quality and the cost of every task and job accomplished in the company are largely impacted by the qualification, creativity, and efforts of the employees involved. A company's human resources make a major contribution to all indicators of the enterprise's performance – from the labour productivity to the size of turnover and profit. Employees contribute decisively to the company's capacity to generate competitive advantage and competitiveness. For this reason, in numerous companies, the training and development of human resources are a priority, with the enterprise management allocating a large amount of money to this. Many companies are already **learning organizations** and the role of learning becomes essential. According to a recent study (Bailey, Reeves, Whitaker, & Hutchinson, 2019), in the coming decade, companies will increasingly need to compete on the rate of learning. To unlock the learning potential of new technologies, leaders need to reinvent the enterprise as a next-generation learning organization (Lesser, Reeves, Whitaker, & Hutchinson, 2018). Every organization needs to look at learning as a core competency (Daugherty, Wilson, & Michelman, 2019).

Development of the powerful educational-formative dimension in the society determines certain significant changes at the level of **company stakeholders**:

- Increased level of education, knowledge, and competences of company stakeholders;

- Amplification of the stakeholders' capacity to understand and to analyze events, individual, and organizational changes and to have innovative undertakings;
- Facilitation of the communication and networking of the company stakeholders inside and outside the organization.

Transition to the knowledge-based economy and society, and digitalization of the main content of the present development, will be permanently associated with the tendency to increase education, training, and lifelong learning, which means human resources with more and a higher level of knowledge. Training and educational processes will take into consideration the rapid changes in technologies, including artificial intelligence, and machine and mobile learning. Already some specialists have formulated new ways to structure education and to use education technology (Ghemawat, 2017; Lyons, 2017; Pyöriä, Ojala, Saari, & Järvinen, 2017).

In the context of the COVID-19 pandemic, decisions and actions regarding education and training should be correlated with those focused on the preservation of people's physical and mental health.

Multidimensional Remodelling of Markets

Markets represent a major component of the business environment, which has changed rapidly and substantially during the last few decades. The largest modifications have occurred in the market for products and services, the labour market, and the financial market. The **main changes** are:

- comprehensive informatization, more than half of the world population being already connected online (Gada, 2016; Hoffmann, Lavie, Reuer, & Shipilov, 2018; Lerider, 2017);
- accelerated digitalization;
- telecommunication expansion;
- business internationalization;
- business and social networking;
- global value chain development;
- population higher level of education;
- improved standard of living;
- proliferation of new types of work organization (hubs, clusters, technological platforms, etc.);
- trade barriers lowered at international, regional, and national level, with some fluctuations in recent years.

Under the impact of the COVID-19 pandemic, these changes have been modified to a certain extent. Some of them, like accelerated digitalization and telecommunication expansion, have developed faster. Others – like global value chain development, standard of living enhancement, population higher level of education, and lowering of trade barriers – have reduced or even stopped increasing.

Today's markets present many new characteristics compared with the "classical" markets: rapid proliferation of e-commerce, increased market fluidity, building of very large, and powerful networks of suppliers and clients, proliferation of concurrence between producers network stakeholders, very high weight of internationalized trade in the global trade, appearance of a new type of concurrence – concurrence based on collaboration and others. Market changes contribute to the design of new business models, which causes **multiple shifts in all company activities.**

The present very developed and functional markets make it possible for companies to have more, faster and lower-cost inputs – raw materials, products, services, labour force, energy, money, etc. The importance and the impact of company activities that deal with markets – marketing, supply, import, export, and sale – are constantly increasing. Other enterprise activities – production, R&D, finance, investment, etc. – will be more oriented to, and connected with, the market dynamic.

Company management should be increasingly open to the market evolution, elaborating and implementing innovative commercial strategies, policies, and mechanisms. Supply chain management (SCM) and Customer Relationship, Management (CRM) will be implemented in more companies, especially large and medium-sized ones. Better company access to markets usually increases the size and the speed of product sales, both being good premises to enlarge the enterprise's turnover and profit. Concomitantly, the company needs to invest in order to digitalize and internationalize activities and to agree to share with network components some of the commercial costs and company profits.

In the near future **markets will increase the speed and size of the impact on companies**, because of continued and fast mutations that happen to them. Among these, we mention the following: trading using digital identity, smart contracts (Lerider, 2017), a neuromarketing approach (Hsu, 2017), extension of hub firms, which control the access of billions of mobile consumers connected by all kinds of products and services providers (Iansiti & Lakhani, 2017), proliferation of competing stakeholder networks (Freeman, Harrison, Wicks, Parmar, & De Colle, 2010), transition to the so-called "era of consumers", proliferation of regional and continental digital markets, like the Digital Single Market in the European Union, and others.

Multidimensional remodelling of the markets influences **company stakeholders** mainly in the following ways:

- increase of the impact of the market evolutions on company stakeholders' decisions, actions, and behaviours;

- developing networks of suppliers, intermediaries, and clients;
- transition from concurrence between producers to concurrence of the producers' networks.

Rapid, complex, and sometimes unexpected changes in the categories of markets – like those provoked by the COVID-19 pandemic – will significantly increase the opportunities, challenges, and threats for companies, involving for their management fast and innovative feedback integrated in a long-term sustainable vision.

Of course, the tendencies formulated by us, using the results of many previous researches from all over the world, are neither exhaustive nor debatable. We have presented them because we believe that they could – to a large extent – be used as major points in order to facilitate the understanding and utilization of the essential evolutions of the changing business environment for management decisions, actions, and behaviours, ensuring the company's survival and competitiveness. **These megashifts could be a very good framework helping to identify and cultivate performant relations with the organization's stakeholders and their management.**

Short Synthesis of the Influences of Megashifts on a Company and Its Stakeholders

Together, the contextual trends briefly presented in the previous sections have many significant and complex influences on companies. We try to synthesize and group them into **two categories:**

a **Influences on the company as an entity,** as an open system, integrated in the environment, mainly in the business environment. In Figure 3.3, we indicate these influences.
b **Influences on company stakeholders.** We enumerate these in Figure 3.4.

There are close connections between a company's influences of contextual changes on the one hand and stakeholders' influences on the other. Practically, they are interwitted, growing mutually.

Company management, in order to be performant, needs to understand, analyze, and take into consideration the main contextual company and stakeholder changes, in an innovative vision and pragmatic approach. Of course, special attention should be paid to the recent changes in the business environment under the influence of the COVID-19 pandemic. Many specialists have already conducted very interesting and useful analysis, proposing new concepts, approaches, and methods (Chaturvedi, Dey, & Singh, 2020; Chima & Gutman, 2020; Dykes, Hughes-Morgan, Kolev, & Ferrier, 2020; Heichler, 2020; Kaplan, 2020; Levenson, 2020;

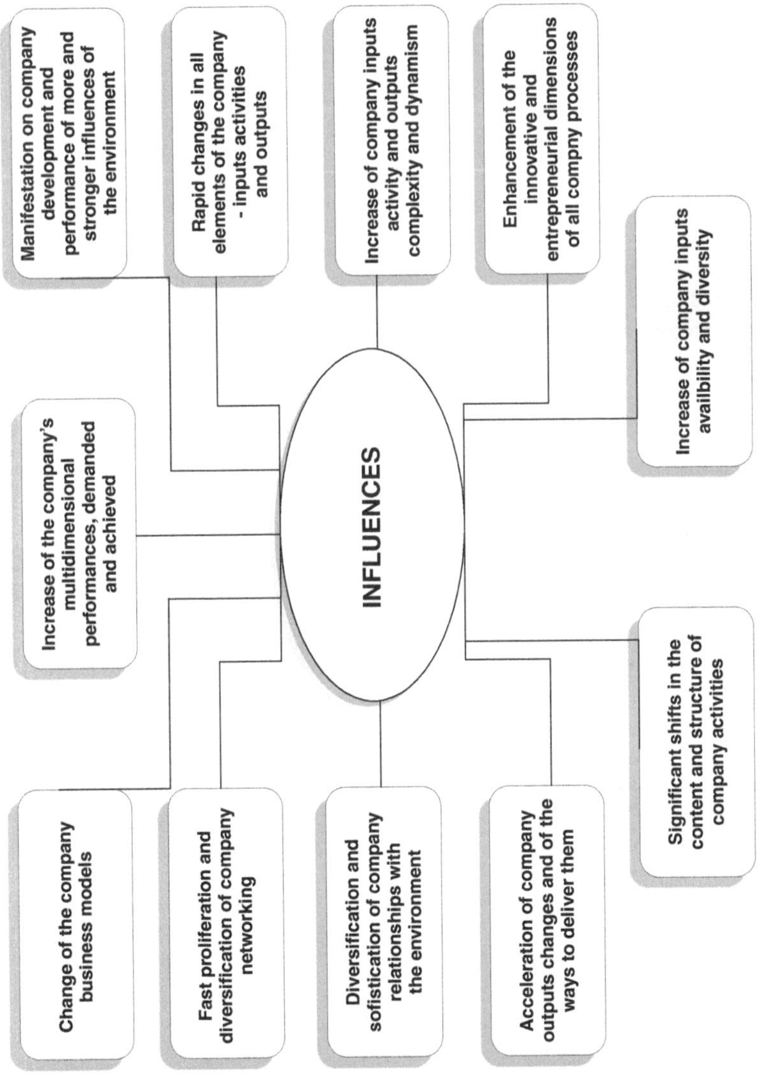

Figure 3.3 Main influences of megashifts on company development and performance.

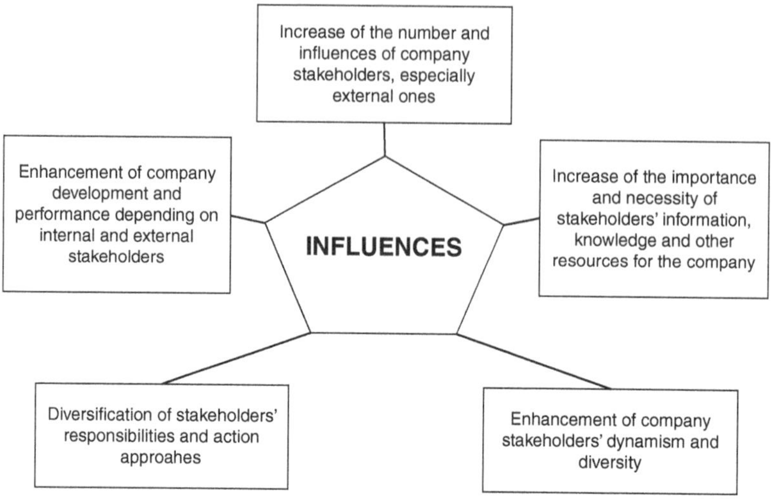

Figure 3.4 Major influences of megashifts on company stakeholders.

Mokyr, 2020; Narayandas, Hebbar, & Li, 2020; Radjou, 2020; Romeo, Moukanas, & Rung, 2020).

In the following chapters, we will present elements that could be useful in rethinking and remodelling company management in accordance with the present and future megashifts in the economy and society.

References

Attali, J. (2007). *Une brève histoire de l'avenir*. Paris, France: Fayard.

Bailey, A., Reeves, M., Whitaker, K., & Hutchinson, R. (2019, April 5). *The company of the future: Winning the '20s*. Retrieved from https://www.bcg.com/publications/2019/company-of-the-future.aspx

Becerra, J. (2017, March 14). The digital revolution is not about technology: It's about people. *World Economic Forum*. Retrieved from https://www.weforum.org/agenda/2017/03/the-digital-revolution-is-not-about-technology-it-s-about-people

Bennett, N., & Lemoine, G. J. (2014). What VUCA really means for you. *Harvard Business Review*, 92(1–2), 27–28.

Birkinshaw, J., Hamel, G., & Mol, M. J. (2008). Management innovation. *Academy of Management Review*, *33*(4), 825–845. doi:10.5465/amr.2008.34421969

Brătianu, C. (2015). *Organizational knowledge dynamics: Managing knowledge creation, acquisition, sharing, and transformation*. Hershey, PA: IGI Global. doi:10.4018/978-1-4666-8318-1

Broadman, H. G. (2015, March 30). Welcome to globalisation 2.0. Or is it 3.0? *Forbes*. Retrieved from https://www.forbes.com/sites/harrybroadman/2015/03/30/welcome-to-globalization-2-0-or-is-it-3-0/#360e603f65a1

Brousseau, E., & Curien, N. (2007). Internet and digital economics: Principles, methods and applications. Cambridge, UK: Cambridge University Press. doi:10.1017/CBO9780511493201

Brown, L. R., Adams, E., Larsen, J., & Roney, M. (2015). *The great transition: Shifting from fossil fuels to solar and wind energy*. New York: W.W. Norton & Company.

Burkus, D. (2013). Innovation isn't an idea problem. *Harvard Business Review*. Retrieved from https://hbr.org/2013/07/innovation-isnt-an-idea-proble

Chaturvedi, H., Dey A. K., & Singh, N. (2020). Coping with COVID-19. *Global Focus the EFMD Business Magazine*. Retrieved from https://www.globalfocusmagazine.com/coping-with-covid-19/

Chima, A., & Gutman, R. (2020). What it takes to lead through an era of exponential change. *Harvard Business Review*. Retrieved from https://hbr.org/2020/10/what-it-takes-to-lead-through-an-era-of-exponential-change

Christensen, C. M., Raynor, M. E., & McDonald, R. (2015). What is disruptive innovation? *Harvard Business Review*, *93*(12), 44–53.

Ciocoiu, N. C., Borisov, D. L., Dobrea, R. C., Burcea, Ș. G., & Târțiu, E. V. (2012). *Modern approaches in exploring the link between digital economy and waste management*. Bucuresti, Romania: ASE Publishing House.

Daugherty, P. R., Wilson, H. J., & Michelman, P. (2019). Revisiting the jobs artificial intelligence will create. *MIT Sloan Management Review*. Retrieved from https://sloanreview.mit.edu/article/revisiting-the-jobs-artificial-intelligence-will-create/?gclid=Cj0KCQjw-_j1BRDkARIsAJcfmTFWo5
DuagUAIhgQJshFIhDY9-el77zsx1903xSTxV2
NbIeWLrEvsWwaApJxEALw_wcB

Day, G. S., & Schoemaker, P. J. H. (2016). Adapting to fast-changing markets and technologies. *California Management Review*, *58*(4), 59–77. doi:10.1525/cmr.2016.58.4.59

Dykes, B. J., Hughes-Morgan, M., Kolev, K. D., & Ferrier W. J. (2020). Responding to crises with speed and agility. *MIT Sloan Management Review*. Retrieved from https://sloanreview.mit.edu/article/responding-to-crises-with-speed-and-agility/

Ernst & Young. (2015). *Redrawing the map: Globalisation and changing the world of business*. Retrieved from https://www.slideshare.net/Management-Thinking/redrawing-the-map-globalization-and-the-changing-world-of-business

Freeman, R. E., Harrison, J. S., Wicks, A. C., Parmar, B. L., & De Colle, S. (2010). *Stakeholder theory: The state of art*. New York: Cambridge University Press.

Gada, K. (2016, June 16). The digital economy in 5 minutes. *Forbes*. Retrieved from https://www.forbes.com/sites/koshagada/2016/06/16/what-is-the-digital-economy/#2088cd737628

Garrow, V., & Varney S. (2015). Organisation design in a VUCA world. A paper from HR in a disordered world: IES perspectives on HR 2015. Retrieved from http://www.employment-studies.co.uk/system/files/resources/files/mp105.pdf

Ghemawat, P. (2017). Strategies for higher education in the digital age. *California Management Review*, *59*(4), 56–78. doi:10.1177/0008125617717706

Griffin, R. W. (2012). *Management: Principles and practices*. Mason, OH: South-Western Cengage Learning.

Grossman, R. (2016). The Industries that are being disrupted the most by digital. *Harvard Business Review*. Retrieved from https://hbr.org/2016/03/the-industries-that-are-being-disrupted-the-most-by-digital.

Hamel, G. (2006). The why, what, and how of management innovation. *Harvard Business Review*, *84*(2), 72–84.

Heichler, E. (2020). Seize the moment. *MIT Sloan Management Review*. Retrieved from https://sloanreview.mit.edu/article/seize-the-moment/?og=Fall+2020+Issue+Horizontal

Hoffmann, W., Lavie, D., Reuer J. J., & Shipilov, A. (2018). The interplay of competition and cooperation. *Strategic Management*, *39*(12), 3033–3053. doi:10.1002/smj.2965

Hsu, M. (2017). Neuromarketing: Inside the mind of the consumer. *California Management Review*, *59*(4), 5–22. doi:10.1177/0008125617720208

Iansiti, M., & Lakhani, K. R. (2017). Managing our hub economy: Strategy, ethics, and network competition in the age of digital superpowers. *Harvard Business Review*, *95*(5), 84–92.

Inkpen, A. C., & Tsang, E. W. K. (2016). Reflections on the 2015 decade award-social capital, networks, and knowledge transfer: An emergent stream of research. *Academy of Management Review*, *41*(4), 573–588. doi:10.5465/amr.2016.0140

Jarvenpaa, S. L., & Välikangas, L. (2014). Opportunity creation in innovation networks: Interactive revealing practices. *California Management Review*, *57*(1), 67–86. doi:10.1525/cmr.2014.57.1.67

Kaplan, S. (2020). Why social responsibility produces more resilient organizations. *MIT Sloan Management Review*. Retrieved from https://sloanreview.mit.edu/article/why-social-responsibility-produces-more-resilient-organizations/

Lerider, M. (2017, August 11). *What is NEO Smart Economy?* Retrieved from https://medium.com/@MalcolmLerider/what-is-neo-smart-economy-381a4c6ee286

Lesser, R., Reeves, M., Whitaker, K., & Hutchinson, R. (2018, December 14). *A leadership agenda for the next decade: Winning the '20s*. Retrieved from https://www.bcg.com/publications/2018/winning-the-20s-leadership-agenda-for-next-decade.aspx

Levenson, A. (2020). A long time until the economic new normal. *MIT Sloan Management Review*. Retrieved from https://sloanreview.mit.edu/article/a-long-time-until-the-economic-new-normal

Lichtenthaler, U. (2016). Six principles for shared management: A framework for the integrated economy. *Journal of Business Strategy*, *37*(4), 3–11. doi:10.1108/JBS-03-2015-0029

Lyons, R. K. (2017). Economics of the ed tech revolution. *California Management Review*, *59*(4), 49–55. doi:10.1177/0008125617717708

Markoff, J. (2016, January 7). Un système d'archivage venu de l'AND. *Courrier International*, *1314*, 37–38.

McIntyre, D. P., & Srinivasan, A. (2017). Networks, platforms, and strategy: Emerging views and next steps. *Strategic Management Journal*, *38*(1), 141–160. doi:10.1002/smj.2596

Mokyr, J. (2020). Why our knowledge economy can survive the new age of pestilence. *MIT Sloan Management Review*. Retrieved from https://sloanreview.mit.edu/article/why-our-knowledge-economy-can-survive-the-new-age-of-pestilence/

Naqvi, A. (2014, April 25). Cities, not countries, are the key to tomorrow's economies. *Financial Times*. Retrieved from https://www.ft.com/content/0221bb6e-cb9d-11e3–8ccf-00144feabdc0

Narayandas, D., Hebbar, V., & Li, L. (2020). Lessons from Chinese companies' response to Covid-19. *Harvard Business Review*. Retrieved from https://hbr.org/2020/06/lessons-from-chinese-companies-response-to-covid-19

Nicolescu, O., Nicolescu, C., Bontea, A., Urîtu, D., Corcodel, S.-F., Samek, D., et al. (2019). *Carta alba a IMM-urilor din Romania 2019*. Bucuresti, Romania: Editura Pro Universitaria.

Nicolescu, O., Popa, I., Nicolescu, C., & Stefan, S. C. (2019). *Starea de sanatate a managementului din Romania in 2018*. Bucuresti, Romania: Pro Universitaria.

Perry-Smith, J. E., & Mannucci, P. V. (2017). From creativity to innovation: The social network drivers of the four phases of the idea journey. *Academy of Management Review*, *42*(1), 53–79. doi:10.5465/amr.2014.0462

Pisano, G. P. (2015). You need an innovation strategy. *Harvard Business Review*, *93*(6), 44–54.

Pyöriä, P., Ojala, S., Saari, T., & Järvinen, K-M. (2017). The millennial generation: A new breed of labour? *Sage Open*, *7*(1), 1–14. Retrieved from https://journals.sagepub.com/doi/pdf/10.1177/2158244017697158 10.1177/2158244017697158

Radjou, N. (2020). The rising frugal economy. *MIT Sloan Management Review*. Retrieved from https://sloanreview.mit.edu/article/the-rising-frugal-economy/

Rifkin, J. (2016, January 14). *The 2016 world economic forum misfires with its fourth industrial revolution theme*. Retrieved from https://www.huffingtonpost.com/jeremy-rifkin/the-2016-world-economic-f_b_8975326.html

Romeo, J., Moukanas, H., & Rung, G. (2020). The age of accelerating strategy breakthroughs. *MIT Sloan Management Review*. Retrieved from https://sloanreview.mit.edu/article/the-age-of-accelerating-strategy-breakthroughs/

Schweer, D., & Sahl, J. C. (2017). The digital transformation of industry: The benefit for Germany. In F. Abolhassan (Ed.), *The drivers of digital transformation. Management for professionals* (pp. 23–31). Cham, DE: Springer. doi:10.1007/978-3-319-31824-0_3

Turcan, R. V. (2013). The philosophy of turning points: A case of de-internationalization. In T. M. Devinney, T. Pedersen & L. Tihanyi (Eds.), *Philosophy of science and meta-knowledge in international business and management* (pp. 219–235). Bingley, UK: Emerald Group Publishing Limited. doi:10.1108/S1571-5027(2013)0000026014

Unruh, G., & Kiron, D. (2017). Digital transformation on purpose. *MIT Sloan Management Review*. Retrieved from https://sloanreview.mit.edu/article/digital-transformation-on-purpose/

Wall, S., Rees, B., & Minocha, S. (2011). *International Business* (4th ed.). London: Pearson Education Limited.

4 Main Aspects of the Stakeholders' Approach Evolution

Short History of the Stakeholders' Approach

The beginning of the stakeholders' approach dates back to before the Second World War. In 1932, the General Electric Company identified four groups with whom they had to deal: shareholders, employees, customers, and the general public. In 1947, Johnson & Johnson identified customers, employees, managers, and the general public. In 1950, the Sears Company named four parties that are very important for any business – customers, employees, the community, and stockholders (Fontaine, Haarman, & Schmid, 2006). Later, in 1963, according to Freeman (1984), in an internal report by the Stanford Research Institute, the first definition of stakeholders was formulated as "those groups without whose support the organization would cease to exist". Stewart and Benepe, who worked with the Stanford Research Institute and Lockheed Aircraft, also deal in some way with the subject of stakeholders (Chartered Management Institute, 2013).

The information regarding the beginning of the stakeholders' approach, until the book by Freeman (1984), describes what we consider could be referred to as the "stakeholders' prehistory approach".

The **"real" history of the stakeholders' approach starts with Freeman's landmark book** (1984), in which he lays down the basic elements regarding the stakeholder concept. In this book, Freeman states that an organization should be thought of as grouping stakeholders and the purpose of the organization should be to manage their interests, needs, and viewpoints. He tried to build a framework capable of responding to the concerns of managers, who were being confronted with unexpected and high levels of environmental turbulence and change. This framework is based on the stakeholder concept. Freeman suggested that company managers must elaborate and implement processes capable of satisfying those groups who have a stake in the business. Later, Freeman generated another important contribution to the stakeholders' approach – the four types of stakeholders' strategy (offensive, defensive, swing, and hold).

DOI: 10.4324/9781003217701-4

A very important contribution was made by Donaldson and Preston (1995) in the study "The Stakeholder Theory of the Corporation: Concepts, Evidence and Implications", where they grouped the stakeholders' theory literature in three fields, namely descriptive, instrumental, and normative, and they argued that "stakeholders theory is managerial" and recommended "the attitudes, structures and practices that taken together constitute a stakeholder managerial philosophy".

In 1997, Mitchell, Agle, and Wood elaborated a model based on three criteria – stakeholders' power to influence a company, the legitimacy of the stakeholders' relationship with the company, and the urgency of the stakeholder claim of the firm – which led to seven stakeholder types – very useful for company management in order to prioritize stakeholders' relationships. They contributed significantly to the elaboration of the theory of stakeholder identification and salience.

Elias and Cavana (2000) from New Zeeland, using some ideas from Freeman's works, launched the concept "stakeholder dynamics", very useful for realistic and performant management of the company–stakeholder strategic relationship.

A few years later, Friedman and Miles (2002) made very relevant contributions to the stakeholder theory development by creating a special typology of organization–stakeholder relationships (type A, type B, type D, and type E), based on two distinctions: compatible/incompatible and necessary/contingent.

Steurer (2006), based on the triple-perspective typology of the stakeholder theory, formulated nine stakeholder approaches, which allows us to frame the contributions of the specialists in the field and to evaluate their impacts on three levels – corporate, stakeholder, and conceptual.

Corporate social responsibility, based largely on Carroll's pyramid (Carroll, 1979), promotes a vision of business accountability to a large range of stakeholders (e.g. Baden, 2016; Carroll, 1991; Chandler & Werther, 2014). Corporate social responsibility refers to the society's expectations – economic, legal, and ethical – of organization stakeholders.

Harrison and Wicks (2013) conceived a stakeholder-based perspective on value, which focuses on four factors that emerge in the context of the company–stakeholder relationships: stakeholder utility, associated with actual goals and services; stakeholder utility, associated with organizational justice; stakeholder utility, from affiliation; and stakeholder utility, associated with perceived opportunity costs.

Garcia-Castro and Aguilera (2015) developed a conceptual framework – based on an analytical taxonomy of value creation and appropriation – consistent with a more complete notion of value and wherein the trade-off in stakeholder value appropriation could be included in a world with multiple stakeholders.

Observing that in theory and practice, social welfare appears to be a multidimensional and pluralistic concept, Mitchell, Weaver, Agle, Bailey, and Carlson (2015) developed an account of multi-objective corporation as a means for enabling a greater range of management decisions and actions, in order to permit more direct organization engagement in the diverse goals of different stakeholders. They argued the consistent advantages of multi-objective corporation, compared with a single-objective corporate function.

Recently, Miles (2017) conducted an analysis via an unparalleled bounded systemic review of 593 stakeholder definitions and produced a comprehensive, multidimensional classification of stakeholder theories, based on four hyponyms, which relate to 16 definitional categories. Her conclusion is that stakeholder theory is indeed a single theory.

Another very interesting approach was presented by Berman and Johnson-Cramer (2017), who analyzed whether stakeholder theory constitutes an established academic field. Their answer is both "yes" and "no", and they outline future directions for stakeholder research.

In the same period, Edward Freeman, "the father" of the modern stakeholders' approach, published a study in which he suggests that there are at least five main challenges to the development of stakeholder theory: understanding what counts as the total performance of a business; accounting for stakeholders, rather than accounting for investors; explaining real stakeholder behaviour; formulating smart public policy in the light of stakeholder theory; and rethinking the basics of ethical theory (Freeman, 2017).

Recently, in the context of the COVID-19 pandemic, we have seen that the focus on the role of stakeholders continues. Many approaches (Levenson, 2020; Narayandas, Hebbar, & Li, 2020; Radjou, 2020; Romeo, Moukanas, & Rung, 2020; Tarabishy & Carayannis, 2020; Teece, Raspin, & Cox, 2020; World Economic Forum, 2020) stress the increasing need to take into consideration organizations' stakeholders in order to solve better the complex challenges and difficulties associated with the COVID-19 pandemic and relaunch the economy.

Finally, we would like to point out that there are many other valuable works and specialists that could be mentioned as contributing significantly to the stakeholder theory and practice development. We select only these, trying to summarize in a few pages the relevant elements from the perspective of stakeholder company management. We try to do this because we fully agree with the thesis that **"stakeholder theory is a genre of management theory"** formulated by Freeman, Harrison, Wicks, Parmar, and De Colle.

Descriptive, Instrumental, and Normative Approaches

Without any doubt, in the rich stakeholder literature, a central position is occupied by Donaldson and Preston's (1995) three approaches of stakeholder theory – descriptive, instrumental, and normative. This systematization is based mainly on the objectives taken into consideration by specialists in stakeholder analysis and the ways to achieve them.

The objective of the **descriptive approach** is to understand how managers deal with organizations' internal and external stakeholders, how they represent stakeholders' interests, and what their impact is on the achievement of each corporation's goals. A corporation is considered as a constellation of cooperative and competitive interests possessing intrinsic value (Lawrence, 2010). The descriptive approach helps to fulfil a realistic map of a company's stakeholder identification. The descriptive approach is an essential process (step) that is necessary in order to understand the complex relationships among the company's multiple stakeholders and how they work. Numerous empirical studies illustrate the usefulness of the descriptive approach.

The **instrumental approach** is focused on the relationships between managers' decisions, the actions and behaviours of the company stakeholders, and the achievement of the organization's objectives regarding profitability, growth, and sustainability. The instrumental approach deals with how company managers should act if they want to favour, and work for, their interests. The instrumental approach is essentially hypothetical. It is based on the supposition that company managers and other agents taking into consideration the stakeholders' interests will generate better company performance in the long run. There are a lot of empirical studies that support this thesis, but not all. Models based on the instrumental approach enable the testing of the connection between managing stakeholders and the accomplishment of the company's objectives and targets. In this respect, the instrumental approach is "prescriptive" too, and it has predictive value. Certain specialists (e.g. Lawrence, 2010) believe that the descriptive approach and the instrumental approach together constitute analytic theory, which answers the question of how to organize stakeholders' interests into a hierarchy.

The main objective of the **normative approach** is to identify moral and philosophical guidelines linked to the activity of management of corporations (Fontaine et al., 2006), supposing that stakeholders have inherent value. It is based, according to Donaldson and Preston (1995), on two "ideas":

a stakeholders are individuals or groups with legitimate interests in procedural and/or substantial aspects of corporate activity. Stakeholders are identified by their interests in a corporation, and whether the corporation has any corresponding functional interests in them;
b the interests of stakeholders are of intrinsic value; that is, each group of stakeholders merits consideration for its own sake and not merely because of its ability to further the interests of some other groups, such as shareholders.

The normative approach focuses on the rights and obligations of company managers and on the fairness and justice of different courses of action and behaviour (Berman & Johnson-Cramer, 2017). The normative approach is used to interpret the function of the corporation, including the identification of moral and philosophical guidelines for the operation and management of the corporation (Donaldson & Preston, 1995). In contrast to the instrumental approach, the normative approach is not hypothetical, but categorical. A large proportion of books and studies on stakeholders are normative (e.g. Freeman, 2017; Freeman et al., 2010; Lawrence, 2010),[1] but according to some specialists in business (Zakhem & Palmer, 2017), it is still a dominant shareholder-centric approach. In the view of Donaldson and Preston (1995), the three approaches – descriptive, instrumental, and normative – are nested within each other (Figure 4.1).

Figure 4.1 illustrates the close connection between the three approaches, which are mutually supportive, the normative approach being at the central core. From a managerial point of view, the model represented by these three interrelated approaches indicates that company managers should acknowledge the validity of different stakeholder interests and should strive to respond to them within a mutually supportive framework, generating multidimensional performance and sustainability for the organization and its stakeholders.

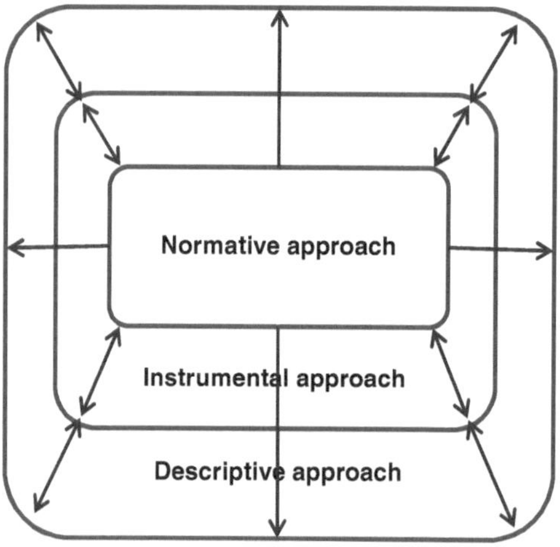

Figure 4.1 Three aspects of stakeholder theory.

Adapted from "The stakeholder theory of the corporation: Concepts, evidence, and implications" by T. Donaldson & L. E. Preston, 1995, *Academy of Management Review*, *20*(1), p. 74. Retrieved from https://www.jstor.org/stable/258887?seq=1#metadata_info_tab_contents.

Main Categories of Stakeholders

The central element in the three main approaches (descriptive, instrumental, and normative) of stakeholders in the stakeholder theory and practice is "the stakeholder concept". Its definition has been very diversified, as we have already mentioned, with almost 600 definitions of stakeholders being identified by Miles (2017). Essentially, a **stakeholder** is a person or group of persons who have an interest or a "stake" in an organization and the performance of that organization that affects it and could also be affected by this (Berman & Johnson-Cramer, 2017). From this definition, it can be gleaned that stakeholders have **three main characteristics:**

- the person or group has an interest or a stake in the company's works and performance;
- the person or group, their decisions, actions, and behaviours, could affect the company's activities and results;
- the person or group could be affected by the company's activities and performance.

In the rich stakeholder literature, based on the different stakeholder definitions, types of approach, specific visions, and the objectives of the specialists, a **large variety of stakeholder categories** is presented. In the following sections, we will synthetically present some of them that are useful for better understanding company stakeholder management.

The oldest classification of stakeholders made by Freeman (1984), and the most frequently used, is based on stakeholder direct interest or stake in an organization. According to this criterion, stakeholders are divided into:

- primary stakeholders, which have a direct interest or stake in the organization and substantially affect and are affected by it;
- secondary stakeholders, which are usually public or special-interest, groups that do not have a direct stake in company but are affected by its operations and performances.

In Table 4.1, we present a **list of the most frequent company stakeholders grouped in these two categories.** We have elaborated this list of stakeholders, and we have divided the stakeholders into two categories, using various approaches of numerous specialists (Buchholtz & Carroll, 2012; Chartered Management Institute, 2013; Coghlan, 2016; Freeman, 1984; Freeman et al., 2010; Harrison & Wicks, 2013; Kumar & Rajan, 2017; Lawrence, 2010; Miles, 2017; Mitchell et al., 1997; Steurer, 2006; Wheeler & Sillanpää, 1997; Wheeler & Sillanpää, 1998; Zakhem & Palmer, 2017), who quite often are partially different. Of course, we assume responsibility for the content of this classification.

Table 4.1 Primary and secondary company stakeholders[2]

Primary	*Secondary*
• Stockholders	• Local, territorial and central governmental bodies
• Top managers	• Media
• Employees (executants)	• Consumer groups
• Customers (strategic)[3]	• Regulatory bodies
• Suppliers (strategic)[3]	• Inspection bodies
• Investors	• Competitors
• Business partners (strategic)[3]	• Consultants
• Communities	• Trainers
• Natural environment	• Designers
• Future generation	• Trade unions
	• Employers' organizations
	• Civic groups

Certain specialists have identified different **subcategories within primary stakeholder groups**. For example, Wheeler and Sillanpää (1997) grouped primary stakeholders into:

- primary social stakeholders (shareholders and investors, managers and employees, customers, etc.);
- primary non-social stakeholders (natural environment, future generation, etc.).

In Table 4.2, we list **other stakeholder classifications**, which could be useful in the management of company stakeholders.

Each stakeholder category involves a specific approach from the company's management in order to valorize their potential and to reduce or eliminate the negative impact.

Stakeholder Identification and Prioritization

From a managerial point of view, one of the most important and difficult aspects regarding company stakeholders is their identification and prioritization. In the stakeholder literature, there are many approaches to this aspect. Without any doubt, the **salient model** elaborated by Mitchell et al. (1997) is the best known. They identified three essential attributes regarding stakeholders:

- power (the impact of the individual or group stakeholder on the organization);
- legitimacy (the legitimacy of the stakeholder claim on the organization);

Table 4.2 Stakeholder classifications

No.	*Criterion*	*Stakeholder Categories*
1.	Company property	• Shareholding stakeholders • Non-shareholding stakeholders
2.	Company appurtenances	• Internal (endogenous) stakeholders • External (exogenous) stakeholders
3.	Number of components of stakeholder	• Individual stakeholders • Group (organizational) stakeholders
4.	Market implications of the stakeholder (Lawrence, 2010)	• Market stakeholders • Non-market (activists) stakeholders
5.	Duration of stakeholders' involvement	• Permanent stakeholders • Occasional stakeholders
6.	Nature of stakeholders' interest	• Private stakeholders • Public stakeholders
7.	Legal basis of stakeholders' relationship with organization (Gautrey, 2013)	• Contractual stakeholders • Community stakeholders
8.	Stakeholder nature of interests and area of influence (Chandler & Werther, 2014)	• Organizational stakeholders • Economic stakeholders • Societal stakeholders
9.	Stakeholder contribution to the company's value generation (Calkoen, 2017)	• Key stakeholders • Ancillary stakeholders
10.	Number of persons that represent an organizational stakeholder	• Single organizational representative • Multi-organizational representative

- urgency (the degree to which an individual or group stakeholder claim should generate immediate action from organization managers).

These attributes provide salience to the stakeholder, which could be defined as how visible or prominent a stakeholder is to the organization's manager.

By combining these three attributes, **seven different types of stakeholders** emerge (see Figure 4.2).

Dormant, discretionary, and demanding stakeholders, which possess only one attribute, form the low-salience classes. For them, the term **"latent" stakeholders** is used, because their influence upon the organization is very small.

Dominant, dangerous, and dependent stakeholders, which possess two attributes, form the moderate-salience classes. For them, the term **"expectant stakeholders"** is employed, because they are stakeholders who "expect something" from the organization.

Definitive stakeholders, which have three attributes, represent the **highly salient stakeholders**, having the most influence on the organization.

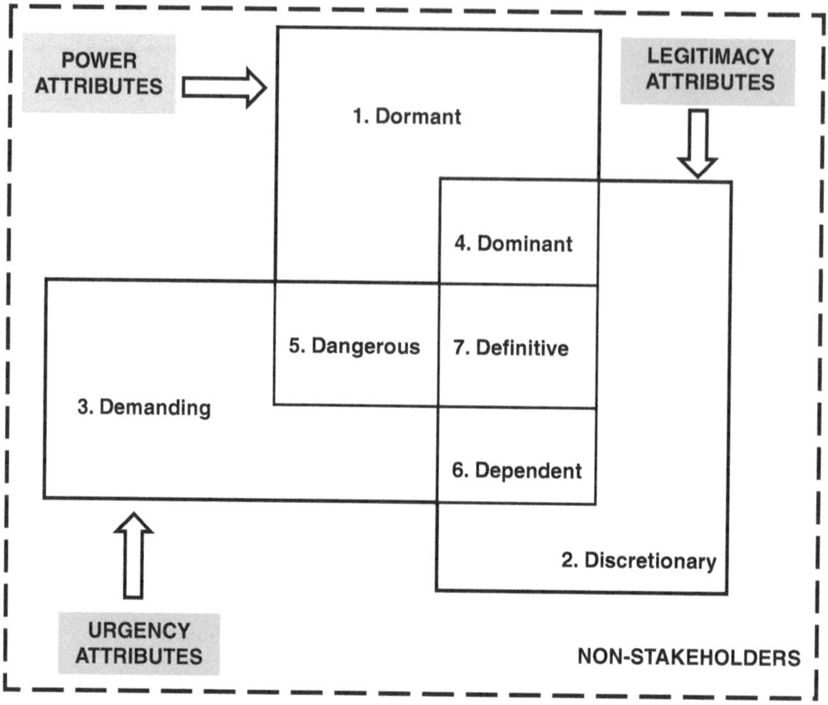

Figure 4.2 Stakeholder typology.

Adapted from "Toward a theory of stakeholders identification and salience: Defining the principle of who and what really counts" by R. K. Mitchell, B. R. Agle, & D. J. Wood, 1997, *Academy of Management Review*, 22(4), 874. Retrieved from https://www.jstor.org/stable/259247?seq=1#metadata_info_tab_contents

The model is based on the idea that the more salient stakeholders are given priority by the organization managers in terms of communication and actions. Normally, the less-salient stakeholders have less priority in relationships with company managers. Without any doubt, the stakeholder salience model is very helpful for organization managers in the identification and prioritization of internal and external stakeholders, although the three attributes taken into consideration do not cover all major characteristics of stakeholders in their rapport with the organization.

Other specialists, such as Bryson, Patton, and Bowman (2011), promote the **evaluation of stakeholders based on many more elements:**

- stakeholders' interests
- stakeholders' needs
- stakeholders' concerns
- stakeholders' power
- stakeholders' priorities
- stakeholders' perspectives

In the authors' opinion, analysis of these characteristics using special techniques – Utilization Focused Evaluation (UFE), SMART, BART, Force Field Analysis, Dennis Triangle Steering Parameters, Time Management Matrix – provides credible stakeholder evaluations to the organization.

In the last few years, specialists have discovered more sophisticated variables in order to evaluate and prioritize stakeholders, such as perceived sustainability of fulfilling stakeholders' interests for companies and assumed costs for (potential) investors' investment intentions (Schwarzmüller, Brosi, & Welpe, 2017).

Company managers, taking into consideration the results of the evaluation, could use different **communication strategies**. Coghlan (2016) recommends three types – informational, persuasive, and dialogue strategies (see Figure 4.3).

Stakeholder identification, prioritization, and communication approaches contribute to the increase of the potential effectiveness of managers in dealing with multiple and various company stakeholders, in an increasingly VUCA environment.

Laws and Principles Regarding Organization Stakeholders

In the approach of any field in economy and in management, there are gradual steps ahead, reflecting the accumulation of information and knowledge, the enhancement and the deepening of analysis, the development of special competences and the vision of the involved specialists, etc. In fact, it is a problem of the maturation of the specific approach

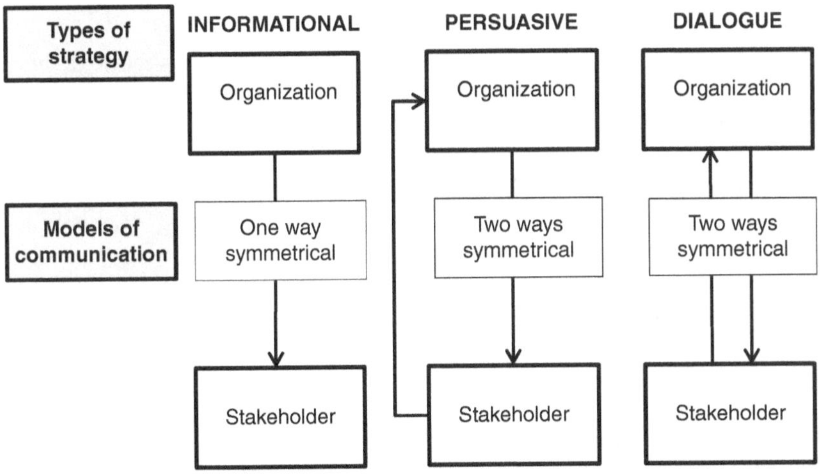

Figure 4.3 Types of communicational strategies.

Adapted from *Inside organizations: Exploring organizational experience* (p. 70), by D. Coghlan, 2016, Sage Publications.

to the respective field. One significant expression of the maturation is the elaboration of specific laws, principles, and axioms. Of course, these elements are valuable for the stakeholder field too.

Recently, two specialists – Garcia-Castro and Francoeur (2016) – formulated **three laws regarding company stakeholders.** The laws present two significant dimensions:

- business dimension, because they are focused on company performance, taking into consideration the investment size and allocation of the investments in the stakeholders. They treat the stakeholders from the perspective of their impact on value creation and are based on the premise that there is not a monotonic relationship between investment in stakeholders and firm performance;
- management dimension, because the laws are focused on the main objective of the company's management – enhancing the organization's performance – and legal requirements should be implemented through the managers decisions.

We present the stakeholder laws exactly as formulated by Castro and Francoeur:

I **Law of stakeholder core balance:** A minimum investment in each primary stakeholder is a necessary condition for achieving high firm performance.

II **Law of decreasing marginal returns to stakeholder investments:** There are decreasing marginal returns, and beyond some point, negative returns to marginal increases in investments in any single stakeholder group.

III **Law of contingent performance:** The optimal investment in a stakeholder (within the lower and upper bounds) is **contingent on firm strategy, industry features and national/legal factors.**

The value of the stakeholder laws has been demonstrated empirically by an analysis of 1,060 multinational companies, which is a representative sample.

In our opinion, the stakeholder laws represent – at least from a pragmatic point of view – an outstanding contribution to the management of company stakeholders. We support our statement with the following four arguments:

a laws refer to the **main stakeholders** from the company point of view. The role and influence of the important stakeholders is appreciated based on their contribution to the company performance and sustainability. Other characteristics of the stakeholder – legitimacy, power, urgency, size, etc. – are taken into consideration only to the extent to which they contribute to the stakeholder impact on the company's performance;

b laws are formulated in a **systemic approach**, because they take into consideration all major stakeholders, bearing in mind the interrelations among them. In the second argument, the laws refer to the general performance of the company, regarded as a system;

c stakeholder laws promote an **equilibrated approach** regarding the size of the investments in stakeholders and the share allocated to the major stakeholders. The authors propose establishing some lower and upper limits to effective investment in stakeholder groups. They argue that a minimum investment should be made in every major stakeholder and a disproportionate high investment in certain stakeholders should be avoid;

d stakeholder laws require stakeholders' investments to be **differentiated in every organization**, taking into consideration the impact of firm strategy, industry features and national/legal factors. Such contextual thinking is an essential element in order to ensure the realism of the stakeholder approach, depending on the specificity of each company, reflected in its strategy and the customized particular conditions in the involved industry and national environment.

Based on these arguments, we feel that the stakeholder laws formulated by Castro and Francoeur are very useful for fulfilling a performant management in companies.

In the same category, of the essential elements regarding the pragmatic management approach of company stakeholders, the **principles of stakeholder management** are included.

Without any doubt the best known are "the Clarkson principles" (The Clarkson Centre for Business Ethics, 1999). **Max Clarkson's seven principles are the following:**

Principle 1: Managers should acknowledge and actively monitor the concerns of all legitimate stakeholders and should take their interests appropriately into account in decision-making and operations.

Principle 2: Managers should listen to and openly communicate with stakeholders about their respective concerns and contributions and about the risks that they assume because of their involvement with the corporation.

Principle 3: Managers should adopt processes and modes of behaviour that are sensitive to the concerns and capabilities of each stakeholder constituency.

Principle 4: Managers should recognize the interdependence of efforts and rewards among stakeholders and should attempt to achieve a fair distribution of the benefits and burdens of corporate activity among them, taking into account their respective risks and vulnerabilities.

Principle 5: Managers should work cooperatively with other entities, both public and private, to ensure that risks and harms arising from corporate activities are minimized and, where they cannot be avoided, appropriately compensated.

Principle 6: Managers should avoid altogether activities that might jeopardize inalienable human rights (e.g. the right to life) or give rise to risks that, if clearly understood, would be patently unacceptable to the relevant stakeholders.

Principle 7: Managers should acknowledge the potential conflicts between (a) their own role as corporate stakeholders and (b) their legal and moral responsibilities for the interests of stakeholders and should address such conflicts through open communication, appropriate reporting and incentive systems, and, where necessary, third-party review.

These principles, which refer to all legitimate company stakeholders, have been largely accepted by stakeholder specialists (e.g. Buchholtz & Carroll, 2012; Clarkson, Donaldson, Preston, & Brooks, 2000; Donaldson, 2002). According to Thomas Donaldson, Clarkson's principles have contributed "to develop[ing] a broad conception of corporation as a vehicle for advancing the interests of, and responding to the concerns of, multiple and diverse stakeholders" (Donaldson, 2002). The Clarkson principles deal with seven major types of actions regarding company stakeholders, which are able to contribute to a large extent to the rationale and effective relationships with them, having a notable ethic dimension. For this reason, they have been intensively used in the analysis of the USA corporation management during the 2009–2010 crisis.

The Clarkson principles deal with the whole management processes of corporation stakeholders.

In the stakeholder literature, sets of **principles regarding especially stakeholder engagement** have also been published, largely disseminated by the Internet. For example, Gautrey (2013) formulated seven guiding principles of stakeholder engagement:

1 Identify the stakeholders;
2 Focus on stakeholders who have the most power to help hinder your goal;
3 Be very clear about what you want from each stakeholder;
4 Connect stakeholders' interests to your goals;
5 Increase your goal's priority;
6 Don't always deal directly with stakeholders;
7 Attain enough agreement to secure your goal.

The stakeholder management laws and principles represent a later stage in the development of the stakeholder theory and practice. They represent very helpful knowledge for the systemic approach to the very complex and difficult aspects associated with organization stakeholder management in a VUCA environment.

The Corporate Governance–Stakeholder Management Relationship

Corporate governance has appeared as an answer to the delimitation between company management and its owners. Traditionally, a company was managed by members of the owners' family. The business, technological, managerial, scientific, financial, etc. mutations, during the second part of the last century, generated the need for professional company management, especially for corporations, and large and medium enterprises, organized frequently as a shareholders' organization. As a result, quite often shareholder companies have hired professional managers in the top company positions. Between the company shareholders and managers, new types of managerial and business relations have developed. **Corporate governance** represents a complex approach – managerial, juridical, and business – used in order to manage the company according to the shareholders' interests. Corporate governance represents a set of rules and stimulants used by the shareholders and company management in order to maximize the company profit and value for the shareholders.

Some companies – like General Motors in 1992 – have faced scandals in their corporate governance. In order to solve such problems, to ensure transparency, accountability, fairness, and responsibility, the Cadbury Code was written and the OECD has produced a model code for corporate governance, which is used in many countries to elaborate national versions.

Corporate governance has contributed to a certain extent to more responsible management of companies, but there have been, and still are, many difficulties and challenges. What happened during the 2008–2009 crisis in the USA with some corporations like Enron provides the relevant facts in this respect.

In a comprehensive book (Calkoen, 2017) regarding the screening of corporate governance, specialists identified a set of "**hot topics**" in this field:

- transparency
- reporting
- compliance
- IT
- accountability and liability
- short termism versus long-run strategy
- shareholder activism

- stakeholders
- sustainability
- measures against climate change
- trust

Other studies have found **other major limitations and difficulties** in corporate governance practice like: negative effects of large shareholders with excess control rights (Boateng & Huang, 2017), top managers' engagement in misconduct, such as illegal insider trading, illegal stock option backdating, bribery, and financial manipulation (Connelly, Shi, & Zyung, 2017), shareholders' coalitions that serve as an instrument for dominant shareholders to extract private benefits (López-Iturriaga and Santana-Martín, 2015).

An analysis conducted in 2015 by Grant Thornton Institute, regarding the practice of corporate governance in 312 FTSE representative companies from Great Britain, showed a very complex situation raising **many questions marks**. They found that only 11 companies, which means less than 4% from all organizations, have truly embraced the spirit of corporate governance (Grant Thornton, 2015).

There are many studies (Fauver, Hung, Li, & Taboada, 2017; Gangi & D'Angelo, 2017; Lafarre, 2017; Salvioni & Gennari, 2016) that increase the need to improve corporate governance significantly, but for the most part, this is mainly from the perspective of shareholders, who represent only one category of stakeholders. Moreover, according to an analysis carried out by a group of specialists (Schwarzmüller, Brosi, Stelkens, Spörrle, & Welpe, 2017), companies regularly have to address opposing interests from their stakeholding and non-shareholding stakeholding groups.

As regards corporate governance, we believe it is necessary to outline **two aspects:**

a Elements described in the previous sections indicate that corporate governance focused on the primordiality of shareholders' interests has not been able to accomplish its objectives: transparency, accountability, fairness, and responsibilities. Even the shareholders' interests have not been sufficiently protected;
b Corporate governance as a rule does not try and does not take into consideration the interests, the stakes and the impact of the company's main stakeholders, although quite a few specialists ask this to be done. For this reason, corporate governance is not able to use the potential of all main company stakeholders and – as a consequence – to generate sustainability for the company and for themselves.

The stakeholder theory provides the framework for overcoming the essential limitations of the corporate governance and shareholders' approach.

There have been several studies in recent decades that contain consistent proposals regarding the development of stakeholder theory and practice, so as to ensure the company's sustainability and the stakeholders' potential valorization. For example, a group of renowned specialists – Mitchell, Weaver, Agle, Bailey, and Carlson (2015) – proposed "develop[ing] a multi-objective corporation as a means of enabling a greater range of management decisions so as to permit more direct corporate engagement in the diverse goals of various stakeholders". Their approach is built on the stakeholder agency framework, wherein corporate actions reflect the outcome of an intercorporate marketplace.

Another study (Mitchell, Van Buren III, Greenwood, & Freeman, 2015) states that

> because present accounting theory and practice does not address the decision-making needs of all stakeholders, who are at risk due to the activities of an organization, it proposes to develop a transdisciplinary theory of value creation stakeholder accounting (VCSA) based on stakeholder risk-sharing, as a superior rationale of stakeholder inclusion.

They introduce "value creation" stakeholder partnerships (VCSPs) as a promising mechanism for the implementation of VCSA, which emerges from distinguishing proprietary-convention (partnership) from entity-convention (corporate) accounting.

Besides the studies dealing with stakeholders, other approaches have been elaborated in order to provide solutions for the present corporate governance problems. "Creating Shared Value (CSV)" by Porter and Kramer (2011) is one that is very popular. Shared value consists in "policies and operating practices that enhance the competitiveness of a company while simultaneously advancing the economic and social conditions in the communities in which it operates". By value they mean benefits relative to cost, not benefits accrued alone. In the authors' opinion, "CSV can give use to the next major transformation of business thinking". In another study, a group of specialists (Crane, Palazzo, Spence, & Matten, 2014), although they appreciated Porter and Kramer's ideas, expressed doubts, with serious arguments, from a theoretical and pragmatic point of view.[4] Crane et al. (2014) believed that "stakeholder theory is probably the long-lasting approach to reconceptualizing the firm as a multi-purpose entity". "Stakeholder theory is fundamentally a theory about how business works at its best and how it could work. It is descriptive, prescriptive and instrumental all at the same time, and as Donaldson and Preston have argued, it is managerial" (Freeman et al., 2010).

Our Proposals Regarding the Development of a New Stakeholder Management Approach

In our opinion, **two main conclusions** can be formulated regarding the situation of stakeholder theory and practice. First, the stakeholders' approach, after more than half a century of history, has demonstrated that it is valuable and could generate multiple benefits for companies, their stakeholders, and the society. Second, the stakeholder theory and practice should be developed consistently and rapidly, in order to be able to generate more benefits for all stakeholders, taking into consideration the deep and rapid contextual mutations modified – to some extent –by the COVID-19 pandemic. So far, the potential of company stakeholders has been valorized only to a small extent by company management.

We propose several elements as a foundation for further development of the stakeholder management approach (see Figure 4.4). Our proposals deal only with **pragmatic managerial aspects of the stakeholder approach.**

A Expanding the use of the stakeholder approach by corporations, big investment projects and public–private partnerships – the current situation in the stakeholder theory and practice – to **all types of companies.** The company operations and performance, notwithstanding size, depend decisively on the main stakeholder-owners (shareholders), managers, executants, clients, suppliers, bankers, etc. As such, there are no reasons for a company to ignore its stakeholders. Of course, when the company size and the complexity increase, the dependence of its performance and sustainability on the stakeholders increases too. In our opinion, the stakeholders' frequency, intensity, and impact on the company require a managerial approach focused on the stakeholders, using new management and business mechanisms – not only for corporation and big projects but also for large and medium-sized companies. Small companies and micro-companies should also be reoriented towards exploiting stakeholders' potential, but without it always being necessary to create specialized business and managerial mechanisms.

B **Systemic stakeholders' approach** taking into consideration all major organization stakeholders. It is necessary to change the present situation, characterized by the placement in the foreground of shareholders and managers, followed, at a certain distance, by some clients and suppliers. In order to ensure a realistic approach on the part of stakeholders, to have effective communication and an

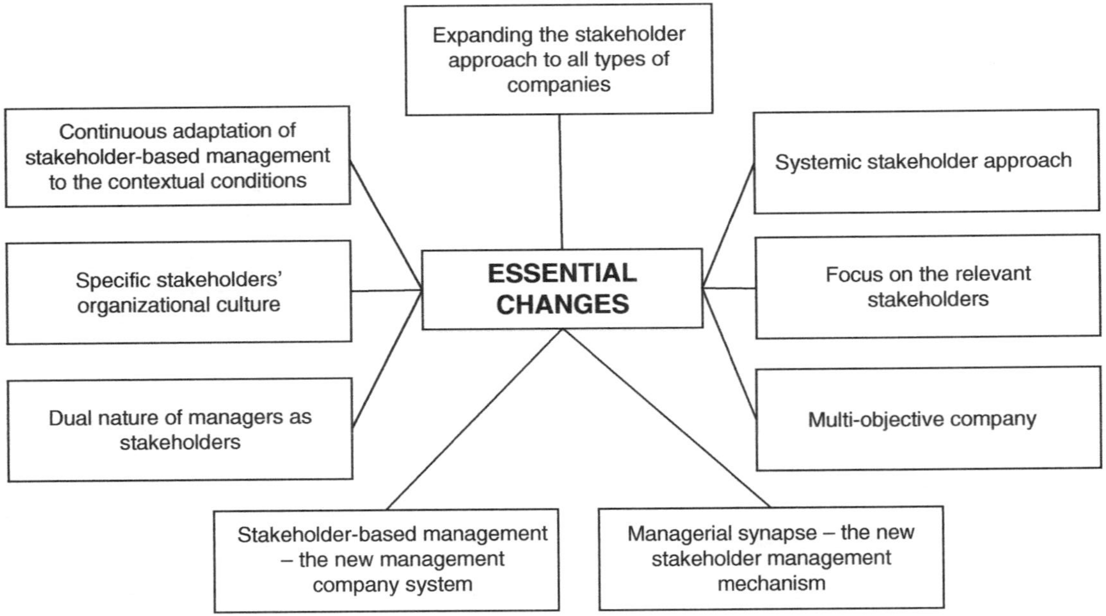

Figure 4.4 New essential elements of stakeholder-based management.

efficient work relationship, it is necessary to take into consideration the diversity of their goals and their characteristics, and the co-opetition among them. Relationships with company stakeholders should be based on win-win negotiations with each main stakeholder, subordinate to the company's sustainability.

C **Company stakeholders should be treated in a differentiated manner, taking into consideration the relevance for the organization. Stakeholder relevance** should be evaluated from two points of view:

- the main stakeholder characteristics – power, legitimacy, urgency, cost involved, impact, etc.
- the correlation between company strategy and policies and the stakeholder capacity and contribution to implement them successfully.

We believe that often the second aspect is more important for company performance and sustainability than the first. In order to avoid making mistakes, both aspects should be taken correlatively into consideration.

D **The company should be approached as an entity with multiple strategic objectives,** determined according to the interests of the relevant stakeholders. Usually, the company's multi-objective should be multi-dimensional – financial, technical, social, ecological, etc. It is recommended that strategic company objectives should be focused on the company and the relevant stakeholders' long-term sustainability. Such objectives motivate the relevant stakeholders to be involved and productive and, concomitantly, to promote in the company a long-term approach that is beneficial for all. A multi-objective approach and the way to plan it should generate stakeholder synergy.

E **Creation in the company of specific managerial business mechanisms at the level of each relevant stakeholder,** in order to exploit at a high level the stakeholder potential and to generate effective win–win relationships. In this study, we propose such a mechanism named by us "**managerial synapse**" (see Chapters 5 and 6).

F **Remodelling of the entire company management through a new management system capable of managing efficiently the entity relationships with all relevant stakeholders.** This system should be designed using the performant concepts and methods provided by the top professional management. Such a system should be innovative, flexible, and dynamic, related to the present fast contextual changes. We call it a "**stakeholder-based management system**", and in this book, we will make a proposal with the main constructive and functional parameters (see Chapters 9, 10 and 11).

G Managers who make a decisive contribution to the design, implementation, and functioning of the managerial synapse and stakeholder-based management system have a dual, very complex, nature. The **dual nature of managers** means:

- managers represent the company, and they have a decisive role in each relevant stakeholder identification, evaluation, communication, and work together. Managers are key factors in the design and implementation of the managerial synapse and stakeholder-based management system;
- managers are themselves relevant company stakeholders, with their own interests and stakes, which are partially different from those of their company.

Between the two sides of managers' nature, there are both convergent and divergent elements. The way in which these two managerial sides are harmonized, in the processes of designing the managerial synapse and stakeholder-based management system, depends to a large extent on the company and stakeholders' performance.

H **New stakeholder-based management involves a new organizational culture,** based on the approach of the company as an open system, which is centred on the relevant internal and external stakeholders. Organizational culture through the values promoted, through the individual and organizational behaviours incorporated, contributes greatly to the development of the stakeholders' cohesion, attachment, and implication in the companies' activities and performances. It is essential in a company "to build trust capital" among the relevant stakeholders.

I **A new stakeholder-based management system should be designed taking into consideration the megashifts in the company environment:**

- Increase of the environment's complexity, dynamism, and volatility;
- Digitalization of the socio-economic procesess;
- Work intellectualization;
- Internationalization of all activities;
- Multiculturalization of the labour force;
- Nanotechnologization and biotechnologization;
- Comprehensive networking in the society and economy;
- Sustainable ecologization;
- Intensification and diversification of state interventions;
- Development of a powerful educational-formative dimension;
- Multidimensional remodelling of the markets.

The recent challenges, difficulties, and opportunities generated by the COVID-19 pandemic should receive special attention in the creation of the new management company system based on stakeholders. This management system will be performant if it succeeds in exploiting to a high degree the most important resource of the smart economy – knowledge – and achieves comprehensive and accelerated digital transformations, related to the last evolutions of the present intensive digitalization.

The elements presented are essential for the transition from the current situation in companies to the next stage focused on the new stakeholder approach. The general framework of this transition is exhibited in Figure 4.5.

This framework indicates **the two axes of the transition:**

- company axis, indicating the change from a company centred on shareholders to an entity centred on stakeholders;
- management axis, revealing the shift from corporate governance to stakeholder-based management.

Between these two axes, there are many interdependencies and influences, which will be analyzed in the following chapters from several perspectives.

The new company management system, based on the relevant stakeholders, exceeds certain limitations of the company salient stakeholders' approach, like being largely static, short-term oriented and firm centred.

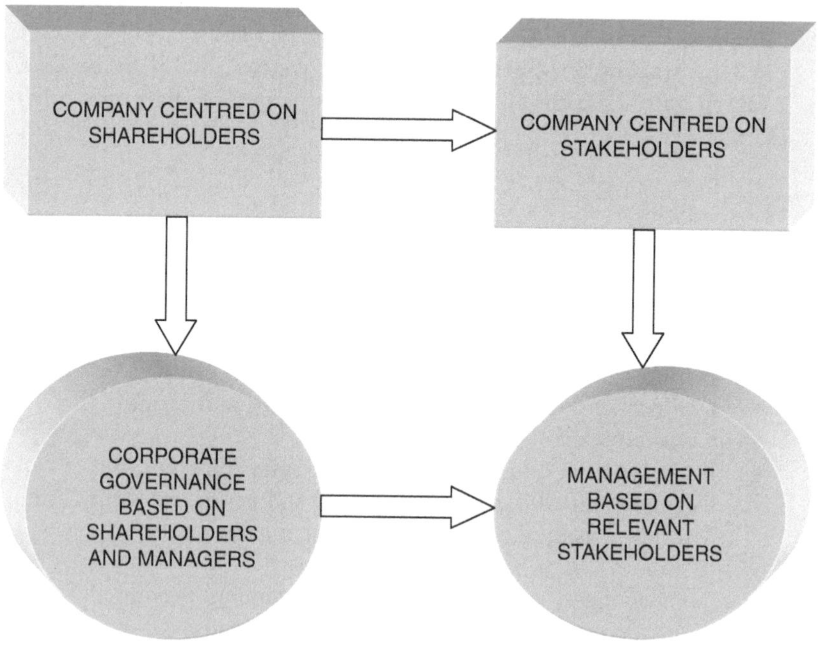

Figure 4.5 The framework of the transition to stakeholder-based management.

Notes

1 It is even a tendency to expand normative perspective from corporation level to other types of entities. In a very interesting paper, Sandra Waddock considers that "humans, institutions, enterprises, other living beings, and ecological systems are all stakeholders of a core focal entity – the Earth, conceived as a living system of Gaya. See Waddock, S. (2011), We are all stakeholders of Gaia: A normative perspective on stakeholder thinking. *Organization & Environment*, *24*(2), 192–212. doi:10.1177/1086026611413933

2 This is a standard classification. At the level of each company, depending on its specificity, certain primary stakeholders could be secondary stakeholders, and vice versa.

3 When they are not strategic, they enter the secondary stakeholders category.

4 Michael Porter and Mark Kramer have formulated a feedback to the comments of these specialists. See a response to Crane et al.'s article by Michael Porter and Mark Kramer (2014) in *California Management Review, 56*(2), between pages 149 and 151. doi:10.1525/cmr.2014.56.2.130

References

Baden, D. (2016). A reconstruction of Carroll's pyramid of corporate social responsibility for 21st century. *International Journal of Corporate Social Responsibility*, *1*(8), 1–15. doi:10.1186/s40991-016-0008-2

Berman, S. L., & Johnson-Cramer, M. E. (2017). Stakeholder theory: Seeing the field through the forest. *Business & Society*, *58*(7), 1358–1375. doi:10.1177/0007650316680039

Boateng, A., & Huang, W. (2017). Multiple large shareholders, excess leverage and tunneling: Evidence from an emerging market. *Corporate Governance: An International Review*, *25*(1), 58–74. doi:10.1111/corg.12184

Bryson, J., Patton, M. Q., & Bowman, R. A. (2011). Working with evaluation stakeholders: A rationale, step-wise approach and toolkit. *Evaluation and Program Planning*, *34*(1), 1–12. doi:10.1016/j.evalprogplan.2010.07.001

Buchholtz, A. K., & Carroll, A. B. (2012). *Business and society: Ethics and stakeholder management* (8th ed.). Mason, OH: South-Western Cengage Learning.

Calkoen, W. J. L. (2017). *The corporate governance review* (7th ed.). London, UK: Law Business Research Ltd.

Carroll, A. B. (1979). A three-dimensional conceptual model of corporate social performance. *Academy of Management Review*, *4*(4), 497–505. doi:10.2307/257850

Carroll, A. B. (1991). The pyramid of corporate social responsibility: Toward the moral management of organizational stakeholders. *Business Horizons*, *34*(4), 39–48. Retrieved from https://www.researchgate.net/publication/4883660_The_Pyramid_of_Corporate_Social_Responsibility_Toward_the_Moral_Management_of_Organizational_Stakeholders 10.1016/0007-6813(91)90005-G

Chandler, D., & Werther, B. W. (2014). *Strategic corporate social responsibility: Stakeholders, globalization and sustainable value creation* (3rd ed.). Los Angeles, CA: Sage Publications.

Chartered Management Institute. (2013). *Stakeholder analysis and management checklist 234*. Retrieved from https://mmclearning.com/elearningdemo/cmi/docs/Stakeholder_Analysis&Management_Checklist_234.pdf
Clarkson, M. B. E., Donaldson, T., Preston, L. E., & Brooks, L. J. (2000). *Principles of stakeholder management*. Retrieved from http://www.rotman.utoronto.ca/~stake/Principles.htm
Coghlan, D. (2016). *Inside organizations: Exploring organizational experience*. London, UK: Sage Publications. doi:10.4135/9781526402424
Connelly, B. L., Shi, W., & Zyung, J. (2017). Managerial response to constitutional constrains on shareholder power. *Strategic Management Journal*, *38*(7), 1499–1517. doi:10.1002/smj.2582
Crane, A., Palazzo, G., Spence, L. J., & Matten, D. (2014). Contesting the value of creating shared value. *California Management Review*, *56*(2), 130–153. doi:10.1525/cmr.2014.56.2.130
Donaldson, T. (2002). The stakeholder revolution and the Clarkson principles. *Business Ethics Quarterly*, *12*(2), 107–111. doi:10.5840/beq200212211
Donaldson, T., & Preston, L. E. (1995). The stakeholder theory of the corporation: Concepts, evidence, and implications. *Academy of Management Review*, *20*(1), 65–91. Retrieved from https://www.jstor.org/stable/258887?seq=1#metadata_info_tab_contents. doi:10.2307/258887
Elias, A. A., & Cavana, R. Y. (2000). *Stakeholder analysis for systems thinking and modeling*. Retrieved from https://pdfs.semanticscholar.org/b52e/0594841aeb6841e4d8c8e0e5b2cd2564385c.pdf?_ga=2.5988149.703572193.1553018223-2027391651.1553018223
Fauver, L., Hung, M., Li, X., & Taboada, A. G. (2017). Board reforms and firm value: Worldwide evidence. *Journal of Financial Economics*, *125*(1), 120–142. doi:10.1016/j.jfineco.2017.04.010
Fontaine, C., Haarman, A., & Schmid, S. (2006). *The stakeholder theory*. Retrieved from https://pdfs.semanticscholar.org/606a/828294dafd62aeda92a77bd7e5d0a39af56f.pdf
Freeman, R. E. (1984). *Strategic management: A stakeholder approach*. Boston, MA: Pitman.
Freeman, R. E. (2017). Five challenges to stakeholder theory: A report on research in progress. In D. M. Wasieleski & J. Weber (Eds.), *Stakeholder Management – Business and Society 360* (pp. 1–20). Bingley, UK: Emerald Publishing Limited.
Freeman, R. E., Harrison, J. S., Wicks, A. C., Parmar, B. L., & De Colle, S. (2010). *Stakeholder theory: The state of art*. New York: Cambridge University Press.
Friedman, A. L., & Miles, S. (2002). Developing stakeholder theory. *Journal of Management Studies*, *39*(1), 1–21. doi:10.1111/1467-6486.00280
Gangi, F., & D'Angelo, E. (2017). "Make" or "buy" the choice of governance modes for corporate social responsibility projects from a stakeholder management perspective. *International Business Research*, *10*(8), 80–92. doi:10.5539/ibr.v10n8p80
Garcia-Castro, R., & Aguilera, R. V. (2015). Incremental value creation and appropriation in a world with multiple stakeholders. Strategic *Management Journal*, *36*(1), 137–147. doi:https://doi.org/10.1002/smj.2241

Garcia-Castro, R., & Francoeur, C. (2016). When more is not better: Complementarities, costs and contingencies in stakeholder management. *Strategic Management Journal*, *37*(2), 406–424. doi:10.1002/smj.2341

Gautrey, C. (2013, June 11). *Seven guiding principles of stakeholder. Association for Talent Development*. Retrieved from https://www.td.org/insights/seven-guiding-principles-of-stakeholder-engagement

Grant Thornton. (2015). *Corporate governance review 2015: Trust and integrity – Loud and clear?* Retrieved from https://www.grantthornton.co.uk/globalassets/1.-member-firms/united-kingdom/pdf/publication/2015/uk-corporate-governance-review-and-trends-2015.pdf

Harrison, J. S., & Wicks, A. (2013). Stakeholder theory, value and firm performance. *Business Ethics Quarterly*, *23*(1), 97–124. doi:10.5840/beq20132314

Kumar, V., & Rajan, B. (2017). What's in it for me? The creation and destruction of value for firms from stakeholders. *Journal of Creation Value*, *3*(2), 142–156. doi:10.1177/2394964317723449

Lafarre, A. (2017). *The AGM in Europe: Theory and practice of shareholders behaviour*. Bingley, UK: Emerald Publishing Limited.

Lawrence, A. T. (2010). Managing disputes with non market stakeholders: Wage a fight, withdraw, wait, or work it out? *California Management Review*, *53*(1), 90–113. doi:10.1525/cmr.2010.53.1.90

Levenson, A. (2020). A long time until the economic new normal. *MIT Sloan Management Review*. Retrieved from https://sloanreview.mit.edu/article/a-long-time-until-the-economic-new-normal

López-Iturriaga, F. J., & Santana-Martín D. J. (2015). Do shareholder coalitions modify the dominant owner's control? The impact on dividend policy. *Corporate Governance: An International Review*, *23*(6), 519–533. doi:10.1111/corg.12126

Miles, S. (2017). Stakeholder theory classification, definitions and essential contestability. In D. M. Wasieleski & J. Weber (Eds.), *Stakeholder Management – Business and Society 360* (pp. 21–47). Bingley, UK: Emerald Publishing Limited.

Mitchell, R. K., Agle, B. R., & Wood, D. J. (1997). Toward a theory of stakeholders identification and salience: Defining the principle of who and what really counts. *Academy of Management Review*, 22(4), 853–886. Retrieved from https://www.jstor.org/stable/259247?seq=1#metadata_info_tab_contents. doi:10.2307/259247

Mitchell, R. K., Van Buren III, H. J., Greenwood M., & Freeman, R. E. (2015). Stakeholder inclusion and accounting for stakeholders. *Journal of Management Studies*, *52*(7), 851–877. doi:10.1111/joms.12151

Mitchell, R. K., Weaver, G. R., Agle, B. R., Bailey, A. D., & Carlson, J. (2015). Stakeholder agency and social welfare: Pluralism and decision making in the multi-objective corporation. *Academy of Management Review*, *41*(2), 252–275. doi:10.5465/amr.2013.0486

Narayandas, D., Hebbar, V., & Li, L. (2020). Lessons from Chinese companies' response to Covid-19. *Harvard Business Review*. Retrieved from https://hbr.org/2020/06/lessons-from-chinese-companies-response-to-covid-19

Porter, M. E., & Kramer, M. R. (2011). Creating shared value. *Harvard Business Review*. Retrieved from https://hbr.org/2011/01/the-big-idea-creating-shared-value

Radjou, N. (2020). The rising frugal economy. *MIT Sloan Management Review*. Retrieved from https://sloanreview.mit.edu/article/the-rising-frugal-economy/

Romeo, J., Moukanas, H., & Rung, G. (2020). The age of accelerating strategy breakthroughs. *MIT Sloan Management Review*. Retrieved from https://sloanreview.mit.edu/article/the-age-of-accelerating-strategy-breakthroughs/

Salvioni, D., & Gennari, F. (2016). Corporate governance, ownership and sustainability. *Corporate Ownership & Control*, *13*(2), 606–612. doi:10.22495/cocv13i2c3p9

Schwarzmüller, T., Brosi, P., Stelkens, V., Spörrle, M., & Welpe, I. M. (2017). Investors' reactions to companies' stakeholder management: The crucial role of assumed costs and perceived sustainability. *Business Research*, *10*(1), 79–96. doi:10.1007/s40685-016-0040-9

Schwarzmüller, T., Brosi, P., & Welpe, I. M. (2017). Führung 4.0 – Wie die Digitalisierung Führung verändert. In A. Hildebrandt & W. Landhäußer (Eds.), *CSR und Digitalisierung: Der digitale Wandel als Chance und Herausforderung für Wirtschaft und Gesellschaft* (pp. 617–628). Berlin, Germany: Springer Gabler. doi:10.1007/978-3-662-53202-7_43

Steurer, R. (2006). Mapping stakeholder theory anew: From a "theory of the firm" to three perspectives on business-society relations. *Business Strategy and the Environment*, *15*(1), 55–69. doi:10.1002/bse.467

Tarabishy A. E., & Carayannis, E. (2020, September 12). *Democratization of knowledge. International Council for Small Business*. Retrieved from https://icsb.org/democratizationofknowledge/

Teece, D. J., Raspin, P. G., & Cox, D. R. (2020). Plotting strategy in a dynamic world. *MIT Sloan Management Review*. Retrieved from https://sloanreview.mit.edu/article/plotting-strategy-in-a-dynamic-world/?gclid=Cj0KCQiAst2BBhDJARIsAGo2ldVOCiF24Hjd9rFWzT7VPsrIVT7GiIgyPbEpHt0NIQbb4uFpMA_8oOsaAlHvEALw_wcB

The Clarkson Centre for Business Ethics. (1999). *Principles of stakeholders management: The Clarkson principles*. Toronto, CA: The Clarkson Centre for Business Ethics.

Wheeler, D., & Sillanpää, M. (1997). *The stakeholder corporation: A blue print for maximizing stakeholder value*. London, UK: Pitman Publishing.

Wheeler, D., & Sillanpää, M. (1998). Including the stakeholders: The business case. *Long Range Planning*, *31*(2), 201–210. doi:10.1016/S0024-6301(98)00004-1

World Economic Forum. (2020). *The global risk report 2020*. Retrieved from http://www3.weforum.org/docs/WEF_Global_Risk_Report_2020.pdf

Zakhem, A., & Palmer, D. E. (2017). Normative stakeholder theory. In D. M. Wasieleski & J. Weber (Eds.), *Stakeholder Management – Business and Society 360* (pp. 49–73). Bingley, UK: Emerald Publishing Limited.

5 Managerial Synapse: New Concept and Innovative Managerial Mechanism

Manager: The Most Important Organizational Stakeholder

Managers are not generally considered to be stakeholders. In our opinion, which is not singular (Tulberg, 2013), the **manager stakeholders' group, which holds the executive power in the company, should be a central topic for stakeholder theory and a key element in the management of any organization.**

The starting point in considering managers as the most important organizational stakeholder is represented by **their dual nature**, mentioned in the previous chapter.

- Managers represent the company in their managerial areas (spans of control), having a decisive role in the identification, evaluation, communication, negotiation, motivation, and collaboration with all other stakeholders. As representatives of the owners/shareholders, according to their work contracts and job descriptions, managers are essential contributors to the design, implementation, and operation of all company mechanisms and instruments (strategy, policy, organizational structure, information systems, management of human resources, management systems, methods and techniques, etc.). Company managers have a decisive impact on the organization's performance and sustainability. They are decisive influencers in the organization (Tulberg, 2013).
- The managers are themselves company stakeholders, having their own interests and stakes that are somewhat different from those of their company and of the other stakeholders. As stakeholders, managers present certain characteristics, which influence their decisions, actions, behaviours, and the results generated by the organization. The manager's characteristics are determined by the manager's job description, vision, knowledge, experience, mentality, etc. and by the company's strategy, culture, performances, etc. Managers, as company stakeholders, are both major claimers and

DOI: 10.4324/9781003217701-5

major influencers. Company managers represent a very important category of stakeholders in each organization.

In our opinion, **the managers are the most important category of company stakeholders.** Our statement is based on several arguments:

- Company managers provide a major, quite often decisive, contribution to the design, construction and implementation of the principal components of the company's management:
    - Strategy and policies;
    - Managerial system and its main sub-systems (decisional, informational, organizational, methodological, and human resources);
    - Company culture and subcultures;
    - Enterprise competitive advantages and performances.
- Company managers offer a major contribution and impact at the strategic level, on the long-term enterprise development and sustainability of the organization, and have a decisive influence at the tactical and operational level on the yearly, monthly, weekly, and daily operations and performance.
- The company managers' visions, decisions, actions, and behaviours influence the content and effectiveness of each managerial function:
    - Prevision to a large extent, because under the guidance of the shareholders' assembly, administration council, management committee etc., managers elaborate all the organization's long-, medium-, and short-term plans;
    - Organization, coordination, motivation, command and control-evaluation functions: managers make a permanent and determinant contribution and impact on these according to the company's strategy and policies.
- Company managers are key players in all phases of an organization's stakeholder approach: identification, prioritisation, contact, communication, establishment of joint objectives, negotiation, collaboration, evaluation, motivation, and sharing results. The company's capacity to have good relationships with its stakeholders, to attract, to use, and to valorize their knowledge and other resources, depend decisively on the organization managers' decisions, actions, and behaviours.
- Managers, because of their powers, responsibilities, and competences, are the most important organizational change agents. Their change capacity and its implications are essential for the innovative development of the company and for achieving sustainable performances. Quite often, managers are transformational leaders in the company.

For all these reasons, the work content and the definition of managers has radically changed. Traditionally, a manager was defined as a person who has a managerial job inside an organization and who, based on the job targets, tasks, competences, and responsibilities, decides and acts on subordinates' work to accomplish the organization's objectives.

From the stakeholders' perspective, the manager is a person who has a managerial job in an organization and who, according to the job targets, tasks, competences, and responsibilities, decides and acts together with other relevant company stakeholders to satisfy stakeholders' major interests, based on their win–win sustainable relationship, to enhance the business and its social and ecological performances. Managers' influence on the company depends to a large extent on the organization level at which they are placed in the company (Figure 5.1). A higher level for managers means more influence on the company's work, functionality, and performance. Managers, as a stakeholder group, have a decisive influence on every major aspect of the company. Managers are essential influencers and claimers of the organization. Management change capacity needs to be a core competence of managers.

There are essential differences between a traditional manager and a modern stakeholder manager, as specified in Table 5.1.

Stakeholder managers should have certain highly developed competences and characteristics, at a much higher level than they are usually found in the traditional manager. Among these we mention: negotiation capacity, dialogic communication, ability to use change management, emotional regulation, cooperative skills, innovative openness, organizational flexibility, and multidisciplinary knowledge.

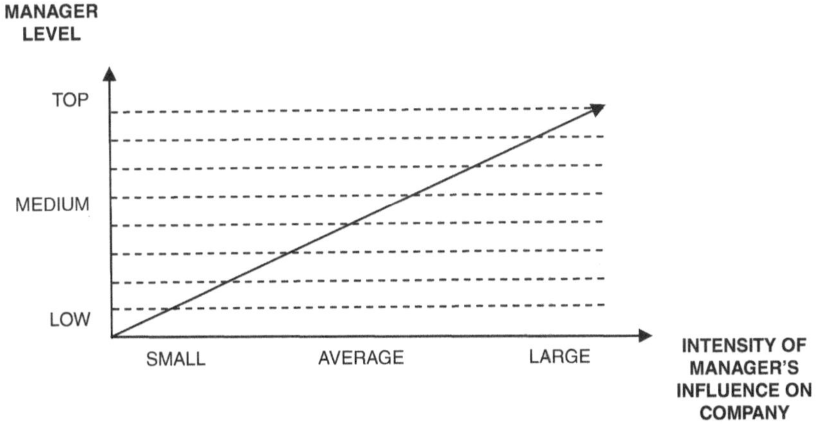

Figure 5.1 Range of managers' influence as representatives of the organization on its work, performances, and sustainability.

Table 5.1 Main differences between a traditional manager and a stakeholder manager

No.	*Elements*	*Traditional Manager*	*Stakeholder Manager*
1.	Objectives	To achieve the company's business objectives	To amplify the company's business, social and ecological performances using a sustainable approach To satisfy the main interests of the relevant company stakeholders
2.	Participants in management relationship	Manager subordinates	Manager All other relevant internal and external company stakeholders
3.	Nature of management relationship	Hierarchical relationship between manager and his subordinates	Complex nature, involving harmonization based on the win-win negotiation between manager and other stakeholders
4.	Performance focus	Predominantly business, focused only on company performance	Multidimensional performance (business, social, ecological and educational), focused on both performance and interests of the company and relevant stakeholders

Today, a **transition from traditional management to stakeholder management is necessary**. To do so successfully requires a new vision, prospective and innovative approaches, effort, agile processes and a relatively long period of time. It is important to emphasize that under the pressure of the needs of the company and society, this transition has already started in many enterprises, especially large ones, with very influential major stakeholders – clients, suppliers, investors, and communities.

A successful transition to stakeholder management requires a systematic approach. It begins with formulating a clear problem statement (Repenning, Kieffer, & Astor, 2017). According to a recent study, before setting the change priorities, managers should analyze three things: the catalyst for transformation, the underlying quest, and the leadership capabilities (Anand & Barsoux, 2017).

Relevant Stakeholder as an Essential Component of Each Company

Any company has many internal and external stakeholders. Bearing in mind the general definition of the stakeholder (see Chapter 4), each stakeholder deserves to be taken into consideration by the company, to receive attention and to develop relationship with him. In the context of COVID-19 pandemic, the intensity of this approach is even higher. The development of performant relationship between the company (managers) and its stakeholders involves **many and complex elements:**

- Allocation of the different company resources – wages, bonuses, buildings, equipments, products, etc. – for the stakeholders and for the relationships with them;
- Time on the part of managers, specialists, and other company human resources to cultivate stakeholders' relationships;
- Special managerial and negotiation skills among the personnel involved in the initiation and development of the relationships with the company stakeholders;
- Certain specific methods and techniques to deal with different types of stakeholders;
- Open and flexible organizational culture;
- Company agility, etc.

The availability of these elements within each company is limited, especially resources and time. A company can afford to allocate and spend only a certain amount of time and money to develop relationships with the stakeholders, and this differs from one organization to another.

Each company has certain thresholds for its resources and other elements that cannot be crossed without jeopardizing the organization's development or even its survival. As a result, a company cannot afford to cultivate and develop relationships with all stakeholders at an equally high intensity. This situation led specialists to recently formulate the necessity of "competing for essential stakeholders" (Priem, Krause, Tantalo, & McFadyen, 2019). A company should be selective; it needs to identify and select the most important stakeholders, to treat them differently, taking into consideration their influence on the company and the other significant individual, organizational, and contextual aspects. The company should establish the relevance of its stakeholders.

Stakeholder relevance can be defined as the direct and indirect significant influence, actual and/or potential which the stakeholder exercises currently or could have later, on the company's functionality, development, and performance that should be taken into consideration to achieve organizational competitiveness and sustainability. Stakeholder relevance denotes the major impact of stakeholders in the company and their strong intertwining. Stakeholder relevance is always multidimensional, with business, social, and ecological aspects being the most prominent dimensions.

Company stakeholders, according to their relevance, could be divided into **two categories:**

- **Relevant stakeholders:** who should receive special attention from the company's management and be approached as major factors in the organization's survival and sustainable development;
- **Irrelevant stakeholders:** who do not merit, at least in this period, significant attention from the company management.

Relevant stakeholders, compared with other stakeholders, present the following **features:**

- Stronger interests in the company's functionality, development and performance;
- Higher motivation for the development of intense relationships with the company and for actions harmonised with it;
- Greater availability of communication and coworking with the company in certain fields;
- Possession of valuable knowledge and competences that are necessary and/or important for the company;
- Use and/or ownership of other resources – financial, technical-material, human, etc. – needed for the company to achieve its strategy and policies;
- Higher interests and influences on the society need to be taken into consideration;
- Powerful impact on certain company activities and results, taking into consideration certain society needs.

Stakeholders relevance is determined according to **two categories of elements.**

A **Company interests, characteristics, and evolution,** reflected in the:

  - Vision and leadership of top managers and main company stakeholders;
  - Company strategy, which establishes the mission, the long-term objectives, strategic options, allocation of resources, final and intermediary terms, and organization's competitive advantage;
  - Policies, which plan medium-term objectives, resources, and terms and main actions for the entire organization and its main fields;
  - Characteristics of the organization's management systems – decisional, organizational, informational, etc.;
  - Managerial methods, techniques, and procedures used in the company;
  - Organizational culture of the company;
  - Evolution and trends in the company's industry and in the organization's actual and potential markets.

These elements, which largely influence the company's activities and performance, depend to a large extent on the parameters of each organization (profile, size, location, available resources, etc.). All these elements should be taken into consideration, using a sustainable vision and approach.

B **Stakeholders' interests, characteristics and potential,** evaluated at the level of every stakeholder category and later, for each relevant stakeholder category, at the level of every stakeholder. Relevance analysis starts with the **identification of the stakeholder categories** and continues with their separation, based on the temporal factor, into two categories:

a **Permanent stakeholders:** usually shareholders, managers, executants, clients, and suppliers.
b **Temporary stakeholders:** the most frequent being the investors, bankers, consultants, designers, informaticians, researchers, analysts, and local community.

Normally, the permanent relevant stakeholders are usually the most important, and the company management pays them special and consistent attention.

Of course, in certain periods, temporary stakeholders, such as investors, can also have a huge relevance and receive special attention if the company's strategic development plan is based on outsourcing. The same is true with designers and researchers when the company plans to innovate massively by introducing new products and technologies using outsourcing.

Within each category of relevant stakeholders, every component should be evaluated to determine the relevant (individual and organizational) stakeholder. The stakeholders' evaluation is based on a **set of parameters,** the most significant being the following:

- Present and future major interests of the stakeholder reflected in strategy and policies, and in the business, managerial, social, and ecological approaches used in the relationships within the company and with other organizations. The approach of the stakeholder interests should consider that the stakes of each stakeholder group are multifaceted and interconnected (Freeman, Harrison, Wicks, Parmar, & De Colle, 2010);
- The main features of the stakeholder behaviour, especially towards the company involved;
- Stakeholder availability in terms of openness to communication, collaboration, and performance achievement;

- Legitimacy or the extent to which the stakeholder`s actions are correct and desirable (Mitchell, Agle, & Wood, 1997);
- Power, referring to the stakeholder's capacity to influence the organization's programme or project, and its business, social, and ecological performance (Mitchell et al., 1997);
- Urgency, which is the extent to which the outcome is interesting and necessary for the stakeholder, and the time pressure involved (Mitchell et al., 1997).

It should be emphasized that the main attributes of the stakeholder, especially the urgency and legitimacy, are not important by themselves, but only to the extent that they have a consistent influence on the company's work and performance. If stakeholder urgency or legitimacy does not really influence the company's performance now or in the future, then consideration of these attributes does not contribute de facto to the existence of stakeholder relevance.

The characteristics considered to determine the stakeholder relevance frequently modify their parameters. As a result, the stakeholder influence on the company changes as well, having a **dynamic dimension**. For this reason, assessment of the stakeholder relevance should be undertaken periodically to account for their dynamism.

Stakeholder relevance, according to the main company and stakeholder interests and expectations, convergence and the nature of the reciprocally impacts, could be divided into **two categories:**

a **Constructive relevance**, which is based on the convergence of the main interests and expectations of the stakeholder, company and society, having as its background a consistent win-win relationship. This relevance generates an increase in performance and business, and in social satisfactions for both the company and the stakeholder. Constructive relevance could be measured by the company and stakeholder trade-off generated.

b **Protective relevance**, involving significant differences between the interests of the company and the stakeholder, usually based on tough negotiations. The result is often the protection of certain major interests of both parties, most frequently of an ecological and social nature. From a business point of view, this type of relevance involves significant time and other resources spent by the organization, which do not contribute to increasing the company's performance but facilitate the continuation of the organization's activity, eventually having a positive impact on its brand and/or the society. Protective relevance can be measured relatively by the company's losses if it does not cultivate relationships with the special stakeholders group.

Based on evaluations, the company's management is able to decide who are the relevant company stakeholders, both organizations and people. It could be useful to evaluate the intensity of the stakeholder relevance using several categories of intensity, such as very high, high, and average. Relative intensity can be useful in designing the management approach to each stakeholder, including the resource type and size allocated to stakeholder coworking, and the dimension and type of stakeholder contribution to the company's functioning and development.

In our opinion, the elements presented so far in this chapter offer an answer to the question of why this study does not use the well-known expressions "salient stakeholder" (Kenny, 2014) or "key stakeholder",[1] instead using "**relevant stakeholder**". Our main arguments are as follows:

- Relevance is specifically contextually determined by the relationships within a certain company, with certain categories of stakeholder, with certain stakeholders and, from a broader perspective, with a specific organizational environment.
- This view of stakeholders, focused on relevance, is more contextually focused, from both a managerial and operational perspective, approaching them as major factors influencing the company performance. It therefore needs and deserves a new term, "relevant", able to suggest the innovative content of this approach.
- The term "relevant", at least in our perception, presents a more consistent and constructive meaning than the term "salient", because relevance suggests two or more parts; relevance is always established by reference to certain elements.

Of course, we know that the term "relevant stakeholder" has been used before but to a small extent and in quite a different approach and context. We could cite as an example Garcia-Castro and Aguilera (2015) and Lelea, Roba, Christinck, and Kaufmann (2016).

The concept "relevant stakeholder" is essential in the approach used in our book, where we will analyze in more depth and detail many other elements useful to better understanding this innovative management concept.

Managerial Synapse Definition and Categories

The stakeholder approach, which has proliferated in recent decades in numerous enterprises, has as a main component the relationship between the manager and important stakeholders. This relationship is quite different from the classic relationship between the manager and the executants, customers, suppliers, etc. It is different in many respects, and, more importantly, it is more productive, generating many and consistent positive effects at the level of stakeholders involved, helping organizations to perform better in the VUCA environment. **The main "secret" of these effects is represented by the win-win approach.**

For this special relationship between the organization manager and the stakeholder, we propose the term **"managerial synapse"**, analogous with electrical and chemical synapses, having the same major role and determinant influence on the functioning of the systems involved. We define the **managerial synapse as a basic managerial mechanism, involving one company manager and one relevant stakeholder; it consists of an intense exchange of information and knowledge, in joint and/or harmonized decisional, operational, and behavioural processes, able to generate superior added value and synergies, satisfying the main interests and objectives** of both parties.

The managerial synapse is an **innovative managerial mechanism** that has started to be developed in recent decades using a range of approaches, especially in multinational corporations, large companies and important projects. The innovative character of the managerial synapses consists in the **change of the management paradigm**. Traditionally, organization management is based predominantly on subordination, a rigid hierarchical relationship from the top to the bottom of the company. **The managerial synapse is based on the win–win relationship, on collaboration, and on real partnership between the parties involved.** Of course, companies continue to have hierarchies, but their main role is to harmonize the decisions, actions, and behaviours of all relevant organizational stakeholders. Within the managerial synapse, the main content of the managerial relationships and processes in the company is radically different, with better results. The managerial synapse represents the basic community of collaboration for each company.

The managerial synapse, like an electrical synapse, is a bilateral mechanism. Managerial synapses, taking into consideration the organizational appurtenance of the two stakeholders involved, can be separated into **two categories:**

- The endogenous managerial synapse, between an organization manager and one relevant stakeholder, a person from the same organization. This type of synapse is entirely fulfilled inside the same organization. In this type of synapse, the relevant stakeholder is usually, an employee or, less frequently, a shareholder.
- The exogenous managerial synapse, between an organization manager and an outside relevant stakeholder. This type of managerial synapse mostly includes as stakeholders, clients, suppliers, intermediaries, bank officials, investors, consultants, etc. This type of synapse is fulfilled both inside and outside the organization, being more complex than the endogenous managerial synapse.

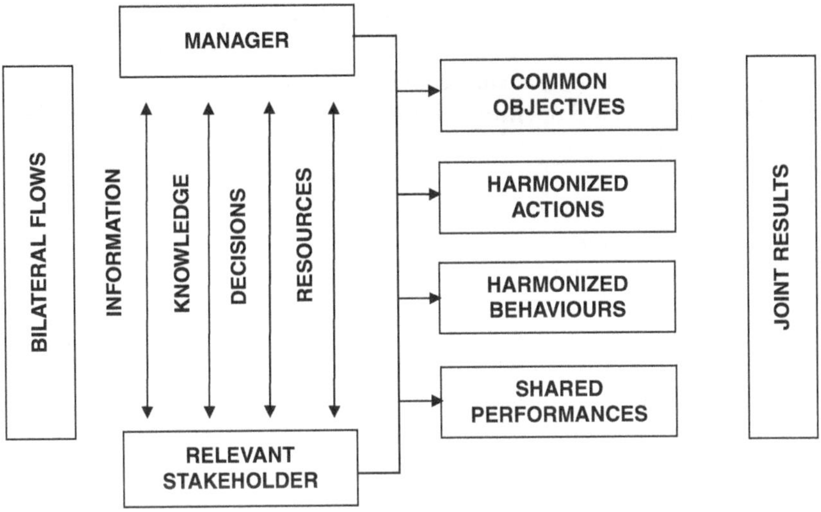

Figure 5.2 The content of the managerial synapse.

A managerial synapse is essentially a **bilateral relationship between one organization manager and one relevant stakeholder.** In the organization, especially for its employees, there are relatively frequent situations when one employee is part of several managerial synapses. In this case, the direct manager of the employee should be the designated manager of all synapses involving the employee in order to harmonise them.

The main content of a managerial synapse is represented by the repeated sending and receiving, between the manager and the stakeholder, of information, knowledge, and other resources and decisions that generate certain harmonized objectives, actions, behaviours, and performances (Figure 5.2). Managerial synapse involves what Sanner and Bunderson (2018) call the "right kind of hierarchy, which can help persons and teams become better innovators and learners and to obtain better performance".

A managerial synapse quite often has entrepreneurial content because both participants have initiatives and have to assume risks and act autonomously.

The content of the managerial synapse is significantly **influenced by the stakeholder type involved,** whether a person (individual) or organization:

- In the case of an individual stakeholder, within the managerial synapse, the managerial and operational processes are usually direct, less complicated, and fulfilled at higher speed.
- In the case of an organizational stakeholder, its representative has a certain mandate and quite often, before providing feedback to the

company manager, he/she should inform, consult, and/or have approval from one manager in his own organization. In such a situation, information and knowledge flows are frequently larger; the decisional and operational processes are more complex and their speed lower.

Essentially, the features of the managerial synapse in both types of stakeholders are the same.

The managerial synapse has in view mainly **two goals**:

- To achieve, based on the joint and/or convergent interests, the common objectives and interests, referring to the direct and indirect obtaining of knowledge, human, technical-material, and financial resources; to the product, services, technology, equipment renewal; to profit, turnover, market share increase, etc.
- To build a collaborative mechanism able to facilitate the joint efforts and contributions, and the fulfillment of certain important needs and interests of the stakeholders involved.

The organization and the relevant stakeholder involved in each managerial synapse collaborate to settle the specific objectives to be achieved together, according to their interests and expectations. The managerial synapse is a special partnership mechanism generating not only better results for each component but also the synergy in the organization.

In our vision, managerial synapse is based on the systemic approach of the organization, its stakeholders, and its environment. The managerial synapse is a dynamic mechanism because its content, work, and performance are constantly changing. For this reason, managerial synapses should be approached and developed as a **dynamic form of organization work**, and it should be designed as an agile organizational entity in the company.

Managerial synapse is an "**autonomous mechanism**" contributing to the increase of the frequency and quality of the entrepreneurial and innovative decisions, actions, and behaviours at the level of the company and its stakeholders. Managerial synapse represents one way to respond to the company need to autonomize significant parts of their business which, according to the specialists from Boston Consulting Group (Bailey, Reeves, Whitaker, & Hutchinson, 2019), shall be a major trend in the coming decade.

It is important to outline that, although the stakeholder approach and stakeholder management have started to proliferate, especially in large organizations and projects, managerial synapses are necessary in every organization. In our vision, considering what occurs in real life in companies and their environment, the managerial synapse is suitable and effective for all types of organization, taking into consideration the specificities of each.

Specificity and Dimensions of the Managerial Synapse

The specificity of the managerial synapse consists in the appearance of the **area where synapses** occurred:

- The share of the information, knowledge, and other resources;
- The harmonised decisional processes;
- The joint and/or coordinated operational processes;
- The deployment of the compatible, convergent, complementary, and/or collaborative stakeholder behaviours.

Managerial synapse is based on the organization–stakeholder fit, which describes the compatibility that exists between an organization and a stakeholder when their characteristics are well matched (Bundy, Vogel, & Zachary, 2018).

The managerial synapse area represents a specific, participative, operational, and entrepreneurial context, favouring the fulfillment of the stakeholders' joint interests. Within this synapse area, the protagonists are the involved manager and relevant stakeholder, but certain colleagues and/or subordinates may also participate. The processes taking place inside the synapses have a deep **participative content.**

The managerial synapse presents **three dimensions** (Figure 5.3).

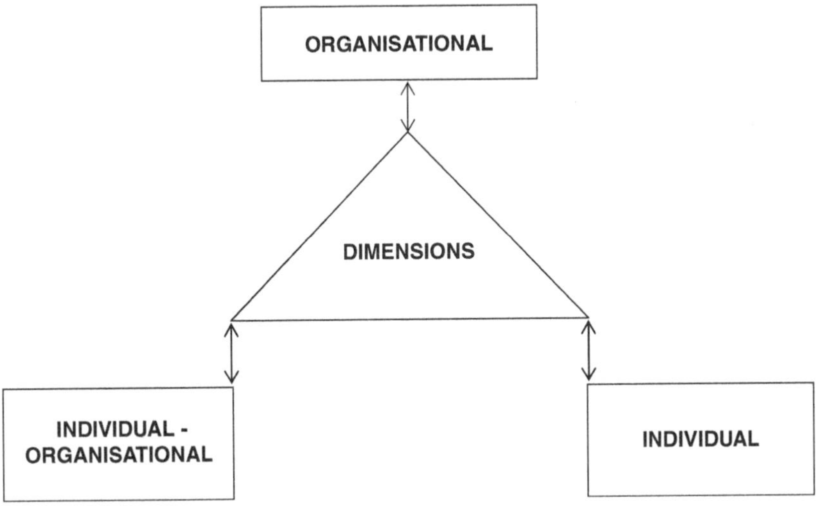

Figure 5.3 The dimensions of the managerial synapse.

The **organizational dimension** is generated by each organization's stakeholder strategies, policies, approaches, objectives, decisions, actions, and behaviours. In every managerial synapse, there is at least one organizational dimension of the involved manager entity. In the managerial synapses within the company, the organizational dimension is the same. In the managerial synapse, where the involved stakeholder is from other organizations, there are normally two organizational dimensions, one for each organization.

The individual dimension, taking place within managerial synapse, involves an individual stakeholder – an employee, shareholder, consultant, etc. The individual dimension reflects the vision, mentality, expectations, aims, knowledge, information, decisions, actions, and behaviours of the person-stakeholder involved in the managerial synapse. The analysis has revealed that the individual dimension is very different among individual stakeholder categories – employee, shareholder, etc. – and, concomitantly, within each stakeholder category.

The individual-organizational dimension reveals the concrete and pragmatic actions in the synapse area of the person representing an organizational stakeholder, influenced by his or her own personality, knowledge, potential, and interests. The individual-organizational dimension changes within the same organization and within the same managerial synapse according to the people involved. Consequently, when the organization changes its representative in a managerial synapse, the characteristics and the results of this synapse partially modify as well.

Within a managerial synapse, these dimensions are harmonised through a **negotiation process based on the win-win approach.** Having as its basis the common and complementary interests, the win-win negotiation generates superior motivation for each stakeholder to communicate, to work, to share, to decide and to benefit together. Each managerial synapse represents a micro-managerial mechanism, intensely participative and operational, able to produce much better results for both the organization and the people involved. The managerial synapse is the basic component of stakeholder-based management, which should be developed in modern companies.

Reciprocity is a very important feature of the managerial synapse. Reciprocity refers to the motivations and efforts regarding the collaboration in order to satisfy the joint interests and expectations of both managerial synapse components. It refers also to the contribution of each party to the fulfillment of the objectives established in a balanced approach and to secure performance for both the company and the relevant stakeholder. We might have **two types** of reciprocity:

- Direct reciprocity – I help you, you help me
- Indirect reciprocity – I help you, and somebody else helps me (Nowak, 2006)

Naturally, in the managerial synapse, direct reciprocity is predominant. Reciprocity could generate reciprocal co-creation of the stakeholder and company involved in many fields (Wallpach, Voyer, Kastanakis, & Mühlbacher, 2017).

Another specificity of the managerial synapse is **dialogic communication**, which means that the two parties alternatively play the role of speaker and listener. Mutual understanding, empathy, and commitment (Cardwell, Williams, & Pyle, 2016) are the hallmarks of dialogic communication. Dialogic communication generates cognitive and emotional resonance (Giorgi, 2017) to the managerial synapse components, favouring the collaboration reflected in joint decisions and actions, and harmonized behaviours.

The managerial synapse **responds to a large extent to the five enablers** proposed by Ganz (as cited in Garrov & Varney, 2015, p. 5) in order to craft agile and performing organizations:

- Shared values that are experienced and communicated emotionally, often through narrative;
- Shared interests based on relational understanding, leading to a commitment to work together;
- Shared structure, creating a space where interaction and creativity can occur, involving shared norms, clear roles, and responsibilities;
- Shared strategy, which turns what you have, into what you need to get what you want;
- Shared actions and the ability to mobilise and deploy resources, including time, effort, and energy.

The elements presented reveal the high specificity of the managerial synapse, which represents the managerial innovation that is quite different from the traditional managerial component of the company.

Psychological–Cultural Background for the Managerial Synapse

Managerial synapses are based mainly on the relationships of collaboration, cooperation and partnership and less on formal relationships. This, as we have already outlined, is quite different from traditional managerial relationships based mainly on a formal approach and on a strong hierarchy. This means that managerial synapses involve different types of human approaches and behaviours. The fundamental question that arises in this context is **whether most people are able and willing to cooperate and to have the partnership relationships necessary in the managerial synapse**. The results of many studies, especially from the last two decades, provide many **valuable arguments** to answer this affirmatively:

- As we have already mentioned, mathematician biologist, Martin Nowak asserts and demonstrates that "natural cooperation is the third fundamental principle of evolution, beside mutation and natural selection" (Nowak, 2006). This means that the present evolution of mankind has the ability to generate comprehensive cooperation in a competitive world.
- According to extensive experimental work, people actually cooperate more than the theory predicts (Benkler, 2011). Fifty percent of the participants in a test regarding cooperative behaviour showed systematic and predictable cooperation: some of them cooperated emotionally, in that they treated kindness with kindness and meanness with meanness; others cooperated unconditionally, even when it came at a personal cost. For this reason, Benkler (2011) states that "we are more cooperative and less selfish than most people believe. Organizations should help us embrace our collaborative sentiments". Referring to this, the well-known specialist Hamel (2009) considers people to be "community minded".
- This century has seen a strong intensification of the participative and collaborative processes. Some specialists (Adler, Heckscher, & Prusak, 2011) consider that we are currently experiencing a "collaborative revolution". As an answer to this revolution, companies have started to develop a new model, a collaborative community type model, "which is organised around a sense of shared purpose and coordinated through to collaboratively development, carefully documented with procedures. Such an organization excels at interdependent knowledge-based work". Recent research has demonstrated that higher levels of collaboration are positively related to perceived improvements in a direct substantial outcome for stakeholders (Conner, 2017).
- Neuroscience provides another argument, showing that when the people cooperate, a reward circuit is triggered in their brains. This means that at least some people want to cooperate because it makes them feel good (Boyd & Richerson, 1988).

In the company, individual and organizational decisions, actions, and behaviours depend heavily on the **organization culture**. It is essential that company culture favours cooperative, collaborative, and partnership behaviour among stakeholders. A very interesting study (Groysberg, Lee, Price, & Cheng, 2018) identified **eight styles of culture**, taking into consideration two dimensions: how people interact, in terms of dependence or interdependence, and their response to change (flexibility and stability). Based on the empirical research, the frequency of their manifestation in the company is highlighted (Table 5.2).

The information presented in the table is very useful in approaching managerial synapse from **two perspectives**:

Table 5.2 The main characteristics, pros, and cons of culture styles

No.	*Culture Style*	*Ranked 1st or 2nd*	*Main Characteristics*	*Major*	
				Advantages	*Disadvantages*
1.	RESULTS	89%	• Achievement driven • Goal focused	• Improved execution • External focus • Capability building • Goal achievement	• Overemphasis on achievement results may lead to communication and collaboration breakdowns and higher level of stress and anxiety
2.	CARING	63%	• Warm • Sincere • Relational	• Improved teamwork • Improved engagement • Improved communication • More trust • Higher sense of belonging	• Overemphasis on consensus building may reduce exploration of options, stifle competitiveness and slow decision making
3.	ORDER	15%	• Rule abiding • Respectful • Cooperative	• Improved operational efficiency • Reduced conflict • Greater civic-mindedness	• Overemphasis on rules and traditions may reduce individualism, stifle creativity and limit organizational agility
4.	PURPOSE	9%	• Purpose driven • Idealistic • Tolerant	• Improved appreciation for diversity, sustainability and social responsibility	• Overemphasis on a long-term purpose and ideals may get in the way of practical and immediate concerns
5.	SAFETY	8%	• Realistic • Careful • Prepared	• Improved risk management • Stability • Business continuity	• Overemphasis on standardization and formalization may lead to bureaucracy, inflexibility and dehumanization of the work environment

(*Continued*)

Table 5.2 (Continued)

No.	Culture Style	Ranked 1st or 2nd	Main Characteristics	Major Advantages	Major Disadvantages
6.	LEARNING	7%	• Open • Inventive • Exploring	• Improved innovation • Improved agility • Organizational learning	• Overemphasis on exploration may lead to a lack of focus and inability to exploit existing advantages
7.	AUTHORITY	4%	• Bold • Decisive • Dominant	• Improved speed of decision making • Better responsiveness to threats or crises	• Overemphasis on strong authority and bold decision making may lead to politics, conflict and a psychologically unsafe work environment
8.	ENJOYMENT	2%	• Playful • Instinctive • Fun loving	• Improved employee morale • Improved engagement • Higher creativity	• Overemphasis on autonomy and engagement may lead to a lack of discipline and create possible compliance or governance issues

Adapted from "The leader's guide to corporate culture: How to manage the eight critical elements of organizational life," by B. Groysberg, J. Lee, J. Price, and J. Cheng, 2018, *Harvard Business Review*, 96(1), p. 49. Retrieved from https://hbr.org/2018/01/the-leaders-guide-to-corporate-culture.

- It reveals that the most used culture styles in companies are **the caring style** (63%) characterized by warm, sincere, and good relations, and **the results style** (89%) characterized by achievement-driven, good-focused value, and behaviour. **The authority culture style**, characterized by bold, decisive, and dominant elements, registers one of the lowest frequencies (4%). The most utilized styles, caring and results, are favourable for the development of managerial synapses. For example, the caring style has the advantages of engagement, communication, trust, sense of belonging, and improved team working, which are very well suited to the managerial synapse.
- The elements in the table represent a very useful guide for the evaluation of the culture styles in a company and for remodeling the organizational culture to enable the reconstruction of the relationships with internal and external relevant stakeholders.

In the study mentioned, there are many other elements that are helpful in the processes of evaluating and remodeling the company culture. Elements from another study regarding the creation of a growth culture based on a specific approach "to liberate infinite energy" in the company are also very useful in this respect (Schwarz, 2018).

Taking into consideration the multiple human aspects involved in the managerial synapse, we can state that its **psychological background is represented by the six elements indicated in** Figure 5.4.

In order to build and develop a performant managerial synapse, all of these elements should be present in each relevant stakeholder component of the managerial synapse and in their mutual relationship.

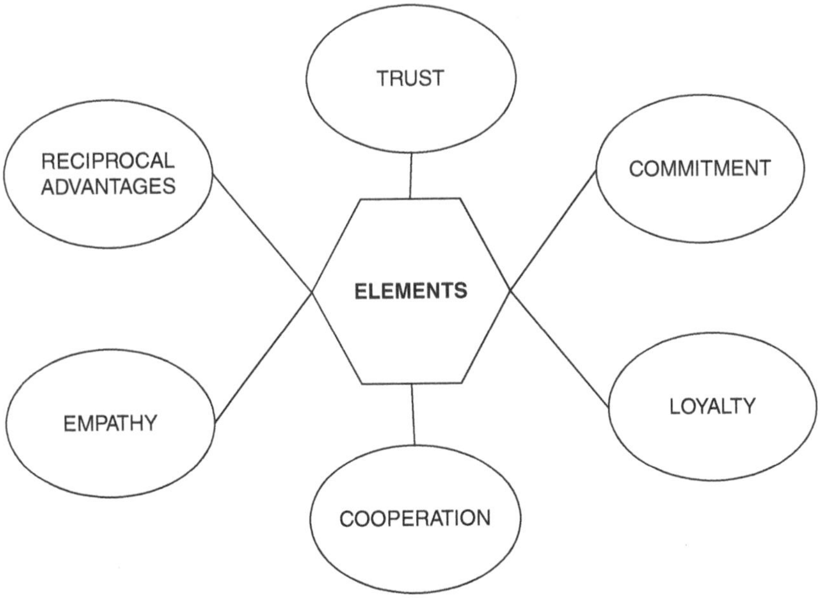

Figure 5.4 The psychological bases of relationships within a managerial synapse.

Stakeholder Trust: Crucial for Managerial Synapse

Without a doubt, trust is a part of the psychological background for the managerial synapse, as indicated in Figure 5.4. We approach it separately because it has an outstanding impact on the building, existence, development, and performance of the managerial synapse. Trust also represents a major component of the intellectual capital of each organization and of every stakeholder.

Stakeholder trust is multidimensional because there are many different stakeholder groups – employees, customers, suppliers, investors, consultants, communities, etc. – with various characteristics. This is one of the main reasons that managing stakeholder trust is very difficult. To help overcome this difficulty, a special analysis should be undertaken for relevant stakeholders, identifying the specific elements (Bassett, 2008).

A large **variety of relationships** are involved in managing relevant stakeholder trust:

- Interpersonal relationships between the individual stakeholders, with one always being a manager in the company;
- Inter-organizational relationships between the company and the other stakeholder organization;
- Mixed relationships between one company and one individual stakeholder.

The approach and the development of trust is quite different among these types of relationships and within each of them, depending on the characteristics of the parties involved in the managerial synapse. Specialists have identified **many factors that influence stakeholder trust.** We group these factors into **two categories.**

The first category refers to the factors that influence trust in an organization, either the company involved or a relevant stakeholder organization of the company. A recent study (Matuleviciene & Stravinskiene, 2015) found two basic factors of trust in an organization: company reputation and organizational trustworthiness. Other factors influencing company trust are the experience of the relevant stakeholder with company and the history of the interactions between the company and the stakeholders involved, etc.

The second category is the factors that influence trust at the level of the individual stakeholder – manager, employee, shareholder, customer, investor, banker, etc. Among these factors, we mention benevolence, integrity, management competence, technical competence, transparency, and value congruence. A study conducted in four different organizations regarding these factors has led to following insights: transparency is overrated, integrity is not enough, the right kind of competence matters, building trust with one group can destroy it with another, and value congruence matters across the board (Pirson & Malhotra, 2008). There are also numerous studies analyzing these factors individually. In relation with organizational transparency, we cite a very complex study by Schnackenberg and Tomlinson (2016) promoting a new perspective on managing trust in organization stakeholders.

Certain specialists have elaborated **models for the impact of the trust.** For example, Matuleviciene and Stravinskiene (2015) designed a very interesting model based on the division of factors into two categories: controllable factors, having a direct impact on stakeholder trust, and uncontrollable factors, having an indirect impact on the stakeholder's trust. In the literature, there are several models regarding organization trust and stakeholder trust (Priston, Martin, & Parmer, 2017; Schwaiger, 2004; Van der Merwe & Puth, 2014), which can be used not only for research but in the management of stakeholders' trust.

Besides models, some specialists have proposed **principles to be used to develop trusting relationships** with stakeholders. Harrison, Bosse, and Phillips (2010) have formulated the principles of distributional, procedural, and integrational justice, especially regarding the allocation of company resources to those areas that will best satisfy the expectations of relevant stakeholders.

The factors, models, principles, and other elements mentioned demonstrate the great importance of stakeholder trust, the need to pay major attention to it in the company, and the availability of a large range of specific approaches and tools to deal with trust. These elements can be used by companies, organization managers, and other relevant stakeholders to evaluate stakeholder trust, to build and develop managerial synapses and other managerial and business mechanisms, and to generate sustainability in the present complex and dynamic times. Trust should be approached based on the realities and not on myths, which are widely disseminated (Sucher & Gupta, 2019).

The elements presented allow us to outline the following **essential aspects from the managerial synapse point of view:**

- Stakeholder trust is a multidimensional, very complex, multifaceted element that is not easy to understand, evaluate and, in particular, to manage.
- Company organizational trust and manager company trust are the key elements in efficiently developing and managing relationships with all relevant company stakeholders.
- Trust, together with joint relevant stakeholders' objectives and expectations, is a precondition to building and utilizing the managerial synapse in any company.
- Many helpful approaches, models, principles, and recommendations regarding the building, use, rebuilding, development, and management

of stakeholder trust have been elaborated and utilized successfully in companies, especially in corporations.

- Stakeholder trust should be personalised in the case of each company and each relevant internal and external stakeholder to be able to achieve performant decisions, actions, and behaviours.
- The managerial synapse is a managerial mechanism that is able to use, develop, and amplify the company and the relevant stakeholder trust, replacing the old "command and control" approach with "trust and empower" (Emmens & Thomson, 2017).
- Company trust and relevant stakeholders' trust represent a major component of the intellectual capital of up-to-date companies, whose importance and impact on organizational and individual performance is constantly increasing.

Trust represents an essential source of company sustainability, which is well valorized by the managerial synapse and by company management based on relevant stakeholders. Trust is a precondition, an essential element, and a permanent source of added value in companies using stakeholder management. Trust generates advantages and sustainability for companies in the present VUCA environment.

Economic Background of the Managerial Synapse

In our approach, we start from the **stakeholder-based perspective of performance** defined by Harrison and Wicks (2013) as "the sum of the utility created by firm for legitimate stakeholders". According to our vision, we have made one change to this definition, replacing legitimate stakeholders with relevant stakeholders. We will not reference the three other popular stakeholder company performance perspectives – shareholder-based financial performance, the balance scorecard and the triple bottom line – because they are not directly in line with the profile of this section, which is focused on the economic background of the managerial synapse.

Our approach is based on the following three perspectives:

- The value created in the company is generated by both the enterprise and its stakeholders.
- Each company has and develops relationships with a stakeholder only if it creates value for the organization or if the stakeholder directly or indirectly facilitates the creation of added value.
- The relationship between stakeholder-oriented management and firm performance is positive and is almost always measured in terms of financial returns (Choi & Wang, 2009; Dorobantu & Odziemkowska, 2017; Hillman & Keim, 2001).

Relevant stakeholders can contribute to value creation within a company in many ways: providing resources (equipment, work, land, building, money, etc.), having knowledge and using it in the company's activities, possessing and using special competences in the company, and providing the company with certain commercial, financial or technical services, etc. The stakeholder's contribution to the company's performance is one criterion in the evaluation of relevance. The most relevant stakeholders usually make a bigger contribution to the company's performance.

Many specialists (Amit & Zott, 2001; Bosse, Phillips, & Harrison, 2009; Bowman & Ambrosini, 2000; Brandenburger & Stuart, 1996; Lepak, Smith, & Taylor, 2007) have contributed to the elaboration of the concept of stakeholders' contribution to the company's performance and their reward for this contribution, which is called **value creation appropriation (VCA)**. Stakeholders are treated as claimants and capturers of value in their interaction with the company. In recent years, there has been a change from the neoclassical economic model, based only on two relevant stakeholders (the consumer and the producer), to the broader-based view of VCA, where multiple stakeholders are considered. Garcia-Castro and Aguilera (2015) made a remarkable contribution in this respect. They developed a conceptual framework based on an analytical taxonomy of value creation and appropriation that is consistent with a more complex notion of value **wherein the trade-off in stakeholders' value appropriation is included**. The concept of total value created by the firm and all its stakeholders is used instead of the previous concept of shareholder value creation. Based on this comprehensive approach of the total value creation in the company, Garcia-Castro and Aguilera (2015) elaborated a model with **value creation and appropriation with multiple stakeholders.**

One important practical aspect is the possibility of applying this model to a company, using only publicly available data referring to prices, costs, inputs, and outputs. This framework can be utilised to measure and redistribute the total value created in the firm to the relevant stakeholders. Moreover, the framework is based on another new concept introduced by Garcia-Castro and Aguilera (2015), **value creation elasticity of stakeholder value appropriation,** which captures the relationships between value appropriated by a stakeholder and the total value added in a period of time. This approach makes it possible to assess whether each dollar appropriated by one stakeholder has a positive, neutral, or negative effect on the total value created by the company. According to the authors, value creation appropriation elasticity can be used by company decision-makers to make investments by selected stakeholders to maintain distributional justice, respect reciprocity norms and build trustworthiness.

Value creation appropriation elasticity represents a good approach for companies to better manage relevant stakeholders, taking into consideration their contribution to the total value created in the firm. In its use, it is important to take into consideration the limits of the approach, as outlined by Garcia-Castro and Aguilera (2015).

Company stakeholder management, in order to use the possibilities created by value creation appropriation elasticity and by other innovative approaches in this field, needs appropriate accounting. According to the specialists Mitchell, Van Buren, Greenwood, and Freeman (2015), the stakeholders' inclusion in organizational decision-making and the resulting issue of value creation, is a thorny problem that stakeholder management has sought to address. **It is necessary that a new branch of accounting** is able:

- To identify the contribution of each relevant stakeholder to the creation of the total value in the company and to reflect it in accounting.
- To allow the appropriation of the value allocated to each relevant stakeholder from the company's value.

Some steps have been made in this direction, but they have been slow and insufficient. There have been some promising studies in recent years, one of which has developed a transdisciplinary theory of value creation stakeholder accounting (Mitchell et al., 2015). This is based on stakeholder risk-sharing as a superior rationale for stakeholder inclusion. The authors propose **a new mechanism – value creation stakeholder partnership** – for the implementation of this new type of stakeholder accounting. The new mechanism is a creative combination of accounting value creation, entrepreneurship and stakeholder theory. A special issue of a well-known management journal was dedicated to this essential field for company stakeholder management (e.g. Andon, Baxter, & Chua, 2015; Brown & Dillard, 2015; Crane, Graham, & Himick, 2015; Harrison & van der Laan Smith, 2015).

The development of a special accounting mechanism, able to reflect both value contribution and appropriation of each relevant stakeholder in the company, is absolute necessary to build performant managerial synapses.

Finally, we want to mention that we only refer to the economic performance of stakeholders in this section because this is our target. As we have mentioned throughout our book, we treat stakeholders' performances multidimensionally, taking into consideration social, ecological, and other aspects.

Criteria for Managerial Synapse Classification and Characterization

Elements presented in the previous sections of this chapter allow us to formulate a **set of criteria for managerial synapse characterization and classification** (see Table 5.3).

The information contained in this table helps to deepen understanding and better approach companies' managerial synapses; the new managerial mechanism is able to contribute to a large extent to the innovative and rapid development of companies, economy, and society in the present turbulent, challenging, and fast-changing times.

Main Advantages and Limits of the Managerial Synapse

Managerial synapses based on the win-win approach generate **many positive effects**, both tangible and intangible, inside and outside the company, and for its relevant stakeholders (Figure 5.5). We can summarize them as follows:

- Building of a joint decisional, actional, and behavioural community of both stakeholders involved in each synapse, based on cooperation and reciprocal advantages;
- Generation of team spirit inside the managerial synapse, having a participative impact on the entire synapse area;
- Construction of the stakeholders' positive identity at work because managerial synapse develops several specific mechanisms. For example "individuals disclose more information, discover shared perspectives, are more authentic and build intimacy" and "enable engagement in multiple domains, increase expose to diverse contacts, [and] create brokering opportunities between contacts" (Dutton, Roberts, & Bednar, 2010);
- New approach of the relevant stakeholders, individual, and organizational, based on the win-win negotiations and correlated decisions, actions, and behaviours, generates higher motivation and involvement, and more creativity, effort and productivity;
- Joint and correlated actions by stakeholders in the managerial synapse, achieved inside and outside company;
- Movement of all type of resources, tangible and intangible – information, knowledge, technical, material, human, and financial – between the stakeholders involved;
- Substantial sharing of knowledge, equipment, technology, building, land, market, licenses, etc. between both stakeholders in the synapse area;
- Direct synergy in the synapse area involved and the indirect synergy at the level of the department or the whole company;

Table 5.3 Characterization of the different types of managerial synapses

No.	*Criteria*	*Types of Managerial Synapses*	*Characteristics*
1.	Components of organizational membership	Internal	• Both managerial synapse components are from the same company • Organizational objectives are the same for both components • Direct and easier relationships between managerial synapse components • Both managerial synapse components are influenced by the same organizational culture
		Internal–external	• One managerial synapse component is from the company and the other from outside the organization • Managerial synapse organizational objectives could be from two organizations • Relationships between the managerial synapse components are more complex and time consuming compared with the previous type of synapse • Certain organizational barriers and organizational cultural differences influence the functionality and performance of the managerial synapse
2.	Type of managerial synapse components	Organizational	• Managerial synapse components represent two organizations • Managerial synapse has a strong organizational dimension • Four categories of interests and objectives should be negotiated and harmonised: company, another organization, company manager and the representative of the second organization • The relationships within managerial synapse are very complex • Content, dynamics and performance of the managerial synapse are heavily influenced by both organizations' strategy, policies, culture etc.

		Organizational–individual	• In the managerial synapse, one component represents the company and the other is an individual relevant stakeholder (subordinate, consultant, etc.) • Managerial synapse has an organizational-individual dimension • Three categories of interests and objectives should be negotiated and harmonised: company, company manager, and the other internal or external individual relevant stakeholder • Relationships within managerial synapse are less complex than in the previous type of synapse • Context, dynamics and performance of the managerial synapse are influenced to a large extent by the company strategies, policies, culture, etc. and by the interests, objectives and personality of the individual stakeholder, the second component of the synapse
3.	Duration of the managerial synapse	Determined	• Period of the existence of managerial synapse and work is determined according to the contract between the company and the relevant stakeholder (supplier, investor, customer, employee, banker, etc.) • Duration of the managerial synapse could be short, medium or long term, depending on the objectives and the contextual conditions • Common objectives and performances are established in a timely manner, facilitating cooperation between the managerial synapse components • Processes and relationships between the two components of the managerial synapse can be precisely planned and organised • Performances – business, social and ecological – are easier to achieve and to evaluate in comparison with the objectives

(Continued)

Table 5.3 (Continued)

No.	*Criteria*	*Types of Managerial Synapses*	*Characteristics*
		Undetermined	• Duration of the managerial synapse is not precisely established from the beginning • The second component of the managerial synapse, usually the external one (local community, NGOs, ecologist body, state administration representative, etc.) is not connected with the company by a formal agreement • Establishment of stakeholders' common objectives, decisions and actions is more complex and difficult than in the previous type of managerial synapse • Managerial synapse content and relationships are largely informal and flexible • Quantitative elements and parameters involved in managerial synapse processes are less presented and are used in a more informal manner
4.	Common types of objectives and interests	Organizational–personal	• Common objectives and interests in the managerial synapse are related to the company and/or the other organization involved, to the persons representing the organizations, and/or to the individual relevant stakeholder acting on his own behalf • Harmonisation of the three categories of interests and objectives is frequently a tough and complicated process • The organizational–personal managerial synapse is the most common in the company, economy and society • This type of managerial synapse is the most complex and difficult to use

		Organizational–social	• Common objectives and interests of the managerial synapse are related mainly to the company's social interests, local community expectations, social ONG, sectorial and/or national social aspects • Harmonisation of the relevant stakeholders' interests is not always very precisely done, often formulating common general aims • This type of managerial synapse is not very common, but the number is increasing rapidly • Informal aspects, qualitative elements and human context are very often more important than the quantitative aspects of the objectives and performance
5.	The nature of the common objectives	Economic	• In companies, business managerial synapses are numerous and sometimes comprise the majority • Business managerial synapses are essential for the company's survival, development and performance • All types of joint objectives involved in the business managerial synapse are of an economic nature: turnover, profit, wage, bonus, dividend, interest, price, sale, productivity, investment, etc. • Objectives are usually quantitative and very precisely determined • All objectives are specified in formal documents signed by both partners of the managerial synapse • Joint objectives of both components of the managerial synapse are usually correlated, favouring an increase of the economic performance of managerial synapse components

(*Continued*)

Table 5.3 (Continued)

No.	*Criteria*	*Types of Managerial Synapses*	*Characteristics*
		Social	• All types of social objectives, referring to the work conditions, labour force security, employees' health, social expectations of the local communities, etc. • The majority of the social objectives are qualitative • In companies, social managerial synapses are not very frequent, but there is a tendency to increase their number • The importance and impact of the social managerial synapse on the company's brand and global performance, on employee productivity and wellbeing, and on the development of the local community and living standards are growing under the conditions of the transition to a knowledge-based economy and digitalisation • Social objectives are for company employees, certain groups of personnel, the entire company, local community, ONGs, etc.
		Ecological	• All types of joint objectives of the ecological managerial synapse refer to internal or external company ecological aspects: types of technical substances used, type of energy produced and/or used, level of CO_2 emissions, soil protection, deposits of waste materials, etc. • Joint objectives of the ecological managerial synapse are both qualitative and quantitative • The ecological managerial synapse is not very frequent in organizations; the most are in industrial and agricultural companies • There is a steady tendency to increase the number of ecological managerial synapses under the impact of the last decade's international agreements regarding the global ecological situation and evolution

		Multidimensional synapse	• There are at least two common objectives of different natures, the most frequent being the economic and social objectives • Joint objectives of the multidimensional managerial synapse are both qualitative and quantitative • Multidimensional managerial synapses are the most used in the majority of companies. There is a growing tendency for multi-dimensional managerial synapses under the condition of the increasing impact of social and ecological factors on companies' work, performance and sustainability • In the near future, the most managerial synapses will be multidimensional, incorporating business, social and ecological objectives
6.	Nature of the processes incorporated	Focused on the procurement of resources	• Processes within managerial synapses provide raw materials, equipment, energy, spare parts, projects, studies, money, knowledge, etc. for the company • Relevant stakeholders frequently involved in this type of managerial synapse are suppliers, bankers, investors, consultants, designers and others • Resource parameters, which should be provided by each stakeholder involved in the managerial synapse, are usually precisely specified qualitatively and quantitatively in contracts • In this type of managerial synapse, an external stakeholder is usually involved • This type of managerial synapse largely influences the company's work and performances • Increases in externalisation of the company's activities and outsourcing contribute to the multiplication of this type of managerial synapse in companies

(Continued)

Table 5.3 (Continued)

No.	*Criteria*	*Types of Managerial Synapses*	*Characteristics*
		Focused on the internal work processes	• Processes involved in this managerial synapse are usually conducted inside the company • Processes are predominantly operational but also decisional or mixed • Stakeholders most frequently involved in this type of managerial synapse are company employees • Frequently, this type of managerial synapse is predominant in the company • In industrial companies, this type of managerial synapse is the most used, especially in the production, storage and account activities, and is very influential on the organization's performance • Company traditions and experience, informal aspects, personality and capacity of the people involved play an essential role in the content and the performance of this type of managerial synapse
		Focused directly on performance fulfillment	• Processes conducted inside the managerial synapse are focused on the attainment of well-defined performance, according to the common objectives negotiated • Common objectives of the managerial synapse components reflect the performances desired by each of them • Common objectives are usually quantitative and precisely formulated, referring to direct sale, percentage of the market, profit, turnover, dividend per share, commission, etc. • The most frequent stakeholder components in this type of managerial synapse are top managers, shareholders, brokers, marketing specialists, salespeople, wholesalers, clients and others

			• This type of managerial synapse makes a direct and major contribution to an increase in the company's and the other stakeholders' performance and sustainability
		Diversified	• Within the managerial synapse, a large variety of work processes are unfolding, with very diverse characteristics • Work processes have features referring to at least two of the previous categories of managerial synapse • This type of managerial synapse is more often used in micro and small companies, where the work processes are less specialised and formal procedures are less used • Often, the performances produced by this type of managerial synapse are below the average of the previous types, especially from an economic perspective
7.	Necessity for the company	Mandatory	• The managerial synapse incorporates work processes without which the company could not exist, such as supply, sale, transportation, maintenance, etc. • This type of managerial synapse has as components the permanent internal and external relevant stakeholders – employees, shareholders, suppliers, clients and others • Usually, the results produced by such managerial synapses directly and permanently condition the survival of the company and contribute significantly to its performance • Companies often have rich experience and know-how, developed from the foundation of the organization, which can be successfully used in this type of synapse • This category of managerial synapse is also plentiful in the company, and a large part of the work processes incorporated are components of the organizational value chain

(*Continued*)

Table 5.3 (Continued)

No.	*Criteria*	*Types of Managerial Synapses*	*Characteristics*
		Optional synapse	• This incorporates work processes that are not mandatory for the company's survival and present performance • Components of this type of managerial synapse are stakeholders who are not permanently necessary and relevant for the company, such as consultants, designers, investors, local community, trainers, experts, etc. • The construction and use of this type of managerial synapse depends decisively on the company vision, on shareholders and managers, on the company strategy and policies, on the company's potential relevant stakeholders approach, and on the evolution of the business environment • Optional managerial synapses play an essential role in the innovative development of the company, in the organization's way out of crises, in the valorisation of the new opportunities like those associated with internationalisation, digitalisation, nanotechnology, etc. • Quite often this type of managerial synapse uses largely tacit knowledge and incorporates less structured work processes and many informal elements inherent to the creative and entrepreneurial approaches implemented within the optional managerial synapse • The frequency, importance and impact of this type of managerial synapse are increasing rapidly, due to the transition to a knowledge-based economy and to the enhancement of the innovative and entrepreneurial processes

Figure 5.5 Positive results of the managerial synapse.

- Increased added value in the synapse area involved and at the organizational level, generated by all previous advantages;
- Sustainability of the two stakeholders' relationships and of the organizations involved.

Of course, the positive effects mentioned are very diverse in nature but essential for each organization. They attain the maximum level when the managerial synapse is professionally constructed and managed according to the new, radically changed vision, specific to the stakeholder-based system, which will be presented later in this book.

A managerial synapse, like any other managerial mechanism, is not perfect and does not present only advantages. The main **limits and disadvantages** of the managerial synapse are as follows:

- Difficulty reshaping stakeholders' mentality and behaviours to be able to (and to desire to) implement win-win decisions and actions constantly within the managerial synapse;
- Great effort is necessary from the individual stakeholders and their organizations to build and implement the managerial synapse;
- The necessity for permanent, intensive, and fair communication between the managerial synapse components;
- High dependence of the managerial synapse development and performance on the organization culture and context characteristics;
- The qualitative effects generated by the managerial synapse to a large extent become visible in the medium and long term.

If we compare the managerial synapse advantages with the limitations and disadvantages, it is obvious that the former are numerous and with much more positive effects on the company and individual and organizational stakeholder performance and sustainability. Furthermore, the advantages are strongly correlated with the major tendencies in the economy that are associated with digitalisation and the building of the knowledge-based economy.

Opportunity and Benefits of the Managerial Synapse in the COVID-19 Pandemic Context

Our approach in this section has the following starting points: (a) recovery of the companies after the crisis generated by the COVID-19 pandemic is not possible with "ad hoc" responses (Pedersen & Ritter, 2020); (b) there are necessary solutions and mechanisms carefully prepared, and we consider that the managerial synapse could represent such a mechanism. We argue this statement in the following sections.

The COVID-19 pandemic has emphasised the VUCA characteristics of the company context, increasing its volatility, uncertainty, complexity, and ambiguity. We are moving into an era of exponential change (Chima & Gutman, 2020). The COVID-19 pandemic has negatively influenced the relationships between the company and many of its internal and external stakeholders. Relationships and collaboration between companies and its employees (managers and consultants) are under pressure because of the practice of working from home, telework, working online, and working in conditions of limited human contact, interrelations, and direct communication. Relationships and collaboration with external stakeholders, especially consultants, trainers, designers, customers, suppliers, intermediaries, and local communities, have been reduced or even suspended. In these conditions, the **managerial synapse is one possible solution to restore and better develop relationships with many company stakeholders.** There are several reasons that support our assertion:

- The managerial synapse is based on the win-win approach, which represents a guarantee for mutual taken into consideration of the most important interests of each stakeholder and the company.
- The managerial synapse specifies the common objectives to be fulfilled by the stakeholder and the company, which represent the right background for a long and fruitful collaboration between them.
- Intense exchange of information, knowledge, and other resources between the company and stakeholders could have a major contribution to the resolution of the complex and sometimes unexpected challenges and difficulties associated with the COVID-19 pandemic and its effects.
- Greater motivation generated by the innovative mechanism of the managerial synapse has a major positive impact on the increased cooperation and performance of each component of the synapse, either internal or external.
- The COVID-19 pandemic has changed to a certain extent many people and organizations, making them more receptive to the new elements, more flexible and cooperative, and less conservative; this represents an important change, enabling implementation of the managerial synapse.

Using the managerial synapse in the COVID-19 pandemic context will generate the positive results mentioned in the previous section, which are very consistent. Moreover, the managerial synapse will have some **immediate benefits**: rapid restoration of the company's collaboration with important external stakeholders; easier and faster access of the company to the stakeholders' knowledge and other resources; increased company stakeholder interests, efforts, and impact on the company's development and performance; acceleration of the relaunching of the companies and of the external organizational stakeholders after the pandemic; development of agility of the company management that will outlast the pandemic (Rigby, Elk, & Berez, 2020) [54]; amplification of the sustainability of the company's relationships with stakeholders; increased organizational resilience of the company; and its organizational shareholders.

In our opinion, these elements explain why the coronavirus period and post-period provide good opportunity to implement the managerial synapse, which is beneficial for both the company and its stakeholders.

Why Is the Managerial Synapse a New Revolutionary Managerial Mechanism?

At the end of this chapter, largely unexpected by its content and approach, we consider it to be necessary to highlight certain essential elements emphasizing the novelty and the revolutionary content of the managerial synapse. The arguments supporting this statement are presented in Table 5.4.

From a scientific point of view, the emergence of a new concept of managerial synapse is not only possible but even necessary. The managerial synapse represents a theorisation of the recent and deep evolutions in managerial practice in many organizations. These evolutions are based on many changes: the strengthening of the open systemic dimension of the organization; the amplified role and impact of the knowledge and information on the managerial relationships and processes; the identification and consideration of the multiple and complex motivations at the individual, group and organizational level; and the proliferation of the multidimensional managerial approaches focused on the competitivity and sustainability; VUCA challenges (Bennett & Lemoine, 2014),

Table 5.4 Why is the managerial synapse a revolutionary management concept and mechanism?

	Arguments
A.	It changes the structure of the management processes and relationships to a large extent by focusing on the manager-relevant stakeholder (internal and external) interface/relationships, instead of focusing on the classic manager-subordinate relationship.
B.	It changes the nature of the managerial process and relationship to a large extent because the manager-relevant stakeholder relationship is based on a win-win approach, which is less hierarchical and more collaborative, motivational and innovative, centred on the accomplishment of the stakeholders' joint objectives and interests.
C.	It represents a new basic management mechanism that is better able to approach and achieve the interests of the company and its relevant stakeholders, building a win-win context.
D.	It focuses on the company's stakeholders' knowledge – the most important resource in the new economy – assuring its intensive, innovative and productive knowledge-sharing, favouring open innovation (Harrison & van der Laan Smith, 2015; Bogers, Chesbrough, & Moedas, 2018).
E.	It valorizes the potential of the internal relevant stakeholder – managers, employees, shareholders – to a higher level by establishing mutual win-win objectives, more harmonised decisions, actions, and behaviours, and much more motivation for effort, creativity and performance.
F.	It valorizes environmental opportunities much better by generating higher motivation and involvement of the company's external relevant stakeholders in its activities.
G.	It faces environmental threads more effectively, with external and internal relevant stakeholders' contributions.
H.	It generates higher and multidimensional performances for the company and its relevant stakeholders in a sustainable way, taking into consideration VUCA contextual elements, which are quickly increasing in this period of digital revolution (Brown & Dillard, 2015).

opportunities and threads for company, etc. The managerial synapse expresses the essential mutations produced at the managerial relationships and processes level and the appearance of the innovative managerial mechanism which is more complex, more motivational and more performant than the traditional, multimillenary subordinate–manager relationship.

The managerial synapse, where information, knowledge, decisions, actions, and behaviours take a new configuration that generates higher functionality and performance, is emerging as a new field of research, which should be analysed and developed further in the coming years. Our study represents just one initial scientific undertaking from this perspective.

From a pragmatic point of view, managerial synapses are essential for the functionality, performance, and sustainability of the modern organization. Management practice over recent decades has provided numerous examples of the utility, effectiveness and efficiency of stakeholders taken into consideration by the organization's management, and of their capacity to generate sustainable competitive advantages. Customer relationship management (CRM) and the supply chain management (SCM) are used successfully in thousands and thousands of companies in many countries. Concomitantly, the development of human resource management (HRM) has demonstrated how productive and innovative the people in organizations can be if they are approached in new constructive and stimulative ways.

For this reason, in many organizations, and more frequently in multinational companies and large enterprises, an intensive use of the stakeholder relationship has become a major component of the organization's management. Managerial synapses offer a solid scientific background for better valorisation of relevant stakeholders – customers, suppliers, employees, managers, investors, and others – using a specific approach, professionally designed, and differentiated for each category of relevant stakeholder. The new managerial mechanism represented by managerial synapses is a crucial element for the organization's increased functionality and performance in a volatile, uncertain, complex, and ambiguous environment in the context of COVID-19 pandemic.

In order to accelerate and to amplify the valorization of the theoretical and methodological elements associated with the managerial synapse, frequent and consistent actions are recommended that are focused on dissemination, training, mentoring, coaching, and tutoring at the level of universities, consulting organizations, companies, employers' organizations, and trade unions, which represent the main knowledge intermediaries in this period of transition to a knowledge-based economy. They should be used by taking into consideration that management simultaneously represents a science and an art, combining resources, activities, and relationships to achieve certain objectives and to obtain sustainable performance in the organization.

Note

1 We mention that other specialists – Weitzner, D., & Deutsch, Y. (2015). Understanding motivation and social influence in stakeholder prioritization. *Organization Studies, 36*(10), 1337–1360. doi:10.1177/0170840615585340 – have renounced to salient approach and have proposed to focus on the prioritization, recognizing that the most important decisions makers are not limited to those found within the classic boundaries of the firm.

References

Adler, P., Heckscher, C., & Prusak, L. (2011). Building a collaborative enterprise. *Harvard Business Review, 89*(7/8), 94–101.

Amit, R., & Zott, C. (2001). Value creation in e-business. *Strategic Management Journal, 22*(6–7), 493–520. doi:10.1002/smj.187

Anand, N., & Barsoux, J. L. (2017). What everyone gets wrong about change management. *Harvard Business Review, 95*(6), 78–85.

Andon, P., Baxter, J., & Chua W. F. (2015). Accounting for stakeholders and making accounting useful. *Journal of Management Studies, 52*(7), 986–1002. doi:10.1111/joms.12142

Bailey, A., Reeves, M., Whitaker, K., & Hutchinson, R. (2019, April 5). *The company of the future – Winning the '20s*. Retrieved from https://www.bcg.com/publications/2019/company-of-the-future.aspx

Bassett, M. (2008, November 25). *Stakeholder trust: A competitive strategy*. Report to the Conference Board of Canada. Retrieved from https://www.conferenceboard.ca/e-library/abstract.aspx?did=2798

Benkler, Y. (2011). The unselfish gene. *Harvard Business Review, 89*(7–8), 76–85.

Bennett, N., & Lemoine, G. J. (2014). What VUCA really means for you. *Harvard Business Review, 92*(1/2), 27–28.

Bogers, M., Chesbrough, H., & Moedas, C. (2018) Open innovation: Research, practices, and policies. *California Management Review, 60*(2), 5–16. doi:10.1177/0008125617745086

Bosse, D. A., Phillips, R. A., & Harrison, J. S. (2009). Stakeholders, reciprocity, and firm performance. *Strategic Management Journal, 30*(4), 447–456. doi:10.1002/smj.743

Bowman, C., & Ambrosini, V. (2000). Value creation versus value capture: Towards a coherent definition of value in strategy. *British Journal of Management, 11*(1), 1–15. doi:10.1111/1467-8551.00147

Boyd, R., & Richerson, P. J. (1988). *Culture and evolutionary process*. Chicago, IL: The University Chicago Press.

Brandenburger, A. M., & Stuart Jr., H. W. (1996). Value-based business strategy. *Journal of Economics & Management Strategy, 5*(1), 5–24. doi:10.1111/j.1430-9134.1996.00005.x

Brown, J., & Dillard, J. (2015). Dialogic accountings for stakeholders: On opening up and closing down participatory governance. *Journal of Management Studies, 52*(7), 961–985. doi:10.1111/joms.12153

Bundy, J., Vogel, R. M., & Zachary, M. A. (2018). Organization–stakeholder fit: A dynamic theory of cooperation, compromise, and conflict between an organization and its stakeholders. *Strategic Management Journal*, *39*(2), 476–501. doi:10.1002/smj.2736

Cardwell, L. A., Williams, S., & Pyle, A. (2016). Corporate public relations dynamics: Internal vs. external stakeholders and the role of the practitioner. *Public Relations Review*, *43*(1), 152–162. doi:10.1016/j.pubrev.2016.11.004

Chima, A., & Gutman, R. (2020). What it takes to lead through an era of exponential change. *Harvard Business Review*. Retrieved from https://hbr.org/2020/10/what-it-takes-to-lead-through-an-era-of-exponential-change

Choi, J., & Wang, H. (2009). Stakeholder relations and the persistence of corporate financial performance. *Strategic Management Journal*, *30*(8), 895–907. doi:10.1002/smj.759

Conner, T. W. (2017). Exploring the diverse effects of stakeholder engagement on organizational performance. *The American Review of Public Administration*, *47*(6), 634–647. doi:10.1177/0275074015618785

Crane, A., Graham, C., & Himick, D. (2015). Financializing stakeholder claims. *Journal of Management Studies*, *52*(7), 878–906. doi:10.1111/joms.12147

Dorobantu, S., & Odziemkowska, K. (2017). Valuing stakeholder governance: Property rights, community mobilization, and firm value. *Strategic Management Journal*, *38*(13), 2682–2703. doi:10.1002/smj.2675

Dutton, J. E., Roberts, L. M., & Bednar, J. (2010). Pathways for positive identity construction at work: Four types of positive identity and the building of social resources. *Academy of Management Review*, *35*(2), 265–293. doi:10.5465/amr.35.2.zok265

Emmens, B., & Thomson, P. (2017). Organizational culture, and the impact of the digital overload. In P. Thomson, M. Johnson, & J. M. Devlin (Eds.), *Conquering digital overload: Leadership strategies that build engaging work cultures* (pp. 39–51). Cham: Palgrave Macmillan. doi:10.1007/978-3-319-63799-0_4

Freeman, R. E., Harrison, J. S., Wicks, A. C., Parmar, B. L., & De Colle, S. (2010). *Stakeholder theory: The state of art*. New York: Cambridge University Press.

Garcia-Castro, R., & Aguilera, R. V. (2015). Incremental value creation and appropriation in a world with multiple stakeholders. *Strategic Management Journal*, *36*(1), 137–147. doi:10.1002/smj.2241

Garrov, V., & Varney, S. (2015). *Organisation design in a VUCA World: A paper from HR in a disorder world: IES perspectives on HR 2015*. Retrieved from http://www.employment-studies.co.uk/system/files/resources/files/mp105.pdf

Giorgi, S. (2017). The mind and heart of resonance: The role of cognition and emotions in frame effectiveness. *Journal of Management Studies*, *54*(5), 711–738. doi:10.1111/joms.12278

Groysberg, B., Lee, J., Price, J., & Cheng, J. (2018). The leader's guide to corporate culture: How to manage the eight critical elements of organizational life. *Harvard Business Review*, *96*(1), 44–52. Retrieved from https://hbr.org/2018/01/the-leaders-guide-to-corporate-culture

Hamel, G. (2009). Moon shots for management. *Harvard Business Review*, *87*(2), 91–98.

Harrison, J. S., Bosse, D. A., & Phillips, R. A. (2010). Managing for stakeholders, stakeholder utility functions and competitive advantage. *Strategic Management Journal*, *31*(1), 58–74. doi:10.1002/smj.801

Harrison, J. S., & van der Laan Smith, J. (2015). Responsible accounting for stakeholders. *Journal of Management Studies*, *52*(7), 935–960. doi:10.1111/joms.12141

Harrison, J. S., & Wicks, A. (2013). Stakeholder theory, value and firm performance. *Business Ethics Quarterly*, *23*(1), 97–124. doi:10.5840/beq20132314

Hillman, A. J., & Keim, G. D. (2001). Shareholder value, stakeholder management, and social issues: What's the bottom line? *Strategic Management Journal*, *22*(2), 125–139. doi:10.1002/1097-0266(200101)22:2<125::AID-SMJ150>3.0.CO;2-H

Kenny, G. (2014). Five questions to identify key stakeholders. *Harvard Business Review*. Retrieved from https://hbr.org/2014/03/five-questions-to-identify-key-stakeholders

Lelea, M. A., Roba, G. M., Christinck, A., & Kaufmann, B. (2016). "All relevant stakeholders": A literature review of stakeholder analysis to support inclusivity of innovation processes in farming and food systems. *Proceedings of 12th European International Farming Systems Association Symposium*, 1–10, Newport, UK. Retrieved from https://www.researchgate.net/publication/305468708_All_relevant_stakeholders_a_literature_review_of_stakeholder_analysis_to_support_inclusivity_of_innovation_processes_in_farming_and_food_systems

Lepak, D. P., Smith, K. G., & Taylor, M. S. (2007). Value creation and value capture: A multilevel perspective. *Academy of Management Review*, *32*(1), 180–194. doi:10.5465/amr.2007.23464011

Matuleviciene, M., & Stravinskiene, J. (2015). Identifying the factors of stakeholder trust: A theoretical study. *Procedia – Social and Behavioral Sciences*, *213*, 599–604. doi:10.1016/j.sbspro.2015.11.456

Mayer, R. C., Davis, J. H., & Schoorman, F. D. (1995). An integrative model of organizational trust. *Academy of Management Review*, *20*(3), 709–734. doi:10.5465/amr.1995.9508080335

Mitchell, R. K., Agle, B. R., & Wood, D. J. (1997). Toward a theory of stakeholders identification and salience: Defining the principle of who and what really counts. *Academy of Management Review*, *22*(4), 853–886. Retrieved from https://www.jstor.org/stable/259247?seq=1#metadata_info_tab_contents. doi:10.2307/259247

Mitchell, R. K., Van Buren, H. J., Greenwood M., & Freeman, R. E. (2015). Stakeholder inclusion and accounting for stakeholders. *Journal of Management Studies*, *52*(7), 851–877. doi:10.1111/joms.12151

Nowak, M. A. (2006). *Evolutionary dynamics*. Cambridge, MA: Harvard Business Press.

Pedersen, C. L., & Ritter, T. (2020). Preparing your business for a post-pandemic world. *Harvard Business Review*. Retrieved from https://hbr.org/2020/04/preparing-your-business-for-a-post-pandemic-world

Pirson, M., & Malhotra, D. (2008). Unconventional insights for managing stakeholder trust. *MIT Sloan Management Review*. Retrieved from https://sloanreview.mit.edu/article/unconventional-insights-for-managing-stakeholder-trust/

Priem, R. L., Krause, R., Tantalo, C., & McFadyen, A. (2019). Promoting long-term shareholder value by "competing" for essential stakeholders: A new, multi-sided market logic for top managers. *Academy of Management Perspectives*. Retrieved from https://journals.aom.org/doi/abs/10.5465/amp.2018.0048. doi:10.5465/amp.2018.0048

Priston, M., Martin, K., & Parmer, B. (2017). Formation of stakeholder trust in business and the role of personal values. *Journal of Business Ethics*, *145*(1), 1–20. doi:10.1007/s10551-015-2839-2

Repenning, N. P., Kieffer, D., & Astor, T. (2017). The most underrated skill in management. *MIT Sloan Management Review*, *58*(3), 39–48.

Rigby, D. K., Elk, S., & Berez, S. (2020). Develop agility that outlasts the pandemic. *Harvard Business Review*. Retrieved from https://hbr.org/2020/05/develop-agility-that-outlasts-the-pandemic

Sanner, B., & Bunderson, J. S. (2018). The truth about hierarchy. *MIT Sloan Management Review*. Retrieved from https://sloanreview.mit.edu/article/the-truth-about-hierarchy/

Schnackenberg, A. K., & Tomlinson, E. C. (2016). Organizational transparency: A new perspective on managing trust in organization-stakeholder relationships. *Journal of Management*, *42*(7), 1784–1810. doi:10.1177/0149206314525202

Schwaiger, M. (2004). Components and parameters of corporate reputation: An empirical study. *Schmalenbach Business Review* *56*, 46–71. doi:10.1007/BF03396685

Schwarz, T. (2018). Create a growth culture, not a performance-obsessed one. *Harvard Business Review*, *96*(2). Retrieved from https://hbr.org/2018/03/create-a-growth-culture-not-a-performance-obsessed-one

Sucher, S. J., & Gupta, S. (2019). The trust crisis. *Harvard Business Review*. Retrieved from https://hbr.org/cover-story/2019/07/the-trust-crisis

Tulberg, J. (2013). Stakeholder theory: Some revisionist suggestions. *The Journal of the Socio-Economics*, *42*, 127–135. doi:10.1016/j.socec.2012.11.014

Van der Merwe, A. W. A. J., & Puth, G. (2014). Towards a conceptual model of the relationship between corporate trust and corporate reputation. *Corporate Reputation Review*, *17*(2), 138–156. doi:10.1057/crr.2014.4

Wallpach, S., Voyer, B., Kastanakis, M., & Mühlbacher, H. (2017). Co-creating stakeholder and brand identities: Introduction to the special section. *Journal of Business Research*, *70*, 395–398. doi:10.1016/j.jbusres.2016.08.028

6 Building of the Managerial Synapse

Main Variables Influencing the Managerial Synapse

Managerial synapse construction, work, functioning, and performance are influenced by many variables (see Figure 6.1), which can be divided into two categories:

a **Direct variables,** whose parameters have a straightforward and major influence on the elements associated with the managerial synapse. They can be separated, taking into consideration their appurtenance, into two groups:

  - Organizational variables, referring to the company involved and – if another relevant stakeholder of the managerial synapse is from an outside entity – to its organization. Hence, in a managerial synapse, it is mandatory to be involved in at least the variables concerning one organization – the company involved;
  - Individual variables, reflecting the characteristics of the people who are acting as relevant stakeholders in the managerial synapse from the company or from the other organization. In a managerial synapse, we always have two sets of individual variables, one for each component.

b **Indirect variables,** which reflect the elements of the environment in which the company and – if such is the case – the other organization with a component in the managerial synapse are integrated. Indirect variables influence the building, work and performance of the managerial synapse mainly through providing – or not – enabling contextual conditions. Usually, the impact of indirect variables on the managerial synapse is smaller than the influence of the direct variables. In certain circumstances – like the crisis generated by the COVID-19 pandemic – the impact of this category of variables could be substantial.

In Figure 6.1, we include the direct and indirect variables that, in our opinion, usually influence, and with substantial intensity, a managerial

DOI: 10.4324/9781003217701-6

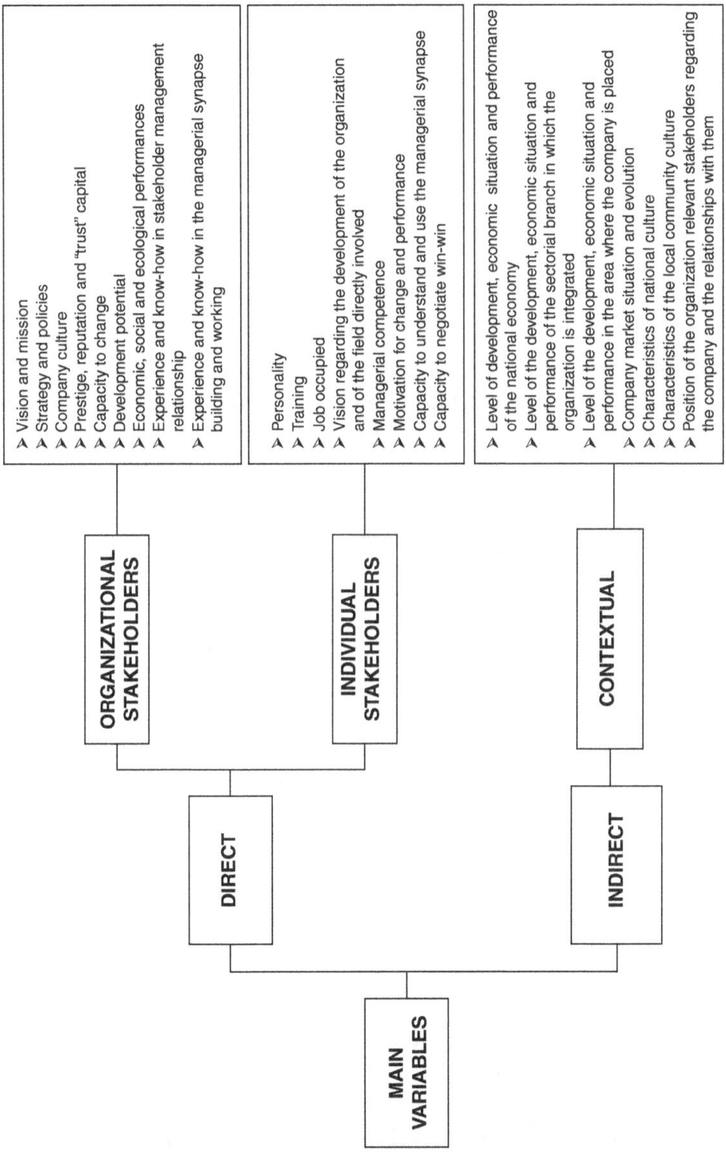

Figure 6.1 Main variables influencing the managerial synapse (building, working, and performances).

synapse. Of course, in special situations, some of these variables could be less relevant and/or other variables, not included in our framework, could have a major influence on the managerial synapse.

The framework with the main variables impacting the managerial synapse could be very helpful, especially at the beginning of building and using the managerial synapses in the company. Also, these variables can contribute to the higher valorization of the huge potential for development and performance increasing of managerial synapse.

The management of the company, together with the individual managers, components of the managerial synapses, should evaluate carefully these variables, in order to valorize their positive characteristics and impact and to avoid and/or reduce the negative aspects regarding the variables. It is recommended that the indirect variables and the organizational variables should be evaluated at the level of the company, and the results used in all managerial synapses. Evaluation of the individual variables should be done at the level of each managerial synapse.

Approaches and Premises in the Managerial Synapse Construction

The managerial synapse, which represents a specific managerial mechanism, in order to be performant, should be constructed using a specific approach that is able to take into consideration its specific particularities, and the company and its relevant stakeholders' strategies and policies.

There are **two ways of approaching the building of a managerial synapse:**

a The construction of the managerial synapse by itself, considering that it is an autonomous entity, connected to other components of the company utilizing the usual type of managerial processes and relationships;
b The construction of the managerial synapse treated as a basic component of the stakeholder management-based system of the company, which is developed, concomitantly, within a comprehensive holistic designing of the entire organization.

We will use the first approach because the building of a managerial synapse as such, as distinct from the other managerial settings, contains the essential elements involved in the case of the second option for its building.

Construction of the managerial synapse is based on **three premises** (see Figure 6.2).

Building a managerial synapse means more than constructing a managerial mechanism. It **means developing a specific multidimensional**

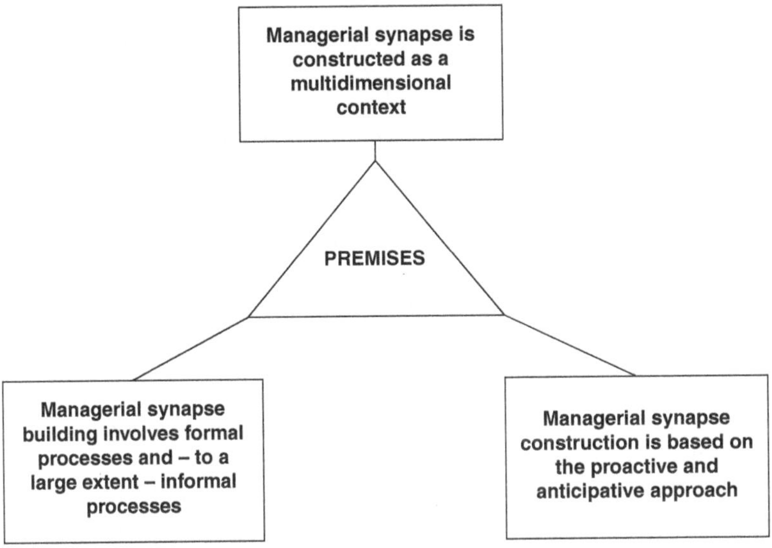

Figure 6.2 Premises for building performant managerial synapse.

context focused on the synapse managerial area. This context is a precondition in order to generate consistent synergy for both components of the synapse and for the company. In fact, increasing the contextual approach in organizations represents a general trend (Johns, 2017), both in social science and in business and managerial praxis.

The design of the managerial synapse should be based on **anticipative and proactive thinking and analysis.** Characteristics of the managerial synapse should be designed and implemented so as to be able to satisfy the challenges and the requirements of the company and relevant stakeholders in the next period. Such an approach makes the managerial synapse not only performant in the next period but also sustainable in the long run.

Construction of the managerial synapse **involves both formal and informal processes.** The essential managerial elements of the synapse – common objectives, main tasks, competences and responsibilities, major methods and techniques to be used, resources allocated, and performance evaluation criteria – should be defined from the beginning by the list of objectives and goals, job description, budgets, list of methods and techniques, etc. The formalized design should determine only the essential elements for each managerial synapse. In order to enhance the innovative approach, flexibility, and entrepreneurial spirit, it is necessary for the many details involved in the managerial synapse to be determined informally, by both components, valorizing their creativity, initiative and desire to be very competitive.

An essential element in the managerial synapse construction is the establishment of joint stakeholders' objectives and/or goals, starting from the company's core mission. There are mainly **three models** that could be used:

- **SMART model of setting objectives**, classical, developed and used in management by objectives (MBO system) (Drucker, 1954; Odiorne, 1965). According to this model, the objectives to be achieved in a company, part of a company, or at the level of an individual component should be specific, measurable, agreed, realistic, and time bounded. The SMART model has been used with very good results, especially in industrial companies, where the production activities have been predominant. The management by objectives system and SMART objectives approach started to be less frequently used at the end of the last century, when creative, innovational and qualitative processes became decisive for performance, and when the information revolution, and later the knowledge revolution, occurred.
- **Process-centred objectives model**, which emerged in the last quarter of the twentieth century in order to overcome the limits of the SMART model. The approach is based on the establishment of a hierarchy of goals, for entire companies, teams, and individuals. The processes are focused on describing each task that an individual manager or executant has to carry out and on establishing operating standards for which individual objectives are determined. This model has been used successfully in the well-known Total Quality Management and Continue Improvement Management Systems (Creech, 1994; Juran, 1995), favouring to a large extent the discovery of weaknesses and errors, and transforming them into opportunities for improvement and development, in spite of the notable bureaucracy involved.
- **Contingency model of objectives**, proposed recently by Manning (2017), which tries to cumulate the advantages of the previous two models and reduce their limits. Essentially, this model divides the tasks to be fulfilled into two categories:
    - clear and straightforward tasks, for which the SMART objectives model is used;
    - complex, ambiguous and changeable tasks, for which an approach based mainly on the process-centred objectives model is used.

There are three stages of the contingent objectives setting: work out the level of straightforwardness or of complexity of the tasks at hand; work out the best type of objectives for the task at hand and level of complexity expected to be encountered; and agree between the manager and stakeholders a set of contingent objectives and goals and how to measure and describe their achievement.

The competitive advantages of this model are:

- the possibility of taking into account the level of complexity, ambiguity, and change inherent to a task, which favours innovative, flexible, and entrepreneurial individual and team actions and behaviours; this type of process is more frequent in the last period of the transition to the knowledge-based economy and digital economy;
- the possibility of getting the maximum results from the straightforward tasks, using mainly the SMART objectives model;
- the possibility of allowing managers and executants to change the nature of the objectives-setting processes, in order to fit to the tasks they should achieve, which, in the present VUCA environment, change quite often.

In the establishment of the objectives of each managerial synapse, one of the three models presented should be chosen. The most suitable model is quite probably the contingency model of objectives. Of course, major attention should be paid to the specificity of the relevant stakeholder involved in the synapse, especially when he(she) is from outside the company.

In Table 6.1, we present an indicative guide regarding the type of objective model setting in the most frequent types of managerial synapse.

Concomitantly with the determination of the joint objectives, it is necessary for both components of the managerial synapse to collaborate, in order to determine the criteria of the evaluation of the objectives fulfilment. Knowing the evaluation criteria from the beginning of the managerial synapse building will increase the stakeholders' motivation to achieve the joint goals and objectives, and the chance of long-run performances and sustainability.

In the setting of the joint goals and objectives using win-win negotiation, the type of relation between the relevant stakeholders should be taken into consideration (Brown, Gianiodis, & Santoro, 2017) in forming the managerial synapse. There **are mainly two types of relationships within a managerial synapse:**

- cooperative relationships;
- co-opetition relationships, which means concomitantly relationships of cooperation, but also relationships of competition between both managerial synapse components.

In the case of exclusive cooperative relationships between components of a managerial synapse, the establishment of joint goals, objectives, and expectations is easier and faster.

Table 6.1 The use of the model's objectives settings for the different types of managerial synapse

No.	*Managerial Synapse Type*[1]	*SMART Objectives Model*	*Process-Centred Objectives Model*	*Convergence Objectives Model*	*Observations*
1.	Company manager – employee	x	x	x	Depends on the type of tasks involved
2.	Company manager – client	x		x	
3.	Company manager – supplier	x			
4.	Company top management body – company manager	x	x	x	Depends on the type of activities of the manager
5.	Company top management body – company shareholder	x		x	
6.	Company top management body – company outside investor	x			Depends on the type of investment
7.	Company manager – banker	x			Depends on the type of activities involved
8.	Company manager – consultant		x	x	
9.	Company manager – trainer		x		
10.	Company manager – researcher		x		
11.	Company manager – designer		x	x	Depends on the type of activities involved
12.	Company manager – local community		x	x	Depends on the type of goals and/or activities involved

In the case of co-opetition relationships, the negotiation is more complicated and difficult because, as well as the common goals, objectives, and expectations, there are divergent or even opposite goals, objectives, and expectations. In such a situation, the successful finalization of the negotiation depends on the importance for each synapse component of the cooperative goals, objectives, and expectations compared with the different or opposite goals, objectives, and expectations. If the first category is more important for both parts – and usually it should be – the capacity to make a compromise for each part is essentially in order to determine joint, feasible, and performant goals and objectives for the managerial synapse.

The approaches presented by us in this section generate the best results when the company is truly a purpose-driven organization, which is based on the management logic of purpose. Fulfilment of personal purposes within organizational purposes is the essence of truly purpose-driven organizations (Rey, Velasco, & Almandoz, 2019). A managerial synapse represents a mechanism that is able to implement this innovative vision.

Stakeholders' Win-Win Negotiation Based on Multifaceted Motivation

In the achievement of a managerial synapse, a **crucial role is played by the negotiation between the two parties – the company manager and the inside or outside organization relevant stakeholder**. Negotiation is a form of social exchange where the negotiators seek to reach an agreement with the other party. It involves, concomitantly, processes of competing and cooperating between the persons involved. Negotiation is dual-purpose, because it consists of both bargaining and problem solving (Bridoux, Coeurderoy, & Durand, 2017).

In our opinion, the negotiation between stakeholders, in order to construct and implement a performant managerial synapse, should be based on the following **premises regarding the individual motivation:**

a **Motivations of the people involved in the negotiation are of multiple natures.** According to the heterogeneity theory of motivation (Hahn, 2015; Ingerson, DeTienne, & Liljenquist, 2015; Olekalns & Druckman, 2014), "human motivation" does not only individualistically conform to the instrumentalism philosophy (Cheng, Huang, & Su, 2017) and practice – which is still predominant today. Very few people are 100% individualistic, focusing only on their self-interests, without paying attention to the needs and interest of family members, friends, organizations, fellows, local community, etc. Concomitantly, very few people are 100% altruistic, not caring at all about their own needs and interests and only focusing on the interests of other people, organizations, communities, etc. Without any doubt, the majority of people – if not all – have mixed motivations, both individualistic and altruistic of course, varying from one person to other, and from one period to another.

b **Motivations are different to a large extent from one person to another, because of many variables**, which can be grouped into three main categories:

- **Individual** – character, education, past experience, health, human models taken into consideration, personal standard of living, etc.
- **Organizational** – company strategies and policies, organizational culture, company manager type (participative, authoritarian, mix), managerial leadership, motivational methods and techniques used, human resources management utilized, etc. Organizational variables refer to the company in which the relevant stakeholder is working and to the partner organization, in the case that the second component of the managerial synapse represents another organization (supplier, investor, client, etc.).
- **Social** – community, territorial and national culture, characteristics of the education and training system, ecological movements, social degree of bureaucracy and corruption, country economic-social development, etc.

All these variables – and not only them – influence the intensity and the structure of the individualistic and altruistic motivations of every person.

c **There are many approaches to be utilized in order to encourage one person to change to a certain degree the motivations and the relationships from individualistic to altruistic ones.** These approaches refer especially to the individual and organizational variables mentioned before, in the short term, and to the social variables in the medium and long term. Among these approaches, we mention: positive communication, training, mentoring, coaching, remodelling of the organization culture, change of the company motivation methods and techniques, new types of organization strategies, and policies focused on the relevant stakeholder's valorization and others.

d **Change at the level of each person of the intensity and types of motivations**, including the relation between individualistic and altruistic motivations, is reflected in the modification of his/her personal behaviours and actions, inside and outside the company. For example, the increase of stakeholders' altruistic motivations will determine more orientation toward the achievement of organizational and social goals using cooperative behaviour and actions, and sharing more intensive their own knowledge and other assets, etc.

e **The negotiation approach in the company should be differentiated according to:**

- Stakeholder category (customers, suppliers, employees, etc.), bearing in mind that each of them has specific types of interests and dominant characteristics of work processes, which make certain specific elements in the negotiation necessary.
- Each relevant stakeholder category has certain strengths and vulnerabilities to consider, in order to get positive results.
- Each individual stakeholder, from every stakeholder category, presents many particular features, interests, approaches, expectations and motivations. Knowing and taking them into consideration is very helpful in order to achieve win-win negotiations.

These five premises indicate that the negotiation between the two relevant stakeholders involved in the managerial synapse might be and should be win-win. Also, they provide many useful elements for the achievement of the win-win negotiation faster, more easily and in a more performant manner. In order to do so, the negotiation with stakeholders **should be reconceptualized.** There are **several ways recommended by specialists to achieve this.** We will briefly present two of them, which are similar in some respects.

The first is **reconceptualization of negotiation focusing more on mediation** (Mehta & Ripol, 2017). Managers and other stakeholders need to replace the classical negotiation, where the win is achieved usually in the form of forcing the other party to accept something of lesser value, with negotiation based on mediation. In this type of negotiation, the company manager and the other relevant stakeholder involved have to see beyond positions and numbers to get what really matters the most. Each participant should have and use a mediator mindset, which facilitates mutual understanding and harmonization of objectives, decisions and actions. For the development of successful negotiation – win-win negotiation based on mediation – it is essential to know the main obstacles, and the techniques to be used in order to overcome them. In Table 6.2, we present a sample of these elements, very well identified by Mehta and Ripol (2017).

Ingerson, DeTienne, and Liljenquist (2015) documented very well another way to reconceptualize negotiation – a **relational approach to negotiation.** They formulated this new approach after profound analysis of instrumentalism, revealing, besides its merits, many serious limitations: extremely selfish approach, cynical interpretation of people's behaviour, disproportionate focus on easily quantified outcomes, usually economic ones, marginalization of the relational and other non-quantified outcomes, pursuit of economic gains at the expense of relational gains, etc.

Relational negotiations are characterized by strong rationality. This means, according to Slife and Wiggins (2009), "the most reality of the

Table 6.2 Major obstacles in company management negotiation, ways and techniques to overcome them

No.	*Obstacles Category*	*Main Obstacles*	*Ways and Techniques to Overcome*
1.	Differences in perceptions of each party regarding:	• Lack of relevant information • The merits of each party's respective position • The risks	• Get basic information regarding your partner before starting negotiations • Exchange information and seek help in interpreting it • Ask for help in interpreting the information • See the strengths of each other's arguments • See the weaknesses of each other's arguments • Anticipate the consequences of not reaching an agreement
2.	Cognitive aspects	• Lack of relevant knowledge • Selective interpretation • Overconfidence • Unrealistic expectations • Lack of interest in the perspective or interest of the other party • Lack of confidence • Loss aversion • Distrust the other party's offers	• Utilize rigorous criteria to analyse arguments/positions • Focus on the weaknesses of your own arguments/positions and the strengths of the other's • Emphasize the benefits of reaching an agreement • Pursue mutually beneficial objectives • Frame offers and concessions in positive, optimistic terms • Be transparent
3.	Emotions and feelings	• Different personalities involved • Feeling the need to vindicate yourself • Negative emotions (anger, frustration, envy, guilt, embarrassment)	• Open with informal discussion • Encourage parties to openly express their feelings • Take the other party's feelings into account • Try to soften the impact of both parties' emotional concerns • Be constructive
4.	Strategic barriers	• Differences between personal and organizational strategies and tactics • Unwillingness to negotiate	• Inform on the organization strategies and tactics • Keep the negotiations period short and sweet • Demand commitment to the process

(*Continued*)

Table 6.2 (Continued)

No.	*Obstacles Category*	*Main Obstacles*	*Ways and Techniques to Overcome*
		• Entrenched positions • Unaligned interests	• Ensure the presence of people with decision-making capacity • Make and demand offers • Identify the other party's intentions and try to clarify ambiguous moves • Warn the other party about the impact of their chosen action on the negotiation • Reformulate the other party's positions • Generate ideas and creative solutions to conflict • Avoid confrontation • Use a win-win approach

Adapted from five ways managers can enhance their mediating skills, by K. Mehta & I. Ripol, 2017, (p. 55), IESE Insight Business Knowledge

work is relationship. Things, events and places are not first self-contained entities – already and always related one to another". As a result, the best way to see an individual is in context, and strong relationality can be used to reframe the negotiation.

A relational approach to negotiation generates many advantages, such as: it enhances perspective-taking ability, increases cooperation, reduces a sinister approach, stimulates creative processes, takes more care of the counterpart's emotions, increases the desire to work together in the future, etc. (Cheng, Huang, & Su, 2017; Ingerson, DeTienne, & Liljenquist, 2015; Slife & Wiggins, 2009).

All elements presented are arguments in order to change in practice, in companies' stakeholder managerial synapse, from the paradigm promoted by instrumentalism – **"competitive approach" – to the new paradigm, "cooperative or distributive approach"**, which is able to satisfy the needs and interests of both relevant stakeholders. The success of using the cooperative paradigm depends heavily on company managers' ability to adopt a relational approach in the negotiation and – to a large degree – on the other relevant stakeholder adoption of the negotiation paradigm.

In the case of a relevant outside company stakeholder, before the negotiation process, it **could be useful to use the** recently introduced new approach known as "**shaking stakeholders**" (Sulkowski, Edwards, & Freeman, 2018). This means proactively initiating cooperation with stakeholders affected by the company, to alter awareness behaviour and networks so as to catalyse change in society and the marketplace, to reward co-creating innovation in the core operation of the company that improves social and environmental impacts. Shaking stakeholders is helpful in initiating and developing win-win negotiation and performant collaboration with relevant stakeholders and in constructing a successful managerial synapse.

Win-win negotiation, based on the multifaceted motivation of the relevant stakeholders involved, has a determinant impact on the managerial synapse construction, work and performance.

Strong Motivation Content and Engagement of the Managerial Synapse Components

A managerial synapse is **one of the most motivational managerial mechanisms** that can be used in a company today. The **main arguments** are as follows:

- managerial synapse objectives, common to both components, are determined by win-win negotiations. This means that the manager and the relevant stakeholder are very strongly motivated to decide, act and behave – each and together – to accomplish the synapse objectives at a very high level;
- targets to be fulfilled by manager and relevant stakeholder are formulated together, taking into consideration common objectives, also using win-win negotiations. Therefore, each synapse component accomplishes the undertaken and desirable work processes, which correspond to individual preferences, expectations and capabilities;
- setting by direct win-win negotiation of the common objectives and tasks, provides the necessary premise, that starting from the beginning of the managerial synapse, to decide the evaluation criteria for the manager and the stakeholder performances. This approach higher motivate them. Such an approach has a positive impact both on the work processes content and on the intense motivation for effort, creativity, and performance;
- in the designing of the managerial synapse, the synapse area is determined, characterized by intense dialogic communication, reciprocity, collaboration, and cooperation, elements that contribute greatly to further motivating the managerial synapse components and, simultaneously, providing better conditions for intense efforts and creativity, favouring the increase of individual and organizational performance;
- in the managerial synapse construction and work, we can use new approaches – like meaningful work, positive identity or agile work – capable of facilitating the design and accomplishment of certain

work processes congruent with the manager and relevant stakeholder's personality and characteristics. This facilitates and enhances the flexible and innovative work processes progress, which is able to generate not only better results, but also a positive attitude and multiple satisfactions, determined by the strong implication of the managerial synapse constituencies;

- a managerial synapse, through all of its characteristics, represents a stimulative work environment for greater efforts and creativity, an environment enabling the better use and valorification of the managerial synapse components' qualities, in order to fulfil the common objectives negotiated.

The above-presented elements, while not exhaustive, demonstrate the high motivational content of the managerial synapse. In this context, we specify that it is recommended to use a comprehensive set of motivations – general and specific – aimed at increasing the manager and relevant stakeholder's intense employment of their qualities, growth potential, work efforts and the contextual conditions. In Table 6.3, we propose a set of such comprehensive elements using **the orientative goals-motivation matrix**. The matrix incorporates two categories of elements grouped in **two lists:**

- a list with the most frequent goals to be achieved in the organizations by the employees. These goals are the background for the determination of the joint concrete objectives for managerial synapse components;
- a list with a set of approaches and tools used in performant companies in order to motivate the employees. This list facilitates the construction of a very powerful incentives system for the managerial synapse components, taking into consideration the fact that stakeholders are multifaceted, dealing with intrinsic and extrinsic motivations. We have selected the motivational tools and approaches from the best practices used in European and North American companies.

The matrix represents a general framework that should be adapted to the conditions of each company – organizational culture or subcultures, general strategy and policies, the human resources management practised in the organization, etc. In the matrix, only the motivational approaches and tools that are in line with the company's motivational approach should remain. A list with the motivational approaches should be analysed and defined by the human resources department, with the approval of the company's top management. This is a very good opportunity for the company to diversify and to enrich the motivational approaches and tools used in the organization. For the company's competitivity and sustainability, it is essential that the organization rewards long-term performance and tolerates early failures (Harrison & Wicks, 2013).

Table 6.3 Orientative goals – motivations matrix

GOAL TYPE	FREQUENT MOTIVATIONAL APPROACHES AND TOOLS																									
	CAR-EER PLAN	TASK FEED-BACK	SIMP-LE "TH-ANK YOU"	WAG-E RISE	BON-USES	PRO-FIT SHA-RING	STO-CK OPTI-ONS	INTE-RNET FAM-OUS[2]	THA-NK-ING EMP-LO-YEE[3]	TRO-PHY	PUBLIC APPRE-CIAT-ION OF WORK WELL DONE	FLEX-IBLE WOR-K SCHE-DULE	OPP-ORT-UNIT-IES FOR ADV-ANC-EM-ENT	GIVI-NG TIME OFF	APPR-ECIA-TION GIFTS	VOU-CH-ERS TAN-GI-BLE GOA-LS[4]	COM-PANY PART-Y AND CELE-BRAT-ION	UPG-RADE WOR-KPL-ACE	COM-PAN-Y-PAID FAMI-LY ACTI-VITY EVE-NTS	FAMI-LY SUPP-ORT PRO-GRA-MME	OPP-ORT-UN-ITY TO WOR-K FRO-M HOM-E	LEAR-NING AND DEV-ELO-PING OPP-ORT-UNIT-IES[5]	PRO-MOT-ION	FIN-ANC-IAL PEN-ALT-IES	MOR-AL SAN-CTI-ONS	OVE-RALL HAPP-IN-ESS[6]
0	1	2	3	4	5	6	7	8	9	10	11	12	13	14	15	16	17	18	19	20	21	22	23	24	25	26
1. TO MAKE PRODUC-T		x	x	x	x				x		x	x	x					x					x	x	x	
2. TO INCRE-ASE PRODUC-TIVITY		x	x	x	x			x	x	x	x	x	x		x	x	x	x					x			x
3. TO SERVICE		x	x	x	x							x	x					x					x	x	x	
4. TO IMPROV-E QUALITY		x	x	x	x			x	x	x	x	x	x		x	x	x	x					x			x
5. TO DEVELOP	x	x	x	x	x			x	x	x	x	x	x		x	x	x	x					x			x
6. TO REDUCE COSTS		x	x	x	x			x	x	x	x	x	x		x	x	x	x					x			x
7. TO SUPPLY		x	x	x	x			x	x		x				x	x							x	x	x	
8. TO BUY		x	x	x	x			x	x		x				x	x							x	x	x	
9. TO SELL		x	x	x	x			x	x	x	x	x	x	x	x	x	x				x	x	x	x	x	x
10. TO STOCK		x	x						x															x	x	
11. TO CREATE NEW...		x	x	x	x	x	x	x	x	x	x	x	x	x	x	x	x	x	x	x	x	x	x			x

12. TO INNOVATE		x	x	x	x	x	x	x	x	x	x	x	x	x	x	x	x	x	x	x	x	x	x			x
13. TO DESIGN		x	x	x	x				x			x	x					x					x	x	x	
14. TO INVEST		x	x			x	x				x				x		x									x
15. TO MODERNIZE		x	x	x	x	x	x	x	x	x	x	x	x	x	x	x	x	x	x	x	x	x	x			x
16. TO BUILD		x	x	x	x				x			x	x										x	x	x	
17. TO MAINTAIN		x	x	x	x				x			x	x					x					x	x	x	
18. TO REPAIR		x	x	x	x				x			x	x										x	x	x	
19. TO TRANSPORT		x	x	x	x				x			x	x										x	x	x	
20. TO SUPPORT		x	x	x	x				x			x	x										x	x	x	
21. TO GET RESOURCES		x	x	x	x	x	x	x	x	x	x	x	x	x	x	x	x	x	x	x	x	x	x			x
22. TO INCREASE INCOME		x	x	x	x	x	x	x	x	x	x	x	x	x	x	x	x	x	x	x	x	x	x			x
23. TO HIRE		x	x	x					x		x													x	x	
24. TO TRAIN	x	x	x	x				x	x	x	x	x	x	x	x	x						x	x	x	x	
25. TO EVALUATE		x	x					x	x		x					x								x	x	
26. TO ANALYSE		x	x	x	x			x	x	x	x		x		x	x							x	x	x	
27. TO REGISTER		x	x							x	x													x	x	
28. TO ELABORATE		x	x	x	x			x	x	x	x		x		x	x							x	x	x	
29. TO COMMUNICATE		x	x					x	x	x	x				x	x								x	x	
30. TO COLABORATE WITH		x	x					x	x	x	x				x	x							x	x	x	
31. TO COOPERATE		x	x					x	x	x	x				x	x							x	x	x	

(*Continued*)

Table 6.3 (Continued)

GOAL TYPE	FREQUENT MOTIVATIONAL APPROACHES AND TOOLS																								
	CAREER PLAN	*TASK FEEDBACK*	*SIMPLE "THANK YOU"*	*WAGE RISE*	*BONUSES*	*PROFIT SHARING*	*STOCK OPTIONS*	*INTERNET FAMOUS*[2]	*THANKING EMPLOYEE*[3]	*TROPHY*	*PUBLIC APPRECIATION OF WORK WELL DONE*	*FLEXIBLE WORK SCHEDULE*	*OPPORTUNITIES FOR ADVANCEMENT*	*GIVING TIME OFF*	*APPRECIATION GIFTS*	*VOUCHERS TANGIBLE GOALS*[4]	*COMPANY PARTY AND CELEBRATION*	*UPGRADE WORKPLACE*	*COMPANY-PAID FAMILY ACTIVITY EVENTS*	*FAMILY SUPPORT PROGRAMME*	*OPPORTUNITY TO WORK FROM HOME*	*LEARNING AND DEVELOPING OPPORTUNITIES*[5]	*PROMOTION*	*FINANCIAL PENALTIES*	*MORAL SANCTIONS*	*OVERALL HAPPINESS*[6]
32. TO SHARE		x	x					x	x	x	x	x	x	x	x	x							x	x	x	
33. TO ASSIST		x	x					x	x	x	x					x	x						x	x	x	
34. TO PLAN	x	x	x	x	x			x	x	x	x	x	x	x	x	x	x				x	x	x	x	x	
35. TO ORGANIZE	x	x	x	x	x			x	x	x	x	x	x	x	x	x	x				x	x	x	x	x	
36. TO COORDINATE		x	x	x	x			x	x	x	x	x	x	x	x	x	x				x	x	x	x	x	
37. TO CONTROL		x	x	x	x			x	x	x	x	x	x	x	x	x	x				x	x	x	x	x	
38. TO MOTIVATE	x	x	x	x	x			x	x	x	x	x	x	x	x	x	x				x	x	x	x	x	
39. TO ENGAGE	x	x	x	x	x			x	x	x	x	x	x	x	x	x	x				x	x	x	x	x	
40. TO PROTECT THE ENVIRONMENT		x	x		x			x	x	x	x			x	x	x	x					x		x	x	
41. TO COOPERATE WITH LOCAL COMMUNITIES		x	x					x	x		x	x			x	x										

Company lists of goals and motivational approaches should be used **in a participative approach** by the components of each managerial synapse. It is useful to employ the list from the beginning in the design of the synapse. The list of goals can help the manager and the stakeholder to select rationally the suitable joint objectives of the synapse. In accordance with the goals taken into consideration and the joint objectives negotiated based on a win-win approach, the synapse components are able to determine – using the matrix – the best motivational approaches and tools for them and for the organizations involved.

Motivational approaches should be differentiated and personalized for each managerial synapse and for each manager and stakeholder, taking into consideration mainly the following elements:

- synapse joint objectives;
- the nature and complexity of the tasks to be accomplished by each component;
- individual characteristics of the manager;
- motivational specificity of the manager;
- individual characteristics of the relevant stakeholder;
- motivational specificity of the relevant stakeholder;
- other special requirements regarding the workplace and organization involved, like those generated by the COVID-19 pandemic.

Such an approach could help in constructing a positive workplace for each component of the synapse that is able to provide a stimulating work environment.

Motivation is dynamic, it changes over time. For this reason, periodically, the motivational approaches and tools used should be analysed and modified, taking into consideration the new elements inside and outside the managerial synapse and in the company and other organizations, in order to enhance the performance of both the components and the company. In the case of exponential changes in the company environment, like those caused by the Covid pandemic, the motivational tools should also be reconsidered.

Recently, a **formal model** has been developed linking the design of firms' incentive structures to their rate growth. The associated dynamics lead to **three distinct approaches of firms' life cycle and of the employees' motivation:**

- rapid growth and high-powered incentive driven by frequent promotion opportunities;
- moderate growth with infrequent promotion opportunities, but large salary increases contingent on promotion;
- finally, stagnant firms with low-powered incentives (Bennett & Levinthal, 2017).

Such a model could be very useful for the development of the motivation system in each company, based on an in-depth analysis of its activities and performance, helping to improve the motivation of the relevant stakeholders.

All elements regarding managerial synapse motivation demonstrate that this new managerial mechanism is able to contribute to a large extent to the individual stakeholders' engagement, which is very beneficial for the company. A research conducted in the last few years has proved that organizations with engaged employees have three times higher profit margins than those with disengaged employees (Sacks, 2017).

Major Role Played by Stakeholder Perceptions in Managerial Synapse Construction and Work

As we know, individual perception regarding what is happening around one is always very important. **Perception, by definition, is subjective**; it reflects how a person obtains, understands, interprets, presents, communicates and uses information regarding an event, activity, other individuals, etc. There are often differences between reality and a person's perceptions of it. The same reality could be perceived more or less exactly the same way depending on the context and, in particular, on the characteristics and the behaviours of the people involved. The emotional intelligence of each person and the specific emotions felt by him or her at the moment of perception have a major influence on the content and significance of that perception. This explains to a large extent why the same reality generates different perceptions in various individuals. Of course, different perceptions are reflected in different information disseminated, decisions taken, actions performed and behaviour adopted.

Perceptions are very important in general, in all activities. The dimension of the importance of perception can be different depending on the nature of the processes involved. In the case of technical, mathematical, informational and other similar processes, which can be very precisely measured using rigorous instruments and methods, the individual perceptions of reality are usually identical or at least similar. In business, social, managerial or administrative activities, where qualitative elements are predominant, they frequently cannot be measured exactly and the perceptions of them can vary to a significant extent from one person to another. A study carried out by a group of very well-known specialists – Peloza, Loock, Cerruti, & Muyot (2012) – based on empirical research in three companies demonstrated that "there is often a major gap between stakeholders' perceptions and firm performance". In all these types of activities – which represent the majority in society and the economy – the perceptions quite often have more of an influence than the reality, the thinking, decisions, actions, and behaviours of the people and groups of people involved.

In the case of a managerial synapse perceptions are even more important than in the daily business and managerial activities of the organization. Three main arguments support this statement:

a The relevant stakeholder of a company's managerial synapse is more sensitive to the decisions, actions and behaviours of the manager who represents the company in the synapse, because usually he/she has more competences and powers concerning the allocation of the organization's resources in achieving the joint goals and expectations and in initiating changes in their bilateral relationships.
b Each relevant stakeholder, each component of the synapse, decides, acts, and behaves based to a large extent on the perceptions regarding the decisions, actions and behaviours of the other component of the managerial synapse. If the perceptions are positive, it is quite probable that his/her feedback inside the managerial synapse will be constructive, contributing to its good work and to the achievement of the joint goals, objectives and expectations. Recent researches have stated that the perception of fairness mediates to a large extent the relationships between stakeholders through positive and negative mutual behaviours (Bosse & Phillips, 2016).
c The perceptions of all internal and external company stakeholders regarding what has happened in each managerial synapse associated with the organization influence their desire and decision to be component, to continue and/or to develop relationships with the company, included the component of a future managerial synapse. The reputation and prestige of each company, which to an important extent reflect the perceptions of the organization's stakeholders – local community, mass media, administrative authority, and public opinion – are essential elements impacting the company's capacity to construct performant managerial synapses. Perceptions are determinant not only of the organization's reputation and prestige, but also of the existence and size of its "trust capital".

The influence of perception on a company's performance is so large that it has led to certain specialists declaring (asserting) that perceptions optimize the total value created in a company more than financial performance (Harrison & Wicks, 2013). The information presented indicates why a company that wants to develop performant managerial synapses valorizing the huge potential of the internal and external stakeholders should pay special attention to the relevant stakeholders' perceptions. The characteristics of company culture, the quality of organizational leadership, the organizational shareholders' and managers' personalities and behaviours play a major role in achieving a realistic and positive perception regarding what happens in the company, as an entity, and at the level of its components. A special programme aimed at making company stakeholders aware of the importance of their perceptions and developing them positively in order to contribute better work and development to the company – including by using managerial synapses – is recommended and could be extremely useful. Such a programme is even more necessary when in the company context there are crises like that created by the COVID-19 pandemic and when people are surrounded by negativity everywhere they turn (Porath & Porath, 2020).

Two Alternative Approaches to Constructing and Implementing a Managerial Synapse

The new managerial mechanism – the managerial synapse – could be used in companies **in two different ways.** The first is to implement the managerial synapse as such, like an autonomous mechanism, within the framework of the current managerial system of the company. This means having separate managerial synapses for some of the company's relevant stakeholders. This is a similar situation to what happens now in companies that utilize CRM and SCM. The second approach is to redesign the whole company management by building managerial synapses for all relevant stakeholders and correlating and integrating them to create a global management system within the organization – a company-relevant stakeholder-based management system.

The **main arguments for the selective use of a managerial synapse for certain relevant stakeholders are presented in** Table 6.4.

There are also many arguments favouring the use of managerial synapses as integrated **components of the relevant company stakeholder-based management system.**[7] In Table 6.5, we formulate these arguments.

Remodelling an organization's management by implementing a relevant stakeholder-based management system is not an easy task. There are a number of difficulties to be overcome: the complexity of the processes involved, the need to learn and apply a new methodology in order to construct a stakeholder-based management system within the organization, the time-consuming nature of the task, the notable costs involved, the relevant stakeholders, their diversity and often the large number of them, among others.

Taking into consideration the advantages and difficulties mentioned, we recommend an **approach to implementing a company-relevant stakeholder-based management system structured in two parts:**

a First, the construction of managerial synapses for the most important relevant stakeholders, when there are good premises to be successful and to rapidly achieve high performances for both synapse components. By doing this, the company can benefit from all the advantages presented in Table 6.5. The know-how and the benefits generated by building and operating these managerial synapses will

Table 6.4 Main advantages of using separate managerial synapses

No.	*Advantages*
1.	It is much easier, faster and less costly to build and use separate managerial synapses than to design, build and implement a stakeholder-based management system throughout the company.
2.	It offers the possibility of remodelling the company's relations with the relevant stakeholders rapidly and benefiting sooner from this managerial innovation.
3.	It provides a very good opportunity for company management and its relevant stakeholders to gain experience and valuable know-how regarding the construction and implementation of the new managerial mechanism – a company stakeholder-based management system.
4.	It proves the openness of the company's management to the relevant stakeholders, based on a win-win relationship, and contributes to the other stakeholders' openness and desire to have a new type of relationship with the organization, implemented by a managerial synapse that is mutually beneficial.
5.	It could help the company to take into consideration faster and better the dynamic opportunities provided by digital transformation, in the context of VUCA.
6.	It represents an important modern managerial achievement, contributing to increasing the company's prestige and trust capital in general and, in particular, in the area of internal and external stakeholders.
7.	It could represent best managerial practice in the organization, facilitating further rapid use of managerial synapses and of the stakeholder-based management system.

represent a very good preparation from all points of view – managerial, psychological, economic, social, ecologic, etc. – for the company management and its relevant stakeholders, leading to the next step of building a stakeholders' company management system.

b Second, continuing with the construction of a company-relevant stakeholder-based management system that will cover the entire organization and all its relevant stakeholders. The complexity of this system is much bigger than a managerial synapse and building it is more complicated and costly as we shall demonstrate in the next chapter. But the experience and know-how gained in the previous step with the managerial synapse will be very useful, contributing to accelerating the building and implementation of the company-relevant stakeholder-based management system and to increasing the business, social and ecological benefits for the organization and the relevant stakeholders.

The top management of each company should decide how to approach and implement the management of the relevant stakeholders, taking into consideration the specific conditions of the organization and the

Table 6.5 Main arguments for implementing a company-relevant stakeholder-based management system

No.	*Arguments*
1.	A company-relevant stakeholder-based management system provides the opportunity to take full advantage of the new approach for all relevant internal and external company stakeholders, without losing none of them.
2.	A company-relevant stakeholder-based management system facilitates more business, social and ecological performances for the company, because of the contribution of all relevant stakeholders.
3.	A company-relevant stakeholder-based management system creates a managerial mechanism capable of correlating and integrating effectively all organization managerial synapses, according to the company strategy.
4.	The work and performance of each managerial synapse are maximized when they are part of the company's stakeholder-based management system.
5.	A company-relevant stakeholder-based management system generates business synergy and sustainability in the company by harmonizing the objectives, decisions, actions and behaviours of the relevant stakeholders, both at the level of each managerial synapse and at the level of the whole organization.
6.	A company-relevant stakeholder-based management system increases the capacity of the organization to face VUCA elements, contributing to taking better advantage of the multiple trends and opportunities and to reducing the effects of threats, which are becoming increasingly frequent under the impact of the present digital revolution.

characteristics of the relevant stakeholders. Analysis of the variables that influence the construction and work of the managerial synapse is strongly recommended (see Figure 6.1).

After deciding what approach is to be used, the company management needs to elaborate, together with the relevant stakeholders involved, a detailed implementation programme.

Guide for Managerial Synapse Construction, Work, and Development

This guide contains the main phases to be completed in order to construct and operate performant managerial synapses in a company (see Figure 6.3). The guide is comprised of 14 phases. The first five phases are focused on the construction of the synapse, the following six phases on its functioning and the last three steps on the generation of performance for both synapse components and, of course, for the entire company.

In the company, as a rule, all phases incorporated in the guide are necessary in the development of a managerial synapse. The content and

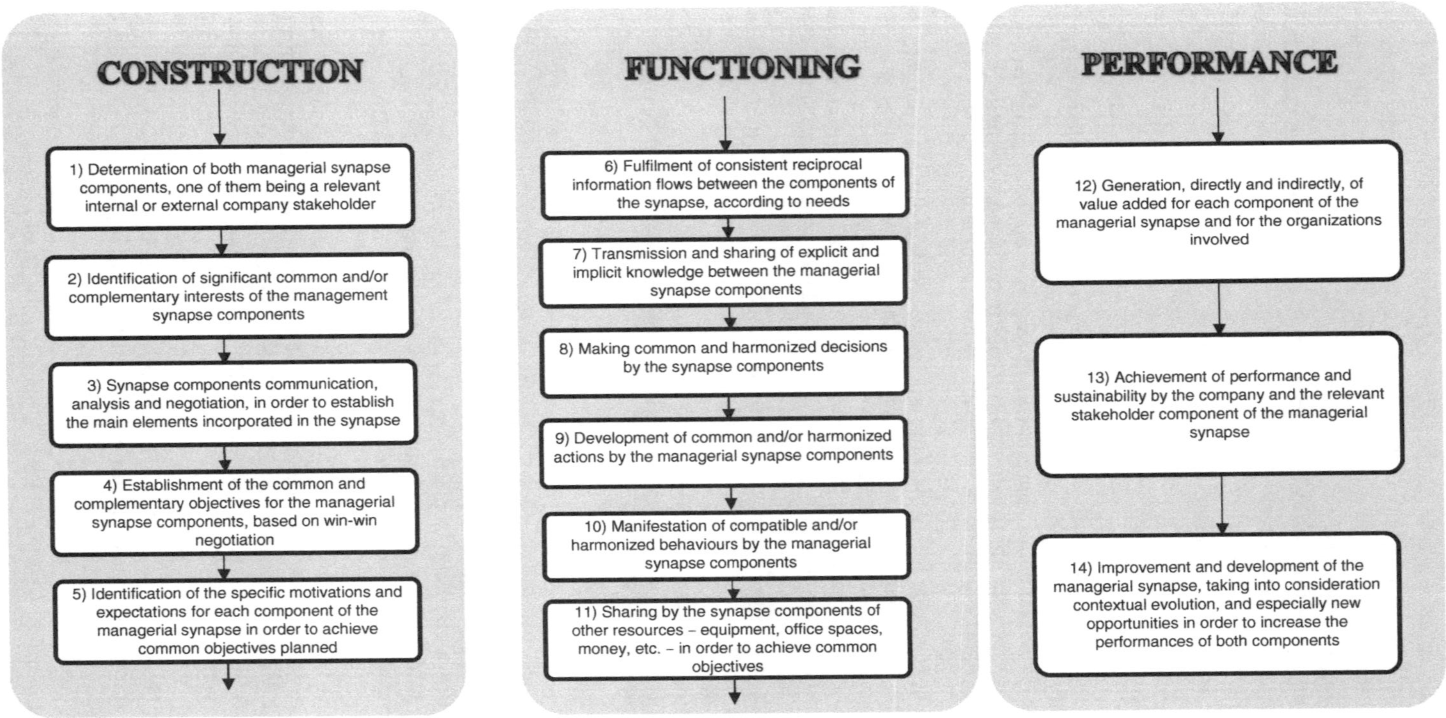

Figure 6.3 Guide for achieving performant managerial synapse construction, work, and performance.

importance of each phase could differ partially from one type of managerial synapse to another. It is essential to take into consideration the logic of the entire guide in a creative and rigorous manner, in the case of each managerial synapse.

In the context of the COVID-19 pandemic crisis, this guide could help to construct or reconstruct functional and performant relationships with some important stakeholders, thereby accelerating the company's recovery and its sustainable development.

Notes

1 Managerial synapses have been grouped taking into consideration, mainly, the frequency of the managerial relationships involved.
2 Internet famous contains: appreciations of employee on the company website, email with employee appreciation to everyone in the company, employee work business impact report on the company website, announcement with star of the month, etc.
3 Thanking employee forms: praising employee, certificate of achievement, announcing an accomplishment at a company meeting, personal note of praise from manager, letter with thanks, handwritten appreciation note, etc.
4 Vouchers tangible goals for: free or subsidized meals, fruits or drinks, sporting events, artistic events, paid group meals, wellness programme, and other holiday vouchers.
5 Learning and development opportunities like: conference participation, training programmes, exhibition visit, mentoring, coaching, tutoring, counselling, etc.
6 Overall happiness, see the analysis of Harrison and Wicks (2013).
7 Company-relevant stakeholders-based management system shall be presented in Chapters 9 and 10 of the book.

References

Bennett, V. M., & Levinthal, D. A. (2017). Firm lifecycles: Linking employee Incentives and firm growth dynamics. *Strategic Management Journal*, *38*(10), 2005–2018. doi:10.1002/smj.2644

Bosse, D. A., & Phillips, R. A. (2016). Agency theory and bounded self-interest. *Academy of Management Review*, *41*(2), 276–297. doi:10.5465/amr.2013.0420

Bridoux, F., Coeurderoy, R., & Durand, R. (2017). Heterogeneous social motives and interactions: The three predictable paths of capability development. *Strategic Management Journal*, *38*(9), 1755–1773. doi:10.1002/smj.2605

Brown, J. A., Gianiodis, P., & Santoro, M. D. (2017). Managing co-opetition for shared stakeholder utility in dynamic environments. *California Management Review*, *59*(4), 114–139. doi:10.1177/0008125617705868

Cheng, J., Huang, Y., & Su, Y. (2017). Relationality in negotiations: Systematic review and propositions for future research. *International Journal of Conflict Management*, *28*(3), 295–321. doi:10.1108/IJCMA-12-2015-0091

Creech, B. (1994). *The five pillars of TQM: How to make total quality management work for you*. New York: Truman Talley Books/Plume.

Drucker, P. F. (1954). *The practice of management*. New York: Harper Business.

Hahn, T. (2015). Reciprocal stakeholder behavior: A motive-based approach to the implementation of normative stakeholder demands. *Business & Society*, *54*(1), 9–51. doi:10.1177/0007650312439029

Harrison, J. S., & Wicks, A. C. (2013). Stakeholder theory, value and firm performance. *Business Ethics Quarterly*, *23*(1), 97–124. doi:10.5840/beq20132314

Ingerson, M. C., DeTienne, K. B., & Liljenquist, K. A. (2015) Beyond instrumentalism: A relational approach to negotiation. *Negotiation Journal*, *31*(1), 31–46. doi:10.1111/nejo.12078

Johns, G. (2017). Reflections on the 2016 decade award: Incorporating context in organizational research. *The Academy of Management Review*, 42(4), 577–595. doi:10.5465/amr.2017.0044

Juran, J. M. (1995). *A history of managing for quality: The evolution, trends, and future directions of managing for quality*. Milwaukee, WI: ASQC Quality Press.

Manning, T. (2017). The development and use of a contingency model of objective setting. *Industrial and Commercial Training*, *49*(6), 288–295. doi:10.1108/ICT-07-2017-0055

Mehta, K., & Ripol, I. (2017). 5 ways managers can enhance their mediating skills. *IESE Insight Business Knowledge*, *34*, 53–60.

Odiorne, G. S. (1965). *Management by objectives: A system of managerial leadership*. New York: Pitman Publishing.

Olekalns, M., & Druckman, D. (2014). With feeling: How emotions shape negotiation. *Negotiation Journal*, *30*(4), 455–478. doi:10.1111/nejo.12071

Peloza J., Loock, M., Cerruti, J., & Muyot, M. (2012). Sustainability: How stakeholder perceptions differ from corporate reality. *California Management Review*, *55*(1), 74–97. doi:10.1525/cmr.2012.55.1.74

Porath, C., & Porath, M. (2020). How to thrive when everything feels terrible. *Harvard Business Review*. Retrieved from https://hbr.org/2020/10/how-to-thrive-when-everything-feels-terrible

Rey, C., Velasco, J. S. C., & Almandoz, J. (2019). *The new logic of purpose within the organization*. In C. Rey, M. Bastons, & P. Sotok (Eds.), *Purpose-driven organizations* (pp. 3–15). Cham: Palgrave MacMillan. Retrieved from https://link.springer.com/content/pdf/10.1007%2F978-3-030-17674-7_1.pdf. 10.1007/978-3-030-17674-7_1

Sacks, A. M. (2017). Translating employee engagement research into practice. *Organizational Dynamics*, *46*(2), 76–86. doi:10.1016/j.orgdyn.2017.04.003

Slife, B. D., & Wiggins, B. J. (2009). Taking relationship seriously in psychotherapy: Radical relationality. *Journal of Contemporary Psychotherapy: On the Cutting Edge of Modern Developments in Psychotherapy*, *39*(1), 17–24. doi:10.1007/s10879-008-9100-6

Sulkowski, A. J., Edwards, M., & Freeman, R. E. (2018). Shake your stakeholder: Firms leading engagement to cocreate sustainable value. *Organization & Environment*, *31*(3), 223–241. doi:10.1177/1086026617722129

7 Manager–Subordinate Managerial Synapse

Premises of the Manager–Subordinate Approach

In most organizations, the majority of managerial processes and relationships involving stakeholders have subordinates as components. For this reason, in this chapter, we choose to deal with the manager–subordinate managerial synapse. Its construction, content and effects are substantially different to the manager–subordinate relationship in classic organizations and traditional management. The construction and the development of the manager–subordinate synapse, both components being employees in the same organization, are based on the following **specific premises:**

a each employee – manager or executant – is approached as a **person that has a major impact on the organization's activities and performances.** For this reason, the management of the organization pays, in many respects, consistent attention to each employee considered to be a relevant stakeholder.

b **each employee is approached as an organization component with a keen interest,** not only in a high personal wage, but also **in the organization's continuity and in its sustainable performance.** The organization management endeavours intensively to ensure that each manager and executant is aware of his/her long- and medium-term interests within the organization and of the high correlation between their fulfilment and the organization's development and performance.

c the organization's motivational system and the organizational behaviour **take into consideration the increase in each employee's effort and work contribution,** based on the correlation between the fulfilment of their motivations and the achievement of the department and organization's objectives.

d each employee is considered and approached, taking **into consideration their multifaceted personality,** their characteristics, expectations, interests and motivations, and not treating them like a simple

DOI: 10.4324/9781003217701-7

executant of certain tasks. As a result, the organization management uses complex motivations – financial (wage, bonus, prizes, free share, etc.), moral (appraisal, distinction, trophy, honorific title, media release, etc.) and mixed (promotion, training, mentoring, coaching, professional conference participation, special invitation to sporting and cultural events, etc.).

e each **employee feels that they represent a major component of the organization,** that they have a significant influence on its functioning and performance and that they are appreciated, encouraged, trained, and stimulated in order to increase their contributions to the organization's development and performance.

f **each employee's decisions, actions, and behaviours are focused on enhancing individual and group performance, on the organization's development,** mainly in their work domain, in their managerial synapse area. All these elements make a substantial and sustainable contribution to the achievement of good performance by the entire organization and to increasing its competitiveness.

g The workforce in the company, both managers and subordinates, are – according to a recent research by Fuller, Wallenstein, Raman, and de Chalendar (2019) – more adaptable than people think, especially where the company creates a learning culture, engaging employees in the transition instead of shepherding them through it.

h The relationships between executants on the one hand and managers on the other **create a solid organizational company structure,** generating positive effects on the organization's existence, functionality and development. It is a new type of structure, made up of numerous managerial synapses, producing a substantial synergy.

The main conclusion, based on the above-mentioned premises, is that managerial synapses, whose components are organization employees, both managers and executants, can represent an innovative managerial micro-system, strongly integrated in the entire organization management, capable of generating multidimensional organization performances – economic, social, educational, and ecological.

Main Differences Between a Manager–Subordinate Synapse and the "Classical Manager–Subordinate Relationship"

In order to facilitate understanding of the content of the manager–subordinate synapse, its specificity and novelty, we have identified the main differences between the classical manager–subordinate relationship and the manager–subordinate managerial synapse (see Table 7.1).

These differences help us to better understand and use of the manager–subordinate managerial synapse in companies.

Table 7.1 Essential differences between managerial synapse and the classical "manager–subordinate relationship"

No.	*Manager–Subordinate Managerial Synapse*	*Manager–Subordinate "Classical" Relationship*
1.	It is based mainly on win-win stakeholder negotiations, and on reasonable compromise	It is based mainly on the organization's hierarchy, on the manager's powerful authority
2.	It is oriented toward achieving common and/or complementary employee objectives, not only the company's	It is focused on the company's objectives and tasks
3.	It is an equilibrated informal and formal managerial mechanism	It is basically a formal mechanism
4.	The motivations used in the managerial synapse are both intrinsic and extrinsic, business and social, the achievement motivation type	Most of the motivations used are extrinsic and economic, quite often with a punitive dimension
5.	The management processes and relationships involved in the managerial synapse are predominantly collaborative, even participative	The management processes and relationships are predominantly hierarchical
6.	Manager–employee bilateral communication within the synapse is dialogic, very intensive and oriented toward both sides	The communication processes involved are predominantly top-down, frequently not intensive
7.	It is a very innovative mechanism based on the stakeholders' (managers and subordinates) motivation to be creative, to use their knowledge, to attain joint objectives in the company's complex internal and external environment	It is often an inertial management relationship, with a heavy emphasis on past experience and continuity, and on respect for hierarchy
8.	It is a flexible and adaptive managerial mechanism in the fast-changing company internal and external environment	It is, to a large extent, slowly responding conservative and rigid relationship, slowly adaptive in the fast-changing environment
9.	The company management considers stakeholders' knowledge to be the most important resource, without neglecting the other stakeholder resources	The company management is primarily preoccupied by the financial and material resources of the company
10.	Stakeholders' balance, in their equilibrated and harmonized relationships, from the main human and business points of view	Disproportional status of the two components, asymmetrical relationship, based on the manager's powerful predominance and on undervalued subordinate potential and motivation

(*Continued*)

Table 7.1 (Continued)

No.	*Manager–Subordinate Managerial Synapse*	*Manager–Subordinate "Classical" Relationship*
11.	The company management is focused on the multidimensional performances – business, social and ecological – of the organization and its stakeholders, and this influences positively the content and the results of the manager–subordinate managerial synapse	The management is focused almost exclusively on the company's business performance and consequently the manager–subordinate relationship is strongly oriented toward the generation of good economic results

Outstanding Role and Importance of the Manager–Subordinate Managerial Synapse

We consider it very useful to start to present and analyze the manager–subordinate managerial synapse by outlining the role and multiple influences of this type of synapse on **two levels** (see Figure 7.1).

a **The role of the company manager–subordinate managerial synapse in, and its influence on, the company's activities and performances** can be summarized as follows:

- This managerial synapse involves two of the three internal essential company components – the manager and the executant (subordinate); the owner is the third essential component of the company.
- Managers and executants fulfil most of the work processes in the company.
- Managers and executants are the largest categories of relevant stakeholders of the company; they usually represent over 80% of its relevant stakeholders. For this reason, they play a central role in implementing the stakeholder-based management in the company and in generating better results.
- In the company, the manager–subordinate managerial synapse represents a milestone for other relevant stakeholders' perception regarding the new managerial approach based on the organization's relevant stakeholders. Organization "trust" capital, from the other stakeholder management point of view, is evaluated to a large extent on the new type of manager–executant relationship and results, incorporated in the company managerial synapses, based on joint interests and objectives, win-win negotiation, equilibrated reciprocal advantages, etc.

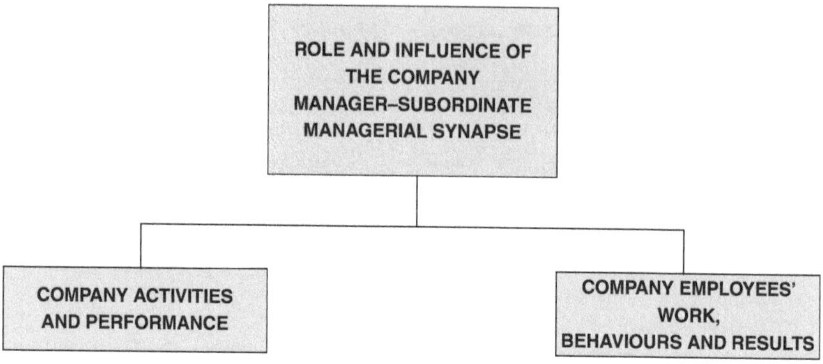

Figure 7.1 Role and influence of the manager–subordinate managerial synapse.

- The components of this managerial synapse – the managers and the executants – decide and use most of the company's tangible resource (machines, equipment, raw materials, buildings, land, money, etc.), influencing significantly their outputs.
- Managers and executants possess and use most of the intangible company resources of the intellectual capital, mainly knowledge, with a major influence on the organization's work and performance.
- The company manager–subordinate synapse contributes to the design of a workplace context that encourages good behaviour, making workers happier and more productive.
- The construction and work of company manager–subordinate synapses influence, directly and indirectly, the creation, use and performance of all other categories of managerial synapses. The company's managers and executants involved in other managerial synapses with external relevant stakeholders will decide, act, and behave within them similarly to how they do in their current managerial work. It is difficult to suppose that company managers who practise a strong hierarchical management inside a company (and not a synapse managerial style) will ever be able to adopt in their relations with other (external) stakeholders a management based on win-win negotiation, intense communication, consultation and cooperation, which is specific to the managerial synapse.
- A manager–subordinate managerial synapse represents a form of relational capital and for this reason the design of such management synapses contributes to increasing the company's intellectual capital.
- In the context of the COVID-19 pandemic, because of the many changes in employees' work (the introduction of social distancing, the increase in working online, telework, hybrid communication, etc.), relationships between managers and executants have become

more complex and challenging and their impact on company functionality and performance has increased.

For all these reasons, company manager–subordinate synapses have a decisive impact on the company's activities and performances, and on its sustainability.

b **The influences of company manager–subordinate synapses on employees' work, behaviour, and results** are mainly as follows:

- A managerial synapse, through a special managerial mechanism and in the specific context created in the synapse area, determines that employees have feelings that are not treated purely like those of a "simple" executant, whose mission is just to execute the tasks required. They feel like significant company constituents, who have, through negotiation, communication, consultation, and cooperation, a voice in the organization and play an active role in this synapse area and managerial synapse;
- The managerial synapse objectives to be achieved are common for the company and the executant, and they reflect their interests, expectations, and particularities, having been established through intensive communication, consultation, cooperation and win-win negotiation;
- Subordinate motivations to fulfil the company's objectives, reflected in the common managerial synapse objectives, to deploy creative and productive work processes, are strong and permanent;
- Subordinate motivations are comprehensive, both moral and material, both intrinsic and extrinsic, etc.
- A company manager–subordinate managerial synapse provides much better conditions, compared with the classical manager–subordinate relationship, in which to efficiently and effectively decide, act and behave, to use all the work time, to valorize the contextual opportunities and to prevent and/or eliminate the potential contextual threats to the synapse area and company;
- A company manager–subordinate synapse provides a very good framework for valorizing subordinate knowledge and potential, and for professional development, facilitating a complex integration in the organization and increasing personal stability in the company;
- For each subordinate, the building and functioning of a managerial synapse represents very good training and very good practice, which helps them to be an effective constituent in the next managerial synapses with external stakeholders, where they represent the company;

- A manager–subordinate managerial synapse, because of all the above-mentioned elements, makes the subordinate more constructive, creative, and entrepreneurial, contributing to enhancing their work productivity. Enhancing subordinates' productivity represents a major element in increasing the company's productivity and other performance indicators – profit, turnover, the value of company shares, the company share market, etc.

Our conclusion, based on the arguments presented, is that the company manager–subordinate synapse could generate, directly and indirectly, large and profound positive mutations in companies, valorizing the many opportunities provided by the transition to a knowledge-based economy and digitalization.

Classification and Characterization of the Company Manager–Subordinate Managerial Synapse

According to the criteria of the classification specified in Section 5.8, the company manager–subordinate managerial synapse can be classified into the categories presented in Figure 7.2. We succinctly describe below the **characteristics of each type of company manager–subordinate managerial synapse:**

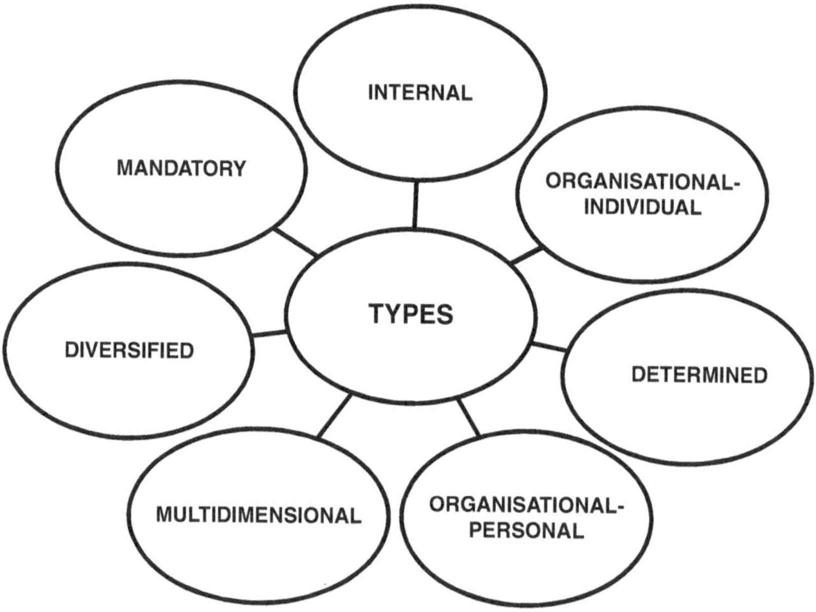

Figure 7.2 Types of company manager–subordinate managerial synapse.

a It is an **internal managerial synapse**, because both components – the manager and their subordinate – are working in the same organization. The company objectives represent the organizational objectives for both and they are influenced by the same organizational culture. The previous elements facilitate direct and easier relations, dialogic communication and intense collaboration between manager and subordinate, favouring a notable reciprocity;

b The company manager–subordinate managerial synapse is, based on the types of constituents, **organizational–individual**. It involves the company through the manager and the individual subordinate, who is a relevant stakeholder. In this type of managerial synapse every manager of the company participates. Low and middle managers participate most frequently because they have many subordinates.

The larger the scope of control of the manager, the greater the number of managerial synapses in which they are integrated. Also, we should point out that a subordinate could also be integrated in more than one managerial synapse with their direct manager if they collaborate or cooperate permanently or for a certain period of time with another manager or specialist from the company or from outside, in order to fulfil certain company objectives. In building a company manager–subordinate managerial synapse and in designing a specific synapse area, three categories of objectives and interests should be taken into consideration and realigned:

- company,
- manager as an individual,
- subordinate as an individual.

In order to achieve this, the manager's ability to negotiate and the availability to communicate and cooperate of both components of the synapse are very important. Win-win negotiation is essential for the successful harmonization of the interests, objectives, decisions, actions, and behaviours of the company manager and the subordinate.

The organization's strategy, policies, culture, managerial approaches, and economic performance have a major impact on the content, dynamics and performance of each company manager–subordinate synapse. They create the specific organization context in which every company manager–subordinate managerial synapse is constructed, works, and performs.

c A company manager–subordinate managerial synapse is classified – based on the duration criteria – as a **determined managerial synapse.** All company employees have work contracts with the organization in which usually the period of work in the organization is specified.

This element is very helpful in the construction and functioning of the managerial synapse for determining the objectives, tasks, and other necessary elements. A long-term labour contract increases the interest of the employee in the company's sustainability and the motivation to work harder and to be performant for the organization. Moreover, for an employee, a long period working with the company increases their specific experience and knowledge of the company, their capacity to understand the organizational values, strategy, culture, mechanisms, etc. and often their attachment to the organization. All these elements contribute to easier and better work processes and relationships inside the company manager–subordinate managerial synapse. It is not mandatory for the duration of the company manager–subordinate managerial synapse to overlap the period of the labour contract. It should be correlated with the objective planning system used in the company. Usually, there are yearly objectives in accordance with the annual policy of the company. If in certain areas of the company other periods are more relevant, they should be used in the planning of the managerial synapses. Such a situation could occur in a production department that makes special products to order, which have durations ranging from a few months to a few years. The company should use the determined manager–subordinate managerial synapse in a way that contributes to the generation of higher productivity and value added in the organization.

d According to the types of common objectives and interests, the company manager–subordinate managerial synapse is **organizational–personal**. This means that the common objectives refer to three parts – the company, the individual company manager and the individual subordinate. Harmonization of these three categories of interests, expectations and objectives is frequently a tough and complicated process, time-consuming and involving high availability of win-win negotiation skills. The degree of complexity and difficulty of the processes of communication, consultation, harmonization and implementation is very high, higher than the organizational–social type of managerial synapse. Acceptance of certain compromises by each of the three parts involved is usually necessary. It is essential not to put high pressure on the subordinate to accept certain objectives because this will transform them into the "classical executant", not sufficiently interested in, and motivated by, the accomplishment of the "common" objectives of the synapse. The common objectives of the managerial synapse should be really motivational for each part – company, manager and the subordinate – generating fully harmonized decisions, actions and behaviours from them.

e A manager company–subordinate managerial synapse taking into consideration the criterion "nature of the common objective" is a

multidimensional synapse. The most frequent common objectives are economic – the majority – and social. The economic objectives deal with the quantity and value of production and sale, acquisition cost, price, productivity, profit, turnover, etc. The majority of them are quantitative objectives. Common social objectives refer to the work conditions – security, health, etc. – for manager and subordinate. In the last few decades, especially in industrial, agricultural and transport enterprises, ecological objectives have been taken into consideration more frequently. The tendency of the increased influence of social and ecological factors on companies will continue in the next period. A large part of this evolution is connected with digital transformation, nanotechnologization, biotechnologization, unconventional energy proliferation, and other major mutations associated with the transition toward the knowledge-based economy. In the company manager–subordinate managerial synapse, this tendency will generate more social and ecologic common objectives, harmonized with business purposes. As a result, the work processes to be fulfilled will be more diversified, involving a larger set of information, knowledge, and abilities. Outputs of the company manager–subordinate managerial synapse will also be more varied and have a greater impact on the synapse area and at the company level. Company sustainability will depend increasingly on the number and quality of company manager–subordinate multidimensional managerial synapses.

f Taking into consideration the nature of the processes incorporated, a company manager–subordinate synapse can be classified mainly into two categories: **the internal work processes managerial synapse** and the **diversified managerial synapse.** Many employees, especially in industrial, construction, and agricultural companies, are focused on internal work processes – production, maintenance, repair, internal transportation, accountancy, storage, etc. Many work processes are task oriented, sometimes with certain specific quantitative objectives. The managers involved in this type of managerial synapse are usually low- and middle-level managers. The content of the work processes usually comprises operational-decisional elements to a small extent. Company traditions, experience and informal organizational elements are very important in the progress of work processes. For the manager–subordinate managerial synapse, the above-mentioned aspects frequently do not favour its performances, because the role of hierarchy is crucial in the traditional manager–subordinate relationship. Remodelling of these relationships according to the new elements of the managerial synapse – win-win negotiation, frequent communication and consultation, intensive collaboration and reciprocity – is not an easy change in the interactions between the manager and the subordinate.

The second very frequent type of manager–subordinate synapse is **the diversified synapse**. Within this type of managerial synapse, a large variety of work processes focused on the procurement of resources, internal activities and performance are fulfilled. The design and the functioning of the diversified manager–subordinate synapse are more complicated and difficult than other types of managerial synapse, because of the variety of common objectives and work processes. Their harmonization and fulfilment are demanding for both components of the synapse – manager and subordinate. They should win-win negotiate quite different common objectives, to provide and receive very diversified information, to use a large variety of knowledge and technical information to accomplish different work processes, to obtain a variety of both qualitative and quantitative performances, etc.

These types of company manager–subordinate synapses are very frequent in micro- and small enterprises and they have the tendency to increase in all categories of organizations, due to the proliferation of the systemic approach, the agile work design and digitalization.

Of course, another two types of company manager–subordinate synapse classified according to the nature of the work processes – a **synapse focused on resources procurement and a synapse directly focused on performance fulfilment** – are also used in companies, albeit generally to a smaller extent.

In the next period, the diversified managerial synapse will have the fastest increase, for the reasons already indicated.

g All, or almost all, manager–subordinate managerial synapses are **mandatory** because they realize work processes that are absolutely essential for the company, like raw materials and energy supply, sale of products and services, transportation of spare parts and goods, equipment maintenance, company finance, personal motivation and training, etc. A company cannot work and survive without these work processes, and for this reason the company manager–subordinate managerial synapses that incorporate them are mandatory or imperative for the organization. In stakeholder-based management, mandatory manager–subordinate managerial synapses are essential, extremely numerous and represent a priority for company managers. Mandatory company manager–subordinate synapses are crucial for the survival and development of the enterprise. Of course, they should be combined with certain optional manager–subordinate synapses, in order to fulfil the innovative processes and to realize organizational transformation.

Numerous elements regarding the characteristics of the most frequent types of company manager–subordinate managerial synapses are very useful for understanding their specificity and complexity and how to approach and use them, enabling the enhancement of the enterprise's performance and sustainability.

Manager and Subordinate Meaningful Work Inside the Managerial Synapse

We believe that the managerial manager–subordinate synapse should be approached, designed and fulfilled from the perspective of **meaningful work**. Recently, the researchers Bailey and Madden (2016) showed that meaningfulness is more important for employees' motivation than any other aspect of work, including pay or rewards, opportunities for promotion and work conditions. It is highly motivational, contributing to enhancing commitment, satisfaction, and personal and organizational performance (Cascio, 2003).

Work meaningfulness differs from one person to another. It tends to be intensely personal and individual. The expectations, desires and requirements of each employee regarding work content, contextual conditions, relationships with managers and other company stakeholders, individual motivations and prestige, personal life, company priorities and culture, etc. vary to a large extent. Employees feeling that their work is meaningful is generated by different combinations of the above-mentioned elements. Frequently, the meaningfulness is connected with helping others and contributing to something beyond the employee themself – such as family, nature or society. Meaningful work is often associated with a sense of pride and achievement and tends to produce more positive and long-term employee feelings than the classical work approach in companies. This not only means greater employee satisfaction but it also contributes to increased productivity, more creativity and better performance.

In order to construct meaningful work, to achieve "job crafting", a study conducted by Gallo (2015) recommends taking into consideration **four categories of aspects** (see Figure 7.3):

a **Legacy**, referring to the concrete outcomes of employee work, to the desire to do the tasks involved and to the satisfaction gained by the employee during and after fulfilment of the tasks.
b **Mastery**, regarding the strengths that the employee wants to improve. It is essential that the employee uses their strengths in a way that is rewarding for them, because they love what they do.
c **Freedom** is about the salary benefits and flexibility that the employee needs in order to live the life they want. This category of aspects is strongly connected with the lifestyle that the employee wants to have.
d **Alignment**, regarding the culture and values of the place where the employee works. It is about how the employee's sense of belonging

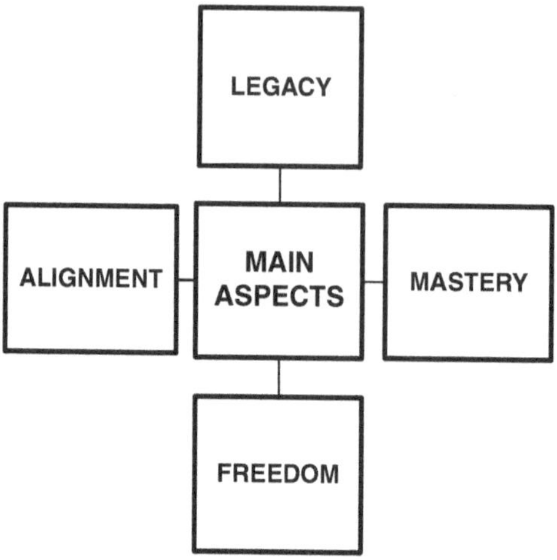

Figure 7.3 Main elements in the construction of meaningful work.

Adapted from "How to build a meaningful career" by A. Gallo, 2015, *Harvard Business Review*. Retrieved from https://hbr.org/2015/02/how-to-build-a-meaningful-career.

matters, taking into consideration the beliefs and priorities of the company and the people they work with and the behaviours and attitudes of the company managers and other employee stakeholders.

In order to identify what meaningful work means, for each component of the managerial synapse – manager and subordinate – it is necessary for everyone to conduct a **self-evaluation**, including using the opinion of other people, like a board of advisors. In this process, the following elements (Gallo, 2015) are very important:

- making a prioritized list of what meaningful careers the employee would like;
- inviting four or five people to serve as a board of advisors, as the employee explores what they want;
- experimenting with different job elements that employees would want in a managerial synapse.

It would be very useful for the managerial synapse components if in this process, in the board of advisors, were included the manager in the case of the subordinate and the subordinate in the case of the manager. Such an approach could help both managerial synapse components to negotiate the common objectives and to harmonize their aspirations, decisions, actions, and behaviours, concomitantly with the development of the meaningful work for them.

A research carried out by Bailey and Madden (2016) demonstrated that the **meaningful work of the employee depends decisively on the quality of the management practised** in the organization. According to this research, "poor management [is] the top destroyer of meaningfulness". A managerial synapse could be one of the main managerial mechanisms capable of contributing to the employees' – managers and executants – meaningful work. The specificity of the managerial synapse is very well suited to taking into consideration, "de facto", the very personal and individual meaningfulness of each employee's work.

In time, the approach of the construction and use of the managerial synapse in a company, based on the meaningful work concept, will enhance the functionality and performance of each workplace and, directly and indirectly, of the entire organization.

Subordinate and Manager Positive Identity Construction and Work

In building a managerial manager–subordinate synapse, one way to develop a cohesive and performant mechanism that has received increasing attention in the last few years **is positive identity construction at work**. According to the specialists Dutton, Roberts, and Bednar (2010), people's identity is a multifaceted and dynamic approach, making a complex and changing representation of self-knowledge and self-understanding, with a broad range of self-relevant feelings and attitudes, modifying work-related processes. Positive identity construction by company employees refers to the way they reconstruct themself in their work domain, resulting in strengthening themself at work. By strengthening themself at work, the employee increases their capacity to generate and share knowledge, to build social resources, to take on new demands and challenges and to endure stress, thereby improving their performance in the company. The construction and development of a positive identity at work is faster and better if it is based on the meaningful work of both components of the manager–subordinate managerial synapse. There are **four types of pathways in constructing a positive identity at work**, each of them focusing on a certain type of element and using specific mechanisms capable of generating multiple positive effects for the employee, their work relationships and the work content. The elements presented in Table 7.2 are relevant in this respect.

Examination of the nine mechanisms included in Table 7.2 from the managerial synapse perspective, indicates that the majority of them are very well suited to its content and specificity, and are able to contribute to strengthening it. **The best suited for use in the manager–employee managerial synapse are the following mechanisms:**

Table 7.2 Main types of positive identity building

No.	*Types*	*Mechanisms*
1.	**VIRTUAL** – based on virtual qualities	P1 – Changes perceptions of ingroup/outgroup boundaries; increases openness to relationships with outgroup members P2 – Promotes identity-consistent behaviours; increases trust and respect in relationships
2.	**EVALUATIVE** – based on high regard	P3 – Generates positive emotions, makes individuals more popular and attractive as relational partners P4 – Generates positive emotions, increases understanding of others, including outgroups P5 – Increases access to self-affirmational resources; enables more open responses to threats
3.	**DEVELOPMENTAL** – based on fit with internal and/or external stakeholders	P6 – Increases cultural alignment; increases attraction due to perceptions or similarity P7 – Increases desire to affirm new identity; encourages the formation of new relationships
4.	**STRUCTURAL** – based on complementary identities	P8 – Enables engagement in multiple domains; increases exposure to diverse contacts; creates brokering opportunities between contacts P9 – Individuals disclose more information, discover shared perspectives, are more authentic and build intimacy

Adapted from "Pathways for positive identity construction at work: four types of positive identity and the building of social resources" by J. E. Dutton, L. M. Roberts & J. Bednar, 2010, *Academy of Management Review*, *35*(2), 277. Retrieved from https://www.researchgate.net/publication/228354753_Pathways_for_Positive_Identity_Construction_at_Work_Four_Types_of_Positive_Identity_and_the_Building_of_Social_Resources.

- **P2**, which increases trust and respect in the relationships for both components of the synapse;
- **P3**, which makes an individual – either a manager or a subordinate – more popular and attractive as a relational partner;
- **P4**, which increases understanding of other individuals within and/or outside the manager–subordinate managerial synapse, for each component of the managerial synapse;
- **P6**, which increases collaboration with other people, due to the perception of similarity;

- **P7**, which encourages subordinate and manager to develop new relationships between themselves and with other stakeholders;
- **P9**, which contributes to the disclosure of more information and discovers shared perspectives and relationships within the managerial synapse with other people.

Without any doubt, it is recommended that the four pathways in constructing a positive work identity are used in the process of building and developing a manager–subordinate managerial synapse.

The construction and the content of the positive identification are influenced significantly by the emotions of the managers and subordinates involved. Employees' emotions can influence positively and/or negatively the positive identity building. In order to minimize the negative influence of emotions and to increase the positive impact, it is useful to appeal to **emotional regulations** (Barrett & Russell, 1998), which involves controlling which emotions are experienced, and when and how they are experienced and used. For regulating emotions, a model of emotions known as the "affective circumplex", centred on two dimensions – degree of energy and degree of pleasantness – can be used (Bailey & Madden, 2016; Cascio, 2003).

For the manager–subordinate managerial synapse, the construction of a positive identity for each component is a complex but very beneficial process that increases the quality of manager–subordinate relationships. A model has been elaborated by Creary, Caza, and Roberts (2015) that demonstrates this relationship improvement generated by positive identities.

During the last few years, several studies (Caza, Moss, & Vough, 2018; Dutton et al., 2010; Gallo, 2015) have emphasized the utility of company employees having **multiple identities.** Of course, for a company employee, having multiple identities could be very helpful in some respects, especially regarding access to supplementary knowledge, information and social capital. In order to avoid neglecting the core tasks involved in the positive identity associated with their manager–subordinate relationship (and managerial synapse), it is necessary to maintain an equilibrium with other actions. In our opinion, the involvement of an employee in multiple identities should be very well justified, based on the job priorities, the potential and the motivation of the employee. Probably, the best results generate multiple identities for company managers and experts, and fewer for "common" company employees.

In terms of work identities, **non-work identities** have an increasing influence (Ramarajan & Reid, 2013) and this aspect should be taken into consideration in the construction of the manager–subordinate managerial synapse work identities.

Special attention should be paid to avoiding and to **solving the conflict between the multiple identities of the managerial synapse.** The specialists

Jones and Hynie (2017) have formulated four approaches that could be used in the case of a managerial synapse:

- reconciliation, where identities are integrated;
- realignment, where one identity is chosen over another;
- retreat, when both identities are avoided;
- reflection, where fit (with other situations) determines identity selection.

With the exception of "retreat", the other three approaches could be useful in the construction and harmonization of employees' multiple identities within the manager–subordinate managerial synapse.

Construction of a positive identity for the constituents of the managerial synapse determines positive manager–subordinate relationships, generating multiple advantages like positive employee attitude, task performance and citizenship behaviour and more effective task organization (Gallo, 2015).

Employee Agile and Dynamic Work

In order to be performant, a manager–subordinate managerial synapse, like any other managerial mechanism, needs to be designed and constructed professionally. **Two different types of approach** can be used:

a **A classical or conventional work design**, based on a mechanistic approach using traditional tools. This is based on work analysis and division, especially for repeated work processes and combining different parts in jobs. Essentially, the job of the employee – manager or executant – is defined in the job description, based on the place occupied by the job in the organizational structure, and on the organization's vision and approach incorporated in the company/organization manual. In the job description the main organizational elements that should be fulfilled by the employee are included – objectives, roles, tasks, competences and responsibilities. In fact, the job description represents a "work plan and guide" for the employee, as it contains the main types of work processes that should be carried out. Quite often, a job description also includes the main requirements regarding the qualities of the person who will take the job. Job descriptions are usually designed by the human resources department for every job in an organization. The job description is reviewed when a new person is hired for the job. Traditionally, the employee endeavours to carry out their work according to the elements of the job description. The classical approach, with its long history, is the most frequently used in companies, contributing significantly to the professionalization of the organization's management and to the company's performance.

In the last few decades, in the context of innovation, informatization and digitalization enhancement, numerous companies' managers and specialists have revealed the limits of this approach in many areas of the organization and have proposed many changes. The limitations are generated largely by the fact that the traditional approach to work processes and organizational design is almost entirely static, because it presumes that the work processes designed will remain unchanged in the next period.

b In recent years, a **new approach – dynamic and agile work design** – has been increasingly used. The agile work approach was launched in 2001 by 17 software developers in a document called the "Manifesto for Agile Software Development", in which they present better ways of developing software by doing it and helping others do it (Beck et al., 2001). The following 12 principles are behind the agile work design (see Figure 7.4).

"Manifesto" has had a huge impact not only on the informatics industry but also on business as a whole. The new vision and practice of the "agile work approach" has proliferated very fast in many industries, generating big advantages. Several **methodologies** have developed in order to redesign work projects in companies like:

- **Screen,** which realizes the planning and implementation of a project at the same time;
- **Extreme,** which is focused on frequent deliverables to ensure that the end product is going to be exactly what the user needs;
- **Agile UX,** which focuses more on how to achieve the project outcome rather than what the project will be;
- **Crystal,** which is focused on major priorities and key properties of projects, providing frequent deliverables.

The agile approach is one of the hottest topics in the management literature and a priority in many companies all over the world. As pointed out by Cappelli and Tavis (2018) in a recent study, agile isn't just for tech anymore and it's been working its way into other areas from product development to manufacturing to marketing and is now transforming how organizations hire, develop and manage their people.

According to a survey conducted by Deloitte in 2017, in IT more than 90% of organizations already use agile practices and 79% of global executives rated agile performance management as a high organizational priority. The major reason for this change is that companies core

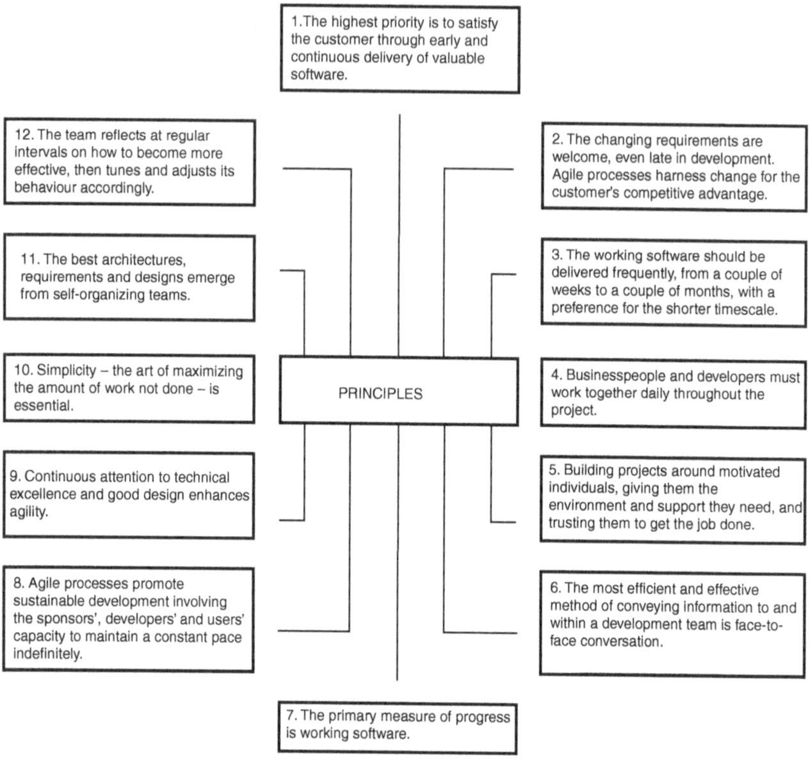

Figure 7.4 Principles behind agile work design.

Adapted from Manifesto for agile software development by Beck et al., 2001. Retrieved from https://www.agilealliance.org/agile101/the-agile-manifesto/.

business and functions have largely replaced long-range planning models with number methods that allow them to adapt and innovate more quickly (Deloitte, 2017).

Recent studies on the agile work approach conducted by Repenning, Kieffer, and Repenning (2018) and Birkinshaw (2018) demonstrated that in companies it is possible to use agile work design to fulfil both agility – in the sense of flexibility – and efficiency. They analysed from several perspectives the multiple aspects involved in this approach and concluded that it could be used with some adaptation to a company's specific profile. It has been pointed out that although an agility and efficiency approach could be very performant in many fields, such as the informatics industry, it is not to be recommended for all types of company activities.

An agile work approach, a **dynamic work design**, is best suited for discrete tasks that are harder to define when the organization relies more on things like training and collaboration and less on routinization and careful specification. It is an organic collaborative approach focused on resolving work problems, taking into consideration the difficulties and shortfalls that are inevitable in real companies (Birkinshaw, 2018; Repenning, Kieffer, & Repenning, 2018). In designing a manager–subordinate managerial synapse both work designs should be used – traditionand agile work.

Agile design work is necessary in a company's activities, **being characterized by intense creative processes, large new flows of information, sharing of knowledge, high task complexity, and fast-changing work requirements and work conditions.** Company activities where these elements occur frequently include R&D, marketing, informatics, management, investment, human resources and others. In such activities the manager– subordinate managerial synapse should be designed based on the **agile work and dynamic work design**, providing a flexible and productive work environment. The designing, construction and development of the managerial synapse should follow the cycle DISCOVERED => PLAN => BUILD => REVIEW, iterated several times, until the degree of agility is feasible and performant (Archer, 2014).

Implementation of the agile work approach is not easy, especially at the beginning, but for certain categories of works – whose frequency and size are increasing fast – it is the best way to generate more flexibility and enhanced performance.

The use of collaborative agile work design in the construction of the manager–subordinate managerial synapse generates **significant advantages** for both components, subordinate, and manager:

- Faster communication between them
- More contribution with ideas and effort in achieving common objectives
- More creativity in the fulfilment of common objectives and tasks
- More flexibility and adaptability to the changing environment
- Contribution to the development of "humanistic management" (Dierksmeier, 2016) in practice
- Facilitation of adaptive planning
- Increased efficiency of the managerial synapse components and of the company

In this section we focus in particular on the use of the agile work approach in the manager–subordinate synapse, because it is new, not sufficiently well known, and its necessity and efficiency will increase rapidly in the near future, under the impact of deep environmental changes, based on knowledge, innovation and digitalization. Rigby, Sutherland, and Takeuchi (2016) emphasized that agile innovation has revolutionized the software industry and it is now poised to transform every function in every industry.

The selection of the type of work design approach – classical or agile – should be made while taking into consideration the characteristics of the work involved. Of course, the approach that is best suited to every managerial synapse should be chosen in order to maximize individual and organizational performances and sustainability.

Innovative Dimension of the Manager–Subordinate Managerial Synapse

Our approach to the relationship between innovation and the manager–subordinate managerial synapse is based **on four premises** (see Figure 7.5).

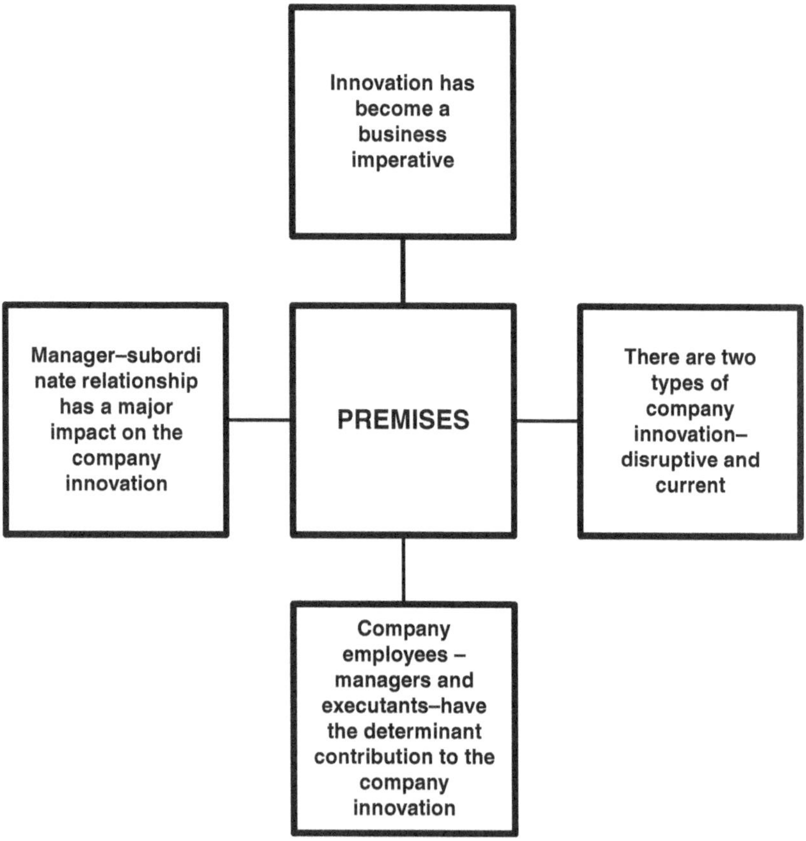

Figure 7.5 Premises of the approach to the relationship between manager–subordinate synapse and company innovation.

a In the present era of fast-paced change – first and foremost, but not only, technological – **innovation has become a business imperative** (Manso, 2017). Accelerated innovation radically changes the environment and generates impressive development of the business and society.[1] For companies, management innovation has become a top priority. According to the 2017 survey of PricewaterhouseCoopers – PwC (2017), based on the answers of 1,379 CEOs from 79 countries, innovation was the aspect of their business they most wanted to strengthen. The main reason for this is that innovation is critical both for company survival and development.

b In most studies regarding innovation, the **focus is on "disruptive innovation"**, which determines profound, often "spectacular" changes in the economy and society. Usually, such disruptive innovations are in the technical and informatics domains, producing original products, technologies and equipment representing major progress in their fields.

We believe that innovation should be approached systemically, taking into consideration all its types and all domains. Innovations, based on their originality, intensity and impact, can be classified into two categories: **disruptive and current.** Although in companies generally, current innovations are less visible, less "salient", they are extremely numerous and often have a notable impact on company processes and results. These innovations are carried out in all company activities – marketing, management, supply, transportation, maintenance, accounting, finance, human resources, etc. – including technical and informatics fields.

In order to better understand the specificity and the role of disruptive and current innovations in a company, in Table 7.3, we present their main characteristics in a contextual approach according to 13 criteria.

Current innovations, taking into consideration their genesis, can be separated into two categories:

- **Current innovations that are associated with disruptive innovations,** which are integrated within new products, technologies, etc. Although quite often they are not perceived as innovative, these current innovations, by making small changes in the processes and elements involved, contribute to the increase of the qualities and performance of disruptive innovations, or even to avoiding the delay or/and even their blockage.
- **Current innovation associated with the fulfilment of employees' daily tasks.** These innovations are frequently created spontaneously by the company's employees, based on their experience and newly acquired, tacit and explicit knowledge. Current innovations help to overcome new difficulties at the workplace or in the department, which occur frequently due to the changing of the contextual

Table 7.3 Significant characteristics of disruptive and current innovation

No.	Criteria	Predominant Characteristics	
		Disruptive Innovation	Current Innovation
	A. REGARDING INNOVATION		
1.	Number	Small	Huge
2.	Complexity	Very large	Small and medium usually
3.	Nature of processes involved	Specialized, narrow, usually in a few selected fields (technics, informatics)	Extremely diverse in all company activities
4.	Time	Long and very long, quite often several years	Very short, short and medium
5.	Human effort	Very large	Small or medium
6.	Resources needed	Large quantity, usually big investments	Small, usually existing company resources
7.	Effects	Huge/determined by studies and specific metrics	Very diverse, the majority not measured separately
8.	Visibility	Very visible, sometimes overwhelming	Small or not visible
	B. REGARDING COMPANIES		
9.	Number	Small number at the beginning of the 20th century, later fast increase	Huge number, implemented practically in every company
10.	Span of use	Some of the companies, the best, the most innovative	All companies, but with unequal frequency and impact
11.	Size of company	Usually large and sometimes medium	All sizes of organizations, but in microcompanies it is frequently the only type of innovation used
12.	Changed activities	Generate huge mutations in organization activities and performance	Generate, usually, small and medium changes, but very necessary and useful in the company
13.	Impact	Generate new business, with huge potential to increase organization performance	Generate continuous adaptability, essential for every company's survival and development

conditions. Quite frequently, current innovations represent improvements in the tasks accomplished, generated by the creative "spark" of the employees.

c Innovation in every company is achieved through the **decisive contribution of its employees – managers and executants**. Their contribution takes **two forms:**

- **Direct creative contribution**, with new ideas and new elements regarding the design of new products, marketing tools, technologies, management approaches, finance sources, etc. In companies that have a strong R&D department, an intensive innovational culture and managerial leadership focused on innovation, the direct creative contribution is high. This is the case for companies from very intensive innovative fields – electronics, informatics, robotics, pharmaceuticals, etc. We should point out that in companies from all fields, the external sources of new ideas – software, consultants, designers, patents, etc. – provide a large proportion of the innovative ideas.
- **Indirect contribution**, managers and consultants participating in the innovation implementation processes in all company activities. Their participation always has some innovational content, which is absolutely necessary in order to facilitate the implementation of the novel elements involved in new products, technologies, etc. invented by others. The company's employees make the decisive contribution in innovation implementation in the organization – either from internal or external sources – firstly because they modify the processes involved and secondly because they implement effectively the new changed processes. Without them, the disruptive and current innovations in the company do not work. Employees' innovation in the workplace is a critical component for any company in order to maintain a distinct competitive advantage in the marketplace (Anderson, Potočnik, & Zhou, 2014).

d Relationships between employees are very important for the designing and implementation of innovations in the company – both disruptive and current. **Manager–subordinate relationships represent the most important component of employees' relationships in the organization.** When these relationships are characterized through mutual trust, effective communications, openness toward changes and new ideas, encouraging initiatives and changes, the generation and implementation of innovations in companies are easier, faster, and greater (Wallace, Butts, Johnson, Stevens, & Smith, 2016). The content of hierarchical manager–subordinate relationships directly influences their thinking, decisions, actions and behaviours regarding company innovations in general, and current innovation in particular. A lot of new good ideas capable of producing valuable innovations in a company are blocked in the beginning phases when there are rigid hierarchical relationships between the managers and their subordinates, when they do not communicate, cooperate, and work effectively. The manager–subordinate relationship represents an essential element in the initiation and development of each innovation. The cooperation and contribution of both managers and subordinates are necessary in order to design and implement successfully any innovation.

Poor-quality manager–subordinate relationships are one of the main reasons why, even in many companies with good innovational strategies and policies, and with substantial resources allocated for innovation, the intensity and quality of innovations are not satisfactory, which has a negative impact on the company's development and performance. Traditional, hierarchical manager–subordinate relationships do not favour either disruptive or current innovations.

A manager–subordinate managerial synapse, due to its specificity and characteristics, is able to take into consideration the innovative premises mentioned. It is necessary from the beginning for the **manager–subordinate managerial synapse to be innovationally designed and built.** The following elements should be taken into consideration in these processes:

- Win-win negotiation between both synapse components needs to be achieved, taking into consideration the requirements to be creative and to renew their work processes;
- Common objectives of synapses should include, either totally or partially, innovative targets and/or having a strong innovative dimension;
- The synapse area should not be a classical workplace but a creative work environment, open to new approaches favouring creativity and the implementation of new elements;
- Reciprocity, dialogic communication and other managerial synapse characteristics should be conceived and practised from an innovative perspective;
- In the set of tasks to be accomplished by the manager and subordinate, targeted innovative work processes should be included; certain tasks regarding obtaining news or acquaintance with new knowledge specific to the work to be done should always be specified;
- The competences and responsibilities of both managerial synapse components should incorporate the facilitation, encouragement and strengthening of creativity and innovation in the work area;
- In order to enhance the innovation within the manager–subordinate synapse, specific incentives should be used, differentiated for exploring and exploiting innovative processes (Manso, 2017);
- Recent approaches regarding the design of the work in the company – meaningful work, positive identity construction, agile work – must be fulfilled in the innovative ways.

Specialists Wallace et al. (2016) determined that opportunities for innovation at work are best taken into consideration and capitalized upon by employees that are willing and able to engage in innovation.

The manager–subordinate synapse, depending on the innovative intensity of their objectives and work processes, can be classified into **three categories:**

- **High innovational synapse,** where all common objectives, or the majority of them, together with work processes, are innovative. Such synapses should be frequently found in R&D, but also in informatics, marketing, public relations, human resources, activities, etc., when company management has innovational strategies and policies. In many cases, within a high innovational managerial synapse, disruptive innovation is fulfilled. High innovational synapses represent a small part of all synapses in the majority of companies, but with a fast-increasing role.
- **Medium innovational synapse,** where some of the objectives and work processes are innovative, but another significant part are not. This type of manager–subordinate synapse should be more frequently found than the previous one. Medium innovational synapses are usually determined by companies' strategies and policies focused on modernization and renewal, but without making radical changes in the organization. Also, this type of synapse is used in highly innovative companies in complementary activities correlated with innovative core activities. There is a strong tendency in many companies to increase medium innovative managerial mechanisms.
- **Low innovational synapses,** where the objectives and work processes are focused on a routine, non-innovative approach, with innovative elements being at a reduced level. When this type of objectives and work activities is predominant in the company, this means a conservative management. Today, low innovational work processes are still predominant in many companies. These companies are striving to survive and/or not oriented toward enhanced development and performance. The number of companies and their activities in which there are predominantly low innovative work processes is decreasing rapidly, because of the danger of bankruptcy and the management reorientation toward innovation, change and performance.

The types of managerial synapse to be created in every company depend largely on its strategy and policies, its managerial approach and organizational culture. In fact, the number and the type of manager–subordinate managerial synapses is not important, but rather their capacity to generate innovative and performant changes in the company suited to the environmental tendencies.

The characteristics of the manager–subordinate managerial synapse make it a very good managerial mechanism – much better than the classical manager–subordinate relationship – capable of accelerating and enhancing companies' innovation and performance in today's fast-changing complex environment, emphasized by the COVID-19 pandemic.

Specific Advantages of the Manager–Subordinate Managerial Synapse

The main advantages of the managerial synapse presented in the previous chapter are also valuable for the manager–subordinate synapse. Moreover, this type of managerial synapse **generates certain specific advantages,** reflecting the particularities of the work processes accomplished inside the company by the employees, and the content and impact of the manager–subordinate relationships within the managerial synapse. Synthetically, these **advantages** are the following:

- decrease of the hierarchical content of the manager–subordinate relationships, which do not always favour personal creativity and initiative;
- manager and subordinate decisions and actions, based on joint win-win negotiated objectives, are better harmonized and more performant;
- more constructive behaviours of both components – manager and subordinate – inside and outside the managerial synapse;
- subordinate and manager knowledge are better shared, used and valorized;
- increased speed of the work processes conducted at the level of the workplaces;
- strengthening both stakeholders – manager and subordinate – at work;
- more participative approach from the manager and their subordinate, having a positive impact on all work processes done by both components of the managerial synapse;
- enhancement of the quality of the work processes inside the company, realized by the managerial synapse components;
- diminution of conflict situations between manager and subordinate;
- decrease of the necessity and intensity of control at the level of subordinate;
- contribution to the development of the "ownership culture" of the management synapse components;
- increase of the manager and subordinate engagement in the company;
- increase of the productivity and value added produced by the managerial synapse components – subordinate and manager;
- better integration of the manager and subordinate work and results in the company activities and performance.

In the context of the COVID-19 pandemic these specific advantages of the manager–subordinate managerial synapse have become more important for the company. They represent strong arguments for using it in order to help companies to recover and to relaunch their development faster and in a more performant manner.

Of course, the construction and the development of the manager–subordinate managerial synapse and the generation of the advantages enumerated are not easily achieved and involve – as we have outlined – complex and difficult processes. Employee efforts, knowledge, and willingness should be large and continuous, and well managed. Top- and middle-level company managers' strong involvement is mandatory.

The widespread use of the manager-subordinate managerial synapse in the company, instead of the classical hierarchical manager–subordinate relationships, could determine profound changes in the company, making it more participative, agile, innovative, and performant. The potential of the largest company human resource – managers and executants – is steadily increasing and better used, contributing to the increase of organizations' competitivity and sustainability.

Note

1 Because it is a very rich literature on this subject, we do not place emphasis on it. Some major aspects regarding the content and the tendencies generated by innovation, in the context of the transition to the knowledge-based economy and digitalization have been approached in Chapters 2 and 3 of our book.

References

Anderson, N., Potočnik, K., & Zhou, J. (2014). Innovation and creativity in organizations: A state-of-the-science review, prospective commentary, and guiding framework. *Journal of Management*, *40*(5), 1297–1333. doi:10.1177/0149206314527128

Archer, J. (2014). *Agile design: What we've learned.* Retrieved from https://crowdfavorite.com/agile-design-what-weve-learned/

Bailey, C., & Madden, A. (2016). What makes work meaningful – or meaningless. *MIT Sloan Management Review*, *57*(4), 53–61.

Barrett, L. F., & Russell, J. A. (1998). Independence and bipolarity in the structure of current affect. *Journal of Personality and Social Psychology*, *74*(4), 967–984. doi:10.1037/0022-3514.74.4.967

Beck, K., Beedle, M., van Bennekum A., Cockburn, A., Cunningham, W., Fowler, M., et al. (2001). *Manifesto for agile software development.* Retrieved from https://www.agilealliance.org/agile101/the-agile-manifesto/

Birkinshaw, J. (2018). What to expect from agile. *MIT Sloan Management Review*, *59*(2), 39–42.

Cappelli, P., & Tavis, A. (2018). HR goes agile. *Harvard Business Review*, *96*(2), 46–52.

Cascio, W. F. (2003). Changes in workers, work, and organizations. In W. Borman, R. Klimoski, & D. Ilgen (Eds.), *Handbook of psychology, volume 12: Industrial and organizational psychology* (pp. 401–422). New York: John Wiley.

Caza, B. B., Moss, S., & Vough H. (2018). From synchronizing to harmonizing: The process of authenticating multiple work identities. *Administrative Science Quarterly*, *63*(4), 703–745. doi:10.1177/0001839217733972

Creary, S. J., Caza, B. B., & Roberts, L. M. (2015). Out of the box? How managing a subordinate's multiple identities affects the quality of a manager-subordinate relationship. *Academy of Management Review*, *40*(4), 538–562. doi:10.5465/amr.2013.0101

Deloitte. (2017). Rewriting the rules for the digital age. *Deloitte Global Human Capital Trends*. Retrieved from https://www2.deloitte.com/content/dam/Deloitte/global/Documents/About-Deloitte/central-europe/ce-global-human-capital-trends.pdf

Dierksmeier, C. (2016). What is "humanistic" about humanistic management? *Humanistic Management Journal*, *1*, 9–32. doi:10.1007/s41463-016-0002-6

Dutton, J. E., Roberts, L. M., & Bednar, J. (2010). Pathways for positive identity construction at work: Four types of positive identity and the building of social resources. *Academy of Management Review*, *35*(2), 265–293. Retrieved from https://www.researchgate.net/publication/228354753_Pathways_for_Positive_Identity_Construction_at_Work_Four_Types_of_Positive_Identity_and_the_Building_of_Social_Resources 10.5465/amr.35.2.zok265

Fuller, J. B., Wallenstein, J. K., Raman, M., & de Chalendar A. (2019). Your workforce is more adaptable than you think. *Harvard Business Review*, *97*(3), 118–126.

Gallo, A. (2015). How to build a meaningful career. *Harvard Business Review*. Retrieved from https://hbr.org/2015/02/how-to-build-a-meaningful-career

Jones, J. M., & Hynie, M. (2017). Similarly torn, differentially shorn? The experience and management of conflict between multiple roles, relationships, and social categories. *Frontiers in Psychology*, *8*, 1732. doi:10.3389/fpsyg.2017.01732

Manso, G. (2017). Creating incentives for innovation. *California Management Review*, *60*(1), 18–32. doi:10.1177/0008125617725287

PricewaterhouseCoopers – PwC. (2017). *20 years inside the mind of the CEO … What's next?* 20th CEO survey. Retrieved from https://www.pwc.com/gx/en/ceo-survey/2017/pwc-ceo-20th-survey-report-2017.pdf

Ramarajan, L., & Reid, E. (2013). Shattering the myth of separate worlds: Negotiating nonwork identities at work. *Academy of Management Review*, *38*(4), 621–644. doi:10.5465/amr.2011.0314

Repenning, N. P., Kieffer, D., & Repenning, J. (2018). A new approach to designing work. *MIT Sloan Management Review*, *59*(2), 29–38.

Rigby, D. K., Sutherland, J., & Takeuchi, H. (2016). Embracing agile. *Harvard Business Review*, *94*(5), 40–50.

Wallace, J. C., Butts, M. M., Johnson, P. D., Stevens, F. G., & Smith, M. B. (2016). A multilevel model of employee innovation: Understanding the effects of regulatory focus, thriving, and employee involvement climate. *Journal of Management*, *42*(4), 982–1004. doi:10.1177/0149206313506462

8 Approach of Customer Relationship Management as a Managerial Synapse

Short Customer Relationship Management (CRM) Genesis and Development (Evolution)

Thousands of years ago people started to trade, first using bartering and later money. The first recorded commercial activity was about 20,000 years ago. Quite quickly traders realized that it is easier to sell to previous customers than to find new ones and that it is advantageous to develop as good relationships as possible with them. Gradually an accounting registration system was developed incorporating information regarding the buyer's name and location, product type and quantity sold, price, etc. This information regarding customers recorded in accounting documents represents an early type of customer database. Such information was used in the first segmentation of customers taking into consideration customers' payment capacity, buying frequency, etc. We can state that the action of recording and grouping customers has a relatively long history and this represents the main reason for the many traders' performant business.

In the twentieth century, because of the keen concurrence in all fields, the attraction, retaining, and loyalization of customers became more and more important for company survival and development. From the old codes, agendas and the famous rolodex used by many companies for customer centralization and coordination in the 70s, with the development of informatics, CRM specialized software was designed and used.

The first CRM programs emerged in the United States between 1970 and 1980, when stand-alone mainframe systems were introduced, containing information regarding sales to customers. These systems provided sales department staff with the tools required for obtaining data regarding customer management. Between 1981 and 1990 North American insurance and finance companies began to use certain software specially designed for them that was able to connect information about customers and trade transactions used in the company business. In 1982, a marketing database was introduced aimed at using some statistical methods for collecting and analysing customer data. In 1986, the first

DOI: 10.4324/9781003217701-8

software for the administration of sale contracts, called ACT, was launched. In the 1990s, as a consequence of the change in business paradigm and of the software focused on customers, the CRM concept was developed and disseminated rapidly.

Significant contributions to the change of business paradigm were made by Kotler (1992a, 1992b) regarding the transition from transactional marketing to relational marketing; Hammer and Champy (1993), who highlighted the need for customer-centric business models; and Peppers and Rogers (1993), through their introduction of the concept of "one-to-one marketing".

In this context, new approaches to organization performance based on the "relationship concept" were elaborated that contributed to other major changes in the marketing field and orientation toward the customer. Kotler emphasized the importance of developing closer relationships with customers, distributors, suppliers, company managers and employees, trade unions, banks, NGOs, governmental bodies, and other major players (stakeholders) in the company business environment. The need for a transition from short-term vision, oriented towards transactions, to a long-term approach, centred on the creation and development of relationships, whose goal is organization competitivity, and enhancement of the local, regional, national, and international markets, has been stressed. **The transition from transactional marketing to relational marketing** has been achieved based on two major mutations (Bălan, 2007):

- the transition from a narrow perspective focused only on the functional area to a vision centred on the correlative approach of several functional areas;
- the objective of attracting customers has proved insufficient for sustainable development and, as result, has led to the transition to a double objective centred on taking into consideration stakeholders' categories (not only customers) and on maintaining customers. It should be noted that various specialists (e.g., Parvatiyar & Sheth, 2001b) believed that the terms "relationship marketing" and CRM were frequently used interchangeably in the academic world.

At the beginning of the 1990s, in the context of the rapid development of informatics, an important step was made toward the **development of software that would later be known as CRM.** Brock Control Systems and Siebel Systems contributed significantly to the evolution of software for contracts management to sales force automation (SFA), which has automated many of the main elements of database marketing and combined them with contracts management, providing companies with very useful information about customers. Over time, SFA and other software for contracts management have had different names, like CRM (Customer Relationship Management), ECM (Enterprise Customer Management), and CIS (Customer Information System). In 1995, the term CRM was definitively accepted in the USA and at international level. Later some companies, such as Oracle and SAP, started to incorporate CRM modules in enterprise resource planning (ERP) software that were initially dedicated to business activities like product planning, manufacturing, transportation, etc. In 1999, the first mobile CRM, with the name Siebel Sales Handheld, was launched, followed by versions made by other top companies like PeopleSoft, SAP, and Oracle. Salesforce.com implemented the first software cloud – SaaS CRM (Software-as-a-Service) ("CRM", n.d.). Between 2000 and 2010, Microsoft entered the CRM market with Dynamics CRM, and SugarCRM developed the first open-source CRM. Cloud-based CRM became dominant and social media was integrated into CRM. After 2010, the most important developments were: CRM integrations with business intelligence services and communication systems, enhancement of CRM customization capabilities based on the activity domain, line of business, sales process or market focus, the appearance of visual, highly intuitive CRM such as Pipedrive, improvements in mobile access, and increased use of AI and machine learning for various purposes (Gaetano, 2018). In summary, the evolution of CRM software can be divided into four main periods or stages: the 1980s or the original stage, the 1990s or the expansion stage, the 2000s or the modern CRM stage, and the last stage, from 2010 to the present, dominated by Cloud-Social-Mobile-Integrated CRM software (Khasenova, 2017). CRM operationalization in companies has developed in a very innovative and successful way both in terms of reconfiguration of the activities within organizations according to a new conception centred on the customer and from the point of view of the use of information and communication technologies. Some specialists refer to customer relationship management as an integrated approach to identifying, acquiring and retaining customers, when the focus of CRM is on managerial elements (Ellatif, 2008), and others see CRM as informatics tools/systems designed to support the relationships between company and customers (Chen & Popovich, 2003). The strategy of a company that focuses on the clients and the CRM software complement each other. But CRM technology is often incorrectly equated with CRM (Reinartz, Krafft, & Hoyer, 2004), and one of the main reasons for the failure of CRM in many organizations is approaching CRM as a technology initiative (Kale, 2004). For this reason, there must be a balance between the integrated approaches of a strategic nature and the use of the elements provided by the ITC industry.

CRM Definition and Mechanism

Surprisingly, **there is no definition of CRM widely accepted at the international level.** Although the term CRM is very frequently used and in many companies CRM systems are implemented as software applications or fuller approaches that deal with many company activities, **the perceptions of scientists and practitioners regarding CRM vary greatly.** Some specialists believe that the best CRM approach derives from the aphorism "the purpose of business is to create and to keep a customer", formulated by Peter Drucker a long time ago (Drucker, 1954).

Starting from the approach levels, the errors regarding the understanding of the concept, the different points of view regarding the content and the contexts of implementation, Francis Buttle identified a number of essential attributes of CRM, which he integrated into the following definition: "CRM is the core business strategy that integrates internal processes and functions, and external networks, to create and deliver value to targeted customers at a profit. It is grounded on high-quality customer data and enabled by IT" (Buttle, 2004, p. 34).

The well-known global research and consulting firm Gartner defined CRM as

> a business strategy that optimizes revenue and profitability while promoting customer satisfaction and loyalty. CRM technologies enable strategy, and identify and manage customer relationships, in person or virtually. CRM software provides functionality to companies in four segments: sales, marketing, customer service and digital commerce. ("Gartner Glossary", n.d.)

A very interesting approach to the definition of CRM was taken by Payne and Frow (2005), who believed that customer relationship management can be defined from at least three perspectives: narrowly and tactically, broadly and tactically, broadly and strategically. Payne and Frow, after a comprehensive review of the specialized literature and intense interaction with managers from many and various companies, formulated a more complex CRM definition:

> CRM is a strategic approach that is concerned with creating improved shareholder value through the development of appropriate relationships with key customers and customer segments. CRM unites the potential of relationship marketing strategies and IT to create profitable, long-term relationships with customers and other key stakeholders. CRM provides enhanced opportunities to use data and information to both understand customers and co-create value with them. This requires a cross-functional integration of processes, people, operations and marketing capabilities that is enabled

through information, technology and applications. (Payne & Frow, 2005, p. 168)

We shall continue by presenting certain CRM definitions very frequently quoted in the specialized literature: "CRM attempts to provide a strategic bridge between information technology and marketing strategies aimed at building long-term relationships and profitability. This requires information-intensive strategies" (Glazer, 1997). "CRM is a management approach that enables organizations to identify, attract and increase the retention of profitable customers by managing relationships with them" (Hobby, 1999). "CRM means being willing and able to change your behaviour toward an individual customer based on what the customer tells you and what else you know about that customer" (Peppers, Rogers, & Dorf, 1993, p. 151). "CRM involves using existing customer information to improve company profitability and customer service" (Couldwell, 1999, p. 14). "CRM is nothing more than an approach that stems from the need to create a new business environment, which allows a more effective management of relationships with customers" (Galbreath & Rogers, 1999). "CRM is an enterprise approach to understanding and influencing customer behaviour through meaningful communication to improve customer acquisition, customer retention, customer loyalty and customer profitability" (Swift, 2000). "CRM is a comprehensive strategy and process of acquiring, retaining and partnering with selective customers to create superior value for the company and the customer" (Parvatiyar & Sheth, 2001b). "CRM is a term for methodologies, technologies and e-commerce capabilities used by companies to manage customer relationships" (Stone & Woodcock, 2001). "CRM is a set of methodologies, processes, software and systems that helps institutions and companies in creating effective and organized management of customer relationships" (Burnett, 2001). "CRM is an ongoing process of identifying and creating new value with individual customers, and then sharing the benefits from this value over a lifetime. It involves the understanding and focused management of ongoing collaboration between an organization and its selected customers for mutual value creation and then sharing this value through interdependence and organizational alignment" (Brunjes & Roderick, 2002, p. 9). "CRM is the infrastructure that enables the delineation of an increase in customer value, and the correct means by which to motivate valuable customers to remain loyal – indeed, to buy again" (Dyché, 2002, p. 4). "CRM is not merely technology applications for marketing, sales and service, but rather, when fully and successfully implemented, a cross-functional, customer-driven, technology-integrated business process management strategy that maximizes relationships and encompasses the entire organization" (Chen & Popovich, 2003, p. 673). "CRM is a business strategy to select and manage customers to optimize long-term value. CRM requires a customer-centric business philosophy and culture to support effective marketing, sales and service processes. CRM applications can enable effective customer relationship management, provided that an enterprise has the right leadership, strategy and culture" (Subhasish, 2007, p. 4). "CRM is a comprehensive sales and marketing approach to building long-term customer relationship management and improving business performance" (Farooqi & Dhusia, 2011).

Various specialists from around the world have identified **several CRM levels, CRM types or perspectives on CRM** strategic, operational, and analytical (e.g., Bălan, 2007; Reiny & Buttle, 2006); operational, analytical, and collaborative (e.g., Karimi, Somers, & Gupta, 2001; Payne, 2005; Tohidi & Jabbari, 2012); functional, customer facing and organizational or strategic (e.g., Kumar & Reinartz, 2018).

According to Buttle (2009), **there are four types of CRM**: strategic, operational, analytical, and collaborative (see Figure 8.1).

1 **Strategic**, which refers to CRM positioning as a major component of the overall organization strategy. Management of the customer relationships involves the development of an organizational culture centred on the customers and the use of customer orientation as a priority at the level of the entire company. Customer acquisition and increase of the customers' degree of satisfaction should not be left only to the marketing and/or sales department. Promises to customers can only be fulfilled continuously and entirely through horizontal integration of all company activities and through orienting organization resources and processes to the satisfaction of the customers' expectations. In each business entity, it is necessary to align and integrate the customer strategy with the company's overall strategy. If there is a gap between strategies, there will be a negative impact on the organization because of the discrepancy between the value provided to the customers and their expectations.
2 **Operational**, which refers to the automation of the company's contact activities with the customers. Automation projects deal with marketing, sales, service and activities using CRM software applications. Marketing automation deals with the following processes: customer segmentation, communication campaigns management and answering customers. Sales force automation refers to opportunities management, contact management, offers management, and the establishment of customer solutions. Service automation deals mainly with operations between customer contact centres and telemarketing centres, services provided by the Internet and partners' activities.
3 **Analytical**, which refers mainly to data mining regarding the customers and evaluation of the organization's performances in the field of customer relationships, in order to elaborate the best

Figure 8.1 Major perspectives on customer relationship management.

Adapted from *Customer relationship management: Concepts and technologies* (p. 4), by F. A. Buttle, 2009, Elsevier Butterworth-Heinemann. Retrieved from https://knowledgestreams.files.wordpress.com/2013/07/francis_buttle-customer_relationship_management_second_edition-butterworth-heinemann2008_2.pdf

strategies, policies, and tactics for each major customer. The analytical level includes processes of information gathering, analysis, interpretation, use, and storage regarding the customers, the most important of which are the following: customer identification, profiling customers from the company portfolio, data analysis, and evaluation of the marketing processes.

4 **A collaborative** approach to CRM refers both to the organization's cooperation with external stakeholders (suppliers, vendors, and distributors) resulting in better alignment in the supply chain of separate enterprises in order to identify, attract, and retain the customers in a performant manner (Buttle, 2009), and also to the internal communications between different departments of an organization (sales, marketing, and technical support) to improve

> the quality of customer service and enhance customer satisfaction/loyalty (Jha, 2008). According to Payne (2005, p. 23), "collaborative CRM involves the use of collaborative services and infrastructure to make interaction between a company and its multiple channels possible. This enables interaction between customers, the enterprise and its employees".

In order to achieve the objectives of CRM regarding value creation both for the company and for the customer, four CRM levels/types should be automated – strategic, operational, analytic, and collaborative.

The development of the Internet and the popularity of social media have generated the emergence of electronic CRM (E-CRM) and social CRM (S-CRM).

Coined in the mid-90s, **E-CRM** has been defined in many ways by diverse specialists. For instance: "Electronic Customer Relationship Management is the use of ICT tools by organizations as a means of building potentially long-lasting relationships with customers" (Kotorov, 2002); "E-CRM refers to the use of the Internet to implement CRM strategies" (Blery & Michalakopoulos, 2006); "E-CRM is actually CRM on the web and involves e-commerce activity and use of email and other Internet-based touch points" (Bergeron, 2004); "Electronic CRM is simply CRM that includes the use of technology" (Harrigan, Ramsey, & Ibbotson, 2012).

Social CRM, which focuses on the use of social media to support and develop the interactions between the organization and customers, has been defined differently by different scholars: "Social CRM is an emerging concept that includes strategies, processes and technologies to link the Social Web with CRM processes" (Reinhold & Alt, 2011); "S-CRM is CRM strategy that encourages customer collaboration and involvement" (Faase, Helms, & Spruit, 2011); "Social CRM is emerging as a new paradigm for integrating social networking in more traditional CRM systems" (Askool & Nakata, 2011); other specialists believed that S-CRM consists in CRM systems that make use of blogs, forums and other social media to broaden the focus of traditional CRM (e.g., Gneiser, 2010; Trainor, Andzulis, Rapp, & Agnihotri, 2014), but the most widely accepted approach belongs to Greenberg (2009, p. 34) who defined social CRM as:

> [a] philosophy and a business strategy, supported by a technology platform, business rules, workflow, processes and social characteristics, designed to engage the customer in a collaborative conversation in order to provide mutually beneficial value in a trusted and transparent business environment. It's the company's programmatic response to the customer's control of the conversation.

CRM consolidation as a management approach was influenced by the major trends that have manifested worldwide since the 1990s (Payne, 2005): transition from transactional marketing to relational-based marketing; awareness to a greater extent of the fact that clients are a business asset; reconfiguration in structuring organizations by moving the accent from functions to processes; increased use of ICT technologies in managing and exploiting the value of information; admission of the need for trade-off between delivering and appropriating customer value; proliferation of one-to-one marketing approaches; and recognition of the advantages of using information proactively than rather in a reactive way.

Main Approaches of CRM in the Specialized Literature and Company Practice

At the international level there are many CRM approaches conducted by scientists and by company specialists, but the objectives and essential elements are, to a large extent, similar. The different approaches are caused mainly by rapid societal changes, which gradually determine updates of CRM systems, the existence of many companies from different branches where CRM is implemented, and the specificity of personal training and experience of the specialists who deal with CRM. We shall briefly present some of the **CRM approaches** that require special attention from the specialists.

The IDIC model, one of the best-known CRM approaches, was elaborated by the consultancy company Peppers & Rogers Group, and has been featured in several books written by the two consultants (e.g., Peppers & Rogers, 1996, 2004). The model focuses on four actions that the company has to undertake in order to build and develop long-term one-to-one relationships with customers:

- **Identify** the customers of the organization and collect as much information or data about them as possible in order to enhance the understanding of their needs and purchase behaviours;
- **Differentiate** the customers on the basis of value (identification of customers that have the most value now or in the future) and according to their needs (serving various customers that have different needs in profitable ways requires more knowledge about their needs);
- **Interact** with customers in order to understand their expectations and their relationships with a brand;
- **Customize** the products and services to be certain that the expectations of customers are met.

The specialists Parvatiyar and Sheth (2001a, 2001b) have developed a broad **framework for the CRM process**, divided into four subprocesses:

- **Customer relationship formation process.** This subprocess refers to setting the purposes of implementing CRM, selecting parties or customer groups for the CRM programme, and developing programmes for relational engagement with the customers;
- **Relationship management and governance process** approaches issues like team structure, role specification, process alignment, communication, motivation of specialists, and employee training;
- **Relationship performance evaluation process.** This is focused on the measurement of the CRM process and comparison with the initial objectives, defined at the start of CRM implementation. The main areas to be assessed are strategic, financial, and marketing issues;
- **CRM enhancement process** refers to the evolutionary process that can occur naturally according to developments occurring in the external environment, and/or based on the experiences accumulated during the implementation of CRM.

Based on many years' theoretical and practical research, renowned professor Francis Buttle elaborated the **CRM value chain** (Buttle, 2001, 2004, 2009), which is one of the best-known CRM models in the world, dedicated to companies that want to develop and implement CRM strategies. Buttle's model focused on **five primary stages** and **four supporting conditions** that lead to the achievement of the main goal of any company – customer profitability enhancement. The primary stages, respectively customer portfolio analysis, customer intimacy, network development, value proposition development and managing the customer life cycle, are approached in a sequential manner in order to ensure that an organization, supported by its network of partners, suppliers, and employees, is able to acquire and retain profitable customers. The main supporting conditions are leadership and culture, information technology, people, and processes, which make the successfully implementation of the CRM strategy possible.

One of the most popular approaches to CRM worldwide was formulated by Payne (2005), who concluded that most companies should take into consideration **five key cross-functional CRM processes:** strategy development process, value creation process, multi-channel integration process, information management process, and performance assessment process (see Figure 8.2).

Based on these cross-functional CRM processes, Payne and Frow (2005) elaborated the **strategic framework for customer relationship management.** According to this approach, CRM is regarded as a strategic set of processes that starts with a detailed review of an organization's strategy (process of strategy elaboration) and ends with an improvement of business results and increase of shareholder value (process of performance assessment). A company's competitive advantage results from the creation of value for the customer and for the

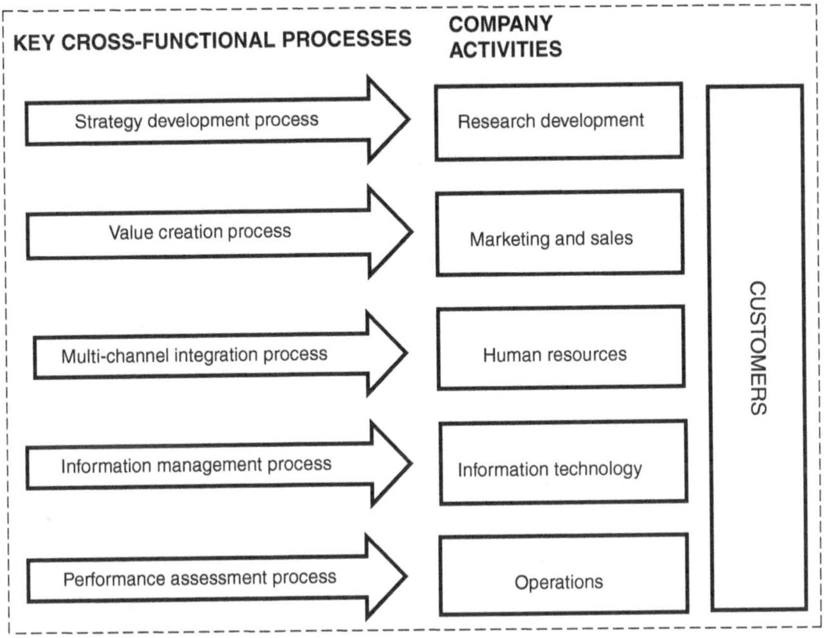

Figure 8.2 CRM as a cross-functional activity – Levels of customer relationship management.

Adapted from *Handbook of CRM: Achieving excellence in customer management* (p. 30) by A. Payne, 2005, Butterworth-Heinemann and Elsevier. Retrieved from https://repository.dinus.ac.id/docs/ajar/Handbook_of_CRM.pdf

organization (process of value creation) through collecting and utilizing in an intelligent manner customer and other relevant data (information management process) in order to build a superior customer experience, at each touchpoint where an interaction between customer and supplier (multi-channel integration process) exists.

With regard to the model elaborated by Payne and Frow, specialist Buttle (2009) mentioned that the strategy development process and the value creation process represent strategic CRM, the multichannel integration process constitutes operational CRM and the information management process signifies analytical CRM.

A very interesting approach is that of Santos and Castelo (2018), who presented **a conceptual model for the adoption of CRM in terms of a strategic perspective.** This approach was developed based on the analysis of over 30 models elaborated between 1999 and 2015 and is focused on elements internal to the organization that are grouped in six dimensions:

- CRM strategy formulation;
- Relational marketing philosophy;

- The application of best practices;
- Organizational and human resources;
- CRM processes;
- CRM technology.

The first two dimensions are related to the design of a CRM strategy and the next four dimensions are approached in terms of implementation. The proposed model includes three functional areas (marketing, sales, and after-sales services) and stresses the need to consider the permanent application of best practices and management of metrics.

In order to support companies that wish to implement electronic CRM or are in the process of implementing E-CRM, Pan and Lee (2003) elaborated **a model focused on five managerial steps:**

- Identify the existing customer relationship management processes within the organization. Detailed knowledge of all processes focused on customers is of great importance, because it will provide answers regarding what specific business benefits are sought from the CRM strategy;
- Formulate an E-CRM vision and strategy. In the second step, an E-CRM strategy and its specific objectives must be established and build upon the existing CRM processes;
- Secure top management support. Depending on the organizational and IT culture as well as their own circumstances, the support level of top management plays a crucial role in the E-CRM implementation process;
- Choose appropriate technology partners. An important challenge for organizations implementing E-CRM is choosing the right technology partner, which must be able to offer a flexible, customized, and scalable product and stay focused on the business objectives and the overall E-CRM vision of the organization;
- Evaluate current information systems and create new mechanisms and metrics to monitor and improve the process. The last step is aimed at the assessment of E-CRM implementation and the adoption of corrective and/or improvement measures.

Alt and Reinhold (2019) developed a **model focused on social CRM** that reveals the design areas of a CRM solution (operational, analytical, communicative, and collaborative), the actors (users, platform provider/providers, companies, and service providers) and the five technological elements (social media, analysis, CRM, interaction, and management/integration). The first element (social media) refers to establishing a presence on a social media platform/platforms (such as forums, wiki, and communities) for the distribution and collaborative generation of information. The second element (analysis) deals with the identification of relevant content, main actors and services on the social web, impact analysis of customer-oriented activities and interpretation of social web content, supported through analytical technique use (e.g., evaluation, filtering, search, aggregation, enrichment, transformation, etc.). The third element (interaction) comprises functionalities for communication between an organization and social media users, on the basis of interaction technique use (e.g., content delivery, dialogue development, publication, dissemination, recommendation). The fourth element (CRM) refers to functionalities for operational, analytical, communicative, and cooperative CRM activities and for using social content in CRM activities. The fifth element (management/integration) refers to operative and strategic control of social media activities and channels, integration between systems and enhancing capabilities to act on the social web.

Presenting several CRM approaches/models is useful for better understanding the major elements referring to CRM and for the analysis of CRM using the features of the managerial synapse.

CRM Evaluation Using the Features of Managerial Synapse

Customer relationship management is widely practised throughout the world and, when implemented professionally, generates high performance, regardless of the field of activity and/or size of organizations. In this section, CRM will be **evaluated in terms of the defining characteristics of the relationship developed within the managerial synapse:** joint interests and objectives, win-win approach, trust capital, reciprocal advantages, reasonable compromise, dialogic communication, loyalty, commitment, collaboration, cooperation, and a new mechanism – value creation stakeholder partnership.

1 Joint interests and objectives

The CRM background is always represented by common and/or complementary interests of the organization and the customers involved. These interests usually refer to the type, quality, price, and quantity of the products provided by the company. Sometimes the location, the size and the prestige of the company and of the stakeholders, the business potential, market evolution, and/or other significant elements in the specific context are important. Based on common interests, the organization and the stakeholders negotiate joint objectives, which are incorporated frequently in the contracts. Joint interests and objectives are mandatory in all CRM. In business there are relatively frequent situations when the joint objectives do not reflect the common and/or complementary interests sufficiently. When such a situation occurs, the sustainability of CRM is not ensured and the continuation of the business between the company and its customers is in danger.

2 Win-win approach

CRM, regardless of the types of programmes (continuity marketing, one-to-one marketing, partnering/co-marketing) and customers (mass markets, distributors, business to business), very frequently focuses on win-win approaches. On the one hand, the companies that sell products/provide services obtain income as a result of transactions with customers, and on the other hand, the clients – natural or legal individuals – gain as a result of the acquisitions, either at the level of psychological satisfaction or from the economic point of view, as a result of carrying out economic activities under the conditions of a convenient ratio between the quality and the price of the purchases. However, not all CRM approaches are based on win-win negotiation; quite frequently some companies or powerful customers do not use win-win negotiation, but "forceful" negotiation, neglecting or not taking into consideration enough the major interests of the other part. There are specialists (e.g., Polonsky & Wood, 2001) who have referred to situations in which companies implemented CRM tactics that increased corporate returns without corresponding benefits for consumers and society. Also, there are situations in which customers do not generate profit, or enough profit, from sales, altering the win-win approach. In such a situation CRM is not able to generate performant and sustainable business for the company and customers involved.

3 Trust capital

Building trust is one of the major areas on which the company needs to focus in order to accomplish strong customer relationships (McKean, 2003; Payne, 2005). Trust is the central element in maintaining and reinforcing the existing relationships and represents the key issue in CRM (Law, Wong, & Lau, 2005). In aiming to build and develop clients' trust, CRM approaches strive to treat customers honestly and ethically, to respond rapidly to their problems and/or queries. Customers are more drawn to trustworthy partners and the most important outcomes of customers' trust are better cooperation, enhanced commitment and prolonged relationship duration. According to Boulding, Staelin, Ehret, and Johnston (2005), the precursor to trust capital is fairness, and for this reason organizations must be very careful that CRM activities do not cross the line regarding what the customers consider fair. Although CRM approaches have proven to be efficient, with a broadly favourable impact on organizations' activities, situations where customers have perceived themselves as being exploited by a company's CRM schemes are frequently encountered. This is due to the fact that CRM is sometimes overused or misused, and to some marketing tactics that are deceptive or manipulative, based on wrong practices that harm customers and increase distrust (Nguyen, Simkin, & Canhoto, 2015). Some specialists (e.g.,

Nguyen, 2012) have referred to the potential hidden costs of customer distrust for organizations (disloyalty, negative word of mouth, diminishing of customer lifetime value, reducing of marketing effectiveness, etc.).

4 Reciprocity/reciprocal advantages

CRM is a managerial approach based on the reciprocal behaviour of the parties involved, namely the organization that sells/provides services and the entity that buys (individual or legal). Specialists (e.g., Payne, 2005) have emphasized that there must be advantages for both parties for successful CRM. Most companies that implement CRM strategies/approaches/systems view customer relationships, especially long-term and B2B-type relationships, as partnerships oriented toward a constant effort to create added value in the mutual exchange of values between buyer and seller. Reciprocal benefits are economic, social, ecological, psychological, etc. There are organizations in which CRM is mistakenly approached, where the focus is on "what the firm could do, not what the customer would get", eluding to the fact that "if there is no benefit to the customer, there can be no benefit to the company" (Payne, 2005, p. XIV). In CRM, reciprocity has a very important behavioural dimension, with the values, fairest attitudes and behaviours of the people who work being quite often determinant for the continuation and performances of the business. There are numerous situations when behavioural elements have a negative impact on CRM, sometimes even stopping the trade relationships.

5 Reasonable compromise

Most of the relationships between organizations and their customers are characterized by mutual concessions, even renunciations, usually within reasonable limits. Thus, on the one hand, CRM schemes incorporate loyalty programmes, bonuses, discounts, deals, staggered payments, personalized products/services tailored to clients' particular needs, etc., and on the other hand, customers are willing to continue buying products/services under conditions of a reasonable price-quality ratio and possibly paying a higher price for the brand, various services, personalization, etc. When there are divergences between the company and the client, it is generally sought to settle them amicably, as litigation in court results in termination of the relationship. Although CRM operationalizes concession-based relationships, many agreements between companies and customers cease due to the impossibility of making reasonable compromises (purchases from an important competitor of the organization, late payments, unethical behaviour, imposing low prices, constraint attempts, requesting too many concessions, etc.). Reasonable compromise makes a major contribution to the fulfilment of joint objectives, win-win negotiations and reciprocal advantages.

6 Dialogic communication

Unlike traditional/transactional marketing, relational marketing focuses on frequent and intense communication with customers. CRM approaches have implemented systems through which representatives of organizations and customers are permanently in dialogue, bearing in mind that communication between partners is essential to the functioning of the relationship. The development of information and communication technologies has generated electronic CRM and social CRM implementation in many organizations, enabling one-to-one dialogue more frequently, both within B2B (business to business) and B2C (business to customer) relationships. Strategic CRM is able to integrate customer interactions across all communication channels, and front-office and back-office applications/business functions. CRM approaches frequently customize communications by tailoring the content and style of customer communications, usually for a particular segment or specific client, to ensure that the expectations of customers are met. Due to fierce competition, in the last few years a tendency for increased frequency of communications with customers in general (including advertising, brochures, and annual reports), and especially increased dialogic communications via the Internet, have been noticed, but also a decrease in face-to-face communications, which are often more efficient. For the sustainability of the company-customer relationship, equilibrium between communication using social media and direct communication, face-to-face, is always necessary.

7 Loyalty and commitment

Without any doubt, CRM is the field in which company managers pay the greatest attention to loyalty. It was obvious more than a century ago that maintaining and increasing company sales depends largely on the organization's capacity to cultivate the customers' loyalty. Customer loyalty means the tendency of customers to continue to buy products and services from the same provider. Loyalty is generated mainly by customer satisfaction.

CRM, in order to obtain customer loyalty, develops loyalty segmentation and loyalty schemes. In loyalty segmentation, customers are evaluated and divided into three segments: very loyal, moderately loyal and disloyal. With these groups, based on analysis, any common characteristics are identified, so the product can be targeted at the prospectively loyal customers (Payne, 2005). Loyalty schemes through credits offered to customers can be used to guide customer acquisition, retention and development and may then serve as an exit barrier to customers. The credits accumulated reflect the value of the investment that a customer has made in the scheme and therefore in the relationship (Buttle, 2009). Customer loyalty has as a consequence **consumer commitment**, which, according to Walter, Mueller, Helfert, and Wilson

(2002, p. 8), is "the intention of a customer to maintain a long-term relationship with a supplier". It is a measure of the future of the relationship. Concomitantly, the commitment of the company employees' managers specialized in customers is necessary, in order to maintain and develop long-term reciprocal advantageous relationships with the clients. This also requires a clear understanding of the potential benefits in terms of customer segment lifetime value (Payne, 2005).

While CRM approaches place in the foreground the increase of the loyalty of the clients, the loyalty of the company towards the clients is, not infrequently, neglected (e.g., promotional deals dedicated to new customers to the detriment of loyal customers, differentiated treatment of loyal clients), and some clients believe that loyalty within their relationship with the organization is not mutual, but is only one way – from the client to the company. Besides these special loyalty actions, customer loyalty is positively influenced by joint objectives, win-win negotiation, reciprocal advantages and dialogic communication.

The CRM approaches favour to a high degree the commitment of customers and employees/managers in dealing with clients, but the unfair or wrong practices of some organizations negatively affect trust, which is an essential component of commitment, both of the clients to the company, and at the level of organization employees' loyalty.

8 Collaboration and cooperation

Any CRM – more or less sophisticated from a technological and/or social point of view – generates performances for company and customers only when it becomes operational. In practice, the main content of the CRM means effective and efficient collaborative and cooperative relationships between customers and company. In order to achieve this, everyone within the business must understand that they perform a role in serving customers (Payne, 2005) and that trust is vital and it should be present in each person and organization involved (Nguyen, 2012).

In practice, companies using CRM do not always succeed in developing relationships with customers based on mutual trust, which creates major difficulties regarding performant and sustainable collaboration and cooperation.

9 Shared performances and rewards

The main goal of CRM, as we have already emphasized in the first part of this chapter, is to increase the sales/buying of the company and its customers under conditions of reciprocal gains and satisfaction. This goal can only be achieved if each part contributes to the creation of enough value added that is able to satisfy reasonably the needs and expectations of the company and the customers. Successful CRM contains mechanisms capable of creating and sharing high performances for each party involved, to provide expected rewards to them. In business, CRM cannot always achieve such mechanisms. This explains why relatively many companies using CRM, after a certain period, do not continue their relationship with many customers. Shared performances mechanism, highly motivating the company and their customers to have sustainable relationships, represents a key element in CRM practices.

Evaluation of CRM from the point of view of the managerial synapse's main characteristics reveals its existence to different extents and in specific ways. CRM in the majority of its types is focused on the joint interests of the company and customers involved and is based, to a certain degree, on win-win negotiation, trust capital, reciprocal advantages, reasonable compromise, dialogic communication, loyalty and commitment, collaboration and cooperation, and shared performances and rewards. Of course, its intensity and approaches vary to a large degree from one type of CRM to another, and from one company to another.

CRM approaches from the last decade, based on relational marketing, long-term vision and relationships with customers, and especially on customization, using to a large extent specific software, including cloud based and social media, are closer to the valuable managerial synapse. CRM, by focusing on the customer, one of the most important stakeholders of the company, achieves one essential step ahead in managing much more performant company stakeholders.

Integration in CRM approaches of the new specific managerial synapse elements can contribute significantly to higher performances for both the company and their relevant customers.

Perspectives and Ways to Develop CRM in Order to Become a Performant Managerial Synapse

In this section, we deal **only with the CRM that is focused on relevant stakeholders,** which need and deserve a special mechanism in order to fully valorize their potential and to develop sustainable relationships with the company. Our proposal regarding the development of CRM in order to become a mature and performant managerial synapse is based mainly on **three elements:**

- features of the managerial synapse and mechanisms of its building and development;
- evaluation of CRM approaches and development in the last few years;
- main trends in the companies and business environment.

The starting point in the remodelling of CRM should be represented by the "Guide for performant managerial synapse construction, work and performance", presented in Chapter 6. All 14 phases incorporated in the guide should be adapted, of course, to the specificity of customers, sales and supply processes and taking into consideration the influences of the recent Covid-19 pandemic. In using this guide, we recommend paying **special attention to the following set of essential elements:**

A **Development of customer value chain**

The vision and the analysis should be based on the virtual value chain. As we have already outlined, in the present and near future the virtual value chain represents a business model capable of integrating the latest business informatics and social development. A virtual value chain focused on knowledge, the most important resource in the smart economy, and on networking, is an outstanding mechanism for connecting and valorizing the relevant external and internal company stakeholders. A specialized value chain for company customers – like the CRM value chain elaborated by Buttle (2009) – can be very helpful in this respect.

B **Determination of joint objectives**

Determination of the joint objectives for a company and relevant stakeholders is very important and frequently a difficult process in the construction of a manager-relevant stakeholders managerial synapse. For this type of managerial synapse, it is recommended to use the SMART model, which helps to determine for each component of the managerial synapse specific, measurable, agreed, realistic and time-bounded objectives. The other two models presented in Chapter 6 of the book – the "process centred objectives model" and the "contingency model of objectives" – are not recommended for this type of managerial synapse. The use of the SMART model should be based on win-win negotiation in order to establish joint objectives, highly motivational for the company and relevant customers, and to help in the development of a sustainable relationship. It is recommended that joint objectives are incorporated in a formal relational type of contract that creates a flexible framework designed with a view to achieving faster collaboration in strategic relationships over the long term (Frydlinger, Hart, & Vitasek, 2019).

C **Positive identity in work construction**

In recent years, many performant companies have focused on constructing a positive identity at work (see Section 7.6 in Chapter 7 of the book). A positive identity construction means that the person involved reconstruct themselves in their work field, resulting in strengthening themselves at work, increasing their capacity to generate and share knowledge, to take on new demands and challenges and to cope with stress, thereby enhancing performances regarding the size of sales, profit, market share, etc. According to the specialists Dutton, Roberts, and

Bednar (2010), there are several pathways to construct a positive identity at work for the customer and the company. For company managers or specialists the following paths are suitable:

- path 2, which increases the trust and respect in the relationships between company manager/specialist and relevant customer;
- path 3, which makes a company representative and customer more attractive as a relational partner;
- path 7, which encourages the component of managerial synapse to develop new relationships between them.

Because it is possible for one person – company manager or customer – to develop multiple identities, it is important to solve potential conflicts among these identities. Specialists (e.g., Jones & Hynie, 2017) recommend several approaches, with reconciliation and realignment being suitable in the case of this managerial synapse.

Building a positive identity for the constituents of the customer–company manager synapse generates many advantages, including a positive company specialist attitude, task performance, citizenship behaviour and more effective task organization (Gallo, 2015).

D Use of a comprehensive set of motivations

The functionality and performance of the managerial synapse with a relevant stakeholder depend largely on the degree of motivation of each individual involved. In Table 8.1, we present an indicative goals–motivation matrix, which might be used in order to increase the motivation of the relevant customers, and the company managers and specialists working with them. Elements incorporated in this matrix have been selected from the general indicative goals–motivation matrix presented in Section 6.9, Chapter 6, projected for all types of company-relevant stakeholders. Motivations, approaches and tools should be differentiated and personalized for each managerial synapse and for each manager, specialist and customer. In the differentiation and personalization of motivations it is recommended to take into consideration the main synapse joint objectives, the nature and complexity of the tasks to be accomplished by each person, the individual characteristics and motivational specificity of each managerial synapse component and the specific market trends (see Table 8.1).

E Focus on the value creation stakeholder partnership with customers

The management and promotion of a company manager/specialist–relevant customer managerial synapse should be based on several new economic and accounting approaches developed by specialists (Amit & Zott, 2001; Andon, Baxter, & Chua, 2015; Bosse, Phillips, & Harrison,

Table 8.1 Orientative goals–motivations matrix for manager/specialist–relevant customer managerial synapse

GOAL TYPE	CAREER PLAN	TASK FEEDBACK	SIMPLE "THANK YOU"	WAGE RISE	BONUSES	PROFIT SHARING	STOCK OPTIONS	INTERNET FAMOUS[1]	THANKING EMPLOYEE[2]	TROPHY	PUBLIC APPRECIATION OF WORK WELL DONE	FLEXIBLE WORK SCHEDULE	OPPORTUNITIES FOR ADVANCEMENT	GIVING TIME OFF	APPRECIATION GIFTS	VOUCHERS TANGIBLE GOALS[3]	COMPANY PARTY AND CELEBRATION	UPGRADE WORKPLACE	COMPANY-PAID FAMILY ACTIVITY EVENTS	FAMILY SUPPORT PROGRAMME	OPPORTUNITY TO WORK FROM HOME	LEARNING AND DEVELOPING OPPORTUNITIES[4]	PROMOTION	FINANCIAL PENALTIES	MORAL SANCTIONS	OVERALL HAPPINESS[5]
0	1	2	3	4	5	6	7	8	9	10	11	12	13	14	15	16	17	18	19	20	21	22	23	24	25	26
1. TO SUPPLY		x	x	x	x			x	x		x				x	x							x	x	x	
2. TO BUY		x	x	x	x			x	x		x				x	x							x	x	x	
3. TO SELL		x	x	x	x			x	x	x	x	x	x	x	x	x	x				x	x	x	x	x	x
4. TO INNOVATE		x	x	x	x	x	x	x	x	x	x	x	x	x	x	x	x	x	x	x	x	x	x			x
5. TO SUPPORT		x	x	x	x				x			x	x										x	x	x	
6. TO INCREASE INCOME		x	x	x	x	x	x	x	x	x	x	x	x	x	x	x	x	x	x	x	x	x	x			x
7. TO TRAIN	x	x	x	x				x	x	x	x	x	x	x	x	x						x	x	x	x	
8. TO COMMUNICATE		x	x					x	x	x	x				x	x								x	x	
9. TO COLABORATE WITH		x	x					x	x	x	x				x	x							x	x	x	
10. TO COOPERATE		x	x					x	x	x	x				x	x							x	x	x	
11. TO SHARE		x	x					x	x	x	x	x	x	x	x	x							x	x	x	

2009; Bowman & Ambrosini, 2000; Brandenburger & Stuart Jr., 1996; Brown & Dillard, 2015; Crane, Graham, & Himick, 2015; Garcia-Castro & Aguilera, 2015; Harrison & van der Laan Smith, 2015; Lepak, Smith, & Taylor, 2007; Mitchell, Van Buren, Greenwood, & Freeman, 2015). These elements are at least the following:

- concept of total value created by the firm and all its stakeholders;
- model of value creation and appropriation with multiple stakeholders;
- value creation elasticity of stakeholder value appropriation;
- new branch of accounting focused on the relationship with stakeholders.

Using these new elements and other theoretical and pragmatic developments a new mechanism has been elaborated – value creation partnership – that helps to measure the contribution of the relevant customers and other stakeholders and to reflect it in accounting. This mechanism, which is in its "infancy", provides the necessary information and knowledge to the company management in order to determine the contribution of relevant customers to the creation of company's total value and to reward them accordingly.

A value creation stakeholder partnership is an expression of the managerial approach reflecting the newly empowered consumers in an evolving economy (Kihlström, 2019).

F Networking the company manager/specialist–relevant customer managerial synapse

A managerial synapse integrating the relevant customer generates better performances when it is networking with other managerial mechanisms. Three types of networking are mainly recommended:

a Integration of the managerial synapse in the individual supply chain management (Miri-Lavassani, Movahedi, & Kumar, 2009) which is used most frequently in small companies. These companies usually represent about 90% of all companies in every country. There are individual supply chains specific to producers, suppliers and customers. By connecting the company manager/specialist–relevant customer managerial synapse with the individual chain of other customers the design, manufacture, distribution, marketing, sales and service for a product can be better correlated;

b Integration of the managerial synapse in the supply chain management that uses a supply chain collaboration platform (Sanders, 2017). This type of approach is usually used in corporations, large and medium-sized companies, valorizing to a high degree the collaborative platform and often generating a great and sustainable increase in sales, profit, market share, etc.

c Integration of the managerial synapse focused on the relevant customer in the company's relevant stakeholder management system. This system will be presented in Chapters 9, 10, and 11 of the book, and it is indicated there how the different company managerial synapses can be integrated within the system. This solution is able to ensure superior performances for a company and its relevant stakeholders.

Classification of Manager-Relevant Customer Synapse

In our opinion the six perspectives and approaches presented above should be the first to be taken into consideration by those who want to develop the CRM as a mature and performant managerial synapse. Each of them should be customized to the particular conditions of each company, its commercial managers and specialists and the relevant customers involved. In Table 8.2, we present the **main types of this synapse and their main characteristics.**

The information presented above can contribute to a better understanding of, and approach to, the manager/specialist–customer managerial synapse, enabling enhanced functionality and competitivity in organizations.

Main Advantages and Limitations of the Customer-Centred Managerial Synapse

The company manager/specialist–relevant consumer managerial synapse, compared with the classical company approach of customers with CRM, has many **potential advantages:**

- Development of a participative approach and team spirit between the company staff in the commercial field and the relevant customers;
- More fruitful win-win negotiation between company and relevant customers;
- Significant increase of the motivation degree of commercial company personnel and relevant stakeholders for higher efforts, productivity and other performances
- Increase of the joint decisions and actions between the managers and specialists on the one hand and relevant customer on the other;
- Contribution to the development of a positive identity at work both in the company commercial field and in the relevant customers' organization;

Table 8.2 Types of manager–relevant customer synapse

No.	*Criteria of Classification*	*Types of Managerial Synapse*	*Types of the Manager–Customer Managerial Synapse*
1.	Components organizational membership	• Internal • Internal–external	**Internal-external** The two managerial synapse components are from different entities: manager or specialist focused on company customer on the one hand, which is an internal component, and customer representative, on the other hand, which is an external component. The objectives of the two organizations are integrated through the managerial synapse into common objectives, in order to co-create value for both organizations. Relationships within the managerial synapse between representatives of two organizations are complex and are influenced by organizational barriers and cultural differences.
2.	Type of managerial synapse components	• Organizational • Organizational–individual	**Organizational** The components of the managerial synapse represent two organizations, one of seller/supplier and the other in the state of buyer. There are four categories of objectives and interests that should be harmonized: of the organization that sells, of the customer, of the seller's manager/specialist and of the customer representative.Managerial synapse is characterized by an intense organizational dimension, and the relationships within the managerial synapse are complex, being deeply influenced by the strategical, political and cultural elements of both entities.

3.	Duration of the managerial synapse	• Determined • Undetermined	**Determined** Duration of the managerial synapse functioning is determined according to the contract between the seller company and customer. Relationships between manager and representative of institutional customer have formal basis, supporting establishment of the common objectives, decisions and actions, as well as intense cooperation within the managerial synapse
4.	Common objectives and interest types	• Organizational–personal • Organizational–social	**Organizational-personal** The harmonization process within the managerial synapse between the common objectives, interests and expectations of seller company or services provider, institutional customer and representatives of these two organizations is very complex and time-consuming, involving a lot of issues like intense communication, negotiation skills, trust, loyalty, commitment, etc.
5.	Nature of the common objectives	• Economic • Social • Ecologic • Multidimensional synapse	**Economic** The common objectives of seller or services provider and customer are mainly oriented to the economic aspects – turnover, profit, return on investment, price, acquisition cost, level of sales, market share, rhythmic supply, quality of products/services, productivity, etc. – that are important for the survival, development and competitivity of both organizations. **Multidimensional** Due to the increasing importance of social aspects and tendency of expanding ecological and social approaches, especially in developed and emerging countries, a significant proportion of manager–customer synapses must incorporate not only economic objectives but also social and ecological ones. The multidimensional managerial synapses are characterized by the establishment of quantitative (profit, turnover, sales, etc.) and qualitative (energetic efficiency, employment of young people, expectations of local communities, etc.) joint objectives whose

(*Continued*)

Table 8.2 (Continued)

No.	*Criteria of Classification*	*Types of Managerial Synapse*	*Types of the Manager–Customer Managerial Synapse*
			achievement impact significantly the company's brand, performance, competitivity and sustainability.
6.	Nature of the processes incorporated	• Focused on the procurement of the resources • Focused on the internal work processes • Focused directly on performance fulfilment • Diversified	**Focused directly on performance fulfilment** This type of synapse places in the foreground the processes oriented towards performances desired to be achieved by the company found in the position of the seller/services provider and the customer according to the negotiated joint objectives. The common objectives are ordinarily precisely formulated and refer mainly to quantitative aspects (profit, level of sales, prices, percentage of the market, etc.), but can also be qualitative (renewal rhythm of products/services, approach of social or ecological issues, etc.).
7.	Necessity for the company	• Mandatory • Optional	**Mandatory** Managerial synapses between company manager/specialist and relevant customer are mandatory type, because improvement of relationships with the most important customers impacts decisively the survival and development of organizations.Development of an intense collaborative mechanism with relevant customer according to managerial synapse defining features must be undertaken on the basis of organization experience and know-how accumulated in previous CRM processes conducted during the existence of the company.

- Strengthening both categories of stakeholders – company employees and relevant customers at work;
- Intensification of the constructive and innovative behaviour of the commercial company managers and specialists and, respectively, relevant customers;
- Increase of the information, knowledge, deposit and transport facilities, etc. sharing between company commercial staff and the relevant customers;
- Increased capacity of the company and relevant customers to implement artificial intelligence, analytical metrics and other new digitalization gadgets for networking;
- Contribution to the development of an open and collaborative organizational culture at the level of company and relevant customers;
- Decrease of the conflict situations between the company's commercial representatives and relevant customers;
- Increase of company sales and relevant customers buying in the short, medium and long term;
- Increased engagement of relevant customers and company commercial managers and specialists in their organizations, in order to achieve joint objectives;
- Increase of sales and added value created by relevant customers and company employees in the commercial field;
- More sustainable relationship between company and relevant customers.

Concomitantly, this managerial synapse presents several **specific limitations:**

- Construction and development of managerial synapse incorporating relevant customers is very demanding in time and effort for those involved;
- Difficulty in reshaping the mentality and work approach of company managers and relevant customers according to the new managerial mechanism contained by managerial synapse;
- The relevant customer, either individual or organizational, has certain specific interests, different from joint interests, which do not always favour the managerial synapse construction, functioning and performance;
- One participant in the managerial synapse – the relevant customer – is not a component of the company, having an organizational culture and work approach different from the company staff involved;
- Managers and specialists from a company that sells products and services do not often have enough knowledge and time in order to properly communicate, understand, negotiate and develop effective relationships with the relevant stakeholder;
- Difficulty in harmonizing the decisions, actions and behaviours of people who work in two organizations and have and other tasks to fulfil;
- Relevant customer is working in another location than the company, sometimes a long distance away, which can negatively influence the communication and cooperation with company representatives;
- The representative of the relevant customer, especially when they

represent a large organization, depends from other manager in his company, which cannot be receptive enough to their integration in a managerial synapse with a representative of another company;

- Advancement of the relevant customer's career depends mainly on their own organization and much less on their work inside the managerial synapse with the representative from the sales company.

Finally, we consider it necessary to make the following **three remarks**:

a We emphasize the advantages of a managerial synapse incorporating relevant customers, because they represent arguments for using it. As we can see, there are 15 such arguments referring to the important elements for the company and relevant customers managerial synapse functioning and performance; these advantages continue to be valuable in the Covid-19 pandemic context.

b We emphasize the limitations faced by constructing and functioning the managerial synapse centred on relevant customers in order to facilitate their taking into consideration and avoiding major mistakes.

c Together, the advantages and the limitations provide a more analytic and realistic perception of this managerial synapse, enabling effective implementation in business.

The current evolution to the smart economy, digitalization, internationalization, artificial intelligence, metric analysis and other trends provides information, knowledge and tools capable of overcoming the limitations and simultaneously increasing and valorizing the specific advantages of this managerial synapse.

In the complex context generated by the Covid-19 pandemic in the CRM approach, and taking into consideration its advantages and limitations, the HEART framework, proposed recently by specialists, could be useful (Waldron & Wetherbe, 2020).

Notes

1 Internet famous means: appreciations of employee on the company website, email with employee appreciation to everyone in the company, employee work business impact report on the company website, announcement with star of the month, etc.

2 Thanking employee by: praising employee, certificate of achievement, announcing an accomplishment at a company meeting, personal note of praise from manager, letter with thanks, handwritten appreciation note, etc.

3 Vouchers for: free or subsidized meals, fruits or drinks, sporting events, artistic events, paid group meals, wellness programmes, and other holiday vouchers.

4 Learning and development opportunities like: conference participation, training programmes, exhibition visits, mentoring, coaching, tutoring, counselling, etc.

5 Overall happiness, see the analysis of Harrison and Wicks (2013).

References

Alt, R., & Reinhold, O. (2019). *Social customer relationship management: Fundamentals, applications, technologies.* Gewerbestrasse, CH: Springer Nature. doi:10.1007/978-3-030-23343-3.

Amit, R., & Zott, C. (2001). Value creation in e-business. *Strategic Management Journal*, *22*(6–7), 493–520. doi:10.1002/smj.187.

Andon, P., Baxter, J., & Chua, W. F. (2015). Accounting for stakeholders and making accounting useful. *Journal of Management Studies*, *52*(7), 986–1002. doi:10.1111/joms.12142.

Askool, S., & Nakata, K. (2011). A conceptual model for acceptance of social CRM systems based on a scoping study. *AI & Society*, *26*(3), 205–220. doi:10.1007/s00146-010-0311-5.

Bălan, C. (2007). Managementul relatiilor cu clientii: valente strategice, operationale si analitice. *Revista de Marketing Online (Journal of Online Marketing)*, *1*(3), 6–17.

Bergeron, B. (2004). *Essentials of CRM: A guide to customer relationship management.* New York: John Wiley & Sons.

Blery, E. K., & Michalakopoulos, M. G. (2006). An e-CRM application in the telecommunications sector: A case study from Greece. *EuroMed Journal of Business*, *1*(2), 5–14. doi:10.1108/14502190610750135.

Bosse, D. A., Phillips, R. A., & Harrison, J. S. (2009). Stakeholders, reciprocity, and firm performance. *Strategic Management Journal*, *30*(4), 447–456. doi:10.1002/smj.743.

Boulding, W., Staelin, R., Ehret, M., & Johnston, W. J. (2005). A customer relationship management roadmap: What is known, potential pitfalls, and where to go. *Journal of Marketing*, *69* (4), 155–166. doi:10.1509/jmkg.2005.69.4.155.

Bowman, C., & Ambrosini, V. (2000). Value creation versus value capture: Towards a coherent definition of value in strategy. *British Journal of Management*, *11*(1), 1–15. doi:10.1111/1467-8551.00147.

Brandenburger, A. M., & Stuart Jr., H. W. (1996). Value-based business strategy. *Journal of Economics & Management Strategy*, *5*(1), 5–24. doi:10.1111/j.1430-9134.1996.00005.x.

Brown, J., & Dillard, J. (2015). Dialogic accountings for stakeholders: On opening up and closing down participatory governance. *Journal of Management Studies*, *52*(7), 961–985. doi:10.1111/joms.12153.

Brunjes, B., & Roderick, R. (2002). *Customer relationship management: Why it does and does not work in South Africa.* Paper presented at the IMM Marketing Educators Conference, South Africa.

Burnett, K. (2001). *The handbook of key customer relationship management: The definitive guide to winning, managing and developing key account business.* Upper Saddle River, NJ: Prentice Hall.

Buttle, F. (2001, February). The CRM value chain. *Marketing Business*, pp. 52–55. Retrieved from https://www.researchgate.net/publication/228396256_The_CRM_value_chain.

Buttle, F. A. (2004). *Customer relationship management: Concepts and tools*. Oxford, UK: Elsevier Butterworth-Heinemann.

Buttle, F. A. (2009). *Customer relationship management: Concepts and technologies* (2nd ed.). Oxford, UK: Elsevier Butterworth-Heinemann. Retrieved from https://knowledgestreams.files.wordpress.com/2013/07/francis_buttle-customer_relationship_management_second_edition-butterworth-heinemann2008_2.pdf.

Chen, I. J., & Popovich, K. (2003). Understanding customer relationship management (CRM): People, process and technology. *Business Process Management Journal*, *9*(5), 672–688. doi:10.1108/14637150310496758.

Couldwell, C. (1999, February 18). Loyalty bonuses. *Marketing Week*, p. 14.

Crane, A., Graham, C., & Himick, D. (2015). Financializing stakeholder claims. *Journal of Management Studies*, *52*(7), 878–906. doi:10.1111/joms.12147.

CRM. (n.d.). *Wikipedia*. Retrieved from https://ro.wikipedia.org/wiki/CRM.

Drucker, P. F. (1954). *The practice of management*. New York: Harper.

Dutton, J. E., Roberts, L. M., & Bednar, J. (2010). Pathways for positive identity construction at work: Four types of positive identity and the building of social resources. *Academy of Management Review*, *35*(2), 265–293. Retrieved from https://www.researchgate.net/publication/228354753_Pathways_for_Positive_Identity_Construction_at_Work_Four_Types_of_Positive_Identity_and_the_Building_of_Social_Resources 10.5465/amr.35.2.zok265.

Dyché, J. (2002). *The CRM handbook: A business guide to customer relationship management*. Boston, MA: Addison-Wesley.

Ellatif, M. M. A. (2008). A cluster technique to evaluate effect of ECRM on customers' satisfaction of e-commerce websites. *SSRN Electronic Journal*. doi:10.2139/ssrn.1128802.

Faase, R., Helms, R., & Spruit, M. (2011). Web 2.0 in the CRM domain: Defining social CRM. *International Journal of Electronic Customer Relationship Management*, *5*(1), 1–22. doi:10.1504/IJECRM.2011.039797.

Farooqi, R., & Dhusia, D. K. (2011). A comparative study of CRM and e-CRM technologies. *Indian Journal of Computer Science and Engineering*, 2(4), 624–627.

Frydlinger, D., Hart, O., & Vitasek, K. (2019). A new approach to contracts. *Harvard Business Review*, *97*(5), 116–124.

Gaetano, N. D. (2018, August 8). *The evolution of CRM (and where it's going) in the future*. Retrieved from https://www.saleshacker.com/evolution-of-customer-relationship-management/.

Galbreath, J., and Rogers, T. (1999). Customer relationship leadership: A leadership and motivation model for the twenty-first century business. *The TQM Magazine*, *11*(3), 161–171. doi:10.1108/09544789910262734.

Gallo, A. (2015). How to build a meaningful career. *Harvard Business Review*. Retrieved from https://hbr.org/2015/02/how-to-build-a-meaningful-career.

Garcia-Castro, R., & Aguilera, R. V. (2015). Incremental value creation and appropriation in a world with multiple stakeholders. *Strategic Management Journal*, *36*(1), 137–147. doi:10.1002/smj.2241.

Gartner. (n.d.). *Gartner glossary*. Retrieved from https://www.gartner.com/en/information-technology/glossary/customer-relationship-management-crm.

Glazer, R. (1997). Strategy and structure in information-intensive markets: The relationship between marketing and IT. *Journal of Market Focused Management*, 2 (1), 65–81. doi:10.1023/A:1009793717081.

Gneiser, M. S. (2010). Value-based CRM: The interaction of the triad of marketing, financial management, and IT. *Business & Information Systems Engineering*, 2(2), 95–103. doi:10.1007/s12599-010-0095-7.

Greenberg, P. (2009). *CRM at the speed of light: Social CRM strategies, tools and techniques for engaging customers*. New York: McGraw-Hill.

Hammer, M., & Champy, J. (1993). *Reengineering the corporation: A manifesto for business revolution*. New York: Harper Business.

Harrigan, P., Ramsey, E., & Ibbotson, P. (2012). Exploring and explaining SME marketing: Investigating e-CRM using a mixed methods approach. *Journal of Strategic Marketing*, *20*(2), 127–163. doi:10.1080/0965254X.2011.606911.

Harrison, J. S., & van der Laan Smith, J. (2015). Responsible accounting for stakeholders. *Journal of Management Studies*, *52*(7), 935–960. doi:10.1111/joms.12141.

Harrison, J. S., & Wicks, A. C. (2013). Stakeholder theory, value and firm performance. *Business Ethics Quarterly*, *23*(1), 97–124. doi:10.5840/beq20132314.

Hobby, J. (1999). Looking after the one who matters. *Accountancy Age* (October 28), pp. 28–30.

Jha, L. (2008). *Customer relationship management: A strategic approach*. New Delhi, India: Global India Publications.

Jones, J. M., & Hynie, M. (2017). Similarly torn, differentially shorn? The experience and management of conflict between multiple roles, relationships, and social categories. Frontiers *in Psychology*, *8*, 1732. doi:10.3389/fpsyg.2017.01732.

Kale, S. (2004). CRM failure and the seven deadly sins. *Marketing Management*, *13* (5), 42–46.

Karimi J., Somers T. M., & Gupta Y. P. (2001). Impact of information technology management practices on customer service. *Journal of Management Information Systems*, *17*(4), 125–158. doi:10.1080/07421222.2001.11045661.

Khasenova, D. (2017). *Development of a software module for order status management at an event management company*. Retrieved from https://bibliotecadigital.ipb.pt/bitstream/10198/14663/1/Dinara%20Khasenova.pdf.

Kihlström, G. (2019). *The agile consumer: Navigating the empowered economy and the future of customer experience*. Arlington, VA: Agile Word.

Kotler, P. (1992a). It's time for total marketing. *Business Week Advance Briefs*, 2, 1–21.

Kotler, P. (1992b). Marketing's new paradigms: What's really happening out there. *Planning Review*, *20*(5), 50–52. doi:10.1108/eb054382.

Kotorov, R. P. (2002). Ubiquitous organization: Organizational design for e-CRM. *Business Process Management Journal*, *8*(3), 218–232. doi:10.1108/14637150210428934.

Kumar, V., & Reinartz, W. (2018). *Customer relationship management: Concept, strategy, and tools* (3rd ed.). Berlin, DE: Springer-Verlag.

Law, M., Wong, Y. H., & Lau, T. (2005). The role of trust in customer relationship management: An example to financial services industry. *Asia Pacific Management Review*, *10*(4), 267–274.

Lepak, D. P., Smith. K. G., & Taylor, M. S. (2007). Value creation and value capture: A multilevel perspective. *Academy of Management Review*, *32*(1), 180–194. doi:10.5465/amr.2007.23464011.

McKean, J. (2003). *Customers are people... The human touch*. Chichester, UK: John Wiley & Sons.

Miri-Lavassani., K., Movahedi, B., & Kumar, V. (2009). Transition to B2B e-marketplace enabled supply chain: Readiness assessment and success factors. *The International Journal of Technology, Knowledge, and Society*, *5*(3), 75–88. doi:10.18848/1832-3669/CGP/v05i03/55999.

Mitchell, R. K., Van Buren, H. J., Greenwood, M., & Freeman, R. E. (2015). Stakeholder inclusion and accounting for stakeholders. *Journal of Management Studies*, *52*(7), 851–877. doi:10.1111/joms.12151.

Nguyen, B. (2012). The dark side of customer relationship management: Exploring the underlying reasons for pitfalls, exploitation and unfairness. *Journal of Database Marketing & Customer Strategy Management*, *19*, 56–70. doi:10.1057/dbm.2012.5.

Nguyen, B., Simkin, L., & Canhoto, A. I. (2015). Introduction. In B. Nguyen, L. Simkin, & A. I. Canhoto (Eds.), *The dark side of CRM: Customers, relationships and management* (pp. 1–19) London, UK: Routledge. doi:10.4324/9781315753737.

Pan, S. L., & Lee J.-N. (2003). Using e-CRM for a unified view of the customer. *Communications of the ACM*, *46*(4), 95–99. doi:10.1145/641205.641212.

Parvatiyar, A., & Sheth, J. N. (2001a). Conceptual framework of customer relationship management. In J. N. Sheth, A. Parvatiyar, & G. Shainesh (Eds.), *Customer relationship management: Emerging concepts, tools and applications* (pp. 3–25). New Delhi, India: Tata/McGraw-Hill.

Parvatiyar, A., & Sheth, J. N. (2001b). Customer relationship management: Emerging practice, process, and discipline. *Journal of Economic and Social Research*, *3*(2), 1–34.

Payne, A. (2005). *Handbook of CRM: Achieving excellence in customer management*. Oxford, UK: Butterworth-Heinemann and Elsevier. Retrieved from https://repository.dinus.ac.id/docs/ajar/Handbook_of_CRM.pdf.

Payne, A., & Frow, P. (2005). A strategic framework for customer relationship management. *Journal of Marketing*, *69*(4), 167–176. doi:10.1509/jmkg.2005.69.4.167.

Peppers, D., & Rogers, M. (1993). *The one to one future: Building relationships one customer at a time*. New York: Currency Doubleday.

Peppers, D., & Rogers, M. (1996). *The one-to-one future: Building business relationships one customer at a time*. London: Piatkus.

Peppers, D., & Rogers, M. (2004). *Managing customer relationships: A strategic framework*. Hoboken, NJ: John Wiley & Sons.

Peppers, D., Rogers, M., & Dorf, B. (1993). Is your company ready for one-to-one marketing? *Harvard Business Review*, *77*(1), 151–160.

Polonsky, M. J., & Wood, G. (2001). Can the overcommercialization of cause-related marketing harm society? *Journal of Macromarketing*, *21*(1), 8–22. doi:10.1177/0276146701211002.

Reinartz, W., Krafft, M., & Hoyer, Wayne D. (2004). The customer relationship management process: Its measurement and impact on performance. *Journal of Marketing Research*, *41*(3), 293–305. doi:10.1509/jmkr.41.3.293.35991.

Reinhold, O., & Alt, R. (2011). Analytical social CRM: Concept and tool support. *24th Bled eConference eFuture: Creating Solutions for the Individual, Organisations and Society*, pp. 226–241.

Reiny, I., & Buttle, F. A. (2006). Strategic, operational, and analytical customer relationship management: Attributes and measures. *Journal of Relationship Marketing*, *5*(4), 23–42. doi:10.1300/J366v05n04_03.

Sanders, N. R. (2017). *Supply chain management: A global perspective* (2nd ed.). Hoboken, NJ: John Wiley & Sons.

Santos, J. D., & Castelo, J. P. (2018). The six dimensions of adoption of a CRM strategy. In I. Lee (Ed.), *Diverse methods in customer relationship marketing and management* (pp. 17–43). Hershey, PA: IGI Global.

Stone, M., & Woodcock, N. (2001). Defining CRM and assessing its quality. In B. Foss & M. Stone (Eds.), *Successful customer relationship marketing* (pp. 3–20). London, UK: Kogan.

Subhasish, D. (2007). *Customer relationship management*. New Delhi, India: Excel Books.

Swift, R. S. (2000). *Accelerating customer relationships: Using CRM and relationship technologies*. Upper Saddle River, NJ: Prentice Hall.

Tohidi, H., & Jabbari, M. M. (2012). CRM as a marketing attitude based on customer's information. *Procedia Technology*, *1*, 565–569. doi:10.1016/j.protcy.2012.02.123.

Trainor, K. J., Andzulis, J., Rapp, A., & Agnihotri, R. (2014). Social media technology usage and customer relationship performance: A capabilities-based examination of social CRM. *Journal of Business Research*, *67*(6), 1201–1208. doi:10.1016/j.jbusres.2013.05.002.

Waldron, T., & Wetherbe, J. (2020). Ensure that your customer relationships outlast coronavirus. *Harvard Business Review*. Retrieved from https://hbr.org/2020/04/ensure-that-your-customer-relationships-outlast-coronavirus.

Walter, A., Mueller, T. A., Helfert, G., & Wilson, D. T. (2002). *Delivering relationship value: Key determinant for customers' commitment*. ISBM Report 8–2002. Retrieved from http://citeseerx.ist.psu.edu/viewdoc/download?doi=10.1.1.202.2179&rep=rep1&type=pdf.

9 Company-Relevant Stakeholders-Based Management System

Company Management System Concept

Organization management is the science and the art to combine resources and work processes to generate performance. The management is a vector of the economic and social development, with a decisive contribution in obtaining multidimensional performances. Organization management contains a set of the management processes and relationships, which involve all employees and work processes.

Management processes mean all the phases that determine the objectives of the company and the subsystems incorporated, the resources, the work processes, and the employees necessary to achieve them, using a set of systems, methods, and techniques to efficiently fulfil the organization's founding purpose. Management processes are characterised by the fact that a part of human resources – the managers – decide and act on the work of the other part – the organization's employees – to achieve the highest performance possible.

Within the management processes, we could separate several main components, the management functions: prevision, organization, coordination, motivation, and control evaluation.[1] These functions represent the content of the standard management processes used in any type of organization, despite their specific features. Although the management processes usually represent only a small percentage of all company work processes, because of the specific content, complexity, and implications, they often have a decisive role in gaining competitiveness. In fact, the management processes and the execution processes are complementary, their separation being the normal result of the work labour division. Management processes determine the enhancement of the execution processes, productivity, and more rational harmonisation of work results, according to economic and social requirements, to the demands of the organization's clients.

Management relationships are the second element of the management and determine its specificity and results. Essentially, the management relationship could be defined as the connection among the company

DOI: 10.4324/9781003217701-9

employees and between them and the components of other systems in the processes of prevision, organization, coordination, motivation, and control evaluation. Analysis of the factors that influence the management relationship characteristics in the company reveals a triple determination: social–economic, technical–material, and human.[2]

Numerous concepts, approaches, principles, systems, methods, techniques, procedures have been elaborated to modelate and exercise effectively and efficiently the management processes and relationships. Gradually, organizations' management become professionalised, substantially increasing their rationality and performance.

Company management systems' design and implementation represent a major contribution to management professionalisation. The first company professional-specific management systems were developed after the Second World War to solve the complex business, social, and political problems generated by the transition from the "war economy" to the "normal" economy in the challenging international context. In Figure 9.1, we indicate the most marketed and used company management systems.

A **company management system** could be defined as a coherent ensemble of elements – principles, rules, structures, methods and procedures – used for the modelation and utilisation in a specific manner of all or most of the management processes and relationships in the entire organization or in a large part of it to amplify the efficacy and efficiency and to achieve sustainable competitiveness (Nicolescu & Verboncu, 2008). We outline that the company management systems are different from management techniques – like SWOT analysis, business plan, job enlargement, career plan, decisional tree, Gant diagram, and managerial simulation – especially regarding the size of the work processes involved and the complexity. Management system covers all or a major part of the entire organization's activities. Management technique usually deals with managerial tasks or a set of tasks, which should be done by one or a few company managers. Management systems have greater complexity, incorporating several managerial techniques to be used independently. Management technique is a basic entity, which could not be divided without breaking down or radically changing its structure, content, and finality.

Management system creation and use represent a superior phase in the development of the management theory and practice (see Figure 9.2) because:

a Management systems approach and remodel a set of management processes and relationships in the company, being a systemic managerial mechanism.
b Management systems focus on the achievement of the company-specific objectives that are well defined and often quantified

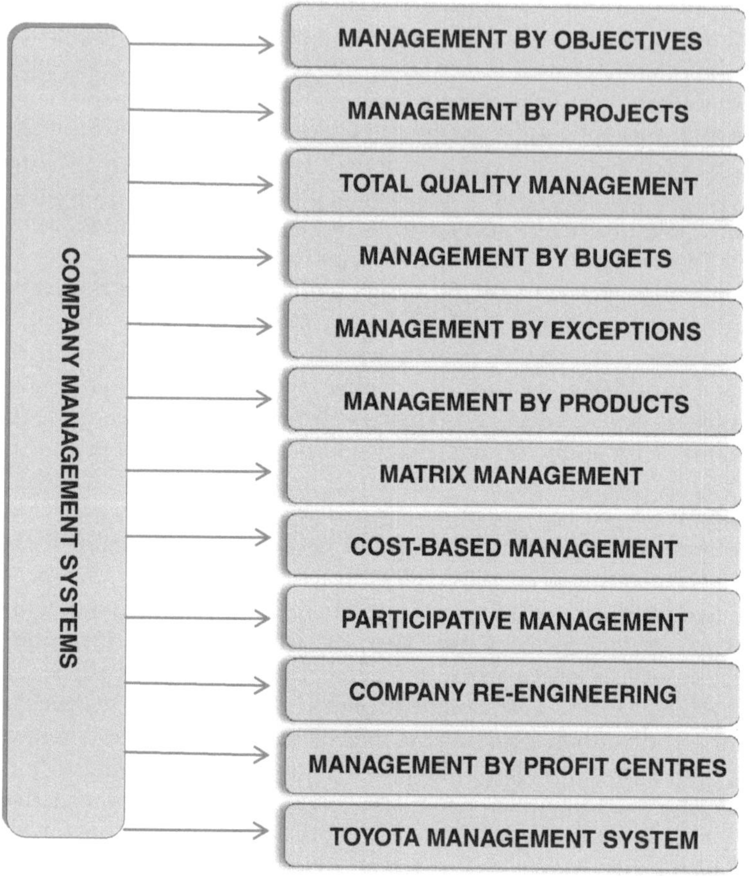

Figure 9.1 Management systems employed in the companies.

regarding the entire or a large part of the organization; all other components of the company management system are determined starting from the management system-specific objectives.

c Management systems represent a methodological undertaking, with a very strong specificity, being rigorously structured in decisional, organizational, informational, motivational, etc. elements precisely defined in implementation and functioning stages and phases, causing deep qualitative changes and better company performance.

d Management systems present high innovational content, generating profound and effective changes in all components of the organization management processes and relationships and a renewal of their approaches and utilisation, which is quite different compared with other managerial systems and mechanisms.

Figure 9.2 Main competitive advantages of the company management systems compared with other methodological approaches.

e Management systems integrate numerous managerial methodological elements that are smaller and less complex (methods, techniques, procedures) and of a different nature (decisional, organizational or informational) that are used in a particular manner, enabling higher company performance.

f Management systems determine deep mutations in all other systems incorporated in the company (technical system, economic system, human system, ecological system, etc.) in their work and performance; management systems are the driving force to change all other elements in the organization.

Management systems are continually improving and renewing under the impact of the organization's exogenous and endogenous evolutions and challenges in all fields: digital, technique, informatic, commercial, financial, human, ecological, social, etc. Every new stage in the development of the society, economy, science, or education demands new managerial approaches and new management systems able to capitalise from the managerial point of view and performance the innovational elements of these phases. The valorisation of the innovational elements is faster, larger, and more performant as the new management systems are professionally designed and used in the companies.

The present transition period to the new economy and digitalisation needs – as many specialists have emphasised (see Chapter 2 of this book) – radical changes in management and requires innovative company management systems that are quite different from the previous systems. According to our analysis, the company stakeholders-based management system represents such a managerial innovation necessary to organizations in the present and future environments.

Necessity of the Stakeholders-Based Management System

Our analysis based on the latest economic and managerial evolutions, on the review of numerous management and business studies and on the trends and challenges in companies, allows us to identify several essential elements that demonstrate the necessity to construct a managerial system focused on the company-relevant stakeholders. We call it **stakeholders-based management.**

We present the **arguments regarding the necessity to use a new stakeholders-based management system in companies** (Figure 9.3).

a **Companies possess only a part of the resources needed to fulfil their objectives,** especially technical, material, and financial resources. Another major part of the necessary resources, especially human, information, and knowledge, is possessed by stakeholders. Also, the company stakeholders comprise significant material resources (suppliers, partners) and financial resources (bankers, investors). All these elements argue the necessity for the company to obtain and use numerous and essential resources from its internal and external stakeholders.

b **The company's own resources, as such, do not create value added only because they exist.** Company resources generate products, services, value added, and profit only if they are employed by human resources, by the stakeholders. The resources, either the company's own or those of stakeholders, are working and producing value through the knowledge and efforts of both internal (managers, executants, and shareholders) and external stakeholders (clients, suppliers, consultants, designers, researchers, investors, and others). Without the work processes done by company stakeholders inside and outside the organization, resources do not produce anything. This means that it is vital for the company to determine the relevant stakeholders to efficiently use the company resources and their own, in the interest of the organization.

c **Company survival and sustainable development depend to a large extent on the organizational stakeholders.** Business reality provides many examples of companies from the same industry having similar resources but with very different development and performances (productivity, costs, sale, profit, environment protection) because of the differences between their stakeholders and the managerial relationships with them. Relevant stakeholders' quality, intensity of motivation, engagement, creativity, and efforts frequently make the difference between companies' development and results. For this reason, it is necessary to approach and manage the relevant company stakeholders in such a way that they intensively and permanently contribute to the company development, using their own knowledge and other resources to a high level.

d **Stakeholders with major influence on the company work and performance are continuously increasing and diversifying in number and quality.** At the beginning of industrial development, company management was focused on the organization and shareholders and on its internal activities, mainly making products and services. Gradually, this managerial approach proved not to be very productive and profitable for companies. Organization management has started slowly to pay more attention to the other stakeholder categories: clients, suppliers, and managers. In recent decades, the influence of these stakeholders increased rapidly, as well as the impact of other stakeholder categories: external investors, business partners, designers, consultants, researchers, local communities and competitors. All these evolutions require the company management to continue to enlarge and diversify the stakeholders taken into consideration. Company management should pay attention to the particularities and specific influence and demand of every relevant stakeholder category and to each relevant stakeholder, based on the organization's strategy.

e **Stakeholders' interests in the company work and performance and, concomitantly, their capacity to significantly impact them are amplifying step by step.** More and more company stakeholders became relevant. Company needs to use more stakeholders' resources (knowledge, raw material, equipment, money, etc.), efforts, and abilities to achieve organization objectives. These elements determine the necessity for the company to deal permanently with relevant stakeholders, taking into consideration their specific interests, requirements, and characteristics. In the company management, relevant stakeholders should be in the central position and approached in specific ways, according to the features of every category of relevant stakeholders and of each relevant stakeholder.

f A major feature of the present time, characterised by the transition to a knowledge-based economy and digitalisation, is transformation of the knowledge in the most important development resource (see Chapter 2).

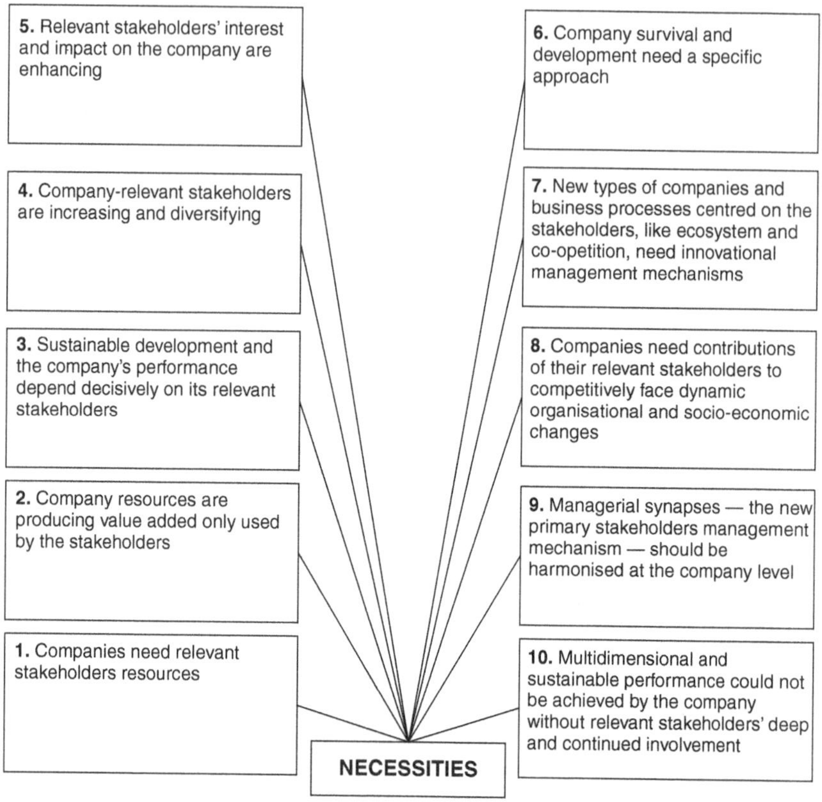

Figure 9.3 The main necessities for the company stakeholders-based management system.

In the company, knowledge is the main raw material and major production means, product, intellectual capital, and competitive advantage. Human resources knowledge – both tacit and explicit – represents major intellectual capital, which determines, more and more, the company's survival and development. **For the activities and performance of every company, the relevant stakeholders' knowledge is essential.**

Determination of the company-relevant stakeholders – internal and external – to mobilise, use, and develop the knowledge, with a special preoccupation with tacit knowledge, is a necessity. For this reason, company management must design and use specific managerial approaches, to determine all relevant stakeholders to fully employ the personal and organizational knowledge[3] for the company development, in a win–win relationship. This is a complex process, as indicated by many studies.[4]

In recent decades, in the transition to a knowledge-based economy and digitalisation, new organization forms have been developed, like ecosystem, networking company, platform network, and cluster, and new economic processes like co-opetition have also been developed. **Stakeholders are playing a decisive role in their creation, development, and performance.** We refer, as an example, to **the ecosystem,** which proliferates quickly and tends to be essential in a new economy.

An ecosystem represents a structure of a multilateral set of partners that interact in order for a focal value proposition to materialise (Adner, 2017). The essential content of an ecosystem is the alignment of activities, actors, positions, and links. This means that an ecosystem involves a set of multiple organizations' stakeholders, which should be managed in specific ways, to generate performance for each of them. A variant of the stakeholders-based management system design, taking into consideration the specificity of the ecosystem, composed of diverse and dispersed partners (Williamson & De Meyer, 2012), could greatly contribute to the ecosystem's sustainable development and high competitivity.

Co-opetition (Peng, Yen, & Bourne, 2017), the new emerging economic process, is a result of the intensification of both cooperation and competition in the new economy. As we have already emphasised, cooperation is the third universal principle of the cosmos and is reflected at the level of person, organization, and social-economic environment through "enough" openness and potential for cooperation. Concomitantly, an increasing number of companies that cooperate are in competition relationships. Co-opetition is developed in this context, which signifies concomitant deployment of the cooperation and competition processes among the same entities among the involved stakeholders. In order to be efficient for the companies involved and their stakeholders, co-opetition needs new specific managerial mechanisms, professionally designed and employed. A stakeholders-based management system, based on win–win negotiation and reasonable compromise, represents such a mechanism.

h The change rate in every field, under the impact of the knowledge revolution, digitalisation, and internationalisation, is rapid. The dynamic character of all systems, despite their nature, size, or localisation, is being enhanced. At the company level, to face the contextual changes, it is necessary the implication of all entities (person or organization), who are interested and have the capacity to significantly influence, this means the company-relevant stakeholders. **The stakeholders could significantly contribute to the rapid perception of the different change necessities and initiate the various decisions and actions to construct efficient solutions.** To achieve this, there are necessary managerial approaches in the company, with the stakeholders-based management system being one such mechanism.

i In the 21st century, the stakeholders present numerous elements, which make necessary radical and different managerial approaches in comparison with the previous mechanisms, focused on the manager–subordinate relationship. The managerial synapse, to which we have dedicated two chapters in the book, represents the primary managerial mechanism to fulfil at the individual stakeholder level a new managerial approach for the company-relevant stakeholders. We want to outline that the managerial synapse deals only with the specific relationships between a company manager and a relevant stakeholder from inside or outside the organization. The managerial synapse deals only with work processes in the workplace. Managerial synapses generate superior results when they are correlated, when the involved inputs and outputs are harmonised, and when at the company level they are based on the strategy and the integrative mechanisms. Hence, a **specific managerial system is necessary to integrate and correlate at the company level all managerial synapses with relevant internal and external stakeholders.**

j To survive and develop, a modern company should achieve multidimensional and sustainable performances. **The company could achieve multidimensional performances – commercial, financial, technical, social or ecological – only with the contribution of the internal relevant stakeholders**, including managers, stakeholders, and executants, **and external relevant stakeholders**, including clients, suppliers, bankers, local community, investors, consultants, public administration and other. Sustainable development and performance over many years need continuous and consistent information, knowledge, resources, and relationship of the company's internal and external stakeholders.

A stakeholders-based management system represents a managerial mechanism able to respond to the above-mentioned necessities effectively and efficiently, taking into consideration the challenges and changes at the level of the company, market, and industry and the other contextual elements.

We consider that the 10 arguments presented, which are not exhaustive, demonstrate that a new management system focused on the relevant stakeholders is necessary in companies to be performant using the huge stakeholders potential. The necessity and performance of such a system are amplified by the transition to a knowledge-based economy and knowledge-based company and the rapid digitalisation. A stakeholders-based management system might be a valuable response to the essential problems raised by the well-known specialist Pfeffer (2009):

> It's clear that the limits of shareholder capitalism are showing themselves like so many cracks in the ages – old foundation

of a house. The question is DO the current repair efforts by the senior executives and policy makers signal a lasting return to the stakeholders capitalism – where CEO feel responsible to all constituencies and not just for investors?

Definition of the Company-Relevant Stakeholders-Based Management System

The definition of the company-relevant stakeholders-based management system **has as background a set of premises regarding the company, management, and stakeholders.** We present these premises in Table 9.1.

Table 9.1 Premises of the stakeholders-based management system

No.	*Premises*	*Content of Premises*
1.	Company is an open system	The updated company is an open system, which has many, varied, and intense relationships (economic, social, and ecological) with the environment. In recent decades, the openness of the company was enhanced quickly, and this tendency will continue in the future.
2.	Relevant stakeholders are essential for the company	Relevant stakeholders are the determinant factors of the company creation, work, and development. Without relevant stakeholders' contributions, no company could exist.
3.	Company is a grouping of stakeholders	A company should and could by defined as an ensemble of many different structural and interrelated stakeholders, which all fulfil the work processes needed in the company.
4.	Company and its stakeholders have multidimensional objectives	A company, in order to work and be sustainable, should plan and fulfil, for itself and its stakeholders, multidimensional objectives. Specifically, a company should use the well-known triple bottom line (TBL) (Searcy, 2018): economic, environmental, and social objectives.
5.	Value shared is the main economic objective	The main economic objective of the company should be value shared for all relevant stakeholders to motivate them, not profit per se.

(*Continued*)

Table 9.1 (Continued)

No.	*Premises*	*Content of Premises*
6.	Company management is focused on the relevant stakeholders	Management focusing on the relevant stakeholders, using specific approaches, represents a valuable solution for increasing organization performance based on the relevant stakeholders' knowledge, work and relationships.
7.	Relevant stakeholders interests, characteristics, and behaviours are dynamic	The array of relevant stakeholders and their interests, characteristics, expectations and motivations is dynamic, and for this reason, the company management, together with the stakeholders, must constantly evaluate the changes and take them into consideration.
8.	A company-relevant stakeholders-based management system is a managerial innovation for management change	A stakeholders-based management system represents an innovative managerial variant for the company and management remodelling to utilise the huge potential of the relevant stakeholders, increasing the company's competitiveness and sustainability. A stakeholders-based management system represents a superior level of maturity in stakeholders' relationship with company management.

The company-relevant stakeholders-based management system consists in all company managerial processes and relationships that predict, organise, coordinate, mobilise, and evaluate the relevant stakeholders' work processes, structured mainly in managerial synapses and based on intense and participative sharing of information, knowledge, and other resources on common and harmonised decisions, actions, and behaviours to achieve sustainable multidimensional interests and objectives of the organization and its relevant stakeholders. Company-relevant stakeholders-based management is emerging as a new management system to utilise the potential of relevant stakeholders in the interest of the organization, to a large extent using emotional intelligence, with beneficial results for all parties involved. In fact, a stakeholders-based management system is a special type of network of internal and external company-relevant stakeholders, in which the managerial synapses play a major role.

In our opinion, the new company-relevant stakeholders-based management system represents the most comprehensive and effective approach to manage a collaborative enterprise. A company-relevant stakeholders-based management system is one of the best managerial feedback to collaborative revolution, which is currently taking place, according to Adler, Heckscher, and Prusak (2011). This system is a possible solution to the present trend outlined recently by a group of specialists (Battilana, Pache, Sengul, & Kimsey, 2019; Ignatius, 2019) regarding the company's change from a simple-minded pursuit of financial gain to consider the interests of all its stakeholders, including employees, customers, communities, and the environment. Companies should focus on four key management practices: setting and monitoring dual goals; structuring the organization to support both goals; hiring and socialising employees to embrace them; and practicing dual-minded leadership.

The company-relevant stakeholders-based management system **aims to fulfil two goals:**

- Achievement of common purposes of the company and relevant stakeholders' categories, based on common and/or complementary interests. Common objectives vary from one stakeholders' category to another (clients, suppliers, executants, shareholders, etc.) and, often, within each category, from one stakeholder to another. Most frequently, they refer to the direct acquisition of knowledge and human, technical, material, and financial resources, the renewal of product, service, technological, managerial, marketing, and environmental tools, etc., and maintaining and increasing sale, market share, and profit to ensure the sustainability of the organizations involved.
- Establishment of a collaborative mechanism, based on the managerial synapses, to facilitate a higher level of accomplishment – through joint efforts and contributions – of the relevant stakeholders' needs arising from major goals of each of them.

Within the company-relevant stakeholders-based management system, there is a new type of stakeholders–manager relationship, usually structured in managerial synapses, which largely replaces the classic manager–subordinate relationship. The manager–subordinate relationship is based on hierarchical dependence and organizational memberships. In contrast, **the new manager–stakeholder relationship is based on the following foundations:**

- the interests of each stakeholders in the proper functioning and performance of the company;
- win–win negotiations between the synapse components;
- the capacity of the stakeholders to significantly influence – positively and/or negatively – the activities of the organization;

- the emotional intelligence of stakeholders, which facilitates interrelations among stakeholders and gives them more consistency;
- the stakeholders' motivation to be useful for the company, contributing to the running of processes and achieving performance, on the basis of a win–win relationship.

Managerial processes and relationships with relevant stakeholders, based on the managerial synapses and guided by a sense of shared purposes, facilitate the committed collaboration in the company, which is beneficial for the parties involved.

Company management processes, modelled through managerial synapses based on win–win negotiations, are powerful managerial processes. This is essential because "firms with strong managerial processes do significantly better on the high metrics such as profitability, growth and productivity" (Sadun, Bloom, & Van Reenen, 2017).

A stakeholders-based management system combines, concomitantly, the focus on the management processes and relationships with the relevant stakeholders' essential stakes. **The company-relevant stakeholders-based management system is a way to move in practice away "from capitalistic to humanistic business"** (Dierksmeier, 2016), reflecting the paradigm shift in the field of theory from mechanistic economics toward humanistic economics. In practice, this involves "human purposes" for a company, broadly defined as the focal points (Wicks & Harrison, 2017).

A company-relevant stakeholders-based management system **should be founded on the open strategy, characterised by transparency and inclusion** (Hautz, Seidl, & Whittington, 2017). These two dimensions of the open strategy are essential for the relevant stakeholders' organic integration in the organization's management and for the fulfilment of the company and its major interests, needs, and expectations. A company-relevant stakeholders-based management system is **founded on the new business model centred on the relevant stakeholders.**[5] A company-relevant stakeholders-based management system could **incorporate mainly the elements presented in** Figure 9.4.

The managerial synapse is the basic component of the stakeholders-based management system. It is the essential mechanism to manage the new type of managerial relationships and processes between relevant stakeholders and the company representative. The quality of managerial synapses, reflected in the strong collaboration between both components and in the fulfilment of the common objectives, is determinant for the performances at the workplace level and has a significant influence at the departmental and company levels.

An autonomous relevant stakeholder refers to the company-relevant stakeholders who is not a part – for certain reasons – of the managerial synapse. An autonomous relevant stakeholder has a special relationship with the company not usually a hierarchical relationship – but without

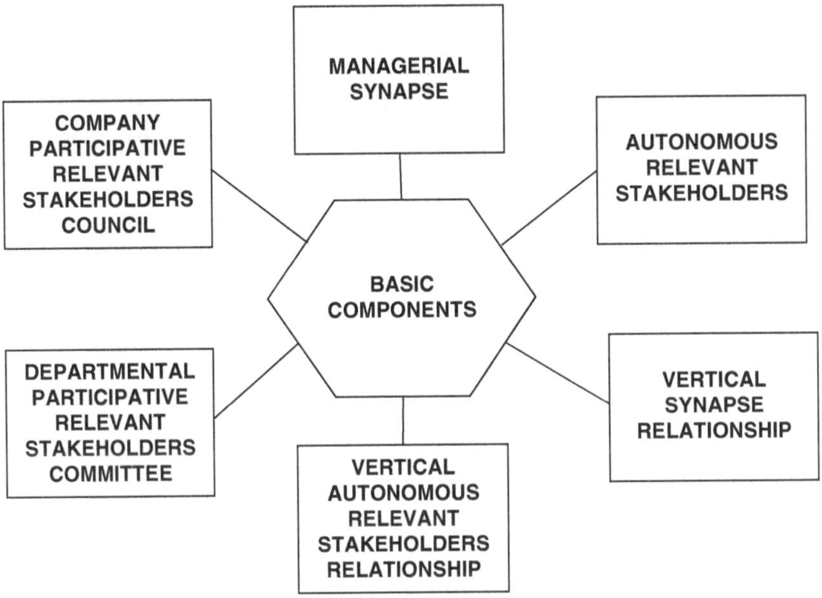

Figure 9.4 Main components of the company-relevant stakeholders-based management system.

being integrated in the synapse. An autonomous relevant stakeholder is not enough influential for the time being on the company work and performance, or is not enough open to be part in the managerial synapse. Also, this category could include the relevant stakeholders who is preparing to be integrated in a managerial synapse.

Each managerial synapse is integrated in the company's organizational structure through a **vertical relationship.** A company representative in the managerial synapse – a manager or specialist – is subordinated to the manager who is responsible for the activities fulfilled by the managerial synapse components. Similarly, the autonomous relevant stakeholders of the company is integrated in the organization's structure by a **special relationship** connecting him/her to the manager responsible for the work processes. Characteristics of this relationship depend largely on whether the stakeholders is an employee of the company. Specific for both types of relationship – regarding the managerial synapse and autonomous relevant stakeholders – are the strong collaborative dimension and the significant presence of informal elements. They are effective only if stakeholders' relationships are trustful.

To facilitate the work and the performance of the stakeholders-based management system, it is necessary to have at **the company level a participative stakeholders council,** which would include representatives of all the relevant stakeholders' categories. Such a council, with periodic meetings, has the main purpose to facilitate the remodelling of the company management according to the relevant stakeholders' specificity and evolution, to improve the stakeholders-based management system's work, and to increase the trust of the internal and external stakeholders in the company management and the owner's dedication to consistent and reciprocal beneficial co-work with them, for the sustainable development of all. A company participative stakeholders council should be connected with the administration council of the organization. Close cooperation of the two bodies is mandatory for the company and the relevant stakeholders, having a major influence on the company and the stakeholders' work and performance.

In large companies, where there are many and diversified relevant stakeholders and activities, it could be useful to create at the level of departments or of the main domains a **departmental participative relevant stakeholders committee.** This organizational body is similar to the previously mentioned council, with the same main objectives but adapted to the specificity of the activities and stakeholders involved. The departmental stakeholders committee is also in a better position to take into consideration the particularities of the domain involved and to contribute to develop it.

Within the stakeholders-based management system it is a hierarchy, but not classic, very authoritarian. A hierarchy is necessary because human beings have a tendency to think and act hierarchically (Zitek & Tiedens, 2012). It is recommended to be called a "**right hierarchy**" (Sanner & Bunderson, 2018), characterised by intense consultation and cooperation, strong informal elements, and team spirit. Such a hierarchy enables initiative, innovation, participative decisions and actions, and flexible approach. An organization in the stakeholders-based management system is recommended to adopt the **new participative centralisation type of authority,** which has proven useful when overlapping spheres of influence (Adler et al., 2011).

The organizational elements presented should determine the development of the collaborative community around a sense of shared purpose and diversity of the stakeholders' capability, stimulating innovation (Adler et al., 2011). A company-relevant stakeholders-based management system may be employed in **two organizational variants:**

a **Integral stakeholders-based management system,** when it incorporates all company-relevant stakeholders – internal and external – structured in managerial synapses. This is an optimal variant able to fully utilise the resources and potential of all company-relevant stakeholders. In the case of this organizational variant, the stakeholders-based management system could be designed and implemented as a global company management system.
b **Partial stakeholders-based management system,** which incorporates – integrated in the managerial synapses – only part of the relevant

stakeholders. Also, it could include some autonomous relevant stakeholders, with special vertical relationships within the company. In the case of this organizational variant, certain relevant stakeholders of the company are approached in the classic manner, without special treatment. A partial stakeholders-based management system might be designed and implemented as a project, taking into consideration the specificity of the stakeholders-based management system. A partial stakeholders-based management system could be used as such for a long time or as a temporary type of organization system during the period of construction of the integral-based management system.

Each company should select the stakeholders organizational variant that is best suited to the organization and its relevant stakeholders.

Main Differences Between the Company-Relevant Stakeholders-Based Management System and "Classic" Company Management Systems

For a better understanding of the content and specificity of the stakeholders-based management system, we find it useful to point out the main elements that the company-relevant stakeholders-based management system distinguishes itself from classic management systems: management by objectives, management by projects, management by budgets, management by exceptions or management by costs. According to our analysis, the **most important differences** refer to the issues presented below:

a The areas of stakeholders-based management are substantially amplified by the individuals, processes, relationships, and organizational entities that previously did not form the subject of the organization's management systems or were tangentially related to it and only random.

b The company-relevant stakeholders-based management goes beyond the frame of the company, taking into account the increasing number and importance of external stakeholders, which is reflected in certain parameters, approaches, processes, mechanisms, methods, etc. that are different from those used in the organization's endogenous framing; the stakeholders-based management system is the first company management system that incorporates elements from outside the organization and that are even numerous.

c The information and knowledge generate a considerably higher impact on the content and modalities of stakeholder management processes and relationships, providing them more consistency, complexity, and effectiveness.

d The personal characteristics of the stakeholders – qualities, knowledge, competencies, emotional intelligence, fairness, sense of responsibility, ability to communicate, desire and capacity to collaborate, team spirit, long term vision, etc. – have a major influence, often decisively, on the content, ways of operationalisation, and effects generated by the new company manager–stakeholder relations, by the managerial synapses.

e In the company-relevant stakeholders-based management system, the informal elements are more numerous and influence to a greater extent the effectiveness of managers' decisions, actions, and behaviours.

f The company-relevant stakeholders-based management system has a stronger motivational dimension because all relevant stakeholders have significant interests in the functioning, development, and competitiveness of the managed organization, whose awareness, consideration, and fulfilment, using managerial synapses, are decisive to achieve the organization's sustainable performance.

g The participative dimension of the company-relevant stakeholders-based management system is substantially amplified because it produces intense interaction not only with its own employees, shareholders, and other owners and representatives, but also with many other outside stakeholders-consumers, wholesalers, retailers, suppliers, consultants, designers, researchers, trainers, risk investors and representatives of banks, local government, employers, and professional organizations.

h The company-relevant stakeholders-based management system is a tense management, because at the level of each company the stakeholders, besides the common interests, have other interests, whose achievement must be allocated time, skills, resources, etc., which are always limited. In addition, in the case of certain stakeholders – usually belonging to the organization or external stakeholders – they may also have competing interests, even if these are less than the common ones, on the basis of which the stakeholder relationship is built.

i Managerial flexibility is intensifying, as a precondition for harmonising a significantly larger and more diverse set of interests, expectations, decisions, actions, and behaviours of company stakeholders.

j The design and work of managerial relationships with individual relevant stakeholders, within managerial synapses are based on the win–win principle, which characterises successful modern negotiations, are rapidly expanding and tend to predominate not only in the organization's relations with external stakeholders, but also with internal ones. Win–win negotiations are likely to contribute substantially to balancing and harmonising the common and particular interests of relevant stakeholders involved.

k Protecting the major interests of the company in its relations with the stakeholders, especially the external ones, becomes a major component of the managerial relationships with them, embracing complex and subtle ways of expression, which is only seldom met in classic management.
l Managers' more extensive, faster, and more accurate information on a broader range of endogenous and exogenous aspects of the company becomes a prerequisite for ensuring the effectiveness and efficiency of managerial processes and relationships with stakeholders. To achieve this, on a large scale and intensively, information and knowledge banks, participative approaches, and integrated informatic systems are used, among other things.
m The complexity, dynamism, and difficulty of the managerial processes and relationships are greatly amplified, being substantially more demanding for the company's managers, involving more and diversified resources, more creative managerial approaches, and superior efforts and skills.
n Organizational leadership within a stakeholders-based management system has much greater importance and partially changed content compared to classic leadership, as it has to compensate for the absence of hierarchical dependence on the relationship of the organization's managers with its exogenous stakeholders. Additionally, it has to lead knowledge-based specialists, characterised by a greater spirit of initiative, creativity, informality, and autonomy.
o The company-relevant stakeholders-based management system has a holistic character, superior to classic management, due to the company's approach as an open system, organically linked to many other independent systems that involve external stakeholders.
p The synergistic long-term effect of the company-relevant stakeholders-based management system is to strengthen the sustainability of the company, due to the contribution of relevant stakeholders and the blending of their strategic interests with the strategic interests of the organization.
q A company-relevant stakeholders-based management system is focused on the achievement of the multidimensional company and stakeholders objectives (economic, social, and ecological) that are different from classic managerial company systems, which, traditionally, are focused mainly on economic objectives.

As a whole, the many highlighted differences demonstrate the high specificity and complexity of the company-relevant stakeholders-based management system compared to classic management systems and contribute to its better perception, understanding, and operationalisation, necessary in the present companies, in the VUCA environment.

Principles of the Company-Relevant Stakeholders-Based Management System

The foundation, work, development, and performance of the company-relevant stakeholders-based management system should be based on a set of **principles** referring to the essential elements involved. The principles are useful in the modelling of the management processes and relationships incorporated by the company-relevant stakeholders-based management system. In Table 9.2, we propose a set of principles, designed in a holistic view, taking into consideration the objectives and specificity of this new company management system, the particularities of the relevant stakeholders, and the recent contextual evolutions, primarily the transition to a knowledge-based economy and digitalisation. In our approach, we employed many recent developments of the management theory and practice and of the company stakeholders approaches.

We want to emphasise that the principles we propose are different from the other stakeholders principles and laws, which we briefly

Table 9.2 Company-relevant stakeholders-based management system principles

No.	*Principles*	*Content of the Principles*
1.	Decisive dependence of the company work and performance on the relevant stakeholders	Every organization depends on many internal and external stakeholders. In order to start, develop, and achieve performance, each company needs to identify and evaluate the relevant stakeholders (managers, specialists, customers, suppliers, investors, bankers or other) and to integrate them in special managerial mechanisms, beneficial for the relevant stakeholders and the organization. The company-relevant stakeholders-based management system is such a mechanism and specially designed.
2.	Multidimensional objectives of the company-relevant stakeholders-based management system and the relevant stakeholders	Objectives to be achieved by the company and its relevant stakeholders in the stakeholders-based management system should be multidimensional (economic, social, ecologic). Objectives should reflect the main interests and necessities of the company and relevant stakeholders. They should be defined carefully, reflecting the realities, and be equilibrated from the company's and relevant stakeholders' points of view.

(*Continued*)

Table 9.2 (Continued)

No.	*Principles*	*Content of the Principles*
3.	Constant individual and organizational cooperation	The company-relevant stakeholders-based management system's foundation, work, development, and performance are based on the permanent cooperation between relevant stakeholders and company managers within the system at the level of managerial synapses, vertical stakeholders' relationships, company stakeholders council, departmental committees, and other components. Cooperation has a triple dimension (decisional, actional, and behavioural)– that is tightly interrelated. Cooperation should be at both the individual and organizational levels and is very complex, with the formal company elements (company plans, job description, organigram, etc.) being combined with informal approaches. Components of the company-relevant stakeholders-based management system require cooperating intensively also with the other components of the company, with the organization's external relevant stakeholders, and with any other interested entities. All cooperation processes and relationships should be subordinated to the achievement of the common multidimensional objectives.
4.	Harmonisation of the company and relevant stakeholders interests and stakes	The company-relevant stakeholders-based management system, in order to work and be performant, should harmonise the main interests and stakes of both the company and the relevant stakeholders. Harmonisation of the interests and stakes is necessary to be done permanently, starting with establishing the objectives and finishing with the share of outputs between the company and relevant stakeholders. This represents a precondition for the significant implication and efforts from the relevant stakeholders and the company's managers.

(*Continued*)

Table 9.2 (Continued)

No.	*Principles*	*Content of the Principles*
5.	Win–win negotiations and relationships between company and relevant stakeholders	The key element in the construction of managerial synapses and of the ensemble of relationships within the company-relevant stakeholders-based management system is win–win negotiation between company managers and relevant stakeholders. Win–win negotiation facilitates formulation of the company's and relevant stakeholders' common objectives. It creates enabling premises and a climate for the next joint activities for the development of reciprocity and feedback.
6.	Intense motivation of the relevant stakeholders and company managers	A milestone of the company-relevant stakeholders-based management system is the constant motivation of company managers and relevant stakeholders to fully employ their knowledge, other resources, and potential for increasing the company's and stakeholders' development and performance. Taking into consideration the company's and stakeholders' essential interests, reflected in common objectives, use of win–win negotiation; planning from the beginning of the work period, of the ways to share the economic and social outputs; permanent communication and consultation; regular use of positive motivation; permanent preoccupation with fairness and equilibrium of interests; and development of an open, innovative, and constructive culture in the company, are approaches and means with powerful motivational impact on the relevant stakeholders and company managers and specialists.
7.	Harmonisation of the company's and relevant stakeholders' decisions, actions, and behaviours	Decisions, actions, and behaviours, through which the company-relevant stakeholders-based management system works, are permanently harmonised at the level of managerial synapses and the entire company system. Tasks, roles, competencies, and responsibilities of the company

(*Continued*)

Table 9.2 (Continued)

No.	*Principles*	*Content of the Principles*
		managers and the relevant stakeholders, at the level of managerial synapses and the whole system, are defined in a specific manner, enabling harmonisation in all aspects. Relevant stakeholders and company managers, using permanent communication and consultation, correlate all work processes within the company-relevant stakeholders-based management system, avoiding dysfunctionalities and conflicts and increasing mutual understanding, cooperation, and synergy at the levels of the workplace, domains, and the entire company and other stakeholders entities.
8.	Achievement of a reasonable and sustainable compromise	Relevant company stakeholders and the company often have different interests, approaches, or perceptions. To avoid divergences, dysfunctionalities, or conflicts, they should be eliminated or drastically reduced. A major way to do this is to look for reasonable compromise. Essentially, a reasonable compromise means a solution, an approach, or an agreement that is not optimum for any participant involved but that represents an acceptable result for all parties, taking into consideration the elements most important for each of them. The reasonable compromise should be made in a sustainable perspective, contributing to continuation of the beneficial stakeholder–company relationships in the long term.
9.	Permanent communication, consultation, and connectivity of the company managers with relevant stakeholders	The creation and work of the managerial synapses and of all relationships within the stakeholders-based management system are determined by the information and knowledge exchanged within the system. Common objectives, win–win negotiations, and harmonisation of the stakeholders' decisions, actions, and behaviours could not be achieved without constant exchange of information and knowledge, openness

(*Continued*)

Table 9.2 (Continued)

No.	*Principles*	*Content of the Principles*
		to the other parties' interests and approaches, and common implication and connectivity in the search and formulation of solutions acceptable for relevant stakeholders and the company. Constant, fair, and intensive communication, consultation, and connectivity help to construct, maintain, and develop trust capital of relevant stakeholders, managers, and the company.
10.	Sharing of the stakeholders' and company's knowledge and other resources	Knowledge and other financial, technical, material, and human resources are the essential "raw materials" in the company and the stakeholders-based management system. To satisfy the necessities of relevant stakeholders and the company, the resources possessed by them should be shared in a fair and mutually beneficial way. In the construction and functioning of the company-relevant stakeholders-based management system, the identification, evaluation, common use, and valorisation of resources represent essential processes that provide "substance" for its successful work. The real desire and the practical availability to share the resources by relevant stakeholders and the company are a complex and learning undertaking not easy to achieve, involving consistent efforts from all parties.
11.	Formal and informal elements "mix" in the company-relevant stakeholders-based management system	The company-relevant stakeholders-based management system, as any other company management system or managerial mechanism, is based on formalised rules, procedures or structures. They are absolutely necessary for the existence and work of any entity. A stakeholders-based management system involves a large number and variety of internal and external company stakeholders; their work processes are dynamic and often even fluid. The current contextual

(*Continued*)

Table 9.2 (Continued)

No.	*Principles*	*Content of the Principles*
		conditions are changing fast and not always in a predictable way. For these reasons, the relevant stakeholders and the company managers need to be flexible, creative, and entrepreneurial. All these positive features are possible only if the formalised managerial elements are reduced to the essentials, leaving enough decisional and operational autonomy for the informal approaches. The present tendencies in the management of almost any type of organization is to increase the use of the informal elements, enabling fast feedback, flexible approaches, and performant innovations.
12.	Sustainable approach and performance of the company and the relevant stakeholders	The company-relevant stakeholders-based management system is a long-term oriented mechanism, aiming at multidimensional economic, social, and ecological performances for the company and the relevant stakeholders. Through the open strategy and in a transparent and inclusive manner involving relevant stakeholders, plans are made for the company's fundamental objectives and the main modalities to achieve them in the next 3–5 years. All work processes at the level of managerial synapses and the whole system are designed and implemented focused on the common multidimensional long-term objectives, which are win–win negotiated. The fundamental implication of the relevant stakeholders (clients, suppliers, managers, investors, consultants, and other) in using the managerial synapses and other elements of the stakeholders-based management system in all managerial and execution processes represents a major contribution to the sustainable approach and performance and a guarantee of achieving them.

discussed in Chapter 4, Section 4.5. Without a doubt, we might find certain resemblances, but the essential content of the principles is not the same and could not be the same, because they deal with two new stakeholders managerial mechanisms:

- managerial synapse, at the level of manager–relevant stakeholder relationships;
- a stakeholders-based management system, at the company level.

Also, our approach to relevant stakeholders, to whom the principles refer, is not the same with previous approaches regarding the salient stakeholders, the primary stakeholders, and others.

The principles included in Table 9.2, **taken together, represent a system.** All should be used in the designing, working, and developing of the company-relevant stakeholders-based management system, taking into consideration their interdependence and complementarity. It is mandatory that every principle be considered and used. Ignoring one of them generates negative effects on the company-relevant stakeholders-based management system's functionality and on the company's and relevant stakeholders' dedication to the common objectives and the sustainable multidimensional performances.

Multiple Advantages of the New System for the Company and Relevant Stakeholders

The company-relevant stakeholders-based management system responds to a large extent to the 25 management's great challenges, formulated in 2009 by the "Renegade brigade" of academics, CEOs, consultants, entrepreneurs, and venture capitalists (Hamel, 2009). Among these, we mention the following: ensure that the work of management serves a higher purpose, reduce fear and increase trust, expand and exploit diversity, expand the scope of employee autonomy, share the work of setting direction, redefine the work of the leadership, reinvent strategy-making as an emergent process, retool management for the open world, and destructure and disaggregate the organization. The stakeholders-based management system has consistent economic, humanistic, and ecological content. In Figure 9.5, we formulate synthetically, in a more pragmatic manner, the main advantages of the stakeholders-based management system, its multiple beneficial effects on the company, and its relevant stakeholders.

The advantage of higher motivation is essential, and a recent study published in Harvard Business Review provides a supplementary argument: "Numerous studies show that close to two-thirds of US employees are bored, detached, or jaded and ready to sabotage plans, projects, and other people" (McKee, 2017). It is very important to stress this amazing

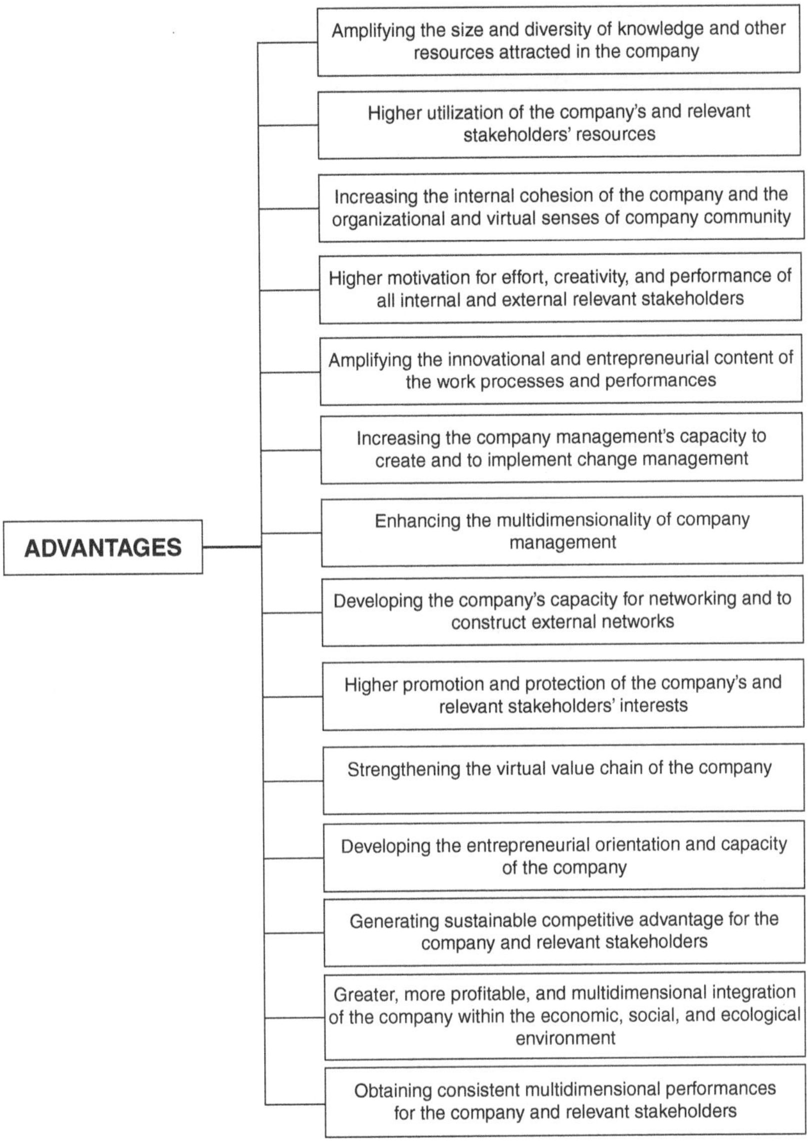

Figure 9.5 Main advantages of the company-relevant stakeholders-based management system.

situation in USA, where is practiced one of the most performant company management in the world.

Besides the numerous and consistent advantages, the company-relevant stakeholders-based management system has **several limits:**

- the dependence of its operation and performances on a large and heterogeneous number of relevant stakeholders, some of whom are located and operate outside the organization
- the high complexity of the management system, generated mainly by many and different relevant stakeholders with multiple and, often, contradictory interests
- major difficulties in implementing the company-relevant stakeholders-based management system due to the many and diversified internal and external variables involved
- the relatively long duration of full implementation of the company-relevant stakeholders-based management system, determined by the previous limits
- high building and operationalisation costs of the new management system, due to the larger scope, represented by all relevant stakeholders, and the need to consider and satisfy the interests of numerous stakeholders, many of them with great impact on the organization.

The advantages of the company-relevant stakeholders-based management system prevail over its limits, reflected by the substantial gain of functionality, competitiveness, and sustainability for the company and its relevant stakeholders. In this context, the following statement of the German specialists Bottenberg, Tuschke, and Flickinger (2016) is pertinent: "Acknowledging potential problems arising from stakeholders orientation, as well as its unique benefits, we call for a modern stakeholders value system".

Comparative Approach of the Company-Relevant Stakeholders-Based Management System with the Stakeholders' Engagement

Stakeholders' engagement has been the main organization management feedback to the necessity to reconsider the relationships with the stakeholders, to use to a larger extent their resources and potential, and to face their challenges. There are many different approaches of stakeholders' engagement, which could be grouped into **two categories:**

- stakeholders' engagement at the company level;
- stakeholders' engagement at the level of a management project, which is more developed and used than the previous category.

Definitions of stakeholders' engagement also differ to a certain extent. We present two definitions of stakeholders' engagement, the first more general and the second focused on the stakeholders' engagement in project management. According to the definition elaborated by specialists from the

Royal Institution of Chartered Surveyors (RICS) in Great Britain, "engagement signifies all the things we might do with stakeholders: consult, listen, understand, communicate, influence, negotiate, etc. with the broader objectives of satisfying their needs, gaining approval and support or at least minimizing their opposition or obstruction" (MacNicol, Giffin, & Mansell, 2014). Another specialist referring to the projects defines stakeholders' engagement as "the process used by an organization to engage relevant stakeholders for a purpose to achieve accepted outcomes" (Worsley, 2016).

There are also many **sets of principles of stakeholders' engagement,** most dealing with stakeholders' engagement in project management. The differences between them are quite substantial, not only in number (6–10) but also, and especially, in content. We present two variants, which are quite different in the number of principles and content.

The first variant was elaborated by the mentioned specialists from the RICS with the definition of stakeholders' engagement. They formulated 10 engagement principles:

- communicate
- consult early and often
- remember they are only human
- plan it
- relationships are the key
- simple, but not easy
- just part of managing risk
- compromise
- understand what success is
- take responsibility (MacNicol et al., 2014).

Another example is the six principles of stakeholders' engagement formulated by Worsley (2016) especially for projects:

- Stakeholders should have a say in decisions that affect them.
- Stakeholders' participation includes the promise that their contributions will influence decisions and they are told how.
- Stakeholders' engagement seeks out those potentially affected by, or interested in, a decision.
- Stakeholders' engagement seeks input on how they may wish to participate.
- Stakeholders' engagement provides information, time, and space to allow stakeholders to participate in a meaningful way.
- It never hurts to be polite.

Other specialists have also elaborated different principles of stakeholders' engagement (Cundy et al., 2013; Gautrey, 2013; Lawrence, 2017). Many specialists have noted the limits of stakeholders' engagement and the necessity to have another approach. For example, Horner and Wilmshurst (2016) noted that "whilst have been instances of successful stakeholders engagement, evidence suggests that the most engagement exercises are for the purpose of reputation and stakeholders management".

Lawrence (2017) emphasised, based on several studies, "[it] is clear that simply engaging with stakeholders is insufficient to build a successful stakeholder strategy. Companies consider as the focal entity in a relationship, also need to actively communicate with stakeholders and manage their relationships".

Stakeholders' engagement has several **important contributions in the management field:**

a It represents the best-known organization management approach, trying to improve and develop relationships with important stakeholders.
b It develops a few specific principles, approaches, methods, and techniques to deal with the stakeholders, especially for the management project.
c It contributes to better relationships between some important stakeholders and the organization, mainly for the project.
d It focuses largely on the external stakeholders, revealing their major impact on the organization's work and performance.
e It reveals the necessity and possibility to deal specifically with the important stakeholders and to pay special attention to them by the company managers, scientists, and media.

In Table 9.3, we present the results of a comparative analysis of the stakeholders-based management system and stakeholders' engagement, which help to understand the **differences between these two approaches of the company stakeholders and their perspectives.**

Differences between the two approaches represent valuable arguments to use in company management, the new company-relevant stakeholders-based management system.

Necessity and Benefits of the Company-Relevant Stakeholders-Based Management System in the COVID-19 Pandemic and Post-Pandemic Contexts

In the authors' opinion, the company-relevant stakeholders-based management system is necessary in companies, especially medium and large companies in the context of the COVID-19 pandemic. **The necessities** are generated by the many and fundamental changes that have occurred during the past year because of this pandemic. They could be divided into **two categories:**

Table 9.3 Main differences between the company-relevant stakeholders-based management system and stakeholders' engagement

No.	*Criteria*	*Company-Relevant Stakeholders-Based Management System*	*Stakeholders' Engagement*
1.	Objectives	Multidimensional for company and relevant stakeholders	Classic targets, mainly economic, usually only for the company or project
2.	Components	All or most of the company-relevant stakeholders	Some of the important stakeholders, often only the stakeholders "creating" tensions or very influential on the company
3.	Background of the stakeholders–organization relationships	Win–win negotiation, cooperative approach	Organizational authority, often of a hierarchical nature
4.	Communication	Comprehensive, intensive, often dialogic communication	Selective communication, focused on the "problems" between the organization and certain stakeholders
5.	Specific organizational–stakeholders mechanisms	Managerial synapses and stakeholders-based management system	——
6.	Motivation	Intense and permanent motivation based on win–win negotiation and use of a wide array of motivation for both the company and relevant stakeholders	Specific temporary motivation to solve the relevant stakeholders' problems with the company
7.	Entity where utilised	Company and any other type of organization	Project management (the most frequent) and large companies
8.	Duration	Permanent, with periodic (recommended yearly) review	Usually temporary until the project is finished or the company has solved the specific relevant-stakeholders problem

(*Continued*)

Table 9.3 (Continued)

No.	*Criteria*	*Company-Relevant Stakeholders-Based Management System*	*Stakeholders' Engagement*
9.	Resources considered	All or most of the company's and relevant stakeholders' resources; knowledge is often considered the most important resource to be shared	Some resources, selectively considered, of the company or important stakeholders; there are relatively frequent situations regarding the non-market stakeholders, when their resources are not taken into consideration
10.	Organizational culture	Specific organizational culture is developed – open, inclusive, intensely communicative, innovative, entrepreneurial, and participative	Organizational culture is not a central element in the engagement approach, sometimes being developed, for influential groups of stakeholders or specific sub-cultures
11.	Complexity	Usually high or average–high complexity	Usually average or low complexity, depending on the number of stakeholders considered and the intensity of the relationships between the project and company, on the one hand, and the stakeholders, on the other hand
12.	Cost	Substantial cost, necessary to construct and to work a comprehensive specific management system with relevant stakeholders	Usually low cost, necessary to solve limited relevant-stakeholders problems

(*Continued*)

Table 9.3 (Continued)

No.	*Criteria*	*Company-Relevant Stakeholders-Based Management System*	*Stakeholders' Engagement*
13.	Specific strategy	Always based on the specific strategy, which should be open, inclusive, and transparent, focused on the construction and work of the stakeholders-based management system	Rarely, the company approach of the important stakeholders represents the target of a special strategy; usually, the company utilises current or short-term approaches
14.	Performance	Multidimensional sustainable performance (economic, social, and ecological) for both the company and the relevant stakeholders	Specific results for a group of stakeholders and/or company; sometimes the results refer to the solving of certain problems (increasing the support of the company activists or minimising communities' resistance to certain company initiatives, and other times referring to obtaining a specific performance)

a **Contextual necessities**, represented by threats and difficulties determined by the negative impact of the COVID-19 pandemic in the company environment. According to the analysis of many specialists (Boston Consulting Group, 2020; Carlsson-Szlezac, Reeves, & Swartz, 2020; Chaturvedi, Dey, & Singh, 2020; Gjaja, Fæste, Hansell, & Hohner, 2020; Heichler, 2020; King, Wald, & Manly, 2020; Narayandas, Hebbar, & Li, 2020; Nicolescu, Popa, & Dumitrascu, 2020; Radjou, 2020; Romeo, Moukanas, & Rung, 2020; Waldron & Wetherbe, 2020), the most frequent and important are the following:

- Substantial decrease or delay in the supply with many raw materials, spare parts, half-finished goods, finished goods, services, etc.
- Great reduction of the direct demand for products and services in many areas (tourism, transportation, sports, shows, restaurants, hotels, etc.)

- Increased risk of the delay and/or blockage for economic and social projects already started, especially those financed from public and state funds
- Reduction of the indirect demand (industry, service, and trade) for numerous products and services, caused by the previous changes
- Substantial and even Brownian fluctuation in the prices and orders for certain product categories (petrol, drugs, medical protection equipment and substances, etc.).
- Significant decrease and reorientation of the alternative finance (stock exchange, venture capital, investment company, etc.) and from banks
- Notable and partially unexpected changes in behaviour of the individual and institutional consumers caused by the previous shifts, reflected in modifications in the size and frequency of the demand for products and services, determined by changes in direct and indirect consumption, by "buffer" stocks, etc.

These contextual changes cause problems in the organization's relationships with all major external stakeholders: clients, suppliers, banks, local communities, consultants, designers, local authorities. There are decreases, tensions, and even blockages or cancellations in the work with external stakeholders, which have a major negative impact on them and on the company's activity and performance.

b **Organizational necessities**, represented by the major changes induced by the COVID-19 pandemic in companies, occur at three levels:

- Workplace – social distance, work from home, telework, hybrid communication, work online, etc.
- Department – hybrid team, hybrid communication, online meetings, jobs lost, incohesive team, etc.
- Organizational level – decrease of sales, profit, jobs, etc.; financial difficulties and/or blockage; tense organizational culture; etc.

The changes and difficulties involve all relevant internal stakeholders – managers, executants, and shareholders – and some external stakeholders, most often consumers, intermediaries, suppliers, banks, local communities, and/or local authorities. In our opinion, these major internal and external threats and difficulties represent arguments for the new managerial mechanisms in companies to be able to face them and to rapidly recover and relaunch their activities and performances. The company-relevant stakeholders-based management system, by its vision and characteristics, could be one of them. The use of this system in a company generates **many benefits, which we divide into two categories:**

- First are the benefits at the level of the company relationship with each relevant stakeholder. We indicated these benefits in Chapter 5, Section 5.10.
- Second are the synergic benefits at the level of the entire company and the ensemble of relevant stakeholders:
  - Faster and more durable recovery of the relationships with the company-relevant stakeholders by eliminating or decreasing the blockages or bottlenecks;
  - Facilitation of new external stakeholders identification with more enabling potential for the company;
  - Boosts the company's integration in the networks using the upstream- and downstream-relevant stakeholders;
  - Provides a new business model that is highly motivational, flexible, and innovative and that is able to attract more knowledge, information, and financial and material resources from the internal and external company stakeholders, and to improve organizational functionality;
  - Faster return of the company to the size of sale and profit from the period before the COVID-19 pandemic crisis;
  - Strengthening and increase of the company's sustainability;
  - Strengthening and increase of the external company-relevant stakeholders' sustainability;
  - Better positioning of the company for capitalisation of the opportunities offered by the transition to a smart economy and digital transformation.

Based on the previous elements and, especially, the benefits for the company and relevant stakeholders, we strongly recommend the use of the company-relevant stakeholders-based management system in the complex context of the COVID-19 period and post-period.

Notes

1 We present our approach of the management functions. (See Nicolescu, O., & Verboncu, I., 2008. *Fundamentele managementului organizației*. București, România: Editura Universitară). In the management literature are many different variants. See for example Longenecker, J. G., &. Pringle, C. D., 1981. *Management*. Columbus, OH: Charles E. Merrill Publishing; Griffin, W. R, 2012. *Management: Principles and practice* (11th ed.). Mason, OH: Thomson South-Western.

2 See more in Nicolescu, O., & Verboncu, I. (2008). *Fundamentele Managementului Organizației*. București, România: Editura Universitară.

3 In this managerial undertaking is very useful to use the new concepts, approaches, tools, provided by the new management discipline – knowledge-based management (See for example Nicolescu, O., & Nicolescu, C., 2011.

Organizația și managementul bazate pe cunoștințe. București, România: Pro Universitaria).

4 See for example Hutzschenreuter, T., & Horstkotte, J. (2010). Knowledge transfer to partners: A firm level perspective. *Journal of Knowledge Management, 14*(3), 428–448. https://doi.org/10.1108/13673271011050148; Ma, Z., & Yu, K. (2010). Research paradigms of contemporary knowledge management studies: 1998–2007. *Journal of Knowledge Management, 14*(2) 175–189. https://doi.org/10.1108/13673271011032337; Nicolescu, O., & Nicolescu, C. (2011). *Organizația și managementul bazate pe cunoștințe*. București, România: Pro Universitaria.

5 We will present this new business model later in.

References

Adler, P., Heckscher, C., & Prusak, L. (2011). Building a collaborative enterprise. *Harvard Business Review*, *89*(7/8), 94–101.

Adner, R. (2017). Ecosystem as structure: An actionable construct for strategy. *Journal of Management*, *43*(1), 39–58. doi:10.1177/0149206316678451

Battilana, J., Pache, A.-C., Sengul, M., & Kimsey, M. (2019). The dual-purpose playbook. *Harvard Business Review*, *97*(2), 124–133.

Boston Consulting Group. (2020). *COVID-19 BCG perspectives series: Facts, scenarios and actions for leaders*. Retrieved from https://media-publications.bcg.com/BCG-COVID-19-BCG-Perspectives-Version13.pdf

Bottenberg, K., Tuschke, A., & Flickinger M. (2016). Corporate governance between shareholder and stakeholder orientation: Lessons from Germany. *Journal of Management Inquiry*, *26*(2), 165–180. doi:10.1177/1056492616672942

Carlsson-Szlezac, P., Reeves M., & Swartz, P. (2020). Understanding the economic shock of coronavirus. *Harvard Business Review*. Retrieved from https://hbr.org/2020/03/understanding-the-economic-shock-of-coronavirus

Chaturvedi, H., Dey A. K., & Singh, N. (2020). Coping with COVID-19. *Global Focus the EFMD Business Magazine*. Retrieved from https://www.globalfocusmagazine.com/coping-with-covid-19/

Cundy, A. B., Bardos, R. P., Church, A., Puschenreiter, M., Friesl-Hanl, W., Muller, I., et al. (2013). Developing principles of sustainability and stakeholder engagement for "gentle" remediation approaches: The European context. *Journal of Environmental Management*, *129*, 283–291. doi:10.1016/j.jenvman.2013.07.032

Dierksmeier, C. (2016). What is "humanistic" about humanistic management? *Humanistic Management Journal*, *1*, 9–32. doi:10.1007/s41463-016-0002-6

Gautrey, C. (2013, June 11). Seven guiding principles of stakeholder engagement. Retrieved from https://www.td.org/insights/seven-guiding-principles-of-stakeholder-engagement

Gjaja, M., Fæste, L., Hansell, G., & Hohner, D. (2020, April 16). COVID-19: *Win the fight, win the future. Boston Consulting Group*. Retrieved from https://www.bcg.com/en-hu/publications/2020/covid-scenario-planning-winning-the-future-series

Hamel, G. (2009). Moon shots for management. *Harvard Business Review*, *87*(2), 91–98. Retrieved from https://hbr.org/2009/02/moon-shots-for-management

Hautz, J., Seidl, D., & Whittington, R. (2017). Open strategy: Dimensions, dilemmas, dynamics. *Long Range Planning*, *50*(3), 298–309. doi:10.1016/j.lrp.2016.12.001

Heichler, E. (2020). Seize the moment. *MIT Sloan Management Review*. Retrieved from https://sloanreview.mit.edu/article/seize-the-moment/?og=Fall+2020+Issue+Horizontal

Horner, C., & Wilmshurst, T. (2016). Stakeholder engagement and the GRI: Implications for effective risk management. *Corporate Ownership & Control*, *13*(3), 209–218. doi:10.22495/cocv13i3c1p7

Ignatius, A. (2019). Profit and purpose. *Harvard Business Review*, 97(2), 10.

King, K., & Wald, D., & Manly, J. (2020, April 21). *Advantage beyond the crisis. Boston Consulting Group*. Retrieved from https://www.bcg.com/en-hu/publications/2020/building-business-advantage-beyond-covid-19-crisis

Lawrence, A. T. (2017). The drivers of stakeholder engagement: Reflections on the case of Royal Dutch/Shell. In J. Andriof, S. Waddock, B. Husted, & S. S. Rahman (Eds.), *Unfolding stakeholder thinking: Theory, responsibility and engagement* (pp. 185–200). New York: Routledge. doi:10.4324/9781351281881

MacNicol, D., Giffin, G., & Mansell, P. (2014). *Stakeholder engagement: RICS guidance note*. London, UK: Royal Institution of Chartered Surveyor. Retrieved from https://www.apm.org.uk/media/6673/stakeholder_engagement_1st_edition_pgguidance_2014.pdf

McKee, A. (2017). Happiness traps. How we sabotage ourselves at work. *Harvard Business Review*, *95*(5), 66–73.

Narayandas, D., Hebbar, V., & Li., L. (2020). Lessons from Chinese companies' response to Covid-19. *Harvard Business Review*. Retrieved from https://hbr.org/2020/06/lessons-from-chinese-companies-response-to-covid-19

Nicolescu, O., Popa, I., & Dumitrascu, D. (2020). *Abordari si Studii de Caz Relevante Privind Managementul Organizatíilor din Romania in Contextul Pandemiei Covid-19*. Bucureşti, România: Editura Pro Universitaria.

Nicolescu, O., & Verboncu, I. (2008). *Fundamentele Managementului Organizației*. Bucureşti, România: Editura Universitară.

Peng, T.-J. A., Yen, M.-H., & Bourne, M. (2017). How rival partners compete based on cooperation? *Long Range Planning*, *51*(2), 351–383. doi:10.1016/j.lrp.2017.10.003

Pfeffer, J. (2009). Shareholders first? Not so fast... *Harvard Business Review*, *87*(7/8), 90–91. Retrieved from https://hbr.org/2009/07/shareholders-first-not-so-fast

Radjou, N. (2020). The rising frugal economy. *MIT Sloan Management Review*. Retrieved from https://sloanreview.mit.edu/article/the-rising-frugal-economy/

Romeo, J., Moukanas, H., & Rung, G. (2020). The age of accelerating strategy breakthroughs. *MIT Sloan Management Review*. Retrieved from https://sloanreview.mit.edu/article/the-age-of-accelerating-strategy-breakthroughs/

Sadun, R., Bloom, N., & Van Reenen, J. (2017). Why do we undervalue competent management? *Harvard Business Review*, *95*(5), 120–127.

Sanner, B., & Bunderson, J. S. (2018). The truth about hierarchy. *MIT Sloan Management Review*. Retrieved from https://sloanreview.mit.edu/article/the-truth-about-hierarchy/

Searcy, C. (2018). Defining true sustainability. *MIT Sloan Management Review*. Retrieved from https://sloanreview.mit.edu/article/defining-true-sustainability/

Waldron, T., & Wetherbe, J. (2020). Ensure that your customer relationships outlast coronavirus. *Harvard Business Review*. Retrieved from https://hbr.org/2020/04/ensure-that-your-customer-relationships-outlast-coronavirus

Wicks, A. C., & Harrison, J. S. (2017). Toward a more productive dialogue between stakeholder theory and strategic management. In D. M. Wasieleski & J. Weber (Eds.), *Stakeholder Management – Business and Society 360* (pp. 249–273). Bingley, UK: Emerald Publishing Limited. 10.1108/S2514-175920170000012

Williamson, P. J., & De Meyer J. A. (2012). Ecosystem advantage: How to successfully harness the power of partners. *California Management Review*, *55*(1), 24–46. Retrieved from https://ink.library.smu.edu.sg/cgi/viewcontent.cgi?article=4518&context=lkcsb_research 10.1525/cmr.2012.55.1.24

Worsley, L. M. (2016). *Stakeholder-led project management: Changing the way we manage projects*. New York: Business Expert Press.

Zitek, E. M., & Tiedens, L. Z. (2012). The fluency of social hierarchy: The ease with which hierarchical relationships are seen, remembered, learned, and liked. *Journal of Personality and Social Psychology*, *102*(1), 98–115. doi:10.1037/a0025345.

10 The Economic, Social, Ecologic, and Psychological Background of the Company-Relevant Stakeholders-Based Management

Holistic Approach to the Company-Relevant Stakeholders-Based Management System Foundations

Our research, from the beginning, has been based on a holistic approach to the environment, company, stakeholders and management. Today, such a vision and approach are mandatory in every research, because without them it is not possible to "grasp", take into consideration, analyse and design realistic and performant solutions to any major problem.

We continue to apply this vision and approach to the causes that make possible and necessary the company stakeholders-based management system. We focus on the essential causes involved, causes that we call the **foundations of the company-relevant stakeholders-based management system**. According to our analysis, there are four essential foundations (see Figure 10.1):

First, there is the **economic foundation**. The company is the main organizational component of each national economy. Most economic activities are developed in companies. Almost all products and services necessary for the society are produced by companies. Most of the value added of the national income in any country is generated in companies. In recent decades, companies have faced many new business situations and many economic challenges.

In our opinion, the main economic challenges for companies are generated by the transition from the "classical value chain" to new types of value chains, mainly **virtual value chains**. The main difference between the "classical value chain" and the virtual value chain is that the latter is more comprehensive, incorporating not only company activities but also outside activities accomplished by external relevant stakeholders – customers, suppliers, intermediaries, investors, bankers, designers, etc. The virtual value chain includes not only physical activities but also information and knowledge processes. Virtual value chains, which proliferated rapidly in companies, are associated with new and very complex problems regarding the **value creation and appropriation in a company with multiple stakeholders.**

DOI: 10.4324/9781003217701-10

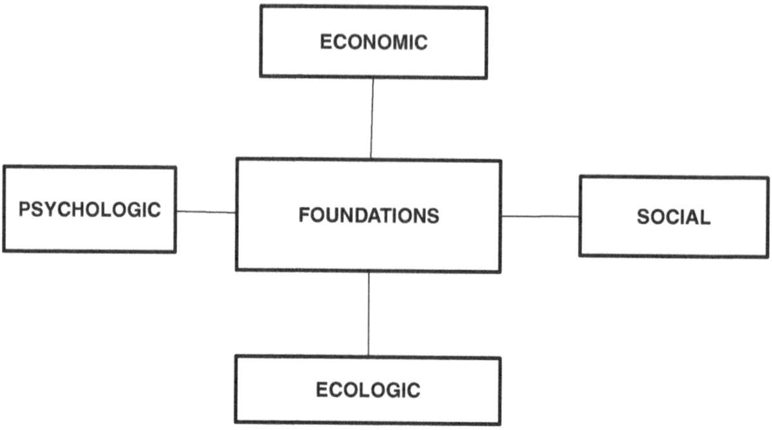

Figure 10.1 Foundations of the company-relevant stakeholders-based management system.

Company management, in order to be able to manage in a performant manner both inside and outside virtual chain activities, which are much more complex and dynamic than the "classical" ones, needs a stakeholders management system. Relevant stakeholders, both internal and external, integrated in managerial synapses are the key players capable of developing virtual value chains.

Social causes represent the second type of foundation. A company, like any other organization, means firstly people. It is composed of individuals who fulfil all necessary inside activities. Multiple and essential external company relations are also fulfilled by the company's own human resources and people representing other outside entities – external relevant stakeholders. All these social relationships are very influential on the company's activities and performance. All these social relationships depend on the persons involved, on their characteristics, feelings, motivations, involvement, satisfaction, engagement, and others. In order to be performant, the company should be able to take all these aspects into consideration, and manage them in efficient and sustainable ways. Hence, companies need new managerial approaches, different from the classical ones. A company stakeholders-based management system represents a possible realistic solution to these social challenges, involving all relevant internal and external stakeholders.

Ecological challenges represent the other essential category of problems that increasingly influence the company's activities and performances. Today, ecological factors have become very important at all levels of the society and economy, starting with the individual person, continuing with all kinds of organizations and up to the level of mankind. Important parts of the society have realized the determinant impact of ecological factors on the world's present and future existence and development. Many communities and NGOs have very useful and numerous ecological initiatives and actions. A large proportion of them are directed at the company level, where most natural resources are used, and where the majority of activities that have an impact on the ecologic environment are fulfilled. In this context, companies should face new types of challenges and deal with many new elements ignored in the previous period. The use of all material resources, protection of the environment, avoidance of pollution and of energy and raw material waste, material recovery, recycling, and reuse have become strategic challenges for any company. The management of a company should deal permanently with these aspects and find and implement the right solutions from ecologic and economic points of view. In order to do this, companies need a new type of management with a strong ecological dimension capable of facing new challenges and finding efficient ecological solutions. A company stakeholders-based management system incorporates the vision and the tools that are able to respond to a large extent to these challenges.

Many companies have already started to generate and implement new approaches focused on social and ecological problems. **Corporate social responsibility** represents the most widely used approach in trying to solve major social and ecological problems. Corporate social responsibility, developed in the last few decades, promotes a new company approach and behaviour regarding some of the most important company stakeholders – society, the ecological environment, local communities, customers, clients, and their own employees. Without any doubt, significant progress has been made in many companies, especially in corporations. But the holistic, permanent, and performant approach and resolution of social and ecological problems remain a huge challenge in companies and also a keen need. A company stakeholders-based management system contains the necessary new decisional, actional, and behavioural elements that are able to satisfy this need.

Human resources, in today's companies, have to a large extent a high level of education, knowledge, and aspirations. Actual company employees are quite different from the labour force employed a few decades ago, and have a different psychology. The typical component of the contemporary company tends to be a highly educated person, possessing a lot of knowledge, with a large array of interests and expectations, possessing valuable intellectual capital, quite often aware of their potential, and demanding to be treated in a new manner. Organization employees and external stakeholders expect from the company management a totally **new approach that is able to take into consideration their psychological particularities** and satisfy specific human and work requirements. Company management, in order to integrate the employees and other stakeholders, to stabilize them and to increase their efforts, satisfaction, creativity, and productivity, should offer new types of approaches and solutions, focused on the human side of people's personality. In this context, management practice and theory have developed **humanistic management.**[1]

Other essential elements, closely associated with humanistic management, include the **reconsideration of people's emotions and emotional intelligence**, helping to promote another individual treatment of these people, much more suited to the individual characteristics of the internal and external company stakeholders. Studies of emotions and emotional intelligence provide better psychological premises in organizations to understand, communicate, and cooperate with the human resources. Humanistic management, the study of emotions and emotional intelligence, has made notable contributions toward a better treatment of employees with beneficial results for the quality of work, manager behaviour, work climate, and individual and organizational performances.

But the reality shows us that these new managerial and psychological approaches are used just in a small number of companies – more frequently in corporations – and usually they are not employed systematically, not integrated in a holistic strategic vision addressed to all company-relevant stakeholders. In order to fully valorize humanistic management, the study of emotions, emotional intelligence and other new elements regarding the "human side" of human resource, they should be integrated in a new management system capable of taking into consideration permanently these "delicate" human aspects. A company-relevant stakeholders-based management system, having a managerial synapse as an essential component, tailored to the specifics of both components, might be able to largely solve these psychological aspects, with significant positive effects on individual and organizational company stakeholders.

Economic, social, ecologic, and psychologic foundations should be approached holistically, taking into consideration the multiple interrelated influences and effects at the level of the whole company and its relevant stakeholders, including the new elements generated by the COVID-19 pandemic. In the following sections we shall deal with each of the main foundations, emphasizing the causal connections between them and the company stakeholders-based management system.

Value Creation and Appropriation in a Company with Multiple Relevant Stakeholders

In our approach we start from the **stakeholder-based perspective of performance**, defined by Harrison and Wicks (2013, p. 108) "as the sum of the utility created by the firm for legitimate stakeholders". In the definition we make one change, replacing the "legitimate" stakeholders with the "relevant" stakeholders, in accordance with our vision regarding management based on relevant stakeholders. We will not make reference to another three popular stakeholder company performance perspectives – Shareholders-Based Financial Performance, the Balance Scorecard, and the Triple Bottom Line – because they are not directly in line with the profile of this paragraph, focused on the economic background of the company stakeholders-based management system (Harrison, Bosse, & Phillips, 2010; Lieberman, Garcia-Castro, & Balasubramanian, 2017; Tantalo & Paton, 2013).

Our approach is based on **the following four perspectives:**

a Value created in the company is generated both by the enterprise and its stakeholders;
b The virtual value chain is the main mechanism of the company stakeholders' value creation;
c Each company has and develops relationships with a stakeholder only if it creates value for the organization or the stakeholder facilitates directly or indirectly the value added creation;
d It is a positive relationship between stakeholders-oriented management and economic firm performance, which can be almost always measured in terms of financial returns (Choi & Wang, 2009; Dorobantu & Odziemkowska, 2017; Hillman & Keim, 2001).

Relevant stakeholders can contribute to the value creation in a company in many ways: providing some resources (equipment, work, land, buildings, money, etc.), having knowledge and using it in the company's activities, possessing and using special competences in the company, providing to the company certain commercial, financial, technical, etc. services. The contribution of the stakeholder to the company's performance is one criterion in the evaluation of its relevance. The most relevant stakeholders are parts of the virtual value chain and usually make a bigger contribution to the company's performance.

Many specialists (Amit & Zott, 2001; Bosse, Phillips, & Harrison, 2009; Bowman & Ambrosini, 2000; Brandenburger & Stuart Jr., 1996; Lepak, Smith, & Taylor, 2007) have contributed to the elaboration of the concept regarding stakeholders' contribution to company performance and their rewarding for this contribution, called **value creation appropriation** (VCA) in the company. Stakeholders are treated as claimants and capturers of value in their interaction with the company. In recent years there has been a change from the neoclassical economic model, based only on two relevant stakeholders (the consumer and the producer), to the broader-based view of value creation appropriation, where multiple stakeholders are considered. Garcia-Castro and Aguilera (2015) make a remarkable contribution in this respect. They developed a conceptual framework based on an analytical taxonomy of value creation and appropriation "consistent with a more complex notion of **value and wherein the trade-offs in stakeholders' value appropriation are included**". The concept of **total value created by the firm and all its stakeholders** is used, instead of the previous concept of shareholder value creation. Based on this comprehensive approach of total value creation in the company, they elaborated a **model value creation and appropriation with multiple stakeholders.**

One important practical aspect is the possibility of applying this model to a company, only using publicly available data referring to prices, costs, inputs, and outputs. This framework could be utilized in order to measure and redistribute the total value created in the firm to the relevant stakeholders. Moreover, it is based on another new concept introduced by Garcia-Castro and Aguilera (2015), **value creation elasticity of stakeholder value appropriation,** which captures the relationships between value appropriated by a stakeholder and the total value added in a period of time. This approach makes it possible to assess whether each dollar appropriated by one stakeholder has a positive, neutral or negative effect on the total value created by the company. According to the authors, value creation appropriation elasticity could be used by company decision-makers to fulfil voluntary investments by selected stakeholders, in order to maintain distributional justice, respect reciprocity norms, and build trustworthiness.

Without any doubt, value creation appropriation elasticity represents a very good approach for companies in order to manage much better relevant stakeholders, taking into consideration their contribution to the total value created in the firm. In its use it is important to take into consideration the limits of the approach, which have been outlined by Castro and Aguilera themselves.

Company-relevant stakeholder management – in order to use the possibilities created by value creation appropriation elasticity and by other innovative approaches in this field – needs an **appropriate accounting.** According to the specialists Mitchell, Van Buren, Greenwood, and Freeman (2015), stakeholders' inclusion in organizational decision-making and the resulting issue of value creation is one of the thorny problems that stakeholder management has sought to address. **A new branch of accounting is needed that is** able:

- to identify the contribution of each relevant stakeholder to the creation of the total value in the company and to reflect it in accounting;
- to allow appropriation of the value allocated to each relevant stakeholder from the company value.

In this regard, some steps ahead have been made, but slowly and not enough. There have been some promising studies in the last few years.

One of them (Mitchell et al., 2015) developed a transdisciplinary theory of value creation stakeholder accounting. This is based on stakeholder risk-sharing as a superior rationale for stakeholder inclusion. In it is proposed **a new mechanism** – the **value creation stakeholder partnership** – for implementing the new type of stakeholder accounting. The new mechanism is a creative combination of accounting value creation, entrepreneurship, and stakeholder theory. In a special issue of a renowned management journal,[2] a set of papers were consecrated to this essential field for company stakeholder management.

The development of the special accounting mechanism that is able to reflect both value contribution and appropriation of each relevant stakeholder in the company is necessary in order to build a performant managerial synapse and stakeholders-based management system.

The elements presented ensure that the company-relevant stakeholders-based management system applies the principles of distributional, procedural, and interactional justice (Harrison et al., 2010), which is essential for the organization relevant stakeholders' engagement and performance.

Value Chain and Virtual Value Chain

The virtual value chain – the main mechanism of the company stakeholders' value creation – represents one of the four premises of the value creation and appropriation approach mentioned in the first paragraph of this chapter. A value chain – as outlined by the very well-known specialists Freeman and Liedtka (1997) – should and could be interpreted in stakeholders' terms.

The **value chain** concept was created and launched in the managerial theory and practice by Michael Porter in his famous book in 1985 (Porter, 1985). Value chains have had a huge impact on business and company management. A value chain is a set of activities that a company, operating in a specific industry, performs in order "to deliver" valuable products or services for market. These activities are divided into two categories:

a primary activities – inbound logistics, operations, outbound logistics, marketing, sales and services;
b support activities – infrastructure, technological development, human resource management and procurement.

A value chain is a powerful management tool for disaggregating a company into its strategically relevant activities, in order to focus on the sources of competitive advantage.

It has revealed the essential role of two categories of external company relevant stakeholders – customers and suppliers – by including them in the primary activities of the company and also by their strong involvement in support activities. Such an approach has had a major impact on reorganizing, in a practical manner, the contribution of these relevant stakeholders to the value creation in the company and on the need to give much more attention, effort, and resources in cultivating special relationships with them.

From the Porter value chain many new variants of value chains have been developed, adapted to the different industries and companies. In 1995, Rayport and Sviokla created a virtual value chain reflecting the profound changes produced in the company, economy, and society, generated mainly by the knowledge revolution and the transition to a knowledge-based economy. They conceived a virtual value chain bearing in mind that every business today competes in two worlds: a physical world of resources that managers can see and touch, and a virtual world made of information (Rayport & Sviokla, 1995).

A virtual value chain is an integrated system rather than a set of related activities; it incorporates five generic value adding steps, which are virtual in that they are performed through and with information on each activity in the value chain:

- gathering, by sifting and extracting, digital information
- organizing, by storing the information in special ways, making it easy to retrieve and use it
- selecting, by choosing the information, to add value to the operation
- synthesizing, by placing the information into context for users
- distributing, through transmission of synthesized information to users

Usually, a virtual value chain represents the results of combining physical and virtual value chain analysis.

The virtual value chain is non-linear; it represents a matrix of potential inputs and outputs that can be accessed and distributed through a wide variety of channels involving a large array of company-relevant stakeholders. Management could use separately the value chain and, respectively, the virtual value chain. In order to maximize performance, it is recommended to use both value chains correlated or – better still – combining them.

In Figure 10.2, we present a variant of virtual value chain which is frequently used in the management company (Van Vliet, 2010; Weiber & Kollmann, 1998). This variant is a combination of a physical value chain and a virtual actual value chain.

Rayport and Sviokla (1995) recommend to company managers a set of **five guiding principles** in the use of a virtual value chain, alone or in combination with a physical value chain:

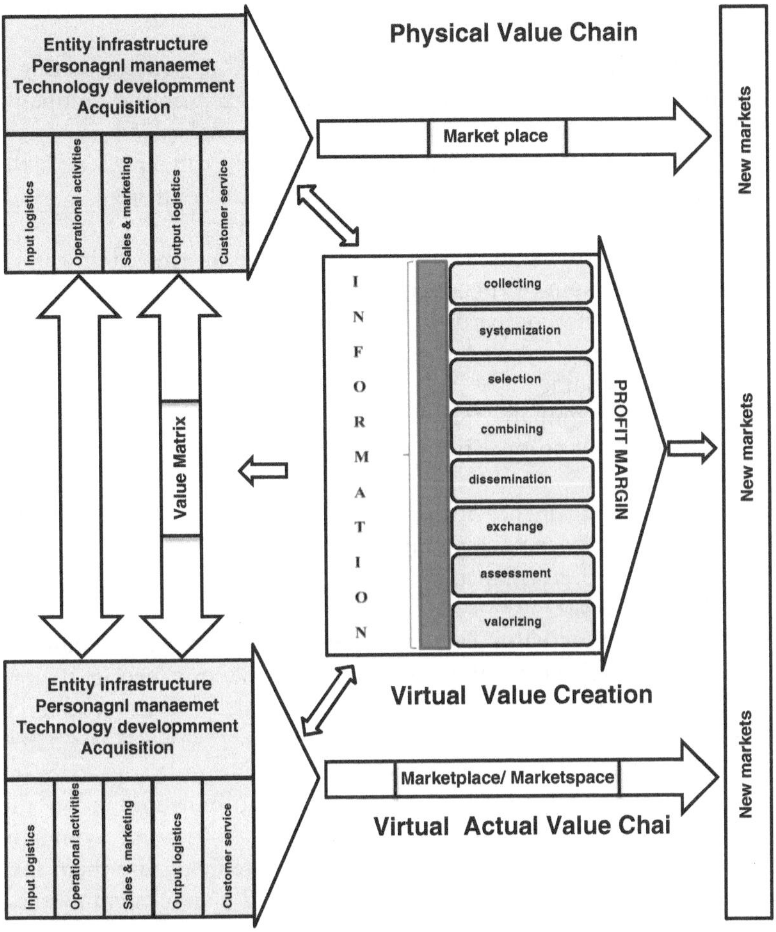

Figure 10.2 Virtual value chain.

Adapted from Virtual value chain model, by V. Van Vliet, 2010. Retrieved from https://www.toolshero.com/problem-solving/virtual-value-chain/.

- the law of digital assets
- new economies of scale
- new economies of scope
- transaction cost compression
- rebalancing supply and demand

The **potential main advantages of company management focused on a virtual value chain** – which could be greatly amplified by using a stakeholders-based management system – are the following:

- physical operations become more effective through a large-scale information system, used to coordinate activities in the physical value chain;
- substitution of physical activities with virtual activities, creating a parallel virtual value chain in the marketplace for the company, which could increase the market share and the sales;
- team that deals with company value chain can transcend the limitations of time and space that characterize the management of physical activities;
- information extracts in every stage of the virtual value chain can be turned in new spin-off products or services;
- placement of the company in a better position in the total value industry process, based on the previous advantages generated by its virtual value chain;
- increase of the company's interorganizational competitive advantage in the context of co-opetition.

Organization management, using a company-relevant stakeholders-based management system, can gain and **increase all these advantages at a superior level** of performance because:

a every relevant activity, every component of the value chain, is fulfilled by a relevant stakeholder, who can be managed in a more performant manner if he/or she is integrated in a managerial synapse;

b the value chain selects and incorporates not only the relevant activities for total company value creation, but, implicitly, the relevant stakeholders; this helps in the evaluation of company stakeholders' relevance and, based on this, in integrating them in a managerial mechanism – a stakeholders-based management system;

c a value matrix specific to the virtual value chain – which represents in fact a matrix of value opportunities – can generate more value for the company and its partners if it is used with a stakeholders-based management system focused on the relevant stakeholders, which in fact could approach and valorize the new opportunities within the value chain;

d a virtual value chain moves relevant activities totally, or a large proportion of them, from the traditional market to the marketplace, increasing the dependence of the performance from the external and internal relevant stakeholders. A stakeholders-based management system can be very useful in the development and fructification of very powerful relationships with these categories of relevant stakeholders;

e a company-relevant stakeholders-based management system due to its specific features – joint objectives, win-win negotiations, reciprocity, etc. – is much more suited to determining the human resources fulfilling the relevant chain of activities, which in fact are company-relevant stakeholders, to operate in new ways required by the virtual value chain.

The value chain and virtual value chain are two economic systems that integrate relevant activities – physical and/or information – fulfilled by relevant internal and external company stakeholders. Consequently, we can conclude that both value chains, in order to generate consistent competitive advantage, need a company-relevant stakeholders-based management system.

Knowledge Value Chain

Without any doubt, a **knowledge value chain** is essentially a virtual value chain. The creation of this specific knowledge value chain has been determined by several causes (see Figure 10.4).

Four main reasons have motivated us to approach it separately, in a special section:

a it presents many very important particularities, which make it different from the consecrated value chain and virtual value chain;
b there are certain categories of companies, especially eco-enterprises – like network companies, virtual enterprises, etc. – in which there are not any physical activities, as all work processes are knowledge processes. In these companies, only the knowledge value chain operates;
c in the future starting with the near future – the knowledge-based companies where only knowledge work processes operate will increase in number very fast and will have a greater impact on business functioning and performances;
d transition to a knowledge-based economy, determined by fast digital transformation, nanotechnologization, biotechnologization, human resources transformation, etc., will increase the frequency and performance of the networks of knowledge value chains at the level of industry, national economy and global economy.

In Figure 10.3, we present the **generic knowledge value chain** adapted from the variant elaborated by Holsapple and Singh (2001), as cited in Holsapple and Jones (2004).

Knowledge value chain creation and fast development are **determined by several causes** presented in Figure 10.4 (Nicolescu & Nicolescu, 2011).

A knowledge value chain is a knowledge management framework (Lee & Yang, 2000) that can contribute to a large extent to increasing the value added generated by the company and its relevant stakeholders.

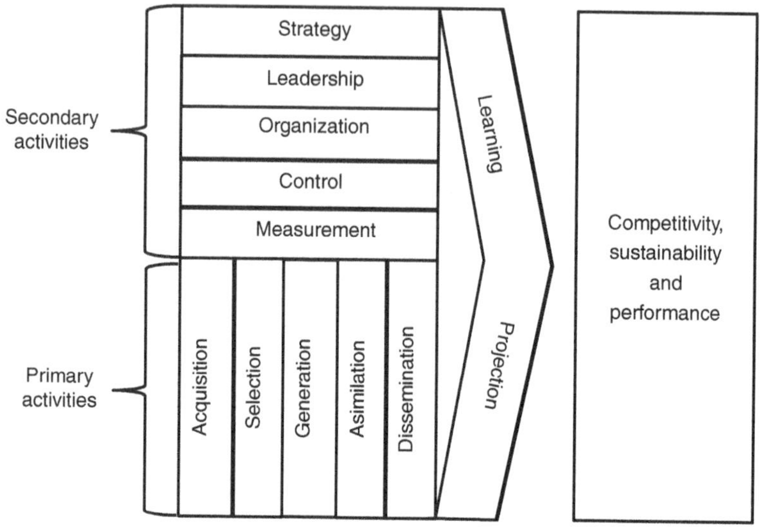

Figure 10.3 Knowledge value chain.

Adapted from "Knowledge chain model: Activities for competitiveness" by C. W. Holsapple & M. Singh, 2001, *Expert Systems with Applications*, *20*(1), p. 80. Retrieved from https://doi.org/10.1016/S0957–4174(00)00050-6.

A knowledge value chain, compared with a virtual value chain, has certain **particularities** (see Table 10.1) that are useful in company management.

The particularities show that the knowledge value chain has huge potential for value creation in companies, through work processes focused on knowledge transformations – creation, access, use, share, organization, dissemination, protection, etc. These knowledge processes generate high performances when they use the tacit and explicit knowledge of all company-relevant stakeholders. The new stakeholders-based management system could help to achieve them successfully. A knowledge value chain focused on knowledge capital (Ermine, 2013), the strategical resource of a company, is – without any doubt – the value chain of the future, in the knowledge-based economy, which is rapidly developing in the context of digitalization.

Taking into consideration the elements regarding the knowledge value chain and virtual value chain, we can conclude that the economic background of modern company management has changed (see Figure 10.5). **The new economic background of the modern company – a knowledge-based company – is represented by the virtual value chain and knowledge value chain.** In order to be performant, managers of the company should focus their decisions and actions on these value

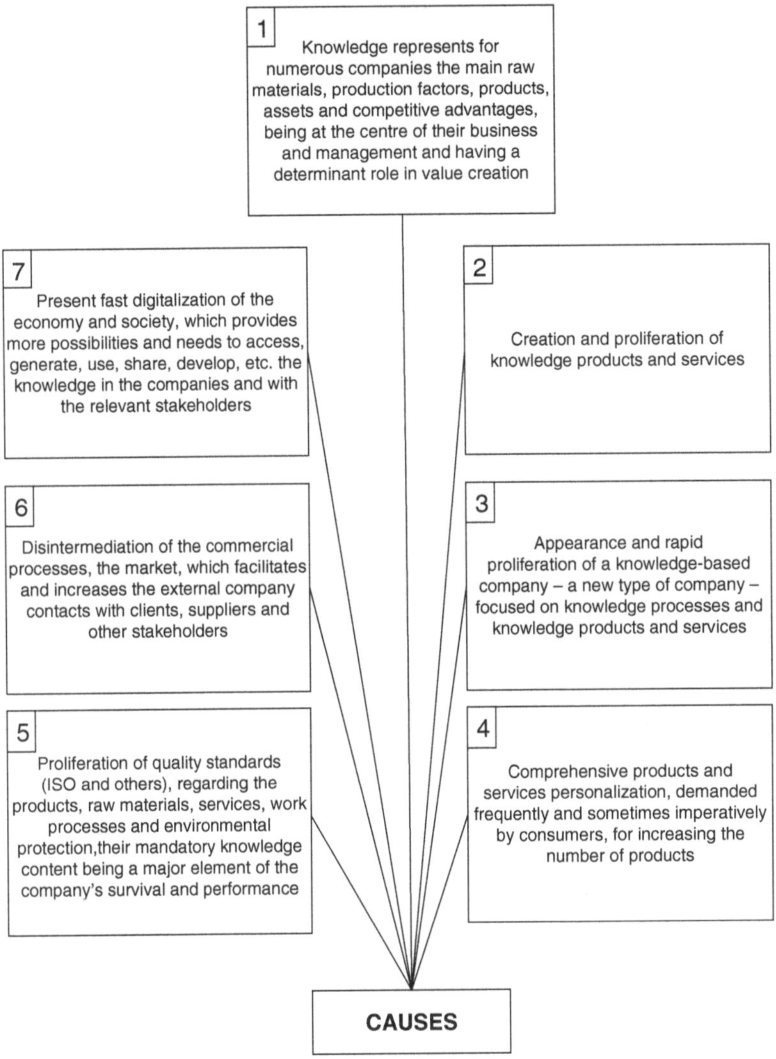

Figure 10.4 Main causes of knowledge value chain creation

chains and on the internal and external relevant stakeholders who operate them.

Interdependencies Between Company Value Chains – Business Environment-Relevant Stakeholders

Approaching each type of value chain separately – as we did in the previous sections – provides only a limited understanding of their role in

Table 10.1 Main particularities of the knowledge value chain

No.	*Particularities*
1.	It works in a new type of enterprise – a knowledge-based company – characterized by the fact that knowledge represents the main raw material, production factor, asset, product, and competitive advantage
2.	It deals only with knowledge products, or products very rich in knowledge
3.	It incorporates only knowledge processes from within the company or outside the company; the most frequent company knowledge processes are the identification, creation, acquisition, organization, sharing, learning, storing, protecting, and selling of the knowledge
4.	It is based on a strong IT background, which is permanently and rapidly developed
5.	It is operated mainly by a new type of human resource – a knowledge-based employee – with rich knowledge and a high capacity to process knowledge and generate value added
6.	It flexibly integrates certain activities from outside the company
7.	It is very dynamic, rapidly operating, and modifying, because of the fast-changing VUCA environment
8.	It involves very specific economic, management, and human structures and approaches, many of them structured as a network
9.	It operates in the marketspace and in the environment space, not directly in the classical marketplace
10.	It is connected with a lot of other knowledge and/or virtual value chains of suppliers, customers, investors, bankers, consultants, designers, etc., being part of many networks of value chains
11.	It is a very performant system, based on the knowledge capacity to be used concomitantly in many places generating value added
12.	It enables the integration of the company and its relevant stakeholders in the industry, markets, global value chains, etc.

companies and the economy, and of the relevant stakeholders' implication. In Figure 10.6, we try to present the main relationships between the transition from one type of value chain to another, the main components of the business environment involved and the categories of relevant company stakeholders directly participating in the activities generating value added in the company. **The premises of our analysis** are the following:

- a value chain represents not only a system of relevant activities but also a network of relevant stakeholders;
- certain components of the company business environment – not only the market – greatly influence the capacity to produce value added for the value chain, relevant activities, and the relevant company stakeholders.

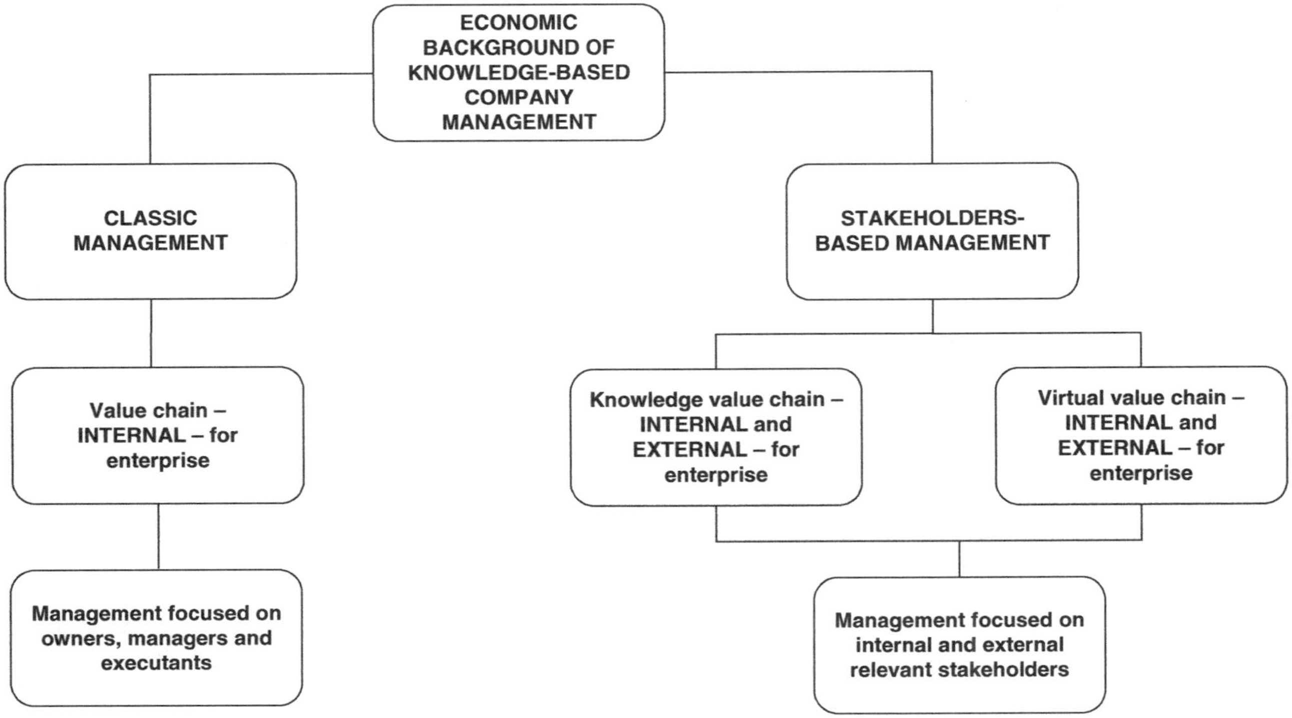

Figure 10.5 New economic background of the knowledge-based company.

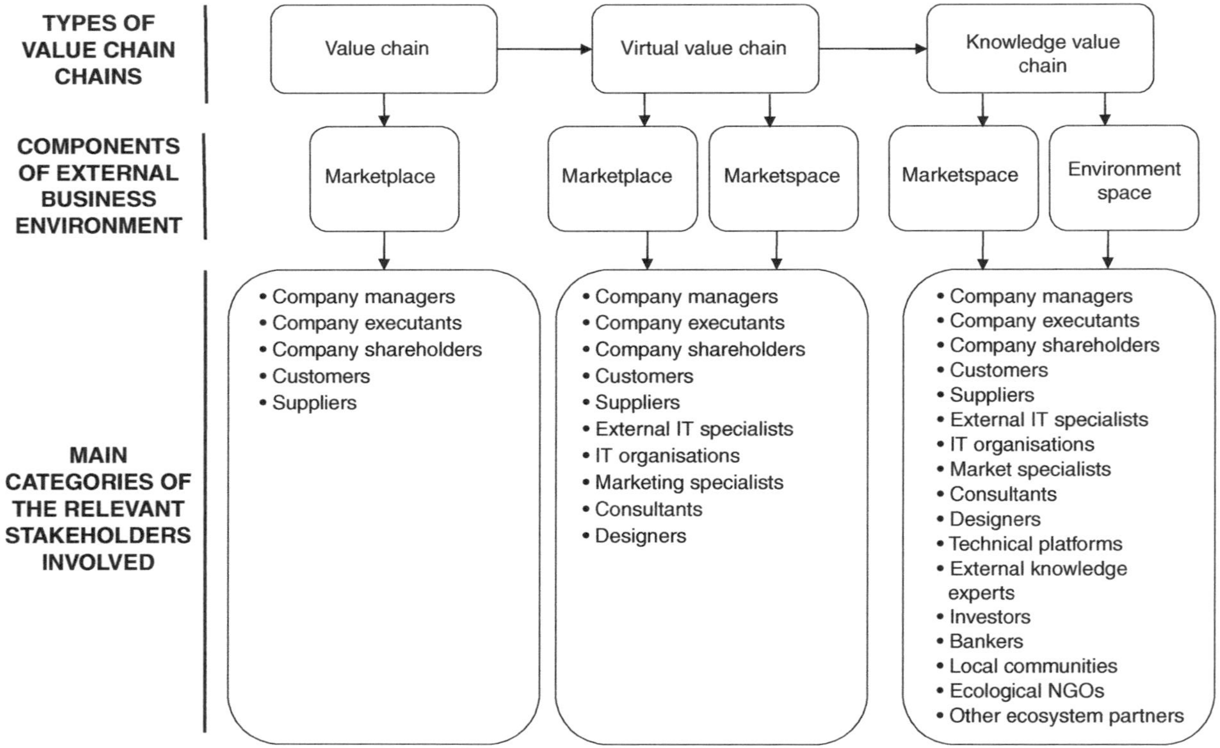

Figure 10.6 Relationships between the different types of value chain, the focus on the business environment components and the relevant stakeholders.

Certain specialists (Lin & Wu, 2010) on the virtual value chain have introduced the **marketspace approach**, which incorporates virtual processes based on the use of information, by the company, in order to sell its products and services on the market. Our analysis has indicated that on the knowledge value chain activities has an increasing impact – positive or negative from profit point of view – many others components of the environment – labor market, local community, company industry, capital market, banking system, ecosystems involved, or industrial platforms. They participate in the company value chain activities, directly and indirectly, with knowledge, which is value chain content that is absolutely essential for the company to gain competitive advantage and be performant. For this reason, we propose the **new approach of environmentspace**, which includes, besides marketspace – which remains a milestone element of a value chain – all other environment components participating in the company knowledge value creation. Environmentspace is the knowledge area outside a company where external parts of the knowledge value chain activities operate that are absolutely essential for the organization's survival and competitive performance. Company access to the environmentspace provides an important part of the tacit and explicit knowledge used within the value chain, sometimes very innovative, from the creative external relevant stakeholders. Environmentspace is an essential element of the company's integration in economy networks, in its ecosystems.

Analysis of the elements incorporated in Figure 10.6 indicates the following **main conclusions:**

a the first horizontal axis indicates the changing of the type of value chain: from the classical value chain focused on physical activities to the virtual value chain focused, totally or partially, on the virtual activities creating value added, and to the knowledge value chain, focused on the knowledge activities generating value added through high utilization and valorization of the company and relevant stakeholders' knowledge;

b the second horizontal axis indicates the changes in environment components, where the value chain operates; it starts with marketplace, the external company area of action of the classical value chain, goes on to marketspace alone or combined with virtual marketplace and, finally, environmentspace, which incorporates all virtual components of the company environment, where a knowledge value chain operates;

c stakeholders are usually involved in each type of value chain; this axis shows the increasing number of company-relevant stakeholder types that participate in the operation of relevant chain activities, enriching their capacity to generate more added value;

d the first vertical axis indicates that the classical value chain acts outside the company mainly in the marketplace and the principal categories of relevant stakeholders involved – managers, shareholders, executants, customers, and suppliers;

e the second vertical axis shows that a virtual value chain works in the business environment, both in marketplace and marketspace, involving more categories of external company-relevant stakeholders; the new categories of external stakeholders are: IT specialists, IT organizations, virtual marketing specialists, consultants, and designers;

f the third vertical axis indicates that the knowledge value chain operates not only in the marketspace but also in the environment space, which includes, as we have demonstrated, other important parts of the company environment. Compared with a virtual value chain, in the knowledge activities generating value added more categories of relevant individual and organizational stakeholders can participate, such as technological platforms, external knowledge experts, investors, bankers, local communities, ecological and social NGOs, and other company ecosystem partners.

The horizontal axis indicates the essential development of the company value chain as a system (first axis), and the changes in the approach of the company environment components, and of the relevant stakeholder categories (third axis). The horizontal axis reveals the major progress of the company value chain approaches in itself and from the perspective of company environment and relevant stakeholders.

The vertical axis shows the essential differences between the three types of value chains and, because of these, the need to adopt different managerial approaches, taking into consideration the environment parts and the relevant stakeholders involved. Each type of value chain needs special managerial mechanisms focused on the relevant activities creating value and on the relevant stakeholders possessing valuable information and knowledge and operating value chain activities.

One final remark: in the economy there are and will be all three types of value chains, reflecting the heterogeneity of companies and the environment. It is a company management duty to select and to apply the type of value chain suited to each company, using special managerial mechanisms that are able to produce high performance, like a managerial synapse and/or a stakeholders-based management system, and to adopt the management tools that generate high performance. Of course, there is a strong tendency to proliferate the virtual value chain and knowledge value chain, the most up-to-date and performant in the context of the new economy – the knowledge-based economy.

Corporate Social Responsibility

Corporate social responsibility represents one of the key concepts and approaches in the management of companies and has a great influence on the treatment of stakeholders. Corporate social responsibility has a long history, starting from the beginning of the nineteenth century, but the major development of the modern corporate social responsibility can be traced back to the 1960s and 1970s (Freeman, Harrison, Wicks, Parmar, & De Colle, 2010). Corporate social responsibility has been defined and approached in a large variety of ways. According to Wang (2015), it has been grouped into four main categories: corporate social responsibility, corporate social performance, corporate citizenship, and corporate philanthropy.

In the first category – **corporate social responsibility** – four types of approaches have been identified. The integrative approach is the most widely used and the most important, being based on systemic vision. The other three approaches of corporate social responsibility are oriented toward certain types of problems – economic, voluntary, and public – each of them important, but neglecting the other essential aspects of corporate social responsibility.

Carroll's approach, reflected in the pyramid of corporate social responsibilities, is the best-known, most widely disseminated and most frequently used integrative approach of corporate social responsibility. For this reason, we shall present it briefly. **Carroll's pyramid**, based on his corporate social responsibility definition from 1979, was published in 1991. According to Carroll (1991), corporate social responsibility encompasses the economic, legal, ethical, and discretionary (philanthropic) expectations that society has of organizations at a given point in time. The definition contains a set of **four responsibilities**, which creates a foundational infrastructure that helps to characterize the nature of a company's responsibilities to the society.

- **Economic responsibility** is a fundamental condition of businesses' existence that permits them to be created, to survive, and to sustain. Society expects and requires companies to be able to sustain themselves and this is not possible without being profitable. A company needs profit in order to reward the owners and to reinvest for growth, making more products, services, and value added. Economic responsibility is a baseline requirement without which the company cannot exist in a competitive economy;
- **Legal responsibilities** reflect the society's view of "codified ethics", containing the ground laws and regulations that have to be applied by the company. Laws and regulations incorporate the fundamental notions of fair business practices, and companies must comply with them as a condition of operating in business;

- **Ethical responsibilities** reflect the society's expectations regarding those activities, norms, standards, and practices that companies should respect when they operate and conduct their affairs. Society's ethical requirements are in addition to the laws and regulatory provisions. Ethical responsibilities are a full range of norms, standard, values, principles and expectations of what consumers, the community, company employees, and owners regard as normal in the protection of stakeholders' moral rights;
- **Philanthropic responsibilities** deal with all forms of company giving, including voluntary and discretionary. Company philanthropic actions do not represent a responsibility in a literal sense. They represent a company's feedback to the public expectation that an organization is a "good citizen". Fulfilment of philanthropic responsibilities involves a variety of giving forms – products and services, donations, gifts of monetary resources, organization employees' voluntarism, etc.

Based on these foundations, Carroll elaborated his pyramid, whose main elements are incorporated in Figure 10.7.

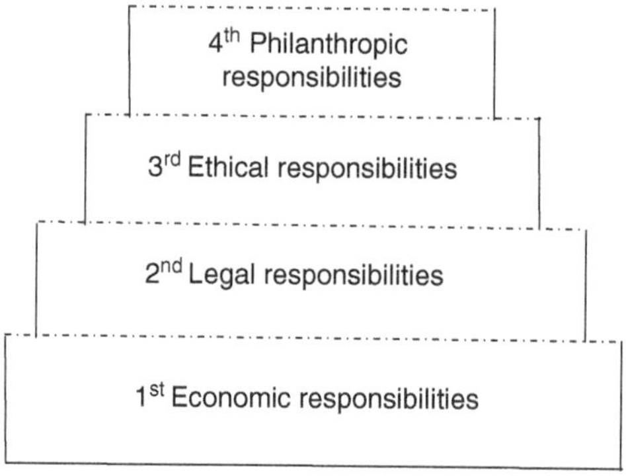

Figure 10.7 Carroll's pyramid of CSR.

Adapted from "The pyramid of corporate social responsibility: Toward the moral management of organizational stakeholders" by A. B. Carroll, 1991, *Business Horizons*, *34*(4), p. 42. Retrieved from https://www.researchgate.net/publication/4883660_The_Pyramid_of_Corporate_Social_Responsibility_Toward_the_Moral_Management_of_Organizational_Stakeholders

Later, Archie Carroll made several changes to his corporate social responsibility definition and pyramid (Carroll, 1999; Carroll, 2004; Carroll, 2016), but the most frequently used remain the variants from 1971 and 1991.

Analyses conducted by certain specialists including a comprehensive empirical fundament (Baden, 2016) or in-depth evaluation (Sachs, Rühli, & Kern, 2009) argued that corporations cannot be seen as purely economic entities, detached from individuals. They proposed that corporate social responsibility is "at heart primarily a moral concept designed to highlight the responsibilities of business (as a minimum), to avoid causing harm to society and environment, or, more proactively, contributing to the welfare of society and its stakeholders" (Baden, 2016). **Denise Baden proposed a new corporate social responsibility pyramid,** whose essential elements are presented in Figure 10.8.

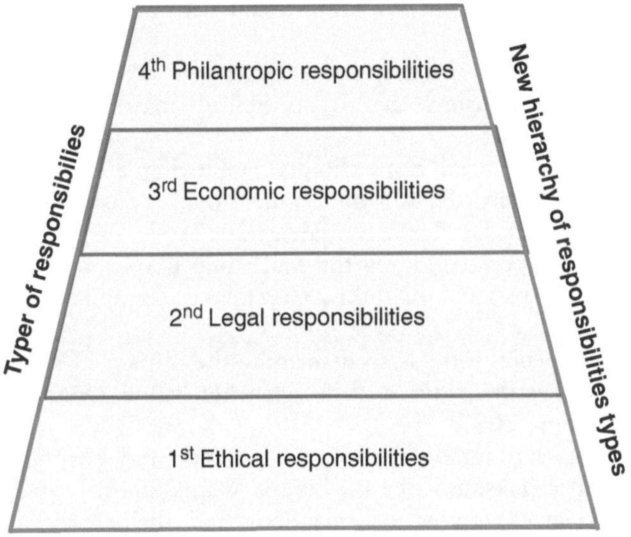

Figure 10.8 Proposed amended pyramid of CSR by Baden.

Adapted from "A reconstruction of Carroll's pyramid of corporate social responsibility for 21st century" by D. Baden, 2016, *International Journal of Corporate Social Responsibility*, *1*(8). Retrieved from https://www.researchgate.net/publication/305801033_A_reconstruction_of_Carroll%27s_Pyramid_of_corporate_social_responsibility_for_the_21st_century.

In her opinion, this pyramid is more powerful and effective, with a **new order of the four types of responsibilities.** The main pragmatic conclusions are:

a Companies, "in order to have licence to operate and to be trusted with the production and allocation of scarce natural resources and inherently valuable human resources, [need] to first and foremost accept ethical responsibilities to not harm and conform to society's ethic norms and expectations";
b A company "needs to be compliant with legal responsibilities". A company is only free to make profit and pursue its economic objectives once it has accepted its moral and legal responsibilities.

During the last few decades, concomitantly with the theoretical developments of corporate social responsibility, in many companies – especially corporations –elements of corporate social responsibilities have been implemented. Specialists' analyses have identified **many elements in which significant progress has been made.** We mention just a few of these aspects:

- institutionalization of corporate social responsibility using certain social mechanisms (Bice, 2017)
- corporate social responsibility organizational learning employing models (Zadek, 2004)
- evaluation of employers' and employees' contribution to corporate social responsibility, using the responsibility matrix (Haski-Leventhal, Roza, & Meijs, 2017)
- measuring corporate social responsibility employing a new tool conceived as a superordinate, multidimensional construct (El Akremi, Gond, Swaen, De Roek, & Igalens, 2018)
- design and use of special indexes for evaluating corporate social responsibility initiatives (Giannarakis, Garefalakis, Lemonakis, & Konteos, 2017)
- construction of special models to determine the impact of social responsibility investment on a firm's market value (Mackey, Mackey, & Barney, 2007)
- relationships between intangibles of productivity and corporate social performance (Hasan, Kobeissi, Liu, & Wang, 2018)
- types of congruence between organizations and their corporate social responsibilities (De Jong & Van der Meer, 2017)
- use of mediating mechanisms in the relationships between corporate social responsibility and corporate financial performance (Karaye, Ishak, & Che-Adam, 2014)
- relationships between corporate social responsibility and employee engagement (Flammer & Luo, 2017; Mirvis, 2012; Rampersad, 2017)
- connection between corporate social responsibility and corporate political responsibilities (Djelic & Etchanchu, 2017; Lyon et al., 2018; Schrempf-Stirling, Palazzo, & Phillips, 2016)
- strategic corporate social responsibility (Chandler & Werther, 2014; Haski-Leventhal, 2018)

This information indicates that the approach of corporate social responsibility is quite comprehensive, dealing with many important elements involved in social corporate responsibility and company management.

Edward Freeman et al. (Freeman et al., 2010) identified in the development of corporate social responsibility from the perspective of stakeholder theory "**two distinct lines of thought** for the integration of financial and social concerns that seem to proceed in parallel and still coexist in ongoing academic research and managerial practice":

a **the residual view** of corporate social responsibility, which is the initial view on it and is still predominant in theory and practice. The residual view conceptualizes corporate social responsibility as a non-strategic activity due to the giving back to society some of the value they created, mainly as a moral obligation;

b **the integrative view** of corporate social responsibility, which conceptualizes its integration of social, ethical and environmental concerns into management criteria as a strategic activity.

The integrative view refers to a deep change in the approach of corporate social responsibility, taking into consideration the multidimensionality of company stakeholders' management as strategic producers and claimants of value created in the company.

The implementation of corporate social responsibility has generated – and this is the predominant specialists' point of view – many positive effects. Specialists from the International Institute for Sustainable Development (2013) elaborated a **comprehensive list of corporate social responsibility benefits**, structured in three categories:

a **Company benefits**

- improved financial performance
- lower operating costs
- enhanced brand image and reputation
- increased sales and customer loyalty
- more ability to attract and retain employees
- reduced regulatory oversight
- access to capital
- workforce diversity
- product safety and decreased liability

b **Benefits for the community and the general public**

- charitable contributions
- employee volunteer programmes
- corporate involvement in community education, employment and home lesson programmes
- product safety and quality

c **Environmental benefits**

- greater material recyclability
- better product durability and functionality
- greater use of renewable resources

  - integration of environment management tools into business, including life cycle assessment and costing, environmental management standards and eco-labelling

Despite these benefits, certain reputed specialists assert, based on comprehensive analysis, that **corporate social responsibility remains a controversial topic** (Chandler & Werther, 2014).

Company-Relevant Stakeholder Responsibilities

The formulation and the idea of "**company stakeholders' responsibilities**" has been very well argued and promoted by renowned specialists Freeman, Harrison, Wicks, Parmar, and De Colle (2010). They proposed "[replacing] corporate social responsibility" with company stakeholders' responsibilities. According to them, a "company signals all forms of value creation and trade, all business and non-profit organizations". Their **main arguments** are the following:

- responsibilities are not contingent on the size and success of one type of organization; all companies should shoulder responsibilities;
- the main goal of corporate social responsibility is to create value for key stakeholders – not only for shareholders – and to fulfil the responsibilities to them;
- company responsibilities imply that we cannot separate business from ethics, because business, ethics, and societal considerations are interdependent and should be integrated.

Based on these arguments, they state that

> company stakeholder responsibility looks at business and society as intertwined, it looks not just at corporations, but at many forms of organizations and promotes a pragmatic view on managing relationships with all the organization's stakeholders, as a primary task toward success (Freeman et al., 2010).

Recently, continuing this approach, Freeman and Elms (2018) argued: "The social responsibility of business is to create value for stakeholders. That means its customers, suppliers, employees and communities, as well as its shareholders".

Business realities provide **other pragmatic elements for the reconsideration of corporate social responsibility**. We shall highlight some of them:

- social corporate responsibility is implemented to different extents in a small number of corporations, especially from Great Britain, the United States, Canada, and a few other developed countries;

- in the use of corporate social responsibility in corporations, frequently not all major elements incorporated by the corporate social responsibility concept are practised (Baden, 2016; Carroll, 2004; Djelic & Etchanchu, 2017; Mirvis, 2012; Rampersad, 2017; Wang, 2015; Zadek, 2004);
- the corporation culture does not usually incorporate corporate social responsibility as a major element;
- in the training and development of managers and other human resources, the topic of corporate social responsibility is not included, or only as a peripheral subject;
- many major stakeholders are not taken into consideration in companies where corporate social responsibility is used;
- the present corporate social responsibility approaches in companies are focused more on the processes involved and less on the stakeholders, on the people, structures or organizations that in practice make/perform the necessary decisions, actions, and behaviours.

The new approach of social responsibility in companies should be holistic in all respects – objectives, responsibilities, organizations, stakeholders, and managerial mechanisms.

We propose, based on the previous elements and other analyses, a **variant of new holistic organization responsibilities**, called **"company stakeholders relevant responsibilities"**, which has the following **features:**

a Responsibility includes all types of social responsibilities, with the condition that they must be relevant. This means that we propose **a new concept of relevant responsibility**. A company responsibility is a relevant responsibility if it respect the criteria incorporated in Table 10.2.
b Company-relevant responsibility deals with every company-relevant stakeholder.
c Company-relevant responsibilities are correlated with multi-objectives of the company and its relevant stakeholders.
d Company-relevant responsibilities take into consideration the relevant responsibilities according to their characteristics and not occasionally, when a crisis occurs, when there is major pressure from powerful relevant stakeholders, etc.
e Different types of responsibilities are correlated taking into consideration their multidimensional nature, and the company and the relevant stakeholders' multi objectives.
f Relevant responsibilities should be reflected in the relevant organizational and individual stakeholders' objectives, roles, tasks, competencies, and responsibilities.
g Relevant responsibilities should be taken into consideration and

Table 10.2 Criteria (requirements) for company-relevant responsibility

No.	*Relevance Criteria*
1.	Responsibility refers to a major "social" need of the society, company and/or the relevant stakeholder
2.	Responsibility could be economic, social, legal, moral, or ecologic
3.	Responsibility accomplishment represents an important element, in order to ensure relationship continuity and stability between the company and relevant stakeholders
4.	Responsibility accomplishment involves, from the company and the relevant stakeholders, specific decisions, actions and behaviours, which consume substantial time, knowledge and other resources
5.	Responsibility has – after fulfilment – a significant positive impact on major elements regarding company and/or relevant stakeholders: organizational performance, individual performance, degree of motivation of the individuals involved, environment protection, social welfare, education, poverty, intellectual capital protection and valorification, prestige and reputation of the organizations, and individual stakeholders involved and others
6.	Responsibility fulfilment contributes significantly to the sustainability of the company and of the relationships between organization and relevant stakeholder, by taking into consideration some grand societal challenges

implemented in all types of companies, regardless of their characteristics (size, profile, performance, location, etc.), because the content of the responsibilities reflects the major interests, objectives, and necessities of the society, economy, and population.

h Relevant responsibilities should be approached and implemented bearing in mind the particularities of each company (size, profile, age, technological level, organizational culture, performances, etc.) and of each relevant individual and organizational stakeholder.

i Company-relevant responsibilities should be realistic and equilibrated, at least in two area:

- the reasonable fulfilment of the relevant responsibilities of the company and the relevant stakeholders
- the enabling of the company and relevant stakeholders' sustainability

In Table 10.3, we have synthesized the **main differences between corporate social responsibilities and the company-relevant stakeholders' responsibilities.**

All the above elements represent reasons for us to propose an alternative to the Carroll pyramid or to other pyramids (see, e.g., Baden, 2016) of corporate social responsibilities – the **responsibilities relevant pentagon of the company** (Figure 10.9).

Table 10.3 The main differences between corporate social responsibilities and company-relevant stakeholders' responsibilities

No.	*Elements*	*Corporate Social Responsibilities*	*Company-Relevant Stakeholders' Responsibilities*
1.	Type of organization	Corporation	All types of organization
2.	Type of responsibility	Social responsibility	All types of relevant responsibilities
3.	Type of stakeholders taken into consideration	Certain primary corporation stakeholders	All relevant company stakeholders
4.	Business objectives	Mainly to create value for company	To create value for company and company-relevant stakeholders
5.	Responsibilities to be fulfilled	Take care of some social responsibilities toward certain stakeholders	All relevant organization responsibilities to all relevant stakeholders

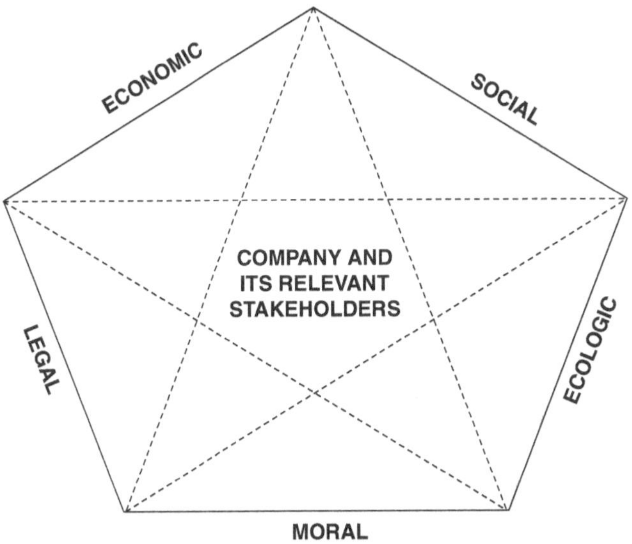

Figure 10.9 Pentagon of company-relevant stakeholders' responsibilities.

Compared with the previous responsibilities pyramids, a company-relevant responsibilities pentagon presents certain **specific features:**

1 It is focused on the company, its relevant stakeholders and relevant responsibilities;

2 It eliminates the mechanical separation and the hierarchical ordination of the different types of social responsibilities;
3 The relevant ecologic responsibilities have been introduced, taking into consideration the recent evolution in the world economy and society, and in science;
4 It is based on the holistic approach taking into consideration all main faces of the relevant responsibility in their systemic interdependences, connected to the company and its relevant stakeholders.

The pentagon of the company-relevant responsibilities represents a good background for a more comprehensive and pragmatic approach in contemporary companies and their environment and for taking into consideration the present and future grand societal challenges. In order to fully achieve this, new systemic management mechanisms are necessary that are able to incorporate and fulfil the organizational and individual objectives, decisions, actions and behaviours, etc. involved in the five types of relevant responsibilities, according to the necessities and expectations of the company and relevant stakeholders, internal and external. A company-**relevant** stakeholder-based management system could be such a managerial mechanism, because through its design and characteristics it is focused on the company and its relevant stakeholders in a holistic and sustainable manner.

Use of the company-relevant stakeholders-based management system, integrating the company-relevant responsibilities, has **multiple advantages:**

a It integrates and operates all types of relevant responsibilities of the company and relevant stakeholders;
b Relevant company responsibilities are permanently approached and implemented based on the specific economic, social, legal, ecologic, and moral criteria, rationally and coherently defined and correlated;
c It is able to operate a proactive approach to company-relevant responsibilities, preventing a crisis and highly tensioned situations at the company and relevant stakeholders level;
d It uses win-win negotiation, reciprocal behaviour and other specific elements of the stakeholders-based management system in the defining and taking into consideration of the relevant company responsibilities, which determine realistic approach and implementation;
e All the above-mentioned elements generate a sustainable implementation and development of the relevant responsibilities at the level of company-relevant stakeholders.

Company-relevant stakeholders' responsibilities overcome corporate social responsibility, having great potential for increasing multidimensional performances at the level of companies, stakeholders, the economy and the entire society. This represents one step ahead in the development of an integrative view of corporate social responsibilities and could be very useful in the context of the pandemic and post-pandemic COVID-19.

Development and Implication of Humanistic Management in Companies

All economic, social or managerial entities or processes are designed, implemented and developed by individuals, such as entrepreneurs, managers, shareholders, executants, etc. For this reason, the interest, native quality, competence, information, knowledge, culture and other characteristics of the people participating in the work processes are essential. **The existence, characteristics, and performances of any business, social, or ecologic processes are decisively influenced by the individuals involved.**

In the present context of the transition to a knowledge-based economy, of the fast digital transformation, the impact of individuals and groups of people on each activity and in every field has increased, becoming determinant because of their knowledge, of their intellectual capital, which are the vectors of development in all organizations.

In the last few decades, the awareness of the huge role and influence of the individual and the society has rapidly increased, in the context of the continuous increase of people's education level and skills, and the demonstration of the efficiency relationship between the quality of human resources and the entity functionality and performance. We can see this awareness in many fields – science, education, health, economy, etc. **In the management of a company this evolution determines that human resources become a central part of it.** In Table 10.4, we present some significant elements showing these **mutations.**

Humanistic management means more than the reconsideration of human resource management. According to certain specialists (e.g. Dierksmeier, 2016), all humanistic management advocates a **paradigm shift in business theory as well as in management practice.** In the field of theory, they suggest a transition from mechanistic economics towards humanistic economics, so as to move in practice away "from capitalistic" to "humanistic business". Humanistic management specialists endorse and affirm the centrality of human rights for all forms and aspects of management (Dierksmeier, 2016). Humanistic management aims to create a more balanced relationship between those things that can be exchanged on markets and those that cannot, but that make life worthwhile, like human dignity and well-being (Pirson, 2017).

Humanistic management involves many changes in organization management, such as: redesigning the company into a vehicle for cultivation of

Table 10.4 Main elements of the company human resource reconsideration

No.	*Elements*
1.	Human resource is considered and treated as an essential company resource
2.	Human resource management has developed rapidly, as a main company function or field, integrating – especially in corporations and large companies – many specialized activities: planning, selection, integration, evaluation, training, motivation, protection, and others
3.	Reconsideration of the company employee, being more frequently treated as having a personality with multifaceted dimensions, needs to be taken into consideration in the organization and its management
4.	Company human resource strategy and policies become more frequent and more influential on the organization's work and performance
5.	Many managerial systems, methods and techniques focused on human resources – like participative management systems and approaches, teamwork, dialogic communication, 360° evaluation, personality texts, management simulation, etc. – have been developed
6.	Continuous and intensive training of company employees inside and outside the organization
7.	Ascension of leadership, including collective leadership, concentrated on communication, implication, and engagement of the company human resource
8.	Organizational and individual culture of the employees in companies tend to become more open, collaborative, and integrative, paying great attention to human resource characteristics

the humanistic relationships inside and outside the organization; promoting self-management-oriented leadership styles; supporting a transformational company culture; avoiding control mechanisms obstructing creativity and initiative; promoting democratic dialogue-based processes and participative management; developing dignity in the workplace in a procedural and participative approach; and transforming human value and virtue in essential components of the organization management (Dierksmeier et al., 2011; Pirson, 2017; Von Kimakowitz, Pirson, Spitzeck, Dierksmeier, & Amann, 2011).

Within humanistic management, special attention is paid to stakeholders. Humanistic management aims to honour the freedom of each business stakeholder, by involving them, as much as possible, in making those decisions that impact their lives. Ideally, everyone who is affected by management should be able to have an effect on it, wherever possible directly, and where impossible, indirectly, by way of representation (Dierksmeier, 2016). Recently, almost 200 CEOs under auspices of the International Council for Small Business (ICSB) (2019) proposed a Human Entrepreneurship Framework within which they share a fundamental commitment to all stakeholders to deliver value to all of them for the future success of companies, communities and countries.

Humanistic management, according to some specialists (e.g. Dierksmeier, 2016; Dierksmeier et al., 2011; Pirson, 2017; Von Kimakowitz et al., 2011), generates **multiple advantages** (see Figure 10.10).

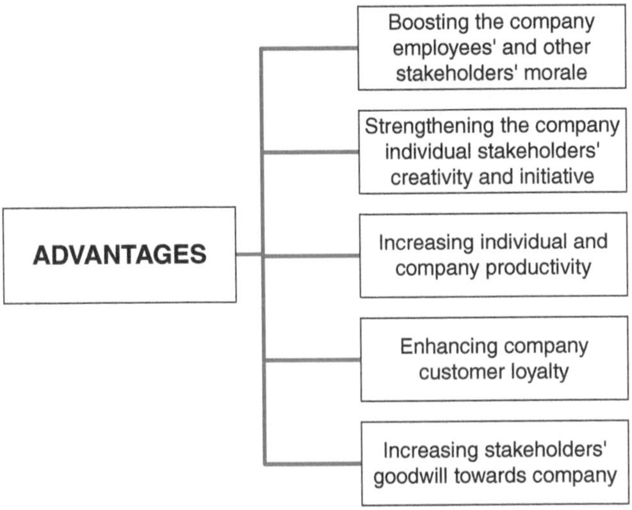

Figure 10.10 Main advantages of implementing humanistic management.

Despite these essential advantages, humanistic management is implemented only to a low extent in companies and, frequently, only in some components that are able to improve certain elements of the organization's activities. Implementation of humanistic management needs radical transformation in the company and its management, which is very complex and difficult to do. In our opinion, managerial synapses and a company-relevant stakeholders-based management system are able to do this. Their nature and main characteristics are fully compatible with humanistic management's aims and means. Integration of the humanistic management vision, which is very helpful in the pandemic context, into the relevant stakeholders-based management system will enhance the work and the performance of the company, concomitantly with the generation of much more satisfaction and many more implications for, and accomplishments by, individual internal and external stakeholders.

Emotions and Emotional Intelligence in Companies

The psychological foundation of the company-relevant stakeholders-based management system is represented by new approaches to people emotions and emotional intelligence in the organization. The study of emotions and affect in organizations started over 20 years ago, revealing their numerous influences on the work of people and on the activities in the company. The prestigious scientific publication *Academy of Management Review* focused a special issue[3] on this subject, publishing eight studies and proposing a new theory regarding emotion in management (Ashkanasy, Humphrey, & Huy, 2017).

The **new science of emotion** contributes to generating practical techniques for helping organizations to enhance their sensing, seizing and transforming capabilities (Forgas, 2000). Researches by Professor Forgas (2008) and Healey and Hodgkinson (2017) demonstrated that the **following these are essential for people's work and performances** in an organization:

- affect and cognition are not separate – thought and emotion are intertwined;
- feelings have a multifaceted influence on everything that we think or do;
- mood affects memory and critical thinking.

From the company management point of view, it is essential to understand the emotions of employees and other stakeholders and to regulate their effects. A very useful tool for doing this is **the model of emotions** known as **the "affective circumplex"**, proposed by Healey and Hodgkinson. They take into consideration a large number of people's emotions – 16 – most frequently encountered in an organization. People's emotions are organized in a circular structure, focused on two major dimensions:

- the first category reflects the degree of energy evoked by particular emotions, which can vary between low and high;
- the second category differentiates emotions in terms of their degree of pleasantness, which can vary between pleasant and unpleasant.

The value of this model consists in providing a comprehensive picture of the main emotions of the people in an organization and of their significance in terms of the energy involved and the pleasantness associated with each of them. Based on these elements their effects, positive or negative, in the organization have been established along with the type of feedback necessary from company managers. The circumplex model of affect helps company managers to regulate the control of emotions, which means what emotions are experienced, when they are experienced and how they are experienced and used. **Emotion regulation** is closely related to people's capabilities of self-control and willpower (Forgas, 2000; Healey & Hodgkinson, 2017) and help managers in managing the emotional dynamics of transformation in the company. Emotion regulation helps organization managers to increase their sensing, seizing and transforming capabilities at the level of workplaces, departments, and entire organizations.

Emotion regulation is very important because of the major influence of emotions on the decisions, actions and behaviours of all managers, executants or other stakeholders. Company components and, generally, people do not make decisions based on fact, information, and knowledge alone. Their emotions contribute substantially to what decisions they make, how they implement them and the results generated. For this reason, company managers should have **emotional competences,** which refers to the ability to experience and display emotions that are deemed appropriate for an actor role in an institutional order (Voronov & Weber, 2015). Emotional competence depends decisively on the **emotional intelligence** of a person. Emotional intelligence involves four main processes:

- emotion identification
- emotion understanding
- emotion regulation
- emotion use

Emotional intelligence is based on specific competencies. In a recent study, the **emotional intelligence competencies** (McKee, 2017) regarding self-awareness, social awareness, self-management and relationship management, have been recommended to be used in the company management.

Managers having and using these emotional competencies determine the development of the healthy emotional climate in the company, which is always an affective climate enabling organizational effectiveness (Ashkanasy et al., 2017). The use of emotional intelligence in a company is not limited to the manager–subordinate relationship. It can also be used in relationships with other internal and external stakeholders. The more you are aware of and understand stakeholders' emotions, the greater the influence you can have (Green, 2015). In approaching a stakeholder, specialists recommend preparing and utilizing **an emotional profile.** So far, this has been used in particular in relationships with major stakeholders within the management of important projects. Our opinion is that the elaboration and use of an emotional profile is recommended in the relationship with each new relevant company stakeholder. In this process, **two emotional intelligence skills are essential for company managers:**

- emotional awareness of others; this means the capacity to read relevant stakeholders' emotions in advance of working with them;
- managing others' emotions, which means the capacity to effectively manage stakeholders' emotions in the work processes fulfilled together.

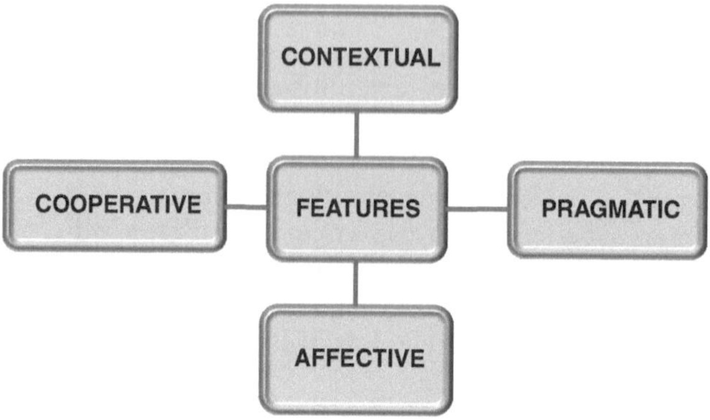

Figure 10.11 Emotional intelligence features, enabling new types of relationship with relevant company stakeholders.

We believe that **emotional intelligence** has **four features** that make it essential in the new management approach to the relationships with relevant company stakeholders (see Figure 10.11).

a Emotional intelligence is **contextual**; it allows the company manager – and other stakeholders too – to perceive, interpret and act taking into consideration the major elements around them in their work and life area. This helps the stakeholder to be open to the specificity of the management synapse, to the common objectives, win-win negotiation, intense communication and consultation, and reciprocity. This contributes to the construction of an enabling emotional climate for the stakeholders' relationships;
b Emotional intelligence is **pragmatic** in the sense that it helps stakeholders, based on the contextual approach, to see and to understand the positive and negative impacts of the different components of their workspace and life space and to generate useful and protective feedback;
c Emotional intelligence is **affective** because it mobilizes stakeholders' affective resources, their feelings, which have the capacity to increase motivation, involvement and engagement, in order to achieve what is necessary and to solve the problems at the workplace and in the company too. The affective dimension of emotional intelligence is a very good psychological support in order to construct performant synapses and to develop a stakeholders-based management system;
d Emotional intelligence has a **cooperative** dimension based on contextual, pragmatic and affective features, because it helps to generate stakeholders' desire and the openness that enables the individual to have contacts, to communicate and to work with other people, to cooperate with them. Emotional intelligence, more than intellectual

intelligence, helps one to have successful win-win negotiations, to achieve reasonable compromises, to work better together within the stakeholders-based management system.

Elements regarding people's emotions, emotion regulation, emotional intelligence, etc. constitute valuable psychological arguments for the stakeholders-based management construction and development.

New Company-Relevant Stakeholders' Business Model Framework

Every company and management system should be based on a business model that synthesizes the economic background of the entity and design logic of the essential business and management processes and relationships to be achieved in order to be performant. We have elaborated for company stakeholders-based management a **new type of business model** that is radically different from classical business models (see Figure 10.12).

Examination of a large number of **classical business models** and their characteristics and approaches (Bodrožić & Adler, 2018; Casadesus-Masanell & Zhu, 2013; Chesbrough, 2010; Demil, Lecocq, Ricart, & Zott, 2015; Garcia-Castro, Ricart, Lieberman, & Balasubramanian, 2017; Green, 2015; Kortmann & Piller, 2016; Laasch, 2018; Zott & Amit, 2010) has revealed the following common features:

- they are focused on profit generation and capture by company shareholders;
- they usually take into consideration only one external stakeholder – the client;
- they treat the client not as an organization stakeholder but as an essential constituent of the market, who should be convinced to buy company products and services;
- they neglect, to a large extent, the social, ecological, and psychological implications of company activities.

The relevant stakeholders' approach involves other types of business models. In Figure 10.12 we present the main elements of a company-relevant "**stakeholders' business model framework**", which has as its strategic objective the achievement of the organization's sustainability, valorizing the relevant internal and external stakeholders' resources and potential. **The main characteristics of the company-relevant stakeholders' company business model**, which makes it different from the classical business model, are the following:

- It is based on the relevant internal and external company stakeholders, integrated into the global network;

STRATEGIC STARTING ELEMENTS	RELEVANT STAKEHOLDERS' EVALUATION AND SELECTION	STAKEHOLDERS' NETWORKING MECHANISM CONSTRUCTION	RELEVANT STAKEHOLDERS' ENGAGEMENT AND RESPONSABILIZATION	VIRTUAL AND/OR KNOWLEDGE VALUE CHAIN	COMPANY AND RELEVANT STAKEHOLDERS' PERFORMANCES	COMPANY AND RELEVANT STAKEHOLDERS' SYNERGETIC RESULTS
- Marketing segment targeted - Products, services beneficial to consumers - Resources available - Intellectual capital needed - Industry main social responsibilities - Humanistic management features - Potential stakeholders' knowledge and other resources - Ecological requirements - Characteristics of company culture - Company leadership styles - Main features of the technologies used - Structure of company value chain - Company position in the industry value chain - Estimated cost structure - Estimated income potential	- Stakeholders - Managers - Employees (executants) - Customers - Suppliers - Production partners - Bankers - Investors - Competitors - Consultants - Trainers - IT experts	- Win-win negotiations with each relevant stakeholder - Joint objectives - Win-win relationships established with each relevant stakeholder - Development of friendly emotional climate with relevant stakeholders - Organization stakeholders' network establishment	- Specific and fair treatment for each relevant stakeholder - Intense communication with stakeholders - Joint stakeholders' previsions - Mutually beneficial contracts for stakeholders (labour, supply, sell, etc.) - Fair stakeholders' behaviour - Specific stakeholders' incentives - Stakeholders' resources share - Joint stakeholders' decision - Joint stakeholders' actions - Harmonization of the relevant stakeholders' behaviours	- Communication - Design - Investments - Financing - Sharing - Innovation - Acquisition (supply) - Production - Marketing - Sell - Capturing value - Motivation - Networking	- More resources attracted and used - Intense work collaboration - Constant information and knowledge share - More innovation - Higher productivity - Cost optimization - Sales increase - Better stakeholders' working and life relationships - Open and innovational organization and stakeholders' culture -Friendly emotional climate - Accomplishment of social responsibilities - Fulfilment of ecological requirements - Better company stakeholders' public image - Competitive company and stakeholders' board	- Increasing company competitivity - Developing organizational sustainability - Fulfilling the main stakeholders' reasonable expectations - Development of the stakeholders' sustainable relationships - Company internal and external relevant stakeholders' community - Valorizing the relevant stakeholders' networks - Multidimensional performances of the company and the relevant stakeholders
WIN-WIN NEGOTIATIONS AND RELATIONSHIPS WITH EACH RELEVANT STAKEHOLDER						

Figure 10.12 Company-relevant stakeholders' business model framework.

- It is based on the virtual and knowledge value chain of the organization;
- It takes into consideration a joint relevant stakeholders' generation and capture of value;
- It integrates the company-relevant stakeholders' responsibilities;
- It incorporates essential elements of humanistic management and emotional intelligence;
- It is conceived and operated based on the stakeholders' win-win negotiations and sustainable relationships;
- It is focused on the sustainable development of a stakeholders' network, centred on the organization;
- It generates sustainable multidimensional performances for the company and its relevant stakeholders.

In order to be operational and to generate performance, **the company-relevant stakeholders' business model framework should be concretized at the level of each entity**, taking into consideration the particularities of the organization, its relevant stakeholders and the environment involved.

The relevant stakeholders business model provides the background for construction and implementation of the company-relevant stakeholders-based management system. The company-relevant stakeholders' business model projected by us is only one variant of the new type of business model. It is always possible to conceive other variants starting from other premises and/or following a different approach.

Without any doubt, in these very complex and fast contextual changes and challenges generated by the transition to the knowledge-based economy, the fast digital transformations and other political, social, ecological, etc. mutations – including those generated by the COVID-19 pandemic – company management should be radically updated, indeed reinvented. Our proposals represent just an attempt to contribute to the development of the new type of management needed and demanded by companies today.

Notes

1 We use for the new necessities and approaches regarding the company employees as individual persons, the concept "humanistic approach", which incorporates quite a few innovational elements [see Pirson, M. (2017). *Humanistic management: Protecting dignity and promoting well-being.* Cambridge, UK: Cambridge University Press. doi:10.1017/9781316675946; Dierksmeier, C. (2016). What is 'humanistic' about humanistic management? *Humanistic Management Journal, 1*, 9–32. doi:10.1007/s41463-016-0002–6; Von Kimakowitz, E., Pirson, M., Spitzeck, H., Dierksmeier, C., & Amann, W. (Eds.) (2011). *Humanistic management in practice.* Basingstoke, UK: Palgrave Macmillan]. We mention the emotional intelligence separately because although it is involved in humanistic management, it has major influence on the other parts of company management. Emotional intelligence decisively affects

the approach of the company stakeholders – both internal and external – deserving a special treatment and needing new management mechanisms in order to fully valorized it.

2 See *Journal of Management Studies* (2015), *52*(7). doi:10.1111/joms.12153

3 We refer to the volume 42, issue 2, 2017 of the *Academy of Management Review*.

References

Amit, R., & Zott, C. (2001). Value creation in e-business. *Strategic Management Journal*, *22*(6–7), 493–520. doi:10.1002/smj.187

Ashkanasy, M., Humphrey, R. H., & Huy, Q. N. (2017). Integrating emotions and affect in theories of management. *Academy of Management Review*, *42*(2), 175–189. doi:10.5465/amr.2016.0474

Baden, D. (2016). A reconstruction of Carroll's pyramid of corporate social responsibility for 21st century. *International Journal of Corporate Social Responsibility*, *1*(8), 1–15. Retrieved from https://www.researchgate.net/publication/305801033_A_reconstruction_of_Carroll%27s_Pyramid_of_corporate_social_responsibility_for_the_21st_century 10.1186/s40991-016-0008-2

Bice, S. (2017). Corporate social responsibility as institution: A social mechanisms framework. *Journal of Business Ethics*, *143*(1), 17–34. doi:10.1007/s10551-015-2791-1

Bodrožić, Z., & Adler, P. S. (2018). The evolution of management models: A neo-schumpeterian theory. *Administrative Science Quarterly*, *63*(1), 85–129. doi:10.1177/0001839217704811

Bosse, D. A., Phillips, R.A., & Harrison, J. S. (2009). Stakeholders, reciprocity, and firm performance. *Strategic Management Journal*, *30*(4), 447–456. doi:10.1002/smj.743

Bowman, C., & Ambrosini, V. (2000). Value creation versus value capture: Towards a coherent definition of value in strategy. *British Journal of Management*, *11*(1), 1–15. doi:10.1111/1467-8551.00147

Brandenburger, A. M., & Stuart Jr., H. W. (1996). Value-based business strategy. *Journal of Economics & Management Strategy*, *5*(1), 5–24. doi:10.1111/j.1430-9134.1996.00005.x

Carroll, A. B. (1991). The pyramid of corporate social responsibility: Toward the moral management of organizational stakeholders. *Business Horizons*, *34*(4), 39–48. Retrieved from https://www.researchgate.net/publication/4883660_The_Pyramid_of_Corporate_Social_Responsibility_Toward_the_Moral_Management_of_Organizational_Stakeholders 10.1016/0007-6813(91)90005-G

Carroll, A. B. (1999). Corporate social responsibility: Evolution of a definitional construct. *Business & Society*, *38*(3), 268–295. doi:10.1177/000765039903800303

Carroll, A. B. (2004). Managing ethically with global stakeholders: A present and future challenge. *Academy of Management Perspectives*, *18*(2), 114–120. doi:10.5465/ame.2004.13836269

Carroll, A. B. (2016). Carroll's pyramid of CSR: Taking another look. *International Journal of Corporate Social Responsibility*, *1*(3), 1–8. doi:10.1186/s40991-016-0004-6

Casadesus-Masanell, R., & Zhu, F. (2013). Business model innovation and competitive imitation: The case of sponsor-based business models. *Strategic Management Journal*, *34*(4), 464–482. doi:10.1002/smj.2022

Chandler, D., & Werther, B. W. (2014). *Strategic corporate social responsibility: Stakeholders, globalization and sustainable value creation* (3rd ed.). Los Angeles, CA: Sage Publications.

Chesbrough, H. (2010). Business model innovation: Opportunities and barriers. *Long Range Planning*, *43*(2–3), 354–363. doi:10.1016/j.lrp.2009.07.010

Choi, J., & Wang, H. (2009). Stakeholder relations and the persistence of corporate financial performance. *Strategic Management Journal*, *30*(8), 895–907. doi:10.1002/smj.759

De Jong, M. D. T., & Van der Meer, M. (2017). How does it fit? Exploring the congruence between organizations and their corporate social responsibility (CSR) activities. *Journal of Business Ethics*, *143*(1), 71–83. doi:10.1007/s10551-015-2782-2

Demil, B., Lecocq, X., Ricart, J. E., & Zott, C. (2015). Introduction to the SEJ special issue on business models: Business models within the domain of strategic entrepreneurship. *Strategic Entrepreneurship Journal*, *9*(1), 1–11. doi:10.1002/sej.1194

Dierksmeier, C. (2016). What is "humanistic" about humanistic management? *Humanistic Management Journal*, *1*, 9–32. doi:10.1007/s41463-016-0002-6

Dierksmeier, C., Amann, W., Kimakowitz, E.V., Spitzeck, H., Pirson, M., Von Kimakowitz, E. (Eds.) (2011). *Humanistic ethics in the age of Globality*. Basingstoke, UK: Palgrave Macmillan. doi:10.1057/9780230314139

Djelic, M.-L., & Etchanchu, H. (2017). Contextualizing corporate political responsibilities: Neoliberal CSR in historical perspective. *Journal of Business Ethics*, *142*(4), 641–661. doi:10.1007/s10551-015-2879-7

Dorobantu, S., & Odziemkowska, K. (2017). Valuing stakeholder governance: Property rights, community mobilization, and firm value. *Strategic Management Journal*, *38*(13), 2682–2703. doi:10.1002/smj.2675

El Akremi, A., Gond, J.-P., Swaen, V., De Roek, K., & Igalens, J. (2018). How do employees perceive corporate responsibility? Development and validation of a multidimensional corporate stakeholder responsibility scale. *Journal of Management*, *44*(2), 619–657. doi:10.1177/0149206315569311

Ermine, J.-L. (2013). A knowledge value chain for knowledge management. *Journal of Knowledge & Communication Management*, *3*(2), 85–101. doi:10.5958/j.2277-7946.3.2.008

Flammer, C., & Luo, J. (2017). Corporate social responsibility as an employee governance tool: Evidence from a quasi-experiment. *Strategic Management Journal*, *38*(2), 163–183. doi:10.1002/smj.2492

Forgas, J. P. (2000). *Feeling and thinking: The role of affect in social cognition*. Cambridge, UK: Cambridge University Press.

Forgas, J. P. (2008). Affect, cognition, and social behavior: The effects of mood on memory, social judgments, and social interaction. In M. A. Gluck, J. R. Anderson, & S. M. Kosslyn (Eds.), *Memory and mind: A festschrift for Gordon H. Bower* (pp. 261–279). New York: Lawrence Erlbaum Associates Publishers.

Freeman, E., & Liedtka, J. (1997). Stakeholder capitalism and the value chain. *European Management Journal*, *15*(3), 286–296. doi:10.1016/S0263-2373(97)00008-X

Freeman, R. E., & Elms, H. (2018). The social responsibility of business is to create value for stakeholders. *MIT Sloan Management Review*. Retrieved from https://sloanreview.mit.edu/article/the-social-responsibility-of-business-is-to-create-value-for-stakeholders/

Freeman, R. E., Harrison, J. S., Wicks, A. C., Parmar, B. L., & De Colle, S. (2010). *Stakeholder theory: The state of art*. New York: Cambridge University Press.

Garcia-Castro, R., & Aguilera, R. V. (2015). Incremental value creation and appropriation in a world with multiple stakeholders. *Strategic Management Journal*, *36*(1), 137–147. doi:10.1002/smj.2241

Garcia-Castro, R., Ricart, J. E., Lieberman, M. B., & Balasubramanian N. (2017). Business model innovation and replication: Implications for the measurement of productivity. In E. Grifell-Tatjé, C. A. K. Lovell, & R. C. Sickles (Eds.), *The Oxford handbook of productivity analysis* (pp. 359–385). New York: Oxford University Press. doi:10.1093/oxfordhb/9780190226718.013.10

Giannarakis, G., Garefalakis, A., Lemonakis, C., & Konteos, G. (2017). The drivers of social responsible stock index: The case of Dow Jones sustainability index world. *Corporate Ownership & Control*, *14*(2-1), 173–180. doi:10.22495/cocv14i2c1p3

Green, R. (2015). *Do stakeholder's emotions matter?* Retrieved from http://www.theeiinstitute.com/emotional-intelligence-leaders/6-do-stakeholders-emotions-matter.html

Harrison, J. S., & Wicks, A. C. (2013). Stakeholder theory, value and firm performance. *Business Ethics Quarterly*, *23*(1), 97–124. doi:10.5840/beq20132314

Harrison, J. S., Bosse, D. A., & Phillips, R.A. (2010). Managing for stakeholders, stakeholder utility functions and competitive advantage. *Strategic Management Journal*, *31*(1), 58–74. doi:10.1002/smj.801

Hasan, I., Kobeissi, N., Liu, L., & Wang, H. (2018). Corporate social responsibility and firm financial performance: The mediating role of productivity. *Journal of Business Ethics*, *149*(3), 671–688. doi:10.1007/s10551-016-3066-1

Haski-Leventhal, D. (2018). *Strategic corporate social responsibility: Tools and theories for responsible management* (1st ed.). London, UK: Sage Publications.

Haski-Leventhal, D., Roza, L., & Meijs, L. C. P. M. (2017). Congruence in corporate social responsibility: Connecting the identity and behavior of employers and employees. *Journal of Business Ethics*, *143*(1), 35–51. doi:10.1007/s10551-015-2793-z

Healey, M. P., & Hodgkinson, G. P. (2017). Making strategy hot. *California Management Review*, *59*(3), 109–134. doi:10.1177/0008125617712258

Hillman, A. J., & Keim, G. D. (2001). Shareholder value, stakeholder management, and social issues: What's the bottom line? *Strategic Management Journal*, *22*(2), 125–139. Retrieved from https://www.jstor.org/stable/3094310

Holsapple, C. W., & Singh, M. (2001). Knowledge chain model: Activities for competitiveness. *Expert Systems with Applications*, *20*(1), 77–98. doi: 10.1016/S0957-4174(00)00050-6

Holsapple, C. W., & Jones, K. (2004). Exploring primary activities of the knowledge chain. *Knowledge and Process Management: The Journal of Corporate Transformation*, *11*(3), 155–174. doi:10.1002/kpm.200

ICSB. (2019, August 20). ICSB's humane entrepreneurship initiative adopted by CEOs of nearly 200 companies. Retrieved from https://icsb.org/200ceos/

International Institute for Sustainable Development. (2013). *Corporate social responsibility (CSR)*. Retrieved from https://www.iisd.org/business/issues/sr.aspx

Karaye, Y. I., Ishak, Z., & Che-Adam, N. (2014). The mediating effect of stakeholder influence capacity on the relationship between corporate social responsibility and corporate financial performance. *Procedia-Social and Behavioral Sciences*, *164*, 528–534. doi:10.1016/j.sbspro.2014.11.142

Kortmann, S., & Piller, F. (2016). Open business models and closed-loop value chains: Redefining the firm-consumer relationship. *California Management Review*, *58*(3), 88–108. doi:10.1525/cmr.2016.58.3.88

Laasch, O. (2018). Beyond the purely commercial business model: Organizational value logics and the heterogeneity of sustainability business models. *Long Range Planning*, *50*(1), 158–183. doi:10.1016/j.lrp.2017.09.002

Lee, C. C., & Yang, J. (2000). Knowledge value chain. *Journal of Management Development*, *19*(9), 783–794. doi:10.1108/02621710010378228

Lepak, D. P., Smith, K. G., & Taylor, M. S. (2007). Value creation and value capture: A multilevel perspective. *Academy of Management Review*, *32*(1), 180–194. doi:10.5465/amr.2007.23464011

Lieberman, M. B., Garcia-Castro, R., & Balasubramanian, N. (2017). Measuring value creation and appropriation in firms: The VCA model. *Strategic Management Journal*, *38*(6), 1193–1211. doi:10.1002/smj.2565

Lin, L., & Wu, J. (2010). Virtual value chain and competitive advantages in the context of e-commerce. Paper presented at 2010 IEEE 17Th International Conference on Industrial Engineering and Engineering Management, Xiamen, China. Retrieved from https://www.researchgate.net/publication/251971660_Virtual_value_chain_and_competitive_advantages_in_the_context_of_e-commerce. DOI: 10.1109/ICIEEM.2010.5646044

Lyon, T. P., Delmas, M. A., Maxwell, J. W., Bansal, P., Chiroleu-Assouline, M, Crifo, P., et al. (2018). CSR needs CPR: Corporate sustainability and politics. *California Management Review*, *60*(4), 5–24. doi:10.1177/0008125618778854

Mackey, A., Mackey, T. B., & Barney, J. B. (2007). Corporate social responsibility and firm performance: Investor preferences and corporate strategies. *Academy of Management Review*, *32*(3), 817–835. doi:10.5465/amr.2007.25275676

McKee, A. (2017). Happiness traps: How we sabotage ourselves at work. *Harvard Business Review*, *95*(5), 66–73.

Mirvis, P. H. (2012). Employee engagement and CSR: Transactional, relational, and developmental approaches. *California Management Review*, *54*(4), 93–117. doi:10.1525/cmr.2012.54.4.93

Mitchell, R. K., Van Buren, H. J., Greenwood M., & Freeman, R. E. (2015). Stakeholder inclusion and accounting for stakeholders. *Journal of Management Studies*, *52*(7), 851–877. doi:10.1111/joms.12151

Nicolescu, O., & Nicolescu, C. (2011). *Organizaţia şi managementul bazate pe cunoştinţe*. Bucureşti, România: Pro Universitaria.

Pirson, M. (2017, June 12). *What is humanistic management?* Retrieved from http://humanisticmanagement.international/what-is-humanistic-management/

Porter, M. (1985). *Competitive advantage: Creating and sustaining superior performance*. New York: Free Press.

Rampersad, R. (2017). Corporate social responsibility: Applying sustainability principles in stakeholder engagement. *Corporate Ownership & Control*, *14*(2-1), 222–229. doi:10.22495/cocv14i2c1p8

Rayport, J. F., & Sviokla, J. (1995). Exploiting the virtual value chain. *Harvard Business Review*, *73*(6), 75–85.

Sachs, S., Rühli, E., & Kern, I. (2009). *Sustainable success with stakeholders: The untapped potential* (1st ed.). Basingstoke, UK: Palgrave Macmillan. doi:10.1057/9780230271746

Schrempf-Stirling, J., Palazzo, G., & Phillips, R. A. (2016). Historic corporate social responsibility. *Academy of Management Review*, *41*(4), 700–719. doi:10.5465/amr.2014.0137

Tantalo, C., & Paton, B. (2013). Value innovation through value co-creation: The stewardship model in an italian SME. *Proceedings of the International Association for Business and Society*, *24*, 240–251. doi:10.5840/iabsproc 20132425

Van Vliet, V. (2010). Virtual value chain model. Retrieved from https://www.toolshero.com/problem-solving/virtual-value-chain/

Von Kimakowitz, E., Pirson, M., Spitzeck, H., Dierksmeier, C., & Amann, W. (Eds.). (2011). *Humanistic management in practice*. Basingstoke, UK: Palgrave Macmillan. doi:10.1057/9780230306585

Voronov, M., & Weber, K. (2015). The heart of institutions: Emotional competence and institutional actorhood. *Academy of Management Review*, *41*(3), 456–478. doi:10.5465/amr.2013.0458

Wang, S. (2015). *Chinese strategic decision-making on CSR*. Berlin Heidelberg, DE: Springer Verlag. doi:10.1007/978-3-662-44997-4

Weiber, R., & Kollmann, T. (1998). Competitive advantages in virtual markets – Perspectives of "information-based marketing" in cyberspace. *European Journal of Marketing*, *32*(7/8), 603–615. Retrieved from https://www.researchgate.net/publication/247614357_Competitive_Advantages_in_Virtual_Markets-Perspectives_of_%27Information-Based_Marketing%27_in_Cyberspace 10.1108/03090569810224010

Zadek, S. (2004). The path to corporate responsibility. *Harvard Business Review*, *82*(12), 125–132.

Zott, C., & Amit, R. (2010). Business model design: An activity system perspective. *Long Range Planning*, *43*(2–3), 216–226. doi:10.1016/j.lrp.2009.07.004

11 How to Design and Build the Company-Relevant Stakeholders-Based Management System

Milestones of Designing and Building the Company-Relevant Stakeholders-Based Management System

Without any doubt, the design and construction of a new company management system based on relevant stakeholders is a very complex undertaking, involving profound changes in the organization and management vision and approaches. It could be considered as a "**breakthrough innovation**", according to the recent approach of Hill and Davis (2017), rethinking traditional methods of governing and management relationships and processes. A relevant stakeholders-based management system needs to design an organization that synergistically combines humans with machines (Lesser, Reeves, Whitaker, & Hutchinson, 2018). In Figure 11.1, we indicate **the essential milestones** that should be taken into consideration by the company management and the relevant stakeholders in this undertaking, in order to develop a company-relevant stakeholders' management system.

In the following sections, we will briefly present the main new elements to be reshaped within each of these milestones.

Premises of the Company-Relevant Stakeholders-Based Management System Construction and Development

Our new approach to company management focused on the relevant stakeholder is based on a **set of premises**. We have formulated these premises bearing in mind the company as an ecosystem, the specificity and complexity of the relevant stakeholders-based management system, and the predominant managerial approaches in the companies.

In the premises, we have introduced certain elements from analysis by other specialists, who have asked (demanded) for the promotion of management centred on the stakeholders. In Table 11.1, we present these premises.

DOI: 10.4324/9781003217701-11

Figure 11.1 Milestones for the new company management system based on relevant stakeholders.

Company Managers' Vision and Leadership Focused on the Relevant Stakeholders

In any company, the starting point in constructing a company-relevant stakeholders-based management system is represented by the new vision and leadership of the company managers and owners. **Without the vision and leadership focused on the relevant stakeholders, the new management system cannot be constructed.** Recently, certain specialists demonstrated that real transformation in companies only occurs when managers' leadership achieves the combination and correlation of three models – mental, business, and measurement (Bonchek & Libert, 2017). The first to be changed is the mental model.

The new leaders, according to Ready, Cohen, Kiron, and Pring (2020), understand that people do not want to be just employees, they want to be active citizens in amazing workplace communities that are doing their best to change the world for the better.

In our opinion, the following elements represent the **main steps** that need to be taken in the company in order to develop a performant vision

Table 11.1 Premises of the company-relevant stakeholders-based management design and construction

No.	*Premises*
1.	Stakeholders are essential for every company foundation, development, and competitivity, and for this reason, organization management should be focused on them.
2.	The organization itself, according to Friedman and Miles (as cited in Fontaine, Haarman, & Schmid, 2006), should be thought of as a grouping of stakeholders and the purpose of the organization should be to manage their interests, needs, and viewpoints, generating high performance for all.
3.	The organization's success or failure depends on the views (perceptions) of stakeholders and also on the passing of time (Bourne, 2009).
4.	Stakeholders' interests, resources and influences on the company are very unequal, varying to a great extent.
5.	Identification of and taking into consideration the company-relevant stakeholders represent the starting point and the background of the stakeholders-based management.
6.	Relevant stakeholder identification and management should be based on the long-term priorities of the company and the stakeholders, combined with their medium- and short-term objectives, which reflect specific needs and requirements for the next and present periods.
7.	Relevant stakeholders' interests, objectives, aspirations, and expectations are multidimensional and dynamic and they should be evaluated and taken into consideration permanently, using a professional approach.
8.	A stakeholders-based management system and managerial synapse represent essential approaches for performant management of the relevant company stakeholders.
9.	New vision and leadership of the company managers, starting with the CEO, represent the crucial elements in the designing of the new managerial system focused on the relevant stakeholders.
10.	A stakeholders-based management system, because of its specificity and complexity, needs professional processes for its design and implementation.
11.	A managerial synapse represents the essential element in the stakeholders-based management design, implementation and development.
12.	Informing and training of internal relevant stakeholders and – as much as is possible – of external relevant stakeholders should precede and accompany the construction of the company stakeholders-based management system.
13.	The construction and development of the stakeholders-based management system should be based on the company-relevant stakeholders' permanent consultation, collaboration, participation, and motivation.
14.	For each relevant stakeholder a specific managerial synapse should be constructed and developed, based on the win-win principle, approached from the sustainable perspective.
15.	The development of an organization culture focused on the relevant stakeholders during the elaboration and implementation of the company strategy focused on the relevant stakeholders is mandatory in order to achieve competitive and sustainable performance.

(*Continued*)

Table 11.1 (Continued)

No.	*Premises*
16.	The functionality and performance of the company-relevant stakeholders' management system depend heavily on the use of specific models, methods, and techniques, focused on the relevant stakeholders, and of certain classical managerial methods and techniques, reshaped according to the new managerial approach.
17.	The company-relevant stakeholders-based management system should be associated with permanent training, consultation, counselling, mentoring, tutoring, and coaching in every key field of the organization.
18.	Relevant internal and external stakeholders should fulfilled periodically, evaluation and self-evaluation of the results generated from their common objectives and win–win relationships perspectives.
19.	Periodically, based on the company-relevant stakeholders' evaluation and self-evaluation, the relevant stakeholders-based management system should be reviewed and developed, eliminating deficiencies and valorizing the new opportunities.
20.	Obtaining information on the multidimensional performances – economic, social, ecologic, and educational – of the company and the relevant stakeholders represents the major criterion used in their evaluation and development.

and leadership capable of determining the building and implementation of a company-relevant stakeholders-based management system:

a CEO and top managers' awareness – supported by the company owners – of the decisive contribution and impact of the relevant stakeholders on the organization's existence, development, performance, and sustainability;

b Employment of consultants and trainers, in order to inform the company managers regarding the relevant stakeholders' role and impact in the company and the main approaches, methods, and techniques to be used for communication and cooperation (co-work) with them;

c Company managers, in order to be able to practise a performant leadership focused on relevant stakeholders, need to develop the following "fundamental" skills:

- share a vision that is exciting and challenging for their team/unit/division/organization;
- translate that vision into a clear strategy about what actions to take and what not to do;
- recruit, develop and reward a team of great people to carry out the strategy;
- focus on measurable results;

- faster innovation and learning to sustain your team for the organization to grow new leaders;
- lead yourself, know yourself, improve yourself, and manage the appropriate balance in your own life (Ashkenas & Manville, 2018).

d Development by company managers of a new approach centred on the relevant stakeholders, capable of seizing the opportunities provided by them, and reducing their challenges and potential negative impact;

e Foundation of a special team in order to elaborate a programme for the remodelling of the organization management focused on the relevant stakeholders, in which it is recommended to include external consultants too;

f In this programme there should be a special module centred on the learning by company managers of the leadership skills necessary for the valorization of the relevant stakeholders' potential and for the development of effective long-term relationships with them;

g Leadership focused on company-relevant stakeholders is recommended to have the **features** (characteristics) presented in Table 11.2.

h Leadership centred on the relevant stakeholders needs to be a permanent feature of the company management and not a temporary campaign performed only at the beginning of the implementation of the relevant stakeholders-based management system.

i Periodically it is recommended to evaluate the leadership practised by the company managers, in order to identify and eliminate the deficiencies and to make improvements. Participation of external consultants and of certain relevant stakeholders in these processes could generate more rigour, creativity, and effectiveness.

In order to be able to design and implement the new vision and leadership, company managers should have five core qualities, the so-called "**ADAPT dimensions**" (Korn Ferry, 2019), which encompass the ability to anticipate, drive, accelerate, develop partnerships, and confer trust. New vision and leadership centred on the company-relevant stakeholders are, concomitantly, a precondition and a permanent feature of the performant company stakeholders-based management system.

Design of the New Company Strategy

Concomitantly with the remodelling of the managers' leadership, based on the new vision regarding the organization's development involving the relevant stakeholders, a new strategy should be designed in the company. The main purpose of this strategy is to enhance the competitivity and sustainability of the multi-objective company (Mitchell, Weaver, Agle, Bailey, & Carlson, 2016) and its relevant stakeholders. A company

Table 11.2 Features of company leadership focused on the relevant stakeholders

No.	*Features*
1.	It should be oriented toward the development of organizational change capacity with heavy involvement of the organization's relevant stakeholders; management change needs to be a core competence of the managers' leadership.
2.	It is focused on the establishment and implementation of joint objectives, determined by win-win negotiation with the company-relevant stakeholders.
3.	It is an "open" leadership, which overcomes the company boundaries, involving external relevant stakeholders.
4.	It is an equilibrated leadership, which emphasizes the affective dimension of human relationships and – concomitantly – the operational side, regarding the fulfilment of common objectives and of the tasks, roles, competencies and responsibilities assigned to each relevant stakeholder.
5.	It is an inclusiveness leadership, characterized by accepting different views, understanding diverse views, integrating other points of view, functioning well across diverse groups, facilitating engagement between fractions, strategically increasing employees' diversity and creating an inclusive culture (Fernández-Aráoz, Roscoe, & Aramaki, 2017).
6.	It is based on intense and permanent communication with all internal and external relevant stakeholders.
7.	It pays respect to the company-relevant stakeholders; respect – both owned and earned – should be one of the most important leadership behaviours (Rogers, 2018).
8.	It should be a transformational leadership, which seeks and explains "why" the actions tend to work well and have a range of positive outcomes.
9.	It is based on emotional intelligence and emotion regulation, which are essential for the construction of an enabling context for continued and effective co-work with company-relevant stakeholders.
10.	It activates shared emotional connection – called by the specialist Hernandez (2019) a "shared passion for place" – with relevant stakeholders.
11.	It fulfils intensively positive motivation of the relevant stakeholders, using a large variety of approaches and tools – bonuses, profit sharing, stock option, trophies, public appreciation of work well done, flexible work schedule, simple "thank you", vouchers, tangible goods, learning and development opportunities, etc.
12.	It has a very strong participative content, both for internal and external relevant stakeholders.
13.	It pays great and permanent attention to valorizing the relevant stakeholders' tacit and explicit knowledge and to their intellectual capital.
14.	It permanently encourages and promotes the relevant stakeholders' creativity, directed toward the achievement of common objectives, negotiated with each of them.
15.	It is a dynamic leadership, continuously modifying itself, according to the stages of the implementation of changes and to the evolution of the relevant stakeholders' "maturity", and that of the other people involved.

(*Continued*)

Table 11.2 (Continued)

No.	*Features*
16.	It fosters empathy and solidarity among all relevant stakeholders and promotes fairness and morality.
17.	It is an "empowering" leadership, which works better, motivating certain types of performance, influencing people's creativity and citizenship behaviour rather than routine task performance (Lee, Willis, & Tian, 2018).
18.	It emphasizes the development of the "feeling of belonging to the company" for all relevant stakeholders, including the external ones.
19.	It takes into consideration valorizing (capitalizing) the multiple possibilities provided by digitalization and digital transformation, from the perspectives of both the company and the relevant stakeholders.[1]
20.	It focuses on the company stakeholders' responsibilities development, which has a powerful multidimensional context (economic, social, ecologic, etc.).
21.	It generates, through all the above-mentioned characteristics – and especially those effectively involved – the dedication of the relevant stakeholders to the achievement of the common objectives and to the other elements win-win negotiated.

strategy based on the relevant stakeholders, in order to generate performances, should present the **characteristics** enumerated in Figure 11.2, briefly described below.

- Focalization on the relevant stakeholders represents the first characteristic of the new company strategy. Selection and focalization on the relevant stakeholders should be done based on the set of parameters established in the Chapter 5, Section 5.2.
- A relevant stakeholders-based strategy should be an open strategy that addresses an organization open to innovation and internal and external stakeholders, and not a "proprietary strategy". An open strategy is characterized by two dimensions – transparency and inclusion (Hautz, Seidl, & Whittington, 2017) – both essential for effective and efficient relationships with company-relevant internal and external stakeholders. Specialists have discovered that an open strategy fosters greater growth compared with the proprietary approach (Appleyard & Chesbrough, 2017).
- In order to generate high business performance, a relevant stakeholders' strategy should be centred on all activities that make up the company's virtual or knowledge value chain and on the relevant stakeholders that fulfilled them. This is a premise in order to maximize the total value created, both for the company and its relevant stakeholders.

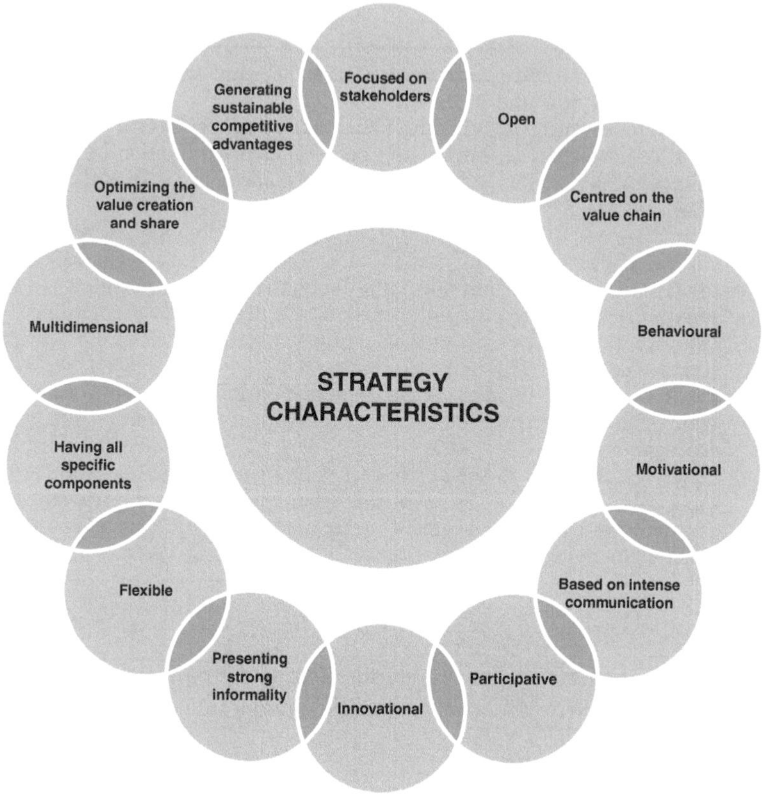

Figure 11.2 Main characteristics of the company strategy based on relevant stakeholders.

- A strategy focused on the relevant stakeholders should be a behavioural strategy that "aims" to bring realistic assumptions about human cognition, emotions, and social behaviour to the strategic management of the organization (Sibony, Lovallo, & Powell, 2017). A behavioural strategy facilitates the "humanistic management" in the organization that is essential for the strong involvement of the internal and external stakeholders in the company's activities and development.
- A company strategy based on the relevant stakeholders should have a high motivational content. In the elaboration of the strategy, the main interests and expectations of each relevant stakeholder should be identified and taken into consideration. Common objectives of companies and relevant stakeholders represent an essential starting point in achieving this. Intrinsic and extrinsic motivations adapted to the specificity of each category of relevant stakeholders should be promoted by the company strategy.

- The construction and implementation of a company strategy focused on the relevant stakeholders is based on intense communication. Each relevant stakeholder should be informed and asked their opinion regarding the elements of the company strategy in which he/she has a major interest and/or influence. In determining the strategy elements, where the relevant stakeholder is directly involved, it is necessary to practise win-win negotiation.
- A company strategy based on the relevant stakeholders should be participative. Each relevant stakeholder should take part in the elaboration of the strategy elements, having a direct influence on their work and performances. Participation of the relevant stakeholders in the elaboration of the company strategy not only increases its realism and potential but also contributes to faster and more effective and efficient implementation.
- The stakeholders' strategy – which itself is a business innovation – should be innovational both for the company and for the relevant stakeholders. The innovation radar (Sawhney, Wolcott, & Arroniz, 2006), which displays the 12 dimensions of business innovation involving the relevant stakeholders, can be very useful in increasing the scope and the performance of innovation.
- Compared with classical strategies, a company strategy based on relevant stakeholders is more informal due to the participation of many relevant stakeholders, especially external ones, in the elaboration of the strategy, which could not be done without using an informal approach. The elements in the strategy that refer directly to the relevant stakeholders also present a certain degree of informality. An informal approach integrated in a "humanistic management" helps to build sustainable and effective relationships with the relevant stakeholders.
- A flexible approach is a mandatory ingredient of the processes involved in the construction and implementation of a company strategy based on the relevant stakeholders. First, it is not possible to communicate and to take into consideration the main interests and expectations of many different relevant stakeholders without a flexible approach. Second, the content of the strategy should also be designed and implemented in a flexible manner, to be realistic, to be able to reflect the changing conditions in the company at the level of the relevant stakeholders and – of course – in the business environment. The VUCA environment is an increasing reality for all companies and cannot be faced without a high degree of informality and flexibility.
- A company strategy focused on the relevant stakeholders should contain all the main components – mission, fundamental objective, strategic option, resource, term, and competitive advantage – rationally correlated and integrated. The absence of one or more

components makes it impossible to operate the strategy effectively and efficiently, to generate the engagement and performance in the company and the relevant stakeholders.

- A company strategy based on the relevant stakeholders should optimize the total value in the company, taking into consideration the main interests, contributions, and expectations of all relevant stakeholders and not only the profit and/or dividend, according to business tradition, which is still predominant in the world economy. Optimization of the total value created by the company and its appropriate share with relevant stakeholders represent the realistic and mandatory business background of the new company management system.
- A strategy focused on the relevant stakeholders should be multidimensional, in terms of both content and performance. Besides the traditional business aspects, the strategy should integrate the main social, ecological, and educational aspects, which are important for the company and demanded by the relevant stakeholders.
- A company strategy based on the relevant stakeholders should be able to generate sustainable competitive advantage and not a temporary advantage (Huang, Dyerson, Wu, & Harindranath, 2015) as has happened quite often. A company is sustainable competitive only if it takes into consideration the major interests and expectations of the relevant stakeholders. Also, the company competitive advantage, as much as is possible, should be harmonized with the competitive advantages of the external relevant stakeholders, this being a condition in order to achieve sustainable performances.

A company strategy based on the relevant stakeholders presents – compared with traditional strategies – **certain particularities at the level of each component** (see Table 11.3).

In all processes involved in the company strategy elaboration, implementation, and operation, **strategic agility** is necessary, which means "the ability to remain flexible in facing new developments, to continuously adjust the company strategic direction and to develop innovative ways to create value" (Weber & Tarba, 2014). A company strategy based on the relevant stakeholders should be coupled with organizational agility, because "only when everything is working well together can value be created and captured and durable competitive advantage realized" (Teece, Peteraf, & Leih, 2016).

A company strategy focused on the relevant stakeholders, like any up-to-date strategy, **should take into consideration the use of digital technologies** (AI, robots, Internet of Things [IOT], and others). In this respect, it is essential to focus the strategy not on digital but on the transformation generated by it. As recently pointed out by a specialist, "technology does not provide value to a business. It never has (except for technology in products).

Table 11.3 Particularities of the company strategy based on the relevant stakeholders, at the level of its components

No.	*Strategy Components*	*Particularities*
1.	Company mission	• It takes into consideration, concomitantly, the future of the company and of the external relevant stakeholders, using an integrative approach;
2.	Fundamental objectives[2]	• All objectives reflect the common essential interests of the company and of the relevant stakeholders; • Common objectives are the result of win-win negotiation between the company and the relevant stakeholders; • In the special circumstances, besides common objectives, certain specific objectives of the most important external relevant stakeholders can be included in the strategy;
3.	Strategic options	• In the strategy is formulated, as the first company strategic option, the construction and the development of sustainable relationships with all relevant stakeholders; • All other strategic options take into consideration the direct and intense participation of the relevant stakeholders in their implementation; • In the special circumstances, a strategic option can be formulated regarding only a certain relevant stakeholder that has an exceptional involvement in, and impact on, the company's performance;
4.	Resources	• Within resources allocated, besides company resources, an important share is represented by the relevant stakeholders' resources, specified as attracted resources; • When the external relevant stakeholders' resources are substantial, they can be specified separately; • Knowledge and information about the company and relevant stakeholders represent a high weight in the total strategy resources;
5.	Terms	• In the strategy, terms can be established separately for certain relevant stakeholders; this usually happens when strategic options are specified in the strategy for the relevant stakeholders; • Terms are reviewed yearly in order to take into consideration the company and the relevant stakeholders' unexpected evolutions and the environmental challenges;

(*Continued*)

Table 11.3 (Continued)

No.	*Strategy Components*	*Particularities*
6.	Competitive advantage	• Company competitive advantage takes into consideration, directly and, especially, indirectly, the specific competitive advantages of the external relevant stakeholders; in fact, competitive advantage planned by a company strategy is a "mixed competitive advantage", reflecting both the company and external relevant stakeholders' interests and potentials; • The company competitive advantage is always multidimensional, reflecting the diversity of the relevant stakeholders' essential interests and contributions.

Instead, technology value comes from doing business differently because technology makes it possible" (Westerman, 2018).

Another significant remark deals with the high **complexity and difficulty in elaborating and implementing a company strategy based on the relevant stakeholders.** There are mainly three causes that generate them:

a The taking into consideration and the participation of many and diversified internal and external relevant stakeholders in the strategic processes;
b Some of the main interests and expectations of certain relevant stakeholders are different from the company ones, or even opposite;
c Among the company's external relevant stakeholders sometimes co-opetition occurs too, and the concurrence involved makes the harmonization of the objectives, strategic options, resources, terms, and competitive advantages within the company strategy based on the relevant stakeholders very difficult.

Finally, we can conclude that a company strategy focused on the relevant stakeholders, with its many particularities and high complexity, represents an essential element without which the design, construction and implementation of a new company management system based on relevant stakeholders is not possible.

Remodelling of the Company Management System

A new company vision, strategy, and leadership focused on the relevant stakeholders are not enough for successful use of the new management system. Remodelling of the company management system and its subsystems should be based on organizational agility, using a flexible approach in all processes involved (Harraf, Wanasika, Tate, & Talbott, 2015; Weber & Tarba, 2014). Concomitantly, it is necessary to employ dynamic responsibilities, "fulfilling the framework that guides managers with respect to when and how to manage" (Teece et al., 2016). Dynamic capabilities are essential for ensuring the enterprise's long-term viability, namely sensing, seizing and transforming (Healey & Hodgkinson, 2017). Remodelling of the organization's management system should be **centred on the company value chain activities,** in order to maximize the contribution to the increase of the company's performance and competitivity. Because the stakeholders-based management system is radically different from "classical" management systems – as we have already argued – it is necessary to redesign all its main components. This means that **its five subsystems** should be **remodelled** (see Figure 11.3).

For each of these subsystems, we will indicate some of the major changes that must be implemented.

a **In the methodological managerial subsystem,** four categories of changes should be operated:

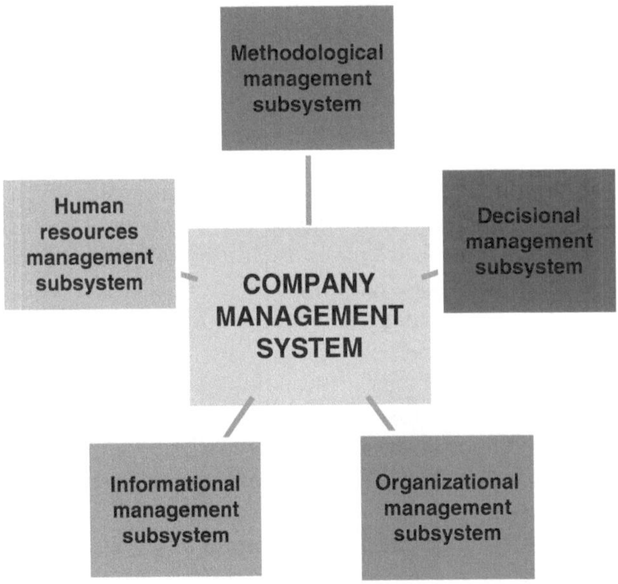

Figure 11.3 Subsystems of the company management system.

- integration in this managerial subsystem of the approaches, methods, and techniques used in recent decades in companies to deal with stakeholders. Of course, these management tools should be adapted to the specificity of the managerial synapse and of the stakeholders-based management system. We want to point out that there are many such methods and techniques, like stakeholder analysis, stakeholder circle, intra-stakeholder alliance, stakeholder co-creative network, stakeholder analysis matrix, four-factor stakeholder model, stakeholder communication template, stakeholder management plan smartsheet, stakeholder strategy matrix, stakeholder focus group, advisory stakeholder panel, stakeholder matrix guide, stakeholder management web, stakeholder performance scorecard, etc. A list of more than 50 such stakeholder management tools is presented in Section 11.6.
- Design of new management tools focused on the relevant internal and external stakeholders. They are essential both for the managerial synapse and relevant stakeholders-based management system in order to fully take advantage of their high specificity and potential to enhance performances.
- Remodelling of some "classical" managerial methods and techniques taking into consideration the specificity of the stakeholders-based management system and of the last development in the company environment. Among these managerial tools we mention: SWOT analysis, business plan, benchmarking, brainstorming, career plan, decisional simulation, delegation, SMART model, root cause analysis, requirement workshop, checklist, job enrichment, organizational chart, scenario method, etc. Of course, not all "classical" management tools can be remodelled in order to be successfully used in the stakeholders-based management system, but for many of these it is possible. In Section 11.5, we make a selection of more than 60 managerial "classical" tools that might be remodelled according to the specificity of the managerial synapse and/or stakeholders-based management system.
- Elimination from the managerial tools integrated in the methodological management subsystem of those methods and techniques, which by their nature are not compatible with the new managerial approach focused on the relevant stakeholders and cannot be successfully used. We mention from this category MTM, work factory, timing technique, instant observations, etc. These managerial tools are based on excessive hierarchy, on constraints, or on the threat to people.

b In the **decisional managerial subsystem**, there are many significant changes, like the following:

- Development of new categories of decisions and decisional flows associated with the relevant stakeholders, most of them with external relevant stakeholders, which could not be found usually in the company management system;
- Major decisions involving the relevant stakeholders are based on win-win negotiation and are focused on the common objectives planned, normally at the beginning of the year. The content and the itinerary of the decisional processes involved are changed to a large extent, compared with the previous period;
- Decisional processes have a highly participative dimension, relevant stakeholders taking part actively in their progress, and communicating intensively in order to harmonize the objectives to be fulfilled and to establish ways to cooperate and to implement them;
- Many decisions involve, relatively frequently, not only company managers and their subordinates but also clients, customers, investors, designers, consultants, trainers, and other relevant stakeholders from outside the company;
- All changes mentioned are necessary for the elaboration of a decisional sheet for every managerial synapse and each company manager. On the decisional sheet (see Table 11.4), it is essential to indicate the methods and techniques to be used in order to make effective and efficient decisions for the company and for the relevant stakeholders.

The changes enumerated determine significant modifications in the decisional subsystem work and performances, making it more complex and performant for the company and its relevant stakeholders.

c **The company organizational management subsystem** should be significantly modified, using an agility approach to dynamic work design (Repenning, Kieffer, & Repenning, 2018). It is recommended to design a "participative centralization" subsystem type (Adler, Heckscher, & Prusak, 2011), which means being based on a new type of authority structure, which involves overlapping spheres of influence between managerial synapses, and between these and other organizational components of the company and of the external relevant stakeholders. We indicate some of the major changes to be made:

Table 11.4 Decisional sheet

No.	*Decisions*	*Periodicity*				*Recommended Decisional Tools*	*Observations*
		Yearly	*Monthly*	*Weekly*	*Daily*		
1.							
2.							
3.							

- Construction of the new organizational component – managerial synapse – which has an essential role and impact in the company organizational structure. A managerial synapse represents the specific organizational way to configure the work processes and relationships at the level of each relevant stakeholder, capable of generating a positive identity at work. A managerial synapse is constructed as a multidimensional context. We do not focus on its characteristics, because these have been presented in Chapter 5, Sections 5.3, 5.4, and 5.5, where we have also proposed a guide for performant managerial synapse construction, work and performance.
- Foundation, within the organization, of new managerial bodies – company participative relevant stakeholders' council and departmental participative relevant stakeholders' committees – specific to the relevant stakeholders-based management system. Information regarding these bodies is presented in Chapter 9, Section 9.3.
- Development of new categories of very intense organizational relationships between the relevant stakeholders inside the managerial synapse and between this and other organizational components of the company.
- Extension of the company's organizational subsystem, beyond the organization boundaries, through the inclusion of external relevant stakeholders.
- Change in the content and functionality of all components of the organizational subsystem – job, function, span of control, department, hierarchical level, organizational relationships – because of the impact of the relevant stakeholders' focalization in the company. Within each of them appear new specific common objectives, roles, tasks, competences, responsibilities, flows, etc.
- Diminution of the hierarchical intensity of the organizational management subsystem, because the establishment of the common objectives and of the set of tasks, competences and responsibilities in every managerial synapse is the result of win-win negotiation and intense consultation, and not imposed by ordering.
- Extension of the frequency of non-hierarchical organizational relationships – functional and cooperative relationships. We point out that in the stakeholders-based management system, in particular, the cooperation relationships are much more frequent and more influential than other types of company management systems. Frequently, the cooperation relationships are integrated in networks that involve relevant stakeholders.
- Increase of the role and impact of informal organizational

elements within the organizational subsystem, which facilitates cooperation among stakeholders and between them and the other company components. Informal organizational elements contribute significantly to the needed flexibility within the stakeholders-based management system.
- All organizational documents of the company – job description, attribution diagrams, organizational handbooks, organigrams, etc. – are redesigned in order to incorporate the new organizational elements of the stakeholders-based management system.

The organizational management subsystem in a company that implements the stakeholders-based management system is radically different from organizational management subsystems in "classical" companies.

d Within the **company's informational management subsystem, the following major changes** should also be made:

- Extension of the informational subsystem beyond company boundaries, external relevant stakeholders becoming major information receivers and issuers for the organization.
- The company's information nature, structure and information procedures also change, due to the incorporation of many new elements generated by the establishment of common objectives, win-win negotiation, reasonable compromise fulfilment, etc.
- Appearance of new information files and databases on the information flows and circuits involved in networking with internal relevant stakeholders and – especially – with external relevant stakeholders.
- Information used in the company comprises, to a large extent, knowledge of the relevant internal and external stakeholders that intensively share it, in accordance with the new management system's specificity.
- The company's information subsystem is characterized by frequent use of the new informational elements generated by digitalization and digital transformation, without which it is not possible to develop intensive and effective relationships with all internal and external company-relevant stakeholders.
- Increase the informational management subsystem informal dimension because of the specificity of human relationships within managerial synapses, and between them and the other company components.

The new company information management subsystem is more complex, flexible, and effective due to the features of the stakeholders-based management system.

e **In the human resources management subsystem**, multiple changes are necessary, including the following:

- Focalization of the human resources management on the company-relevant stakeholders, both internal and external, increasing their scope and changing partially the content and how it operates. It is recommended to use the agile approach, which, according to some specialists (Cappelli & Tavis, 2018), "is now transforming how organizations hire, develop and manage their people".
- Modification to a certain extent of the criteria for internal stakeholders' selection, integration, motivation, evaluation, training, promotion, etc., taking into consideration the specificity of human relationships within the managerial synapse, which are characterized by intense communication and consultation, win-win negotiation, reciprocity, high participation in decisional processes and actions, etc.
- Foundation in the human resources management of a new field, dealing with the external relevant stakeholders, which will integrate many elements of human resources management that are quite different from the management of company managers and subordinates. The mission of this new field should be to facilitate the creation and the development of effective and efficient sustainable relationships with internal and external relevant stakeholders, to increase the meaningfulness work for each of them (Bailey & Madden, 2016) and to develop company-relevant stakeholders' responsibilities.
- Increase of the importance and intensity of motivation, approached as a multifaceted process and designed taking into consideration the specificity of the managerial synapses and of the stakeholders-based management system as a whole. Moral motivations tend to increase and diversify concomitantly with the increase of relevant stakeholders' participation in sharing the total value created by the company.
- Design and fulfilment of special approaches and programmes for training, mentoring, coaching, counselling, etc. the company employees and the external relevant stakeholders, with the aim of developing their qualities, skills, and knowledge with a major impact on the creation and development of managerial synapses.

The company management human resources subsystem plays a very important role in the successful implementation of the stakeholders-based management system.

Reshaping of the five main components of the company management system should be achieved using a combination of "top-down" and "bottom-up" approaches (Heyden, Fourné, Koene, Werkman, &

Ansari, 2017), with **intense participation by all relevant stakeholders.** Such participation is indispensable for the construction of the stakeholders-based management system. Without comprehensive and continued participation of each relevant stakeholder in all phases of the managerial synapse construction, in all management system components – decisional, organizational, informational, etc. – it is not possible to generate an effective and efficient company managerial mechanism. Nothing can replace the direct and intense participation of each relevant stakeholder in determining the common objectives, win-win negotiation or reciprocal compromise fulfilment. Relevant stakeholders' participation in the managerial synapse construction and in the other elements of the stakeholders-based management system has a powerful motivational content. At the same time, the participation is an irreplaceable condition so that relevant stakeholders can continue to make a great contribution with all their resources to the company work and to maximum use of their qualities, energy and competences to achieve the common objectives, generating high performance for them and the organization. Participation develops "stakeholder organization ownership" and responsibility of the new management mechanisms.

High functionality and performance of the stakeholders-based management system is conditioned by the **harmonization at the level of the whole company between all its components.** In order to accomplish harmonization it is essential to operate on the following two levels:

- Harmonization among the five managerial subsystems – methodological-managerial, decisional, organizational, informational and human resources management. Harmonization should be done at the level of each company component, every external relevant stakeholder, and each managerial synapse. Special attention should be paid to the harmonization of those elements in every company department and at the level of the entire organization.
- Harmonization between the new management elements, specific to the stakeholders-based management system, and the other elements of the company management. At the level of every organization component, of each relevant internal and external stakeholder, the new organizational, decisional, informational, etc. elements should be strongly correlated with the other processes and relationships fulfilled in the company. This harmonization should be fully completed, in order to accomplish "de facto" integration of all work processes and relationships involved. It is absolutely essential that mismatches do not exist between the management elements specific to the stakeholders' management and the other managerial processes and relationships.

Harmonization of all components of the company stakeholders-based management system, using an **agile approach**, can contribute in the development of the organization's internal innovative environment, centred on the relevant stakeholders.

The elements presented reflect the novelty and the complexity of the company-relevant stakeholders-based management achievement. Companies – especially large and medium-sized ones – in order to build a performant new management system, an agile organization, need to use a professional undertaking involving consultants specialized in the design and development of organization managerial systems who have the vision, know-how and the dynamic capabilities demanded by such a project, and are able to take into consideration the complex changes generated by the COVID-19 pandemic.

Approaches, Methods, and Techniques Useful in the Construction and Operation of the Company-Relevant Stakeholders-Based Management System

As we have argued, the company-relevant stakeholders-based management system is a new organization management system that is completely different from all previous management systems used in companies. Moreover, in the construction, use and development of this system, **quite a large number of the managerial approaches, methods and techniques from the present company practice might be employed.** Taking into consideration their content, they can be grouped into **two categories:**

- approaches, methods and techniques created in the last few decades, focused on the organization stakeholders. These take into consideration more or less stakeholders' specificity;
- methods and techniques from "classical" management, which could be used, of course, with adaptation in the stakeholders-based management system.

In the next few pages, we will selectively enumerate both categories of methodological tools, which could be very helpful in the new company management system.

I Specific stakeholder managerial approaches, models, methods, and techniques

In the international literature dedicated to stakeholders and their approaches, thousands of studies and books have been published in recent decades. The majority of them have a theoretical content and – to a less extent – they present results of empirical research. The review of a few hundred studies and books elaborated by well-known specialists in their field and of organization consultant sites and of other bodies that deal with company management and stakeholders allows us to identify quite a few stakeholders' approaches, models, methods, and techniques. We have made a selection of some methodological tools that might be used in the stakeholders-based management system. In Table 11.5, we list them, indicating whether they are useful for the managerial synapse and/or for the stakeholders-based management system.

We want to make it clear that we do not pretend that we have selected the most representative or the best stakeholder approaches, models, methods, and techniques to be employed in companies. Our selection – like any qualitative selection – is subjective. But the tools selected are useful in the building and functioning of a stakeholders' management system. Also, they can help practitioners from the companies in stakeholder management, even if they do not utilize the new specific managerial mechanisms proposed by us – the stakeholders-based management system and managerial synapse.

In regard to the use of specific tools for the company stakeholders' approach incorporated in Table 11.5, in the company-relevant stakeholders-based management system, we should outline **two aspects:**

a In every company, these tools should be used in a specific manner, taking into consideration organization and stakeholders' particularities. Each of them should be adapted to company-relevant stakeholders-based management specificity, taking into consideration at least the following elements:

   - The stakeholders involved are relevant stakeholders, who need to be approached in a specific manner, different from other types of the company stakeholder (salient, primary, etc.) used by other specialists;
   - The managerial synapse, the basic component of the new system used for each relevant stakeholder, is an innovational managerial mechanism with very high particularities, which determines quite often profound changes in the employment of the previous managerial stakeholder tools;
   - The company-relevant stakeholders-based management system has a specific structural and functional content, and the management processes and relationships are remodelled differently compared with the management processes and relationships used so far in the previous stakeholder approaches.

For this reason, the managerial tools should be modified in order to fit and to generate performance within the company stakeholders-based

Table 11.5 Specific stakeholders' management approaches, models, methods, and techniques recommended for the management of relevant stakeholders

No.	*Stakeholders' Management Tools*	*Field/Specificity*	*Where to Be Used*	
			Managerial Synapse	*Company-Relevant Stakeholders-Based Management System*
A. Methodological approaches				
1.	Capability Maturity Model Integration (CMMI) (Bourne, 2009)	Tool for assessment and improvement of an organization's ability to choose the right stakeholder project and to do it correctly in a consistent manner		x
2.	Organizational Project Management Maturity Model (OPM_3) (Bourne, 2009)	Tool for assessment and improvement of an organization's ability to choose the right stakeholder project and then to do it correctly in a consistent manner		x
3.	Portfolio Programme And Project Management Maturity Model (P_3M_3) (Bourne, 2009)	Reference guide for structuring best stakeholder project and organization practice		x
4.	Stakeholder Circle (Bourne, 2009)	Methodology for stakeholder engagement		x
5.	Large Multi-Stakeholder Partnership (Clarke & MacDonald, 2019)	Stakeholders' approach designed to address and prioritize a social problem and build capacity by developing and leveraging the diverse perspectives and resources of each partner stakeholder		x
6.	Selective Revealing Practice (Alexy, George, & Salter, 2003; Jarvenpaa & Välikangas, 2014)	Key collaboration strategy that involves sharing part of the firm's knowledge or its intentions, focusing on commercial exploitation		x

7.	Long-Term Plan For Value Creation With Investors (Youmans & Tomlinson, 2018)	New tool for periodic corporate shareholder communication, leading company and investors together to drive sustainable value creation		x
8.	Analytical Framework For Collaborative Planning Processes (Vandenbussche, Edelenbos, & Eshuis, 2017)	Analytical framework for studying stakeholders relating dynamics in collaborative planning		x
9.	Intra-Stakeholder Alliance (Fassin, De Colle, & Freeman, 2017)	Alliance among the various stakeholder groups in a specific company, in reaction to the organization decision to terminate production locally		x
10.	Stakeholders Co-Creative Network (Calton, 2013)	Stakeholders' network, which engages in a co-creative process for constructing mutual value		x
11.	Social Return On Investment (SROI) (Hall, Millo, & Barman, 2015)	Accounting methodology intended to permit managers both to incorporate stakeholders' voices and to communicate the special value created by the firm for those stakeholders		x
12.	Dialogic Accountings (Brown & Dillard, 2015)	Dialogic accountings aim to counter narrow managerial framings and address stakeholders poorly served by traditional accounting, taking pluralism seriously and enabling critical reflection on the organizational practices from diverse socio-political perspectives		x
13.	Stakeholders Analysis ("Stakeholder Analysis, Project Management, Templates and Advice", n.d.)	Stakeholders' analysis is a systematic way to analyse stakeholders by their power and interest	x	x
14.	Stakeholders Analysis Matrix ("Stakeholder Management Strategy Template", n.d.)	Approach used to capture stakeholders' concerns, level of involvement and management strategy, based on the stakeholders' analysis and power/ interest matrix		x

(Continued)

Table 11.5 (Continued)

No.	*Stakeholders' Management Tools*	*Field/Specificity*	*Where to Be Used*	
			Managerial Synapse	*Company-Relevant Stakeholders-Based Management System*
B. Models				
1.	Relationship Management Maturity (RMM) (Bourne, 2009)	Model to assist the implementation of stakeholder management processes and practices that most meet the organization's current level of readiness for stakeholder relationship management		x
2.	Four Factors Stakeholder Model (Harrison & Wicks, 2013)	Model has five essential ingredients: recognition that the purpose of the firm is based on the amount of value that the firm provides to its stakeholders; inclusion of both economic and non-economic factors that provide utility to stakeholders; inclusion of measures for all of a firm's primary stakeholders; recognition that the different stakeholders are likely to value different things; measures having the capacity to recognize a level of utility to stakeholders that exceeds more satisfaction with the firm		x
3.	Leadership Communal Sharing Model (Wellman, 2017)	Model in which leadership is the company collective responsibilities of all members		x
4.	"Six Market" Model (Freeman, Harrison, Wicks, Parmar, & De Colle, 2010)	Model for relationships with traditional stakeholders, taking into consideration six markets: customer markets, referral markets, supplier markets, influencer markets, employee markets and internal market	x	x

C. Methods				
1.	Stakeholder Management Place Smart-Sheet ("How to Create Stakeholder Management and Communication Plans", n.d.)	Method that produces a template that contains a list with stakeholders and seven elements to be specified for each of them	x	x
2.	Stakeholder Communication Plan Template ("How to Create Stakeholder Management and Communication Plans", n.d.)	Method that produces a template that contains a list with stakeholders and ten elements to specify for each of them	x	x
3.	Value Creation Stakeholder Partnership (VCSP) (Mitchell, Van Buren, Greenwood, & Freeman, 2015)	Mechanism for implementation of value creation stakeholder accounting, which is derived from a fusion of accounting, value creation, entrepreneurship and stakeholder theory		x
4.	Stakeholder Strategy Matrix (Freeman et al., 2010)	Method that produces a matrix that determines the stakeholder ability to cooperate with the firm on the one hand, and their ten organizational goals on the other		x
5.	BABOK stakeholder concern ("Brandenburg", n.d.)	Method that provides the business analyst's understanding of issues identified by stakeholders – risks, assumptions, constraints and other relevant information – that may be used in business analysis	x	x
6.	Conduct Stakeholder Analysis (International Institute of Business Analysis, 2009)	Method that covers the identification of stakeholders who may be affected by a proposed initiative or who share a common business need, identifying appropriate stakeholders for a project phase and determining stakeholder influence and/or authority regarding the approval of project deliverables	x	x

(*Continued*)

Table 11.5 (Continued)

No.	*Stakeholders' Management Tools*	*Field/Specificity*	*Where to Be Used*	
			Managerial Synapse	*Company-Relevant Stakeholders-Based Management System*
7.	Social Responsibilities Matrix (Haski-Leventhal, Roza, & Meijs, 2017)	Method consisting of four patterns for classifying the social responsibility of employees and employers – low social responsibility, identity-based social responsibility, behaviour-based responsibility and entwined responsibility – which allows to the level of congruence between these two key categories of stakeholders to be assessed		x
D. Techniques				
1.	Stakeholder Interview (Cummings, 2002; Owen, 2003)	Interview focused on stakeholder relevant information and feedback	x	x
2.	Stakeholder Focus Group (Cummings, 2002; Owen, 2003)	Focus group specifically organized in order to communicate and consult with important stakeholders		x
3.	Stakeholder Public Meeting (Cummings, 2002; Owen, 2003)	Public meeting with non-economic stakeholders in order to communicate and consult on very important ecological and social issues	x	x
4.	Stakeholder Consultation (Cummings, 2002; Owen, 2003)	Special consultation session with certain category of stakeholders regarding the approaching and the solution of very important well-defined topic		x
5.	Advisory Stakeholders Panel (Owen, 2003)	Advisory panel with important stakeholders regarding the approach of specific major aspects in the relationships with the company		x

6.	Stakeholder Evaluation Hotline (Skolits & Boser, 2018)	Mechanism based on the evaluation hotline for identifying and reaching community stakeholders and enabling their participation		x
7.	Stakeholder Performance Scorecard (Ashworth et al., 2011)	Special technique that sets the satisfaction norms for key stakeholders – employees, suppliers, retailers and distributors – and tracks the satisfaction of the company management, taking action when one of these groups shows an increased level of dissatisfaction		x
8.	Stakeholder Matrix Diagram or Grid (Ashworth et al., 2011; Bryson, 2004)	Stakeholders are placed in the grid according to how much influence and interest they have on the company or on the project	x	x
9.	Power Versus Interest Grid or Matrix ("Stakeholder Analysis, Project Management, Templates and Advice", n.d.; "Stakeholder Analysis", n.d.)	Grid having three columns and rows with interest/influence either high, medium or low, helping to make stakeholder analysis	x	x
10.	Stakeholder Analysis Mindmap Template ("Stakeholder Analysis, Project Management, Templates and Advice", n.d.)	It uses a mind-mapping tool, first branches organize stakeholders into impact and influencing groupings, and stakeholders are then mapped by adding branches to each group		x
11.	Stakeholder Map (Ashworth et al., 2011)	Diagram with the organization in the centre and the primary stakeholders round it and secondary stakeholders in a second tier		x
12.	Stakeholder Influence Network (Ackermann & Eden, 2011)	Technique for capturing the interactions between stakeholders, indicating which players are important and which relationships are the most pronounced	x	x

(Continued)

Table 11.5 (Continued)

No.	*Stakeholders' Management Tools*	*Field/Specificity*	*Where to Be Used*	
			Managerial Synapse	*Company-Relevant Stakeholders-Based Management System*
13.	Stakeholder Management Web (Ackermann & Eden, 2011)	Technique that is focused on a single stakeholder, designed to record, in a structured and detailed manner, information about specific key stakeholder actions, objectives and motivations; this technique, which explicates the stakeholder basis of power and interest, suggests stakeholder management options more clearly than many other techniques	x	x
14.	Acceptance And Evaluation Criteria Definition (International Institute of Business Analysis, 2009)	Technique that defines the requirements that must be met in order for a solution to be considered acceptable to key stakeholders, using the acceptance criteria and evaluation criteria	x	x
15.	Alignment, Interest, Influence Matrix (Hearn, 2014)	Stakeholders' analysis technique that can be used for identifying and classifying boundary partners, which is useful in monitoring changes in stakeholders' work	x	
16.	Dow Jones Sustainability Index World DJSIW (Giannarakis, Garefalakis, Lemonakis, & Konteos, 2017)	DJSIW is a special technique employed to identify companies that incorporate socially responsible initiatives in their business operations, helping to explain the investor's behaviour in response to stock index returns	x	x

17.	List Evaluation Stakeholders (Bryson, Patton, & Bowman, 2011)	Technique to develop initial list of stakeholders using brainstorming, which conducts iterative process of narrowing the field of key stakeholders	x	x
18.	Basic Stakeholders Analysis Technique (Bryson et al., 2011)	This technique offers a quick and useful way of identifying each stakeholder and comparing and contrasting their interest(s) in the programme versus their interest(s) in the evaluation	x	x
19.	Stakeholder Influence Diagram (Bryson et al., 2011)	Technique that indicates how stakeholders influence one another, taking into consideration their power and interests	x	x
20.	Bases of Power – Directing of Interest Diagram (Bryson et al., 2011)	This technique takes the analysis in the power versus interest grid to a deeper level by identifying: a the sources of different evaluation stakeholders' power and b what the actual interests or goals of different evaluation stakeholders are	x	x
21.	Participation Planning Matrix (Bryson et al., 2011)	Technique that indicates probable level of stakeholder participation and relationship of evaluator to stakeholder; it can be used to create a sort of evaluation contract with selected stakeholders who are important to engage in the company	x	x
22.	Stakeholder Role Plays (Bryson et al., 2011)	This technique contributes to the understanding of how different stakeholders respond to different methods, measurements and designs	x	x
23.	Recommendation Attractiveness Versus Stakeholder Capability Grid (Bryson, 2004; Bryson et al., 2011)	Technique that identifies recommendations that are likely to be implemented due to stakeholder capacity, and those that will fail due to lack of capacity	x	x

(*Continued*)

Table 11.5 (Continued)

No.	*Stakeholders' Management Tools*	*Field/Specificity*	*Where to Be Used*	
			Managerial Synapse	*Company-Relevant Stakeholders-Based Management System*
24.	Recommendation Implementation Strategy Development Grid (Bryson et al., 2011)	This technique helps stakeholders to gain a clear picture of what will be required for company strategy implementation, and helps to develop action plans that will tap stakeholders' interests and resources	x	x
25.	Ethical Analysis Grid (Bryson, 2004)	This technique indicates which proposals or options regarding company stakeholders should be eliminated or altered on ethical grounds	x	x

management system. In practice, it is necessary to adopt a creative approach and use each stakeholder tool in order to obtain the maximum positive effects at the level of the company and every relevant stakeholder.

b In using these tools, company **managers should integrate, as much as possible, the new communication technologies** – including blogging, texting, podcasting, and video posting – especially in the relationships with external stakeholders. Such an approach is very useful in order to communicate better with company stakeholders, to use the stakeholders' knowledge and information to a higher level, and to develop faster and better work relationships with them.

II Classical managerial methods and techniques recommended to be used in the company-relevant stakeholders-based management system

As a result of our management analysis of the list of 136 management classical methodological tools (International Institute of Business Analysis, 2009; Nicolescu & Verboncu, 2008) relatively frequently used in companies, we completed a selection of 62 items incorporated in Table 11.6, indicating where we believe they should be used at the level of the stakeholders-based management system and/or the managerial synapse.

We want to specify that some of these methods and techniques have already been used by company management in the stakeholders' approach – brainstorming, benchmarking, interview, questionnaire, SWOT analysis, focus group, flow diagram, document analysis, etc. They have been employed either as such or integrated in the specific stakeholder tools. Of course, this list is just a limited selection of managerial approaches, methods, and techniques. Without any doubt, there are other managerial "classical" management tools that could be used in the stakeholders-based management system. In order to use them within this new management system and to obtain maximum positive effects, are recommended **to adapt them to the specificity of the new system.** Adaptation should be based on in-depth analysis of each company management and its internal and external environment, of the relevant stakeholders taken into consideration. Quite often, adaptation should have a consistent innovational content in order to generate sustainable development and performances for the company and the relevant stakeholders.

Table 11.6 "Classical" managerial tools that could be used in the company-relevant stakeholders-based management system

	Management Tools *1*	*Managerial Synapse* *2*	*Company-Relevant Stakeholders-Based Management System* *3*
1.	ABC	x	x
2.	Algorithm Deutsch Martin	x	–
3.	ASME diagram	x	–
4.	Benchmarking	–	x
5.	Brainstorming	x	x
6.	Brainwriting (635)	–	x
7.	Break point	x	x
8.	Business plan	–	x
9.	Career plan	x	–
10.	Check list	x	x
11.	Crawford technique	–	x
12.	Critical path	–	x
13.	Data flow diagram	x	x
14.	Decisional simulation	x	–
15.	Decisional table	x	–
16.	Decisional tree	x	x
17.	Delbecq	x	x
18.	Delegation	x	x
19.	Diagnosis analysis	x	x
20.	Discovery matrix	x	–
21.	Document analysis	x	x
22.	ELECTRE	x	x
23.	Extrapolation	x	x
24.	Focus group	x	x
25.	Functional evaluation	x	–
26.	Gantt graphic	–	x
27.	Global evaluation	x	–
28.	Gordon technique	–	–
29.	Hyjmans graphic	–	x
30.	Interface analysis	–	x
31.	Interview	x	x
32.	Job analysis	x	–
33.	Job enrichment	x	–
34.	Just in time	x	–
35.	KAIZEN	–	x
36.	LIFO	x	–
37.	Management by project	–	x
38.	Management by budgets	–	x
39.	Manager diagram	x	x
40.	Markowicz method	x	–
41.	Meeting technique	x	x
42.	Monte Carlo technique	x	–
43.	Organigram	–	x
44.	Organizational culture audit	–	x

(*Continued*)

Table 11.6 (Continued)

	Management Tools 1	*Managerial Synapse* 2	*Company-Relevant Stakeholders-Based Management System* 3
45.	ORTID	x	x
46.	PERT	–	x
47.	Phil Carol	–	x
48.	Phillips 66	x	x
49.	Planus graphic	–	x
50.	Problem tracking	x	x
51.	Questionnaire	x	x
52.	Requirement workshop	–	x
53.	Root cause analysis	x	x
54.	Scenario method	–	x
55.	SMART model	x	–
56.	Strategic alliance	–	x
57.	SWOT analysis	–	x
58.	Synectic	x	x
59.	TEMPLATE grid	–	x
60.	Value analysis	x	–
61.	Value chain	–	x
62.	Vendor assessment	x	–

Construction of the New Company Organizational Culture and Subcultures

The essential role played by the organizational culture in the building and development of a performant organization was demonstrated years ago. For example, a study reported by Harvard Business School in 2003 that examined the management practice in 160 organizations over ten years found that organizational culture has significant effects on long-term economic performance. In order to generate high performance, organizational culture should be correlated with all other major components of the management system and of the company. Of course, a stakeholders-based management system also involves a specific organizational culture, enabling it to work normally and be competitive. This new culture does not appear spontaneously; it should be constructed and developed in correlation with strategy, leadership, a stakeholders-based management system, managerial methods, and techniques, all being reshaped under a new vision focused on the company-relevant stakeholders.

Construction of the specific company organizational culture should be based on a **holistic approach**, considering a company as an open system and dealing with and modelling all the components of the organizational culture. In the conception of the company organizational culture focused on relevant stakeholders, it is necessary to start from the **following premises:**

- stakeholders-based management system is quite different from all other "classical" management systems, the main differences being specified in Section 9.4;
- stakeholders-based management construction and work are based on the 12 new principles formulated in Section 9.5;
- stakeholders-based management system characteristics reflect the essential elements of the new "humanistic management" mentioned in Section 10.8, which should be taken into consideration in the remodelling of the organizational culture;
- specific features and components of the company organizational culture need to be changed according to the characteristics of the stakeholders-based management system.

These premises allow the **main characteristics of the organizational culture in the company implementing the company-relevant stakeholders-based management system** to be formulated. According to our analysis, there are 12 characteristics, enumerated in Figure 11.4 and briefly presented further below.

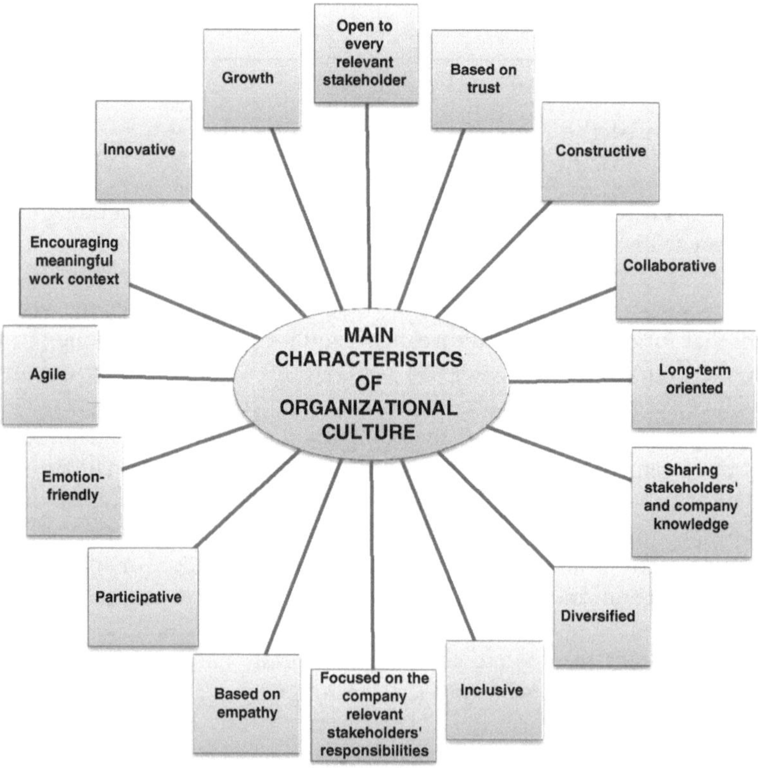

Figure 11.4 Main characteristics of organizational culture focused on the relevant stakeholders.

- Organizational culture is open to every relevant stakeholder, internal and external, without any restriction, treating each as an important company component and encouraging the development and manifestation of company-relevant stakeholders' responsibilities.
- Trust is considered of crucial importance in the company and it is cultivated constantly at all levels – between individuals, between the organization and its components, between the company and internal and external stakeholders.
- Organizational culture is constructive, being focused on the positive approach, on the development of the company and each relevant stakeholder, encouraging everyone people implication, innovation, and performance.
- Organizational culture is collaborative, striving always to facilitate and increase positive communication, collaboration, and cooperation among all company components, at every level, centred on the internal and external relevant stakeholders. This characteristic helps company and relevant stakeholders to become a collaborative community (Adler et al., 2011).
- Performances to be achieved by the company there are approached multidimensional not only economic ones.
- Organizational culture through its values, symbols, norms, rituals, behaviours, etc. should facilitate and encourage the relevant internal and external stakeholders and, of course, the company to share their explicit and implicit knowledge, in order to generate performances and value added for all entities involved.
- Organizational culture takes into consideration and values diversity of human resources involved, of the internal and external relevant stakeholders, considering it a major source for the company development, and for "enriching" humanistic management practice.
- Inclusiveness is a major value and preoccupation for the company management, with integration of all company components, of every relevant internal and external stakeholder, being centred in managerial vision, decisions, actions, and behaviours, facilitating the increase of company synergy.
- The new approach of the company and relevant stakeholders' responsibilities (see Section 10.7) will only become operational if it is incorporated in the company's organizational culture and subcultures. Focusing the organizational culture on the company-relevant stakeholders' responsibilities is essential for the harmonized and sustainable development of the company, internal and external stakeholders, local community, environment, etc.
- Developing empathy with the ability of company components, starting with managers, to understand and to share feelings with others is essential for the company and for each relevant stakeholder. Without constant empathy a managerial synapse, the basic

component of the stakeholders-based management system, cannot be constructed.

- Organizational culture participative feature means a superior step in the cooperation among company human resources, involving the direct participation of every relevant stakeholder in the decisional processes regarding its activity and status in the company. A managerial synapse cannot be built and work without real participation of the relevant stakeholders involved.
- An emotion-friendly organizational culture pays major attention to the perceptions, emotions and feelings of individuals, taking care that each person feels well and is available to communicate and to cooperate with others in the work process, contributing to the development of a pleasant and productive working context for all relevant stakeholders.
- Emotional intelligence competences of managers and other individuals involved in the company work processes play a major role in the development of the emotion-friendly culture in the company.
- The agility of an organizational culture, based on the understanding of cultural dynamics (Vogel, 2017), provides to the company the necessary flexibility and speeds up its evolution in order to integrate all relevant stakeholders, including the external ones, in the company mechanisms and to enhance their functionality and performance in the conditions of win-win results.
- All the previous characteristics of a stakeholders-based organizational culture contribute to creating for company components, for its relevant stakeholders, a meaningful work context, which means an environment where they become part of creating success, cohesiveness and culture at work. Meaningful work is very motivational for the effort and the performance contributing to the individual accomplishment of relevant internal and external stakeholders.
- An innovative company culture is characterized (Pisano, 2019) by the following five features: tolerance of failure but not tolerance of incompetence, willingness to experiment but highly disciplined, psychologically save but brutal candid, collaboration but with individual accountability, and flat but strong leadership
- Organizational culture based on the relevant stakeholders is recommended to be a growth culture and not a performance-obsessed one; a growth culture, based on multifaceted motivations, involves a blend of individual and organizational components – an internal environment that is safe, a continuous learning, time limited manageable experiments with new behaviour, continuous feedback (Schwarz, 2018) – up, down, and across the organization and its relevant stakeholders.

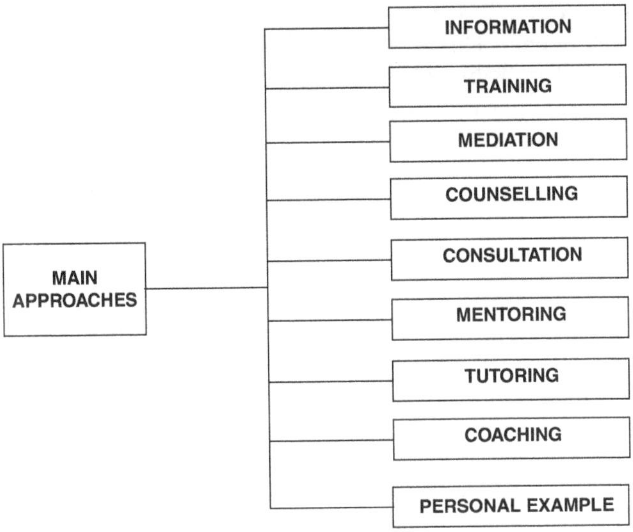

Figure 11.5 Main approaches to be used with human resources in order to re-shape the company organizational culture.

In order to develop an organizational culture with the characteristics presented, it is necessary to use a **set of approaches**. In Figure 11.5, we enumerate a selection of them that have so far been successfully used in companies for human resources information, training and remodelling of their values, skills, behaviours, etc. We do not consider it necessary to comment on these ways, because they are used frequently in companies, being generally well known by managers and human resources management. As regards the specific aspects involved in their utilization for the development of organizational culture focused on relevant stakeholders, we formulate the **following specific requirements:**

- to be focused on the creation and increase of all specific characteristics of this new type of company organizational culture;
- to evaluate the organizational culture of the company in order to identify their characteristics, and its main strengths and weaknesses;
- to evaluate the features of the relevant internal and external company stakeholders, and the particular cultural problems with them;
- to identify the main subcultures inside the organizational culture of the company and of the external relevant stakeholders and their specific significant characteristics;
- to select, based on the previous elements, what ways to be used in order to develop the organizational culture at the level of the entire company and at the level of its main fields and relevant stakeholders, where subcultures have been identified;

- to elaborate a programme for the use of the ways selected to reshape organizational culture, based on the consultation of all company-relevant stakeholders. This programme might incorporate the elements indicated in Table 11.7. In the case of a large company, two special programmes can be elaborated – one for reshaping the entire organization culture, and the second for the reshaping of subcultures identified.
- to precede the establishment of each way and action by determining the specific content and forms to be used, based on all previous analysis, in order to maximize the positive effects on the company's organizational culture and subcultures, with reasonable costs and time consumption.

Company organizational culture reshaping should start with company **managers and internal relevant stakeholders**, who play a major role in the design and implementation of the stakeholders-based management system. Their personal example has a great influence on the organizational culture change, and on the operation of the managerial system focused on the company-relevant stakeholders. It is obvious that the most important is the personal example of the company CEO and of other top managers.

A major aspect to be considered in the organizational culture remodelling is the **harmonization of the company organizational culture with the main subcultures involved** – from the own organization and from external stakeholders. Their major characteristics should be harmonized or at least made fully compatible, developing a company stakeholders' community. Within the company, it is recommended to use predominantly the care culture style and culture results style, which are more performant (Groysberg, Lee, Price, & Cheng, 2018).

For company managers, in order to develop the organizational culture focused on the relevant stakeholders, it could be helpful to use some **methodological approaches** recommended by specialists in the field for the remodelling of the company organizational culture. There are many such approaches in the speciality literature, like those elaborated by Cameron and Quinn (2011), Connors and Smith (2011), Edmonds (2014), Knight (2014), Schein (2010) and, more recently, by Groysberg et al. (2018).

The integration of the specific elements regarding company organizational culture focused on the stakeholders, indicated by us, should be very useful in improving the results achieved by company management.

Without any doubt, constructing a company organizational culture focused on the relevant stakeholders is a very complex and difficult process that needs significant costs and time. Despite these problems, the new company organizational culture should be constructed, because

Table 11.7 Programme with the approaches to be used in order to remodel company organizational culture and subcultures

No.	*Approaches*	*Actions*[3]	*Level of Utilization*		*Action Responsible*	*Action Period*	*Observations*[4]
			Organizational Culture[5]	*Organizational Subculture*[6]			
0.	1	2	3	4	5	6	7
1.							
2.							
3.							
4.							

without it the company management system cannot work properly and in a performant manner. When organizational culture is properly aligned with the other components of the company it "can unleash tremendous amounts of energy toward a shared purpose and foster an organization's capacity to thrive" (Groysberg et al., 2018).

The building of the new **organizational culture should be correlated with the implementation of all other major elements involved, mentioned at the beginning of this chapter** – new vision and leadership, specific organization strategy, redesigned company management system, and the "arsenal" of stakeholder-focused approaches, methods, and techniques. Together, all these essential management fields represent the content of the company-relevant stakeholder-based management system.

One final remark: the **design and implementation of the relevant stakeholder system is a personalized process** for each interested company. Elements presented in this chapter of the book, there are just major landmarks to be used in this process. In order to achieve a competitive relevant stakeholders' company management system, the concrete approach to each organization management process and relationship is decisive, taking into consideration company and relevant stakeholders' particularities, using agile and innovative approaches.

Concomitantly, the last changes and challenges in the company environment should be taken into consideration, including those generated by the COVID-19 pandemic (see, e.g., Boston Consulting Group, 2020; Carlson-Szlezac, Reeves, & Swartz, 2020; Chaturvedi, Dey, & Singh, 2020; Chima & Gutman, 2020; Gjaja, Fæste, Hansell, & Hohner, 2020; King & Wald, 2020; Narayandas, Hebbar, & Li, 2020; Nicolescu, Popa, & Dumitrascu, 2020; Pedersen & Ritter, 2020; Radjou, 2020; Romeo, Moukanas, & Rung, 2020; Waldron & Wetherbe, 2020) and their major influences on the company and the internal and external relevant stakeholders.

Notes

1 Certain specialists have introduced the term "digital leadership", which is about enabling the organization to provide vision and purpose, to create conditions to experiment, to empower people to think differently and to get people to collaborate across boundaries, being quite often a distributed leadership (Kane, Palmer, Phillips, Kiron, & Buckley, 2018).

2 For forecasting the strategic objectives and for all other quantitative elements of the strategy we recommend using not the classical "point" prediction but the "range of plausible estimates", which leave some margin of error, producing more realistic previsions, helping to create better management of the company and its relevant stakeholders. SPIES is a method specially developed by Haran and Moore (2014) for this new approach.

3 All concrete actions in order to use each approach selected will be indicated, like information meeting, seminar, training course, round table, mediation session, mentoring session, etc.

4 Other very important aspects to be taken into consideration in the preparation of action shall be mentioned – if it is the case.
5 Participants selected for each action shall be indicated.
6 Subcultures involved, and the person who shall participate in each action shall be specified.

References

Ackermann, F., & Eden, C. (2011). Strategic management of stakeholders: Theory and practice. *Long Range Planning*, *44*(3), 179–196. doi:10.1016/j.lrp.2010.08.001

Adler, P., Heckscher, C., & Prusak, L. (2011). Building a collaborative enterprise. *Harvard Business Review*, *89* (7/8), 94–101.

Alexy, O., George, G., & Salter, A. J. (2003). Cui bono? The selective revealing of knowledge and its implications for innovative activity. *Academy of Management Review*, *38*(2), 270–291. doi:10.5465/amr.2011.0193

Appleyard, M. M., & Chesbrough, H. W. (2017). The dynamics of open strategy: From adoption to reversion. *Long Range Planning*, *50*(3), 310–321. doi:10.1016/j.lrp.2016.07.004

Ashkenas, R., & Manville, B. (2018). The 6 fundamental skills every leader should practice. *Harvard Business Review*, *96*(5). Retrieved from https://hbr.org/2018/10/the-6-fundamental-skills-every-leader-should-practice

Ashworth, P., Bradbury, J., Feenstra, C. F. J., Greenberg, S., Hund, G., Mikunda, T., et al. (2011). *Communication/engagement toolkit for CCS projects*. Australia: Commonwealth Scientific and Industrial Research Organisation. Retrieved from https://www.globalccsinstitute.com/archive/hub/publications/13571/publication-20110601-communication-engagement-toolkit.pdf

Bailey, C., & Madden, A. (2016). What makes work meaningful – or meaningless. *MIT Sloan Management Review*, *57*(4), 53–61.

Bonchek, M., & Libert, B. (2017). To change your strategy, first change how you think. *Harvard Business Review*. Retrieved from https://hbr.org/2017/05/to-change-your-strategy-first-change-how-you-think

Boston Consulting Group. (2020). *COVID-19 BCG perspectives series: Facts, scenarios and actions for leaders*. Retrieved from https://media-publications.bcg.com/BCG-COVID-19-BCG-Perspectives-Version13.pdf

Bourne, L. (2009). *Stakeholder relationship management: A maturity model for organisational implementation*. Farnham, UK: Gower Publishing.

Brandenburg, L. (n.d.). *How to capture stakeholder concerns*. Retrieved from https://www.bridging-the-gap.com/capture-stakeholder-concerns/

Brown, J., & Dillard, J. (2015). Dialogic accountings for stakeholders: On opening up and closing down participatory governance. *Journal of Management Studies*, *52*(7), 961–985. doi:10.1111/joms.12153

Bryson, J., Patton, M. Q., & Bowman, R. A. (2011). Working with evaluation stakeholders: A rationale, step-wise approach and toolkit. *Evaluation and Program Planning*, *34*(1), 1–12. doi:10.1016/j.evalprogplan.2010.07.001

Bryson, J. M. (2004). What to do when stakeholders matter: A guide to stakeholder identification and analysis techniques. *Public Management Review*, 6(1), 21–53. doi:10.1080/14719030410001675722

Calton, J. M. (2013). A de-centered stakeholder network path to creating mutual value: Is Wal-Mart showing the way? *Proceedings of the International Association for Business and Society*, *24*, 200–207. doi:10.5840/iabsproc20132421

Cameron, K. S., & Quinn, R. E. (2011). *Diagnosing and changing organizational culture: Based on the competing values framework* (3rd ed.). San Francisco, CA: Jossey-Bass.

Cappelli, P., & Tavis, A. (2018). HR goes agile. *Harvard Business Review*, *96*(2), 46–52.

Chaturvedi, H., Dey A. K., & Singh, N. (2020). Coping with COVID-19. *Global Focus the EFMD Business Magazine*. Retrieved from https://www.globalfocusmagazine.com/coping-with-covid-19/

Chima, A., & Gutman, R. (2020). What it takes to lead through an era of exponential change. *Harvard Business Review*. Retrieved from https://hbr.org/2020/10/what-it-takes-to-lead-through-an-era-of-exponential-change

Clarke, A., & MacDonald, A. (2019). Outcomes to partners in multi-stakeholder cross-sector partnerships: A resource-based view. *Business & Society*, *58*(2), 298–332. doi:10.1177/0007650316660534

Connors, R., & Smith, T. (2011). *Change the culture change the game*. New York: Penguin Group.

Cummings, J. (2002). Engaging stakeholders in corporate accountability programmes: A cross-sectoral analysis of UK and transnational experience. *Business Ethics A European Review*, *10*(1), 40–52. doi:10.1111/1467-8608.00211

Edmonds, S. C. (2014). *The culture engine: A framework for driving results, inspiring your employees, and transforming your workplace*. Hoboken, NJ: John Wiley & Sons.

Fassin, Y., De Colle, S., & Freeman, R. E. (2017). Intra-stakeholder alliances in plant-closing decisions: A stakeholder theory approach. *Business Ethics A European Review*, *26*(2), 97–111. doi:10.1111/beer.12136

Fernández-Aráoz, C., Roscoe, A., & Aramaki, K. (2017). Turning potential into success: The missing link in leadership development. *Harvard Business Review*, *95*(6), 86–94.

Fontaine, C., Haarman, A., & Schmid, S. (2006). *The stakeholder theory*. Retrieved from https://pdfs.semanticscholar.org/606a/828294dafd62aeda92a77bd7e5d0a39af56f.pdf

Freeman, R. E., Harrison, J. S., Wicks, A. C., Parmar, B. L., & De Colle, S. (2010). *Stakeholder theory: The state of art*. New York: Cambridge University Press.

Giannarakis, G., Garefalakis, A., Lemonakis, C., & Konteos, G. (2017). The drivers of social responsible stock index: The case of Dow Jones sustainability index world. Corporate. *Ownership & Control*, *14*(2-1), 173–180. doi:10.22495/cocv14i2c1p3

Gjaja, M., Fæste, L., Hansell, G., & Hohner, D. (2020, April 16). COVID-19: *Win the fight, win the future. Boston Consulting Group*. Retrieved from https://www.bcg.com/en-hu/publications/2020/covid-scenario-planning-winning-the-future-series

Groysberg, B., Lee, J., Price, J., & Cheng, J. Y.-J. (2018). The leader's guide to corporate culture. *Harvard Business Review*, *96*(1), 44–52.

Hall, M., Millo, Y., & Barman, E. (2015). Who and what really counts? Stakeholder prioritization and accounting for social value. *Journal of Management Studies*, *52*(7), 907–934. doi:10.1111/joms.12146

Haran, U., & Moore, D. A. (2014). A better way to forecast. *California Management Journal*, *57*(1), 5–15. doi:10.1525/cmr.2014.57.1.5

Harraf, A., Wanasika, I., Tate, K., & Talbott, K. (2015). Organizational agility. *Journal of Applied Business Research*, *31*(2), 675–686. doi:10.19030/jabr.v31i2.9160

Harrison, J. S., & Wicks, A. C. (2013). Stakeholder theory, value and firm performance. *Business Ethics Quarterly*, *23*(1), 97–124. doi:10.5840/beq20132314

Haski-Leventhal, D., Roza, L., & Meijs, L. C. P. M. (2017). Congruence in corporate social responsibility: Connecting the identity and behavior of employers and employees. *Journal of Business Ethics*, *143*(1), 35–51. doi:10.1007/s10551-015-2793-z

Hautz, J., Seidl, D., & Whittington, R. (2017). Open strategy: Dimensions, dilemmas, dynamics. *Long Range Planning*, *50*(3), 298–309. doi:10.1016/j.lrp.2016.12.001

Healey, M. P., & Hodgkinson, G. P. (2017). Making strategy hot. *California Management Review*, *59*(3), 109–134. doi:10.1177/0008125617712258

Hearn, S. (2014, September 15). Alignment, interest, influence matrix. Retrieved from https://www.outcomemapping.ca/nuggets/alignment-interest-influence-matrix

Hernandez, M. (2019). A shared passion for place can make a business more resilient. *MIT Sloan Management Review*. Retrieved from https://sloanreview.mit.edu/article/a-shared-passion-for-place-can-make-a-business-more-resilient/

Heyden, M. L. M., Fourné, S. P. L., Koene, B. A. S., Werkman, R., & Ansari, S. (2017). Rethinking "top-down" and "bottom-up" roles of top and middle managers in organizational change: Implications for employee support. *Journal of Management Studies*, *54*(7), 961–985. doi:10.1111/joms.12258

Hill, L. A., & Davis, G. (2017). The board's new innovation imperative: Directors need to rethink their roles and their attitude to risk. *Harvard Business Review*, *95*(6), 102–109.

How to Create Stakeholder Management and Communication Plans. (n.d.). Retrieved from https://www.smartsheet.com/how-create-stakeholder-management-and-communication-plans

Huang, K.-F., Dyerson, R., Wu, L.-Y., & Harindranath, G. (2015). From temporary competitive advantage to sustainable competitive advantage. *British Journal of Management*, *26*(4), 617–636. doi:10.1111/1467-8551.12104

International Institute of Business Analysis. (2009). *A guide to the business analysis body of knowledge (BABOK Guide). Version 2.0*. Totonto, Canada: International Institute of Business Analysis.

Jarvenpaa, S. L., & Välikangas, L. (2014). Opportunity creation in innovation networks: Interactive revealing practices. *California Management Review*, *57*(1), 67–87. doi:10.1525/cmr.2014.57.1.67

Kane, G. C., Palmer, D., Phillips, A. N., Kiron, D., & Buckley, N. (2018). Coming of age digitally: Learning, leadership, and legacy. *MIT Sloan*

Management Review. Retrieved from https://sloanreview.mit.edu/projects/coming-of-age-digitally/

Knight, J. (2014). *Culture that rocks: How to revolutionize your Company's culture*. Winter Garden, FL: Knight Speaker LLC.

Korn Ferry. (2019). *Self disrupt or be disrupted*. Retrieved from https://www.kornferry.com/self-disrupt

Lee, A., Willis, S., & Tian, A. W. (2018). When empowering employees works, and when it doesn't. *Harvard Business Review*, *96*(2). https://hbr.org/2018/03/when-empowering-employees-works-and-when-it-doesnt

Lesser, R., Reeves, M., Whitaker, K., & Hutchinson, R. (2018, December 14). *A leadership agenda for the next decade - Winning the '20s*. Retrieved from https://www.bcg.com/publications/2018/winning-the-20s-leadership-agenda-for-next-decade.aspx

Mitchell, R. K., Van Buren, H. J., Greenwood M., & Freeman, R. E. (2015). Stakeholder inclusion and accounting for stakeholders. *Journal of Management Studies*, *52*(7), 851–877. doi:10.1111/joms.12151

Mitchell, R. K., Weaver, G. R., Agle, B. R., Bailey, A. D., & Carlson, J. (2016). Stakeholder agency and social welfare: Pluralism and decision making in the multi-objective corporation. *Academy of Management Review*, *41*(2), 252–275. doi:10.5465/amr.2013.0486

Narayandas, D., Hebbar, V., & Li., L. (2020). Lessons from Chinese companies' response to Covid-19. *Harvard Business Review*. Retrieved from https://hbr.org/2020/06/lessons-from-chinese-companies-response-to-covid-19

Nicolescu, O., & Verboncu, I. (2008). *Fundamentele Managementului Organizatiei*. Bucuresti, Romania: Editura Universitara.

Pisano, G. P. (2019). The hard truth about innovative cultures. *Harvard Business Review*, *97*(1), 62–71.

Radjou, N. (2020). The rising frugal economy. *MIT Sloan Management Review*. Retrieved from https://sloanreview.mit.edu/article/the-rising-frugal-economy/

Ready, D. A., Cohen, C., Kiron, D., & Pring, B. (2020, January). The new leadership playbook for digital age. *MIT Sloan Management Review*. Retrieved from https://sloanreview.mit.edu/projects/the-new-leadership-playbook-for-the-digital-age/?gclid=CjwKCAjwg6b0BRBMEiwANd1_SE8dUmZetK_peLCkKBI6abknYo6vYcKUtSDNbE_MYo5CTuqs4SF6yRoCxlwQAvD_BwE

Repenning, N. P., Kieffer, D., & Repenning, J. (2018). A new approach to designing work. *MIT Sloan Management Review*, *59*(2), 29–38.

Rogers, K. (2018). Do your employees feel respected? *Harvard Business Review*, *96*(4), 62–71.

Romeo, J., Moukanas, H., & Rung, G. (2020). The age of accelerating strategy breakthroughs. *MIT Sloan Management Review*. Retrieved from https://sloanreview.mit.edu/article/the-age-of-accelerating-strategy-breakthroughs/

Sawhney, M., Wolcott, R. C., & Arroniz, I. (2006). The 12 different ways for companies to innovate. *MIT Sloan Management Review*, *47*(3), 75–81.

Schein, E. H. (2010). *Organizational Culture and Leadership* (4th ed.). San Francisco, CA: Jossey-Bass.

Schwarz, T. (2018). Create a growth culture, not a performance-obsessed one.

Harvard Business Review, *96*(2). Retrieved from https://hbr.org/2018/03/create-a-growth-culture-not-a-performance-obsessed-one

Sibony, O., Lovallo, D., & Powell, T. C. (2017). Behavioral strategy and the strategic decision architecture of the firm. *California Management Review*, *59*(3), 5–21. doi:10.1177/0008125617712256

Skolits, G. J., & Boser, J. A. (2018). Using an evaluation hotline to promote stakeholders involvement. *American Journal of Evaluation*, *29*(1), 58–70. doi:10.1177/1098214007312777

Stakeholder Analysis. (n.d.). Retrieved from https://www.slideshare.net/dsaadeddin/stakeholder-analysis-52893836

Stakeholder Analysis, Project Management, Templates and Advice. (n.d). Retrieved from https://www.stakeholdermap.com/stakeholder-analysis.html

Stakeholder Management Strategy Template. (n.d.). Retrieved from https://www.projectmanagementdocs.com/template/project-initiation/stakeholder-management-strategy/#axzz6NTp7qXI3

Teece, D., Peteraf, M., & Leih, S. (2016). Dynamic capabilities and organizational agility: Risk, uncertainty and entrepreneurial management in the innovation economy. *California Management Review*, *58*(4), 13–35. 10.1525/cmr.2016.58.4.13

Vandenbussche, L., Edelenbos, J., & Eshuis, J. (2017). Pathways of stakeholders' relations and frames in collaborative planning practices: A framework to analyse relating and framing dynamics. *Planning Theory*, *16*(3), 233–254. doi:10.1177/1473095215620150

Vogel, D. J. (2017). Haas research on leadership: An introduction. *California Management Review*, *60*(1), 5–7. doi:10.1177/0008125617735339

Waldron, T., & Wetherbe, J. (2020). Ensure that your customer relationships outlast coronavirus. *Harvard Business Review*. Retrieved from https://hbr.org/2020/04/ensure-that-your-customer-relationships-outlast-coronavirus

Weber, Y., & Tarba, S. Y. (2014). Strategic agility: A state of the art introduction to the special section on strategic agility. *California Management Review*, *56*(3), 5–12. doi:10.1525/cmr.2014.56.3.5

Wellman, N. (2017). Authority or community? A relational models theory of group-level leadership emergence. *Academy of Management Review*, 42(4), 596–617. doi:10.5465/amr.2015.0375

Westerman, G. (2018). Your company doesn't need a digital strategy. *MIT Sloan Management Review*, *59*(3), 14–15.

Youmans, T., & Tomlinson. B. (2018). Six reasons why companies should start sharing their long-term thinking with investors. *MIT Sloan Management Review*. Retrieved from https://sloanreview.mit.edu/article/six-reasons-why-companies-should-start-sharing-their-long-term-thinking-with-investors/

12 Instead of Conclusions: Why the New Vision and Approaches Regarding Company Management, Relevant Stakeholders, and Social Responsibility Should Be Implemented in Numerous Companies?

This final part of our book contains the essential points to be considered by company managers in order to take the decision to design and implement the new company management system based on the relevant stakeholders.

The arguments regarding the huge beneficial effects of the implementation of the company-relevant stakeholders-based management system can be grouped into **three categories:**

- Supplementary resources for the company;
- Better work processes in the company;
- Higher multidimensional and sustainable performances for the company and its external and internal relevant stakeholders (see Figure 12.1).

Supplementary Resources for the Company

Reshaping the company management system focusing on the relevant stakeholders **increases the resources available for the organization,** mostly without supplementary cost. These resources are provided by the relevant stakeholders because of the common and convergent company and relevant stakeholder objectives, of the harmonization of their main interests and expectations, of the win-win negotiations, of the strong reciprocity between them and of all other specific characteristics of the new management system. For this reason, the relevant stakeholders are motivated and able to provide to the company more and better resources than before.

Internal relevant stakeholders – managers, executants, and shareholders – contribute mainly with more information, knowledge, and relationships. This means that they use their intellectual capital to a larger extent in favour of the company.

DOI: 10.4324/9781003217701-12

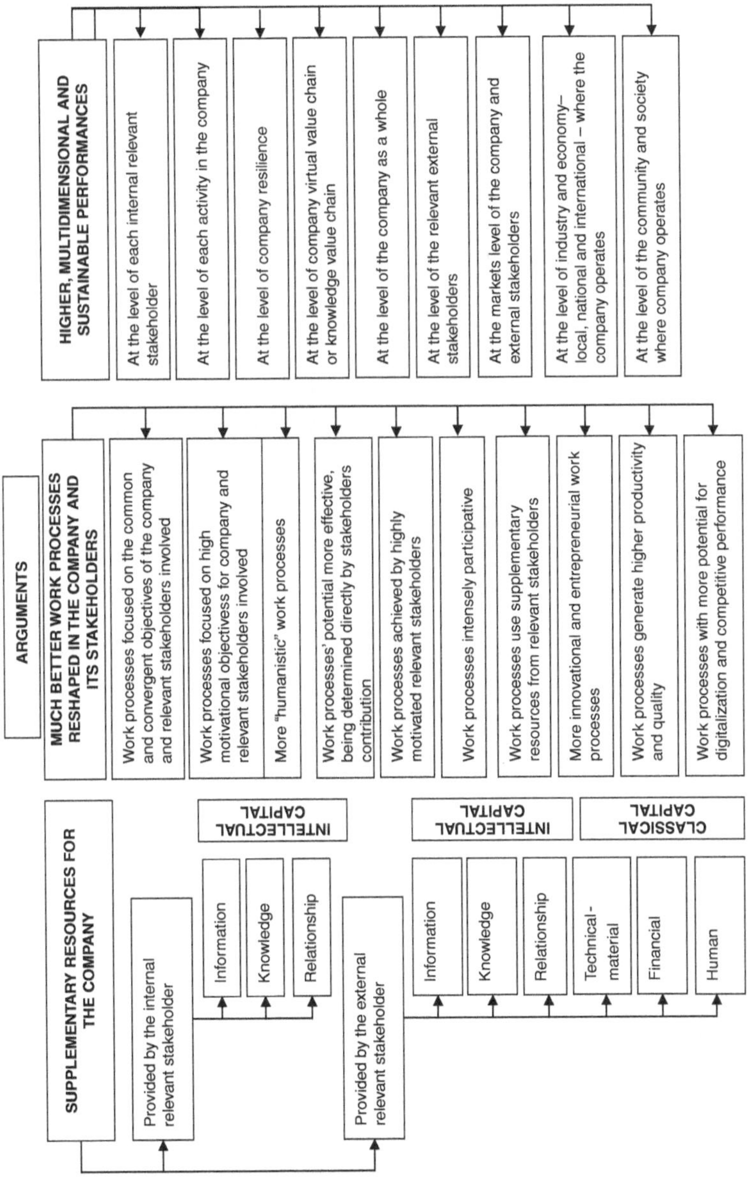

Figure 12.1 Arguments demonstrating why the company-relevant stakeholders-based management system is needed in companies.

External relevant stakeholders – customers, suppliers, banks, informaticians, designers, consultants, trainers, local communities etc. – provide the same type of intellectual capital resource and also more "classical" tangible resources – raw materials, services, products, money, specialists, etc. Some of these resources can be offered without supplementary cost and others with some additional cost or in more favourable conditions in terms of time, quality, costs, easiness, places, etc.

Supplementary and better and cheaper resources, both tangible and intangible, increase their economic, social, and ecologic performances.

Better Processes in the Company and at the External Stakeholders Level

The second category of arguments refers to **the work processes** in the company. The new management system determines much better and higher productive work processes in the organization. There are at **least 10 arguments** that support this statement:

- the objectives that should be fulfilled through work processes operated by the relevant stakeholders and the company are common and convergent, being determined by them;
- work processes focused on the common and convergent objectives are highly motivational, because they reflect the interests and expectations of the relevant stakeholders and the company;
- work processes based on the relevant stakeholders' approach are more "humanistic", because of taking into consideration the stakeholders' characteristics, desires, and expectations;
- work processes are potentially more effective and efficient being determined by the direct contribution of the stakeholders that perform them, and taking into consideration to a high level of their particularities and specific requirements;
- work processes are intensely participative, the relevant stakeholders being involved in their construction and operation;
- work processes are conducted by highly motivated relevant internal and external stakeholders;
- work processes are more prospective and sustainable, because of taking into consideration the relevant stakeholders' demands and expectations in the short, medium, and long term;
- work processes are more innovative and entrepreneurial because of the above-mentioned elements;
- work processes generate higher productivity and quality of the products and services, because relevant stakeholders provide – as we have already mentioned – substantial supplementary intangible and tangible resources;

- company work processes, remodelled and operated by the relevant stakeholders, using to a large extent their intellectual capital, have a much higher potential for digitalization and competitive performance for the whole value chain involved.

Higher, Multidimensional, and Sustainable Performances for the Company and Its Internal and External Stakeholders

The third category of arguments deals with **multidimensional and sustainable company and relevant stakeholders' performances.** In fact, this category of elements is the most important for the company and stakeholders, because for each of them, the performance is usually the most important objective. Of course, when we are referring to multidimensional performance, we look at the economic, social, ecologic, educational, and other fields. Performances improve because of the supplementary resources provided by the relevant stakeholders, and of better and more productive activities in the company and to the external relevant stakeholders, determined by the managerial synapses and by the company-relevant stakeholders-based management system.

The improvement in performances **can be identified at eight levels:**

a Internal company-relevant stakeholders:

  - managers – quality of decisions, actions and behaviours, fulfilment of objectives referring to products, costs, sales, profit, etc.
  - executants – quality of products and services offered, individual productivity, new ideas, etc.
  - shareholders – the value of the dividends, company value share, company asset value, etc.

b Each company activity – quality of specific outputs generated, costs associated with the activity, activity ecological effects, etc.

c Company value chain (virtual and knowledge) – quantity of the products and services offered, duration of the production cycle, productivity, etc.

d Company resilience, essential in the present environment, strongly affected by the coronavirus pandemic, which means its ability to recover from difficulties, to spring back into shape after a shock.

e Company as a whole entity – technological change, innovation capacity, rate of learning, turnover, market share, profit, brand value, etc.

f External company-relevant stakeholders:

- clients – value of acquisition, profit obtained, degree of satisfaction associated with the company products and services, etc.
- suppliers – value of sales, profit obtained, future orders for raw materials, etc.
- investors – value of the investment in the company, profit obtained, efficiency of investment, etc.
- consultants – value of the income, profit obtained, future contracts, etc.
- designers – value of income, profit obtained, future contracts, etc.

g Markets of the company and of the external relevant stakeholders – demands for their products and services, increased sales, increase in their market shares, etc.

h Company industry and economy (local, national, international) – company rating in the industry and the economy involved, evolution of the company sales, brand value, export, import, etc.

i Community and society involved – contribution to the development of the local community, diminishing unemployment, protection of environment, labour force hired, sponsorships provided by the company for the community and the societal actions, taxes paid, etc.

In our opinion, the elements mentioned above represent convincing arguments for taking into consideration the vision regarding relevant stakeholder company management, relevant stakeholder, company social and relevant stakeholder responsibility, and the utilization of the new company-relevant stakeholders-based management system. It can contribute significantly to overcoming many of the difficulties faced by numerous companies, revealed and recognized by many specialists. The company-relevant stakeholders-based management system is very well equipped to contribute to **"revolutionizing" the company and its management and responsibility**, under the impact of the fast digital transformation and the transition to the knowledge-based economy. It can contribute significantly to reinventing the enterprise according to the new challenges, threats, and opportunities, including those generated by the COVID-19 pandemic.

Index

References to figures appear in *italic* type; those in **bold** type refer to tables